The 'Vedas' are the oldest known human documents in terms of religion, philosophy and literature. The term 'Veda' signifies the sacred knowledge and wisdom. These so valuable documents of Indian sacred lore and learning were composed in the dim hoary past and show the path of ultimate release from human bondage through righteousness, self-knowledge and surrender to the Universal Soul. As such their teachings cut across all the imaginable boundaries of caste, creed, country, climate and age. In their appeal and application they are universal and belong to all the ages and the entire humanity.

⚛ DIAMOND POCKET BOOKS PRESENTS

RELIGION & SPIRITUALITY BOOKS

Essence of Vedas

Dr. B. R. Kishore

DIAMOND BOOKS

ISBN— 81-288-0668-8

© **Publisher**

Publisher	:	**Diamond Pocket Books (P) Ltd.** X-30 Okhla Industrial Area, Phase-II, New Delhi-110020
Phone	:	011-5161861-865
Fax	:	011-26386124, 51611866
E-mail	:	sales@diamondpublication.com
Web site	:	www.diamondpublication.com
Edition	:	2004
Price	:	Rs. 195/-
Laser Typsetting	:	Tact Computer Graphics, Krishna Nagar, Delhi-51
Printed At	:	Adarsh Printers, Shahdara, Delhi

Essence of Vedas

By Dr. B. R. Kishore   Rs 195/-

Table of Contents

Preface

The Vedas are the oldest tomes of the most ancient civilization and culture broadly called Hinduism. They record what man felt at the dawn of human consciousness when having fully developed as 'Homo sapiens' he started to comprehend the environs enveloping his existence. Believed to have been compiled a few millennia ago— although the scholars still debate on their actual time of compilation— the Vedas reveal the human curiosity about life, nature and all its supporting agencies.

The Rig (or Rik) Veda, the first of the four Vedas, the oldest religious text, is a collection of hymns for use at the sacrifices (the Yagyas) of the aristocratic Aryan cult. The three later Vedas, viz. the Yajur, Sama and Atharva, are of somewhat different character. The Sama Veda, believed to be the origin of Indian school of music, is in fact a collection of certain verses of the Rig Veda arranged for liturgical purposes. The Yajur Veda, compiled a century or two later than the Rig Veda, contains sacrificial formulae in prose and verse to be pronounced by the 'Adhvaryu' or priest who performs the manual part of the sacrifice. It exists in various recensions ('Samhitas') which are of two types: the 'Black'–giving the formulae with rubricated instructions–and the 'White', adding detailed instructions in a lengthy appendix called a 'Brahmana'. The AtharvaVeda consists mainly of magic spells and the Mantras (incantations) in verse, which was certainly compiled after the Rig and Yajur Vedas. It possesses, however, an atmosphere of simple or sympathetic magic on a lower cultural level than that of the Rig Veda, deriving from the plebeian religion of the Aryan and containing many non-Aryan elements as well. The massive Brahmanas, which were looked down upon as appendices to the Vedas and the mystical Aranyakas and the Upanishads, are in turn appendices to the Brahmanas. This complete set of literature is called Vedic literature.

Incidentally, the term Upanishad itself shows that these were originally not in the written form. Literally Upanishad means 'sitting close by (Upa+Nishada)'. When the Vedas were being compiled, their terse aphorisms were not easily understandable. In order to explain them the seers used to expound on them to let their disciples understand their real meaning. Hence the term Upanishad which means a commentary on the Vedas. Perhaps from that stage the term 'Shruti' must have become synonymous whith the Vedic leterature. This led to the common belief that the Vedas are 'Apaurusheya', i.e. their authorship cannot be assigned to any human being and the Vedas are the divine revelation emanating from Brahman (Supreme Being). But the fact cannot be denied that the seers were those who brought their collection in the written form as they could comprehend by virtue of being blessed by the Brahman or God.

These Vedic 'Richas' or the hymns are given in the Sookta form. A 'Sookta' is like an aphorism which gives a pithy saying based upon the author's experience and comprehension of the truth as he perceived. There are hymns and general prayers to various gods that were popular in that time, like Indra, Agni, Varuna and goddesses like Aditi, Ushas, Aranyani, Ratri, Prithvi. Thus during the Vedic time the chief objects of worship were the 'devas'. The root from the word derived is 'div' which is connected with brightness and radiance. Thus the divinities were the 'shining ones' showing a clear prejudice towards darkness which still exists as it was then in the human ken.

The Vedic man believed that with the gratification of the gods he might ensure a better life for himself. So he would often invite these divinities to grace his sacrifice and drink 'Soma', a mysterious drink repeatedly eulogised by the Vedic text. This drink is so revered in almost all the Vedas that it has acquired the form of divinity of special character. Soma is believed to have been a plant or hemp not yet definitively identified. It has been described to be a plant with 15 leaves which the tree shed, one at a time during the bright half of the lunar month. Its leaves used to be ceremoniously collected, ground with water to secrete the juice which caused most invigorating effect on the drinker. However, the drink prepared from the plant can scarcely have been alcoholic as it had to be consumed soon after its preparation, giving no time for fermentation which is a must for any alcoholic beverage. The drink was thought to be the best potion of which even the divinities were greedy. It is described to be only next to ambrosia which could not only cure all illnesses whether mental or physical but also to grant a feeling of perfection.

The Vedas contain knowledge that is given in a symbolical form through terse allusions. It was in order to explain the real meaning that the subsequent commentaries like Upanishads came to be appended with the original text. Explaining the symbolism employed to describe a scarifice (yagya), the Brihadaaranyaka Upanishad says: "Dawn is the head of the sacrificial horse, the sun its eye, the wind its breath, fire its mouth, the year its body, heaven its back, the sky its belly, earth its chest, the four quarters its inside .... etc." It is this terse symbolism and frequent use of continued metaphors that made a yagya more than a mere endeavour for ensuring physical pleasures. It means any act done with full dedication.

But the confusion created by a hundred interpretations and commentaries became a hurdle for the common man to realise the real import of the Vedas. That is the precise reason behind bringing out this book 'Essence of Vedas'. Instead of explaining the meaning of the text Sooktawise, it was decided to check the various aphorisms together with a similarity of image under one group.[1] This book is aimed at letting the discerning readers get the real message of the Vedas which beams across the words describing rather baser desires. When these are seen or read in the total perspective they highlight the human ingenuity for better living—both physical and spiritual.

A little careful perusal of them would make the reader realise that the Rig Veda period was the time when the Vedic man had barely become aware of his environs and he started questioning the existence which created the world. So it is full of prayers revealing his curiosity about nature and fervently praying to the 'Devas' to ensure his enjoying the bare necessities of life without any hindrance. Not only that, these prayers also have a negative request as well. That "I may get wealth, health, riches, progeny (etc.) but not my enemy" was the tone and tenor of many prayers of this period. No doubt they might look a bit offensive style to the modern readership

---

1. We have also published the Vadas' Sookta-wise original text and translation and the desirous readers may get them from us—Publisher.

but when judged against the background of that 'primitive stage' these prayers might appear quite normal.

In order to settle down in those primeval stages the Vedic seers prayed for a hassle-free living. Indra, Varuna and other deities that seemed to control natural agencies have most prayers dedicated to them in this stage. In fact Indra was deemed the greatest god who is believed to fulfil the dual functions of war-god and weather-god. As Indra 'torans' he rode at the head of the Aryan host, and destroyed the fortresses of the 'Daasas'; as Indra 'pluvius' he slew the dragon Vritra who held back the waters and, thus, brought rain to the parched land. He was a dragon-slayer and a wild rider of the storm. 'Surya' drove across the sky in a flaming chariot; Savita (or Savitr), the stimulator, another solar god having the most holy Mantra (Gayatri) dedicated to him; Pusan, yet another solar god driving daily across the sky, depicted as guardian of roads, herdsmen and straying cattle. In fact the Vedic deities hymned in the initial phase have much greater importance ascribed to than even the three super-gods (Brahma, Vishnu, Mahesh) who have dominated the Hindu pantheism of the present phase.

By the time Sama Veda came to be compiled, the Vedic man must have learnt the effect of music on the human consciousness. He learnt that if the same matter is converged in a sonorous manner, it has lasting and more profound effect on the listeners. So they made most of the early Richas converted to musical metres. It was the stage when the words and syllables were analysed and though the texts were still unwritten, the letters of the alphabet were recognised and personified as eternal divinities. Even the metres used in the Vedas were also thought of as gods. Later certain syllables were believed to be particularly holy—notably OM (or AUM) (also known as Pranava) which is believed to contain the essence of the Vedas and hence pregnant with the utmost power of mystery.

Even though the Sama Veda may appear as a musical version of the Rig Veda, the method of pronunciations of the Sama Veda and the Rig Veda hymns are so different that there appears a huge time-gap between their creation. However, traditionally it is held that there is no repetitions in the Vedas because a sacred incantation (Mantra) in different texts and contexts reveals different meanings.

By the time the Yajur Veda came to be compiled the Vedic man had learned that apart from prayers, even by action he could improve his life style and live in a more awakened manner. Thus the Yajur Veda is a kind of sacrificial prayer book containing hymns that are essentially ritualistic but also embody the loftiest sentiments that man can ever feel for his god or goddess. The Yajur Veda heralds the advent of spiritual consciousness of man that bloomed fully in the last of the Vedas, the Atharva Veda. It, however, must be understood clearly that to do a 'Yagna' is not only to do a 'havan' or 'feed the fire' or 'invoke the gods' but to perform any action with full dedication and concentration.

The Atharva Veda shows the Vedic man, having ensured his settled living to great extent, becoming philosophical and developing a scientific temperament. On account of its sublime metaphysical contents it is also known as Brahma Veda. It is at this stage that the man of the primeval times began the quest of knowing his Maker. Although part of it is again taken from the Rig Veda—the source of all the later Vedas—the Atharva Veda deals not only with the philosophical but very practical problems of human life like security, destruction of the enemies, the use of magic charms, exorcism of evil spirits, anointment of kings, political affairs, welfare of the common man, funeral and the like. Its chief importance lies in its being one of our richest heritage sources, representing the mundane, secular, philosophical and intellectual aspects of our ancient life and culture—all rolled into one.

These Vedas are our prime source of knowledge. It is not surprising that eons before the arrival of Copernicus, Galileo etc. the Vedic seers knew that the moon is devoid of its own light and reflects only the solar light. They knew much before the west learnt about the basics of surgery as to how and why a part of human body should be amputated and what is the technique of setting a displaced bone.

As a matter of fact, besides the physical or metaphysical concepts or knowledge, the Vedas are also the sources that moulded our psyche—nay the oriental man's psyche—and hammered in some of the beliefs as much as to make them our axioms—like the transmigration of the soul, the karma theory and the need to live together with consideration for each other. The Sooktas or the Richas of the Vedas teach us that no matter what man achieves he cannot neglect God—echoing the famous observation of most renowned scientist of the modern world, Albert Einstein, that "there is something that keeps in chaos in order!" It is enough to blunt the edges of the egoistic exuberance that right since the dawn of human consciousness to now, there is a Supreme authority whom no one can challenge. The Vedas, this way, also enlighten us to sift and discriminate between what is permanent and what is impermanent; between the fey and eternal and between self and Self.

It is chiefly for letting the real and unsullied message of the Vedas reach the comman man that this work has been undertaken. A plethora of the Vedic commentaries written in various eras with quite arbitrary and at times ambiguous interpretations have driven the normally awakened man from the real contents of the Vedas. It was for this very reason that the doyen among the modern enlightened seers, Swami Dayananda, advised the people to go to the very fount, the Vedas, and not to their interpretations. Hence our taking special care to skip relatively less tangible and obscure passages which add confusion and whose details have outlived their relevance in the general context. Our target has been removing the slough and revealing the substance, highlighting the eternal and deleting the transitory.

We must present before our readers as to what is the basic purpose for which our ancestors insisted on our learning the Vedas, how they could maintain their relevance for so many millennia and how can we still make our life better by learning their message. We have deliberately skipped the details about their authorship, their form and the format of divisions and have concentrated more on their contents. After all what the Vedas contain that drew the western scholars such as Max Muller and Winternitz like iron filings to magnet? Why doing a 'homa' is still neccessary? Why must chanting of the sacred syllabus 'OM' or the Gayatri Mantra is necessary even for a modern youth? Why the disciplines of Yoga and our indigenous school of medicine 'Ayurveda' are gaining popularity all over the world? Needless to emphasise that these two unique schools that strive to unite mind and matter, the subjective and objective in an unparalleled way trace their origin to the Vedas only.

The Vedas' eternal message of 'Tat twam asi' is the basic concept that developed into our belief of universal brotherhood, the very premise of modern India's foreign policy. Our other belief 'Sarva dharma samabhava' or showing equal respect to all faiths also had its seed in the Veda teachings. The idea behind this book is inspired by the same urge that Goswami Tulsidas might have felt before putting the essence of the Hindu teachings in his 'magnum opus' 'Sri Ramacharita Manas'—that the readers should have an easy accessibility of these treasured teachings sans their verbose, arbitrary and confusing interpretations. We do not claim to have interpreted all the Vedas rightly for there are hundreds of the Vedic Sooktas that have not been properly understood by anyone. But what we have presented in this work is after much study of the Vedas and in a planned manner.

Written in easy-to-comprehend and flowing style, we are sure, this work, 'Essence of Vedas', would provide our curious readers a peep into the gems that our ancients had bequeathed to us. Let us polish out the slough of antiquity and dazzle them further with our present knowledge and understanding.

It has, indeed, been a stupendous task: checking the authenticity, the meaning and ensuring the right interpretations of a pithy observation made eons ago. We owe our special gratitude to Shri Narendra Ji of Diamond Pocket Books whose zeal in unveiling the treasures of our heritage has almost no parallel in the modern publication field. We shall be delighted to receive our readers' response because the ultimate satifaction of compiling the book of this genre is not received as much by the sale of their copies as by the readers' response. May the wisdom of our ancient seers enlighten our modern youth confused by the occidental invasion upon our culture.

—**Dr. B.R. Kishore**

Rig Veda

Book First

I glorify God Agni, the chief priest, minister of the sacrifice, the bounteous giver of wealth. Praiseworthy is the effulgent lord by living and ancient sages. He brings the Gods hither. He brings us wealth and food increasing daily, fame and heroic sons to gladden our hearts. Only the sacrifice that you Lord encompass and guard reacheth the Gods in heaven. To you, dispeller of darkness, O Agni, we come with daily prayer, bringing our reverence. O Lord of Sacrifice, nourisher of the world, thou waxeth mighty in thine own dwelling. Be easy to us of access, like a sire to his son, be with us for our weal and joy.

O friends, come and sit ye down all here together to hymn Indra. Sing his praise who is the Lord of all things, the best and the richest, the showerer of wealth. May he help us in acquiring abundant wealth and grant nourishing food for our health and strength. Praise Indra, whose strength foemen in battle dare not challenge. Come ye near him, the Soma enjoyer for whose enjoyment the juices have been shed mingled with curds. O Indra, born to enjoy the juices, thou hath grown strong to perform noble deeds. Let the speedy Soma enter thee, O Indra, the lover of song, to make you happy. May these our songs of praise increase the powers, and may our Vedic hymns magnify thee, O God, full of never failing power. May thou Indra of infinite strength accept our food offerings of thousands of kinds containing manly strength, the source of true delight. O Lord, let not men harm our body, thou keep violence far away from us.

O men, learn ye that Indra made light where there was no light and form where there was no form. He was born with the Dawns. Thou, Indra, pierced the cave and discovered the kine like the fierce Wind Gods who break down things that are firm.

The singers, the reciters and the choirs have glorified Indra. Indra the golden, thunder-armed, with his two bay steeds hath the world as his car. He hath placed the Sun on high that people may see by his light. Clouds he bursts to shower the rain. O awful Indra, help us by your fierce acids in battles to win thousand spoils. We invoke Indra in frays small and great, our unfailing friend who hurls his thunderbolt at wicked powers. Unclose for us, our irresistible Hero, thou bounteous Indra, the yonder cloud. Higher and still higher I sing his praise, but I find no praise worthy of him. He, the irresistible, drives the people with his might, as the bull drives the herd onward. He is the sovereign of wealth and fivefold race, of men that dwells upon the earth. Indra, we call thee away from all other men, may he be ours and none others.

Our hymns extol Indra, vast as the ocean, the best hero borne on chariots, the Lord of strength and protector of men. We bow before Indra and glorify him, in whose mighty friendship we never fear. Thou art, O hero, ever conqueror but never conquered. The gifts of him from of yore, his saving succour, never fail, when to his devotees, who laud him, he gives land, kine and wealth. Indra the wielder of thunderbolt, the young, the wise, of limitless strength, the sustainer of all sacred acts, much extolled, is the crasher of enemies and their forts by birth.

Every day in the morning, we invoke Indra, during the sacrifice of drinking Soma juice. Come here with thy bay steeds, the juice is effused. Come thou to our sacrifice where thy songs of praise are sung, to juices shed for thee, drink of it like a thirsty stag and increase thy strength.

I invoke Indra and Agni, the great Soma drinkers for the fame of Mitra, the friend and benefactor of all. We call upon strong and mighty Indra and Agni to enjoy the oblations offered here in the Yajna. O mighty Gods, protectors of men, come to us, destroy the wicked ones. Let the wicked foes, the devourers of men be destitute of progeny. May Indra and Agni, who are well known for their truthfulness, fill us with joy and happiness.

May Heaven and Earth grant sweet nourishment to our sacrifice. May the Earth be without thorns and pits to provide us dwellings. May she, spreading wide, the resting place for all, grant us delight and pleasure by providing shelter. May the learned protect us by teaching about the all-pervading God, who created this world with seven substances, and sustains all comprising earth, water, fire, air, etc. God alone should be adored who made this visible earth, the invisible subtle world and the brilliant solar world. He, the omnipresent and protector of all upholds the threefold world, which follows the eternal law ordained by Him. Look ye, O men at the works of God, the true friend of the soul, the giver of bliss, the creator, sustainer and disintegrator of the world. The righteous and learned men behold God within their hearts, as the ordinary mortals see the Sun in the sky. These learned men, singing His songs of praise, attain the blissful light, of all-pervading God that is the goal of all.

These Lords of Law, of light, I call who uphold law by law, Mitra and Varuna, I invoke. May Varuna be our chief guardian, may Mitra defend us with all his aids. May both the Gods help us grow rich. May Waters contiguous to the Sun or its light and those with which the Sun is associated be propitious to our sacrifices. I invoke the Waters for the performance of the sacrifice, wherein our cattle quench their thirst; offer ye the oblations to Rivers. Know ye learned men, there is Amrita in the Waters, there is healing balm. Know this and be enlightened. Soma hath told me, there dwells within Waters all balms that heal. Agni, also benefits and blesses all. O Waters, keep my body safe from harm with your medicinal qualities, that I live long to see the Sun. Whatever sin is found in me, whatever evil I have done, if I have falsely sworn or lied, Waters, remove this sin from me.

Who is he, what God, the giver of bliss, whose auspicious name we may invoke and remember? Who will send us back to Aditi, the great Boundless that I may see my father and my mother? He is Agni, the God omniscient, his auspicious name let us invoke. It is he who restores us to Aditi, that we may again see our parents. Varuna of pure vigour, abiding in the baseless sky, sustains the rays whose base is high above. There are streams below, may they be concentrated within us as a source of healthy existence. He hath made a spacious pathway, for the Sun footstep, and drove far away the unrighteous. O Varuna, thou hast a hundred, nay a thousand healing balms, deep be your favours, keep away the unrighteous, put away the sin committed by us and liberate us from it. The stars that appear on high in the sky at night, by day they disappear, whither we know not. Varuna's laws are immutable and inviolable by whose command the Moon sails forth at night in splendour. Loosen the bonds, O Varuna, which hold and crush us. Make us sinless in your holy law, unbound us, thou Son of Aditi.

Whatever law of thine, O God Varuna, we being mortals, may violate day after day. Consign us not, we beg, as prey to death, or to thy wrath to be destroyed when displeased. Just as a charioteer tethers his horse, so shall our hymns bind thy heart to obtain thy mercy. As to their nests the birds fly, so do my desires fly away in search of happiness. He, the lord of sea, knows all the ships that are thereon. True to his holy laws, he knows the twelve months with their progeny the days. He knows the pathway of winds sweeping high with might, he knows the Gods who abide in heavens. Varuna, hear this call of mine, grant us your favour, longing for help I have cried to thee. Thou sovereign and wise lord ruling over the Earth and Heaven, hear me, as you pass on your way. Release me from bonds all that I may live.

O God, ever true, though we faint in utter despair, do thou Indra grant us hope of thousands of cows, horses and land, O lord of treasures. O Lord of strength, subdue the malevolent spirits that haunt, let them sleep. Grant us hope of thousands of fine cows and horses.

O radiant and immortal Dawn, who is he that does not approach you to obtain delight and true happiness? O wonderful, red-hued and brilliant Dawn, thou have, had been in our thoughts whether nigh or far away. O daughter of the Sky, thou Dawn come unto us with thy nourishments and grant us riches.

O Agni, I call first for our prosperity, I call on Mitra, Varuna, they may aid us here. I invoke Night who provides the world with rest, and on Savitar I call that may lend us aid. Wheeling through the dusky sky, on his golden chariot cometh Savitar, laying to rest both men and Gods and gazing on all created beings. Adorable Savitar comes from far distance, journeying along the upward and downward path with his resplendent steeds. He comes chasing away every danger and distress. The mighty car adorned and decked with pearls, with golden pole, he hath mounted. The radiant One, God Savitar, the mightly, comes sweeping darkness away. Drawing the car with golden pole, his bay steeds, white footed, have shed the light over the whole world. All men, all beings abide for ever in divine Savitar's bosom. Savitar, the farseeing, golden handed God, marches on between the Heaven and Earth, driving away sickness, bidding the Sun to approach us, and soars up in the sky from the darksome region. O Gods, thy ancient paths are well established and dustless in the atmosphere. Now, come unto us along these paths so fair and protect us from harm, and bless.

We choose Agni our envoy, the omniscient God, our Hotar priest. The flames of the mighty Agni spread wide around and reach the sky. The Gods awaken thee, their messenger of old. The sacrificers gain wealth by proffered oblations unto thee. Thou effulgent God, lord of the house, men's envoy, all noble and inviolable deeds and the laws observed by the enlightened men, are aggregated and harmonised in thee.

When will ye, O Maruts uphold our sacrifice as a father holds by both his hands a son, Gods for whom sacred grass is spread? O Gods now whither? Where do ye go to attain your goal like the beams of the Sun reaching the Earth? Where are your roars that sound like a low of a cow to her calf ? Where are your latest favours and happiness? Where is, O Gods, your prosperity? O Maruts, as a deer is never indifferent to pasture, so let not your admirer suffer censure, nor let him go to Yama's path soon. Let never diseases destroy us, let them depart from us. May health and happiness be attained by us. May ye mighty Maruts, sons of Rudra, send pleasant rains over even the desert. The lightning which roars like a mother cow lowing for her calf, and the Maruts set free the rains. They spread darkness over even the day with the water bearing clouds and then inundate the Earth. When the Maruts roar, the seat of earth shakes and men begin to tremble. Come ye Maruts along the beautifully embanked river fronts, with strong-hoofed steeds unobstructed. May the fellies of your wheels be firm, steady your chariots and steeds and may your reins be fashioned well.

Never is he harmed whom Varuna, Mitra and Aryaman protect. He ever prospers and is free from obstacles whom the Gods Varuna, Mitra and Aryaman safeguard as with both arms and preserve from foemen. These Gods drive away the enemy and lead the righteous safely over distress.Where Adityas are the preservers, and where the path has been made thornless, there is no fear. That man, unsubdued, leads a righteous life long and full of happiness.

Shorten our path. O God, remove all obstacles, be close unto us to show the path. Scare away from our path the wicked wolf, the inauspicious wolf that lies in wait to harm. Chase the robber away from our way who lurks there with a guileful heart. Tread under thy feet the burning brand of the wicked, the double tongued, whoever he be. O wonder-working God, we claim from you that sain aid which you did give to our fathers of old. So, granter of favours, wielder of golden sword, make for us riches easy to be won. Aid us, elude the pursuers, make our way easy and smooth, lead us to pastures rich, protect us from heat, show thou thy power for this. Be gracious, fulfil us all, give us food and nourishment, show thy power for this. All that ye do for us, O God, shall win our laud. We magnify thee with songs of praise. We seek the Mighty one for boons!

Now Dawn with her earliest radiance shines forth, beloved daughter of the Sky. Lofty Ashvins, I praise you much. O ye sons of the Ocean, full of abundant knowledge, you give us much wealth. Your mighty horses speed forth through the glorious heavens with the chariot flying like birds. O Ashvins, truthful, and circumambient. Dawn follow ye, grant us prosperity and royal wealth. O Ashvini, drink this nectareous Soma juice offered in libation and with your irresistible protective aids bestow upon us bliss and fine residence.

O brilliant Dawn, the daughter of the Sky, diffuser of light, dawn on us with radiance, prosperity and riches. O admirable Beauty! O Dawn, utter the sweet and joyous words to make me happy. Take away the wealth of those rich who go astray and give it to the noble men and thereby make me happy. The Goddess Dawn travels on pleasant cars, on whom thy have fixed their thoughts, who desirous of wealth send their ships to the sea. The learned men sing aloud the glories of the Gods. The princes, at the approach, O Dawn, fix their thoughts on higher things. Dawn comes carefully tending everything, stirring all creatures, all the creeping and winged things. She sends the busy forth, each man to his pursuit, being active, delay she knows not. O Radiant one, after thy rising, the birds that have flown forth no longer rest. The Ushas have harnessed the cars afar, before the rising of the Sun. Borne on hundred chariots of rays she marches on her way to men, the auspicious Dawn. Dawn, the daughter of the sky, an excellent leader of the day, to meet whose glance all beings bend down, who drives away the malevolent and the wicked. Shine on us, O Dawn, thou the daughter of the Sky, bringing happiness in abundance and scattering darkness away. O thou, Lady of Light, each creature's breath and life, cometh borne on thy lofty car, now listen, thou of wondrous wealth, to our call. O Dawn, as thou hast set open today the doors of the heaven, so thou grant us spacious and secure dwellings, free from the fear of wild beasts. Fulfil our noble desires and give us food and milch kine. Make us happy with abundant wealth of many kinds and gladdening plentiful food.

Dawn comes by auspicious ways from high sky's bright realm. Let thy red steeds bring thee down to the house where Soma is poured in oblation. O daughter of the Sky, come mounting the chariot, beautiful, pleasant and ample, to aid and protect a noble man from all evils. Brilliant Dawn, when your rays appear, all living beings start to stir, both bipeds and quadrupeds, and the birds fly in the sky to and fro.

His bright rays now bear him aloft, the God who knows all living things, the Sun, that all may see him. Now, steal away the stars with Night, at the all-beholding Sun's approach. The beams that herald him are seen from afar, shining over homes of men like tongues of fire, that burn and blaze. Swift and beautiful art thou, O Sun, father of the light, who illumines all the radiant realm. Thou shinest upon the hosts of Gods, and likewise on mankind, that the heavenly light may be beheld. With this same eye, O brilliant Varuna, you keep watch upon the busy race of men. Moving across the sky, and the realm of space, thou measure the days by means of your light, seeing all things that have birth. Seven bay steeds drawing your car carry you, O farseeing God, Surya with flaming hair.

Though even this heaven's wide space and earth have spread out, neither heaven nor earth may be Indra's match in greatness. He, mighty and awful like a bull among the herd of cows, whets his thunderbolt. He is like the ocean who receives rivers spread out on all sides. He is like the mighty bull to drink the Soma juice and he being a powerful hero is ever praised for strength.

O Agni, the source of energy, all other fires are thy different branches. All immortals delight in thee. Thou art the centre of all living beings and support of all the creatures, giving them power sustenance. Thou art the centre of the earth and the forehead of heaven and illuminator of all. The sages manifest thee. May we ever adore thee, O God Agni. Thou art sovereign of all the universe, the lord of all objects that mountains hold, of herbs, of the waters and of men. All these objects abide in these, O Vaishvanara, like the rays of light set in the Sun.

The Hotar priest, the lord of all the treasures, Agni is the foremost in sacrifice. The sacrificers who desire their offspring to continue their line are disappointed not in their desire. They all quickly obey the commands of this Agni like sons obedient to their fathers. He, possessing abundant food and wealth, unbars the same like a door, he is to be honoured and served by all.

We the pious men meditate upon God Agni, the omniscient who knows all our acts old or new, all divine laws which regulate the race of mortal men. Let us worship him, who is present as a germ in the waters, in the woods, the rays of the sun and moon, within all movable and immovable things, even in the mountain and mansions. The immortal God is the controller of the objects and cares for all men. Agni, lord of riches, gives wealth to him who serves him with songs. O God, protect all these many creatures on earth, thou being omniscient, knowest the origin of both the Gods and mortal men.

We sing a hymn of praise to Agni as to Yajna we go forth. He listens to our words everywhere far and near. We chant our hymn for him, who preserves his wealth for those who give themselves up to God Agni. Let men speak of him to one another who is the dispeller of darkness, and causes victory to his devotees in every strife.

Accept thou our resounding praise, and the food delightful to the Gods, poured in thy mouth as oblations to be consumed. O Agni, the wisest and the noblest, the best mediator, may we utter to thee an acceptable and much precious prayer. Who among men is your kind? Who are you? On whom dependent? You are of all men the brother and their dear companion, a friend whom friends may supplicate. Bring to us thou Agni, Mitra and Varuna, bring the Gods to honour to thy own hearth.

What is that which may please you? What song of praise shall bring us your divine blessings? With what oblation should we attain you? Come to us Agni, and take your seat. Be our leader. May Earth and Heaven that gratify all protect you, worship the Gods to win their favour for us. Burn all the wicked, O Agni, to protect our Yajna from violence.Bring hither with his steeds the lord of Soma, the giver of prosperity. O thou, our officiating Hotar priest, I invoke you, come to us and be seated among the Gods. I praise you with my lips as noble controller, generator of riches, giver of progeny, O Purifier.

When at thy roar, O Indra, all objects both movable and immovable shook and even Tvashtar became agitated at thy wrath and trembled with fear, did thou, then honour thy sovereign authority and imperial sway. There is none to emulate Indra in his might. In him the Gods have treasured many boons like industry, perseverance and power, which laud his own imperial authority.

O Indra, refresh thee with the Soma juice effused for thy joy and strength. We know thee well to be the lord of ample wealth, therefore, be our protector. We approach thee for the attainment and increase of our strength. These thy subjects, keep for thee all that is worthy of ye. Thou, lord of all, knowest what are the possessions of those men who offer no gifts. Thou bring us this wealth of theirs.

O Indra, yoke your two bay steeds. O Maghavan, listen to our request and do not be negligent to us. When we solicit felicity from you, make us full of joy and happiness. Quickly yoke thy bay steeds, O Indra, for us. The wise men, resplendent like the Sun, have lauded thee with their hymns, the friends have risen and gone after having enjoyed the meals. We bow before you, Indra, thou art so beautiful to look upon. So adored by us and bound with full and true bond of love, subdue our adversaries, yoke your steeds and drive thy car for gaining victory over the wicked. Now, yoke thy Car, O Indra, containing all material of war, arms, weapons and other requisite things, the chariot which brings wealth and kine. O Lord of hundred powers, let thy steeds be harnessed on the right and left of your car. Therefore in the ecstasy of Soma juice, riding the chariot draw thou nigh your consort and gladden her. O lord of mighty arms, I yoke in your chariot the steeds of long and shining manes like the beams of the Sun. Now hold in your hands the reins. The Soma juices have gladdened you, thou thunderer has rejoiced with thy beloved.

Show respects to indra, sing his glory you men. Let the juice of Soma make him glad, pay adoration to his superior strength. When you, O Indra, harness your chariot, there is no better warrior than you, none equal to you in strength, none although well-horsed has overtaken you. He is Indra indeed, who alone bestows wealth on charitably disposed men. His heroism is undisputed, and he is lord of immense strength. When will you trample upon the godless men who have no gifts to offer, as if upon a coiled snake? When will you, verily, listen to our praise? With bones of Dadhichya for his weapon, Indra of indomitable power, has struck ninety-nine Vritras dead.

The Maruts, the loud singers, endowed with great vigour, unbending, immovable, unflinching, impetuous, absolutely fearless, the most beloved, the most manly, have manifested themselves, like the heavens studded with stars, when on the steep they pile the clouds, they look like birds flying along a certain path. The clouds pour sweet rain upon your cars. Rain riches him who sings your laud. When the Maruts march on the path of victory sportfully, roaring loudly and armed with flashing weapons, they magnify their glory. Then, at their march the earth shakes under the wheels of their chariots like a girl suffering from cold fever. Swift moving are your spotted steeds, O youthful Maruts, revered, true and endowed with vigour, sincere, liberator from debt, lords of the army, irreproachable are you and therefore, be our protector.

Come here, ye Maruts on your lightning cars, stored with various weapons and nourishing wholesome food. Fly into us like birds and then go wherever you list. Their tawny or perhaps red-hued horses which speed their cars, they have come for victory. Bright, brave and wonderful is he, who is armed with strong weapons, and who annihilates his enemies with sharp edge of the wheel which is like a thunderbolt. O Maruts, shining with swords upon your bodies, men amass for you wealth like a mountain. You should also bring about their weal. As you stir tall trees in the forest, so may you stir our spirits.

May auspicious, benevolent grace of Gods be ours, may the Gods shower on us their unhindred favours from all sides. May they be our protectors every day for our progress, never failing in their care, being ever alert. May the righteous Gods gladden our hearts with the warmth of their love. We invoke them with Vedic hymns of ancient times Bhaga the prosperous, Mitra Aditi, Daksha, Aryaman, Varuna and Soma. May Goddess Saraswati grant us prosperity and good progeny. May the Wind waft to us beneficial, disease-destroying medicine. May mother Earth grant it, and our father Heaven. May the twain Ashvins, and the stones that press out the Soma juice, hear this our call. May the grace of the Gods encompass us, their friendship we seek. May the grace of the Gods grant us life that we may live! May the illustrious Indra give us prosperity and happiness, may Pushan grant us bliss, the sustainer of the world. May Tarkshya with his firm and unharmed fellies prosper us, may Brihaspati grant us prosperity! May the Maruts, borne by graceful spotted horses, come to us in our rites, moving in their majesty. May Agni whose tongues are flames, radiant like the Sun, come here for our protection. May we ever hear, O Gods, what is good, may we ever see what is good. May we attain such stage of life as is appointed by Gods, through our bodies firm, helpful to the cause of righteousness. A hundred autumns are there for us. O Gods, kindly do not interpose in the midst of these years of our fleeting existence, by inflicting infirmities in our bodies, so that we may gain the age when our sons become fathers in their turn. Aditi is eternal, Aditi is the Sun, the sky, mother, knowledge, father, guardian and son. Whatever has been and shall be in the course of time is all Aditi; Aditi is immortal God and the five classes of men.

May Varuna lead us on the path of Dharma, and Mitra, a friend of all and Aryaman straight on the path of righteousness in accord with the Law. They, the virtuous Gods, protect all evermore the noble persons. May they bestow upon us mortals, shelter and happiness destroying our enemies. May they, Indra, Maruts, Pushan and Bhaga lead us to bliss and prosperity. Ye Gods, our nourishers, enrich our songs with kine and grant us prosperity and happiness. May the winds blow sweetness, the rivers flow sweetness, the herbs be sweet for us, the men of Law. Sweet be the nights, and sweet be the dawns, sweet be the atmosphere, sweet be the Father Heaven. May the tall trees afford sweetness, the Sun shine sweetness. May our kine be sweet for us and milk in plenty! May Mitra, the friend to all, be gracious to us, may Varuna bestow peace on us. May Aryaman, Indra, Brihaspati and Vishnu the almighty, be pleased to grant us peace.

O Soma, endowed with all the glories displayed in heaven, on earth, on the mountains, in the plants and in the waters, do thou, being kind, and devoid of anger, accept our oblations. O Soma, thou art sovereign lord, protector of the noble, Vritra slayer. Thou art most auspicious and omniscient. May we live long and not die prematurely, O God Soma, praise loving lord of herbs and plants. O God, Soma, be glad to dwell in our hearts as cows in milk, in grassy meads, or as a bridegroom in his own house. O God, when in your friendship a mortal man finds delight, then you mighty sage grants him favour. Save us, O Soma, from distress and reproach, be unto us a loving friend. Let your virility come to us from all sides, wax strong at the time of battle between the armies, be thou the destroyer of disease.

The Dawns have spread light over the eastern firmament, they have raised their radiant banner, like warriors brandishing their weapons, onward they march, red-hued, the mother cows. The purple rays of the Dawns have shot up unhindered, yoking to their cars the red clouds. The red-hued Dawns in their splendour have restored, as of old, to sentient beings their clear perception. They sing a song like women engaged in some task, along the same path, coming from afar. They bring refreshment to the liberal devotee and grant all good gifts to those who effuse the juice. She, like a dancer puts her ornaments on, as a cow yields her udder, so she bares her bosom. Creating light for all animate beings, she hath laid the gates of darkness open, as cows their stall. We have beheld the radiance of her face, it spreads driving away the monstrous night. Like a tinted post, decorated at the sacrifice, the Heaven's daughter hath attained the wonderful splendour.

Now we are on the other side of the darkness. Dawn, shining forth again gives clear vision. She smiles like a flatterer, immersed in glory, her face hath awakened us to joy. The chanting sacrificers have praised the Heaven's radiant daughter, the lady of charms. Dawn, thou grant us strength with offspring and men, make us rich in steeds and kine. Dawn, thou shines forth in wisdom and splendour, urged by your own strength. O auspicious one, grant us ample wealth, renown, brave sons, servants and possession of horses. Having lighted up the whole world with her gaze, she spreads her radiance towards west. She awakens all living beings to the labour and pays heed to the call of every worshipper. This ancient of days, born anew again and again, decking herself with the same ornaments, she wastes away the life of mortal men like a skilled bird catcher who holds in his clutches the feathery creatures. Discovering the heaven's borders, she has chased away her sister Night to the far distance. She reflects the splendour of her lover, the Sun and dwindles the days of human mortals. She, the blessed, the radiant, shines forth spreading her rays like grazing kine, as floods rolling, never transgressing the divine laws, she is beheld by all, being escorted by the rays.

O Dawn, of ample wealth, bestow on us the wondrous gifts that we may nourish therewith our children and children's sons. O auspicious lady, uttering sweet sounds, shine on us now with wealth of cattle and steeds. O Dawn, enriched with sacred sacrifice, harness to thy car purple steeds and bring to us all felicities. O Ashvins, with one mind and intention drive your car to our home, enriching us with cattle and gold. You who brought down the sweet song from heaven, a light that lights up the world of men, give us strength now, O Ashvins! May they who wake at dawn, bring here Soma juice for Gods to drink, the bestowers of health, doers of wondrous deeds, borne on paths of gold.

O Agni to you, worthy of our laud, we send this eulogy as it were a car. Auspicious is thy love for us. Let us not suffer harm in your assembly and friendship. The man whom thou favours, prospers, achieves success, strength and lives without a foe. Poverty touch him not, he grows strong. Let us not suffer in thy friendship. O Agni, may we have power to kindle thee. Grant our desires, through you the Gods acquire good food. Bring hither the Adityas. for whom we long. May we never suffer harm in thy friendship. We bring fuel and offering for the sacrifice, acquiring virtues with perfect means. Grant us our desires and longevity. May we never suffer harm in thy friendship. O God, desired by all, thou knowest how to grant prosperity, prolong our life here. May Varuna grant our prayers, and Aditi, Sindhu, Mitra, Earth and Heaven.

Shine, thou Agni, wealth on us and chase away our sins. May Agni burn down our sins! We make our sacrifice to you for fair fields, goodly homes and for wealth. May Agni burn up our sins! He and others who surpass in devotion are the best. May Agni burn up our sins! O Agni, let high priests spring from you. May we be reborn in you. May Agni burn up our sins! The mighty Agni's flames penetrate universally, his visage shines bright in every direction. May the God burn up our sins! Your face is turned to every side. Thou art immanent in every thing. May the God burn up our sins! The God whose glory shines in every direction may take us across safely as in a boat. May the lord burn up our sins! O God, take us across safely, across the stream, as in a boat. May the Lord burn up our sins!

May we subsist in Vaishvanara's favour. He is sovereign Lord of living beings, the leader of all the creatures, verily the rival of the

Sun. He is present in the sky, present upon the earth, he pervades all the herbs. May that all-pervading God, with his vigour, guard us night and day against all violent men. May we acquire your vow of truth, may wealth collect around us in profusion. May Mitra, Varuna, Aditi, Sindhu, Earth and Heaven grant this prayer of ours!

Let us effuse the Soma juice for Jatvedas, may he consume the wealth of a wicked man. May he carry us beyond all difficulties and troubles, as if in a boat crossing a river!

May Indra, the cause of rains, resplendent King of the earth and heaven, the home of strength, associated with the Maruts, worthy of acceptance, be invoked for our protection! May Indra whose glory is like the Sun, the slayer of Vritra, present in every fray, the mightiest, girt by the Maruts, be ever for our protection. The limits of Indra's powers cannot be reached, neither by the Gods, however divine, nor by men, nor yet by the Waters. In might he surpasses both Heaven and Earth. May he, in association with Maruts, be our protector.

Mighty Indra's power shines in the heaven in one form, the other shines on the earth, and is possessed by the sages of yore. The one in the heaven and the other on the earth, both manifest his glory like a bright banner in a battle. Indra who spread the earth wide and sustains it, struck the lightning with his bolt and unloosed the floods, he also struck dead the demons. To Indra, the mighty and true hero, who is the author of many noble deeds, to him verily we pour out our Soma juice. It is he who takes away wealth from the godless men who do not perform the Yajna. O Indra, thou did a glorious deed when you awoke the slumbering foe with thy bolt. Then the divine Dames were delighted, the Maruts and all the other Gods were overjoyed, much pleased and exulted were they, when you destroyed the enemy forts as the Sun destroys the mighty clouds. May this prayer of ours Varuna grant, and Mitra, Aditi, Sindhu, Earth and Heaven!

We have made an altar for Indra to rest upon. Hasten thou hither to sit upon it as a panting horse. Loosen your steeds, set free your flying coursers, who bear you day and night to distant places. Grant us, Indra, a share of sunlight, of waters, freedom from sin, and good reputation. Do not in any way harm our heart-desired joys for we have great trust in thy mighty powers! We place our trust in you and your truthfulness. Do not deprive us of good food and noble offspring. O Indra, invoked by many, do not consign us to destitute houses. Lead thou to ample riches and provide us with food and drink when hungry. Harm us not, O Indra, forsake us not, deprive us not of the enjoyments dear to us, nor injure our unborn offspring, nor take away our vessels of gold and steel. Come to us, O lover of Soma, we have it ready for you. Drink it for joy. Let the juice be within you and when called upon, listen us as a father does his sons.

Those who desire wealth gain it, wife enjoys the closeness of her husband, and they entwined in each others embrace, both share the bliss. Mark this my hymn, O Earth and Heaven! I ask, the Sacrifice should be as a messenger tell me the truth. Where is the ancient law divine? Who bears it amongst the modern men? Mark this my hymn, O Earth and Heaven! O Gods, abiding in the three lucid regions of the heaven, tell me, what is truth and untruth? Where is my call on you of yore? Mark this hymn, O Varun's watchful eye! How can we go beyond the wicked on the path to Aryaman? Mark this my hymn, O Earth and Heaven! I the thoughtful sang many a laud of old when Soma was effused, yet carrion crows consume me like a wolf who attacks a thirsty deer. Mark this my hymn, O Earth and Heaven!

The Radiant, the Fair has come, to her the dark Night has consigned her home. Both akin and allied to the Sun, immortal, succeeding and effacing each other mutually, traverse the heavens. These sisters have a common and unending pathway, they travel it alternately guided by the Sun combined in purpose, though of diverse forms, Dawn and Night of the endless morns that have gone by and first of the endless mornings to come, being the dispenser of darkness, urges and awakens every living being, but she awakes not one from his slumber who is dead. The men who looked upon the rising Dawn of yore have departed. We the living now see her and feel happy. Those who shall behold her hereafter will also feel happy. From times immemorial the radiant Usha has been rising with her splendour of light, full of wealth. So will she shine hereafter in future times. Eternal, she moves on with her own strength. On the sky's border she has appeared in foil splendour, the Goddess has thrown off the veil of darkness. Her well yoked chariot of purple steeds, heralding her approach, has awakened the world.

Bringing all the life-sustaining blessings with her, brilliantly she shines sending forth her radiance. She is the last of countless mornings that have disappeared, she is the first of bright ones yet to arrive. Arise, the breath of life is again here, darkness has fled and light approaches. For the Sun she has left a pathway to travel. We have arrived where men's existence continues. With the web of songs for Dawns, the priest, the bard rises. They drive onward steering their way, the radiant ones. Shine then today, O bounteous Dawn on him who sing thy praise, shine on us the gifts of life and children! Mother of Gods. Aditi's radiant form, token of sacrifice, shine forth exalted. Rise up, looking on our devotion with favour and be gracious to make us chief among the people. Whatever marvellous wealth the Dawns bestow as blessings to bless a devotee, who offers oblations, that may Mitra and Varuna vouchsafe us, and Aditi, Sindhu, Earth and Heaven!

The Sun follows the radiant Usha, the Goddess, as a youth follows an elegant maiden. In whose auspicious presence learned men calculate the ages for happy days to come. Auspicious are his bay steeds, splendid, swift, changing colours and praiseworthy are they. Bearing our prayers they circumambulate the Earth and Heaven with speed. When the mighty Sun withdraws his majesty which spreads all over the world, people stop their labour leaving the work even unfinished. Then, Night spreads her veil of darkness over all the world.

The same today, the same tomorrow, the joyous Dawns do not transgress the eternal law. The irreproachable, they traverse the long and distant space in a moment and can be seen across the thirty regions. Though born out of gloom but she is shining, white and refulgent and marks the advent of the day. This Maiden transgresses not the eternal law, and comes day by day to the appointed place. The noble Dawn manifests herself like an ever active maiden, and goes to her loving husband, the Sun. She being youthful and maiden meets the Sun smiling and uncovering her bosom and shining lustrously. Radiant as a bride, well embellished by her mother, she displays her beautiful form that all may behold. Blessed are you, O Dawn, shine yet more splendidly. May thy joy never decay. Opulent in kine, steeds and wealth, she is ever possessed of the rays of the Sun, the Dawn goes away and returns again in her usual form sending down her happy gifts.

This Dawn, first of many and radiant to look on, debars from her light neither kinsman nor stranger. Proud of her pure form, she shining brightly, spurns not the great nor the humble. She seeks man like a maiden without a brother and ascends her car as if to gather riches. She shining forth and well ornamented, bares her beauty like a loving woman to her husbands. The sister Night relinquishes her place to her elder sister. The Dawn having seen Night departed, decks herself with shining rays of the Sun, like a girl going to keep a date in a festival. Of these sisters of whom one has just now vanished, a later one succeeds the former in the course of days. So, may these Dawns shine wealth on us as of yore and bring us a happy day.

Ask of him, the God Agni, he comes, he knows it, he the wise is implored. In him are commands, in him are counsels and requests. He is the Lord of power and strength. All men ask him not as seekers of truth, and yet fewer learn. The Sage has all things in his grasp, he goes with his mind composed, for he knows the first word and the last. To him ascend these oblations, these prayers reach him like speedy mares. He listens to my prayers, all-conquering, all-speeding, perfector of sacrifice, the Child, ever helpful, he has assumed great powers. Whatever he meets, he grasps and marches on, and thus newly born advances farther straight way. He bestows joy and pleasure to the weary, accepting their gifts as he comes. He, the true lord, is a thing of flood and forest. He has been laid on the highest at the altar. He, the wise, knows the law and directs the mortal men to right action.

I laud Agni, the wise seven rayed who pervades all the regions, the higher, the middle and the lower ones. Seated in the lap of his parents and pervading all the luminous realms of heaven and all objects he is perfect. He is a great sustainer grand and undecaying. He keeps his feet firm over the world, his red tongues lick the clouds in the heaven. Like the milch kine, the Earth and Heaven move together towards their common child and fully nourish it. They measure out and uphold the path free from all that is to be avoided, the path that is to be traversed. The learned men escort him to his dwelling, protecting him the ever youthful. They turn him with reverence and are shown the Sun. He is accessible and inspirer of all, the great and the small alike.

I will declare the mighty deeds of Vishnu, of him who measured out the earthly realms and propped the heavens, accomplishing all in three mighty strides. For this mighty deed is Vishnu acclaimed. He roams the mountains, like a wild beast, wandering as he will, he in whose three mighty paces are the three worlds. Let my song of praise ascend to Vishnu, the Bull of mighty strides who dwells the mountains, to him who with triple stride has measured out these far spread regions. Him whose three paces are filled with such sweetness, imperishable, the cause of joy. He alone verily sustains the three—the Earth, the Heaven, and all the living beings. May I attain to his glorious abode, where men devoted to Gods live in bliss, where close to the Strider, in Vishnu's footstep, springs the well, pure and sweet. O Lord! For your abode, where dwell the oxen ever fresh and possessed of many horns, for there shines down upon the world, from the highest, the Hero of wide strides!

How noteworthy and wonderful hath been your advent, O Steed, when you emerged from the ocean or space and neighed seeing the light. You possessed the limbs of a deer and pinions of an eagle. Your birth must be lauded indeed. This Steed, Yama's gift, Trita harnessed and Indra was the first to mount. The Gandharva first of all held its reins. From the substance of the Sun, O Gods, you fashioned forth this Steed. You are Yama, O Steed, you are Aditya, you are Trita by a secret operation. You are distinguished from Soma only a little. You are said to have three connections in heaven. Three bonds you are said to possess, three bonds in heaven, three in water and three in the ocean. You resemble Lord Varuna, O Steed, there they say is your highest birth place. Here, O courser, are the place where you have been groomed, here are the prints of your winning hooves. Here I have seen your auspicious reins that guide you, which, those who guard the cosmic law, protect. I perceive from far your soul, a bird that soars high in the heaven. I have seen your form soaring higher and higher along the paths free from dust and pleasant to travel. Behind you, O Steed, come a car, the hero and an offering of kine, and then the maidens. Desiring your friendship they follow with vigour have the Gods blessed you. His horns are of gold, his feet are of iron. He is as swift as thought, but less swift than Indra. The Gods have assembled to taste the sacred oblation, offered to him who mounted the Steed first to all. Like swans flying in a row the celestial steeds put forth their might when they reach the heavenly pathway, the horses symmetrical in form, of thin bellies and of fiery spirit. Your body, O Steed, is made to fly as on wings, your spirit moves fast as the wind, your horns are spread wide in space, they speed with restless motion in wilderness. The mighty Steed has come to the place of sacrifice, with his mind composed and thoughts directed towards God. The goat of his kin is led before him, the sages and singers follow next. The Steed has attained the highest abode, he has reached the place of his Father and his Mother. May he receive utmost welcome today from the Gods and win good gifts for him who offers.

The Earth standing up below the upper region, and above the lowest one, bears her calf like a cow. Whither and to what place does she go? How calves she? Not amid this herd of cattle. Two birds with beauteous wings, knit together in bonds of friendship, reside on the self same eternal tree. One of the twain enjoys the sweet and ripe fruit of the tree, whereas the other eating not simply observes.

I ask you about the farthest limit of the earth? Where is the navel of the world? What is the Stallion's prolific seed? Tell me about the highest heaven where abides the speech? This altar is the earth's farthest limit, this sacrifice of ours the world's navel, the Soma is the Stallion's prolific seed, and Brahma is the highest heaven where the speech abides.

The speech is measured out in four quarters, the sages with insight know it. The three kept in close secret cause no movement, the fourth is the division that is talked about by men.

God is one but sages call Him by various names. They call Him Indra, Mitra, Varuna, the mighty universal spirit Garutmat. They call Him Agni, Yama and Matarishvan.

It is not today, nor is it tomorrow. Who knows the mystery? It (the soul) has motion and action in the consciousness of another, but when approached by the thought, it vanishes. Why do thou seek Indra to strike us? The Maruts are your brothers. Achieve perfection with their help, slay us not in our struggle. Why O Agastya, my brother and friend, dost thou neglect us? Well we know the nature of thy mind and that thou will give us naught. Let them set the altar, let them kindle Agni in front. We two are here to extend to you our sacrifice that the Gods would observe. O Lord of wealth, Master of power and love, thou art the strongest. Do thou, O Indra, agree with the Maruts and enjoy the oblations in their proper seasons.

To you I come with my obeisance and by this hymn I seek the Strong One's grace. Take delight, O Maruts, in my hymn, lay your anger aside and unyoke your steeds. This laud full of my obeisance, framed by my heart and mind, is offered to ye, O Maruts. Come unto us, ye rejoicing to make our prayer fruitful. Let the Maruts, lauded be gracious to us. Let Indra, be propitious, praised by us. Let our days, O Maruts, that are to follow be full of delight. Trembling with fear of Indra I fled. O Maruts, the oblations meant for you were put aside. Forgive and be gracious to us.

By whom the mind grows conscient and sharp, in the mornings through the powers of the Dawns, give us thou, O Bull amidst the herd, the glorious energy with Maruts, thou fierce with the fierce, steadfast and giver of strength. Do thou protect the Heroes with their increased strength, O Indra, put aside thy wrath against the Maruts. With the wise Maruts be victorious. May be find nourishing food in abundance.

Which of these two came earlier, which later? How were they born? Who, O Seers, knoweth it? These of themselves support and contain all that bears a name, and days and nights revolve as on a wheel. These two, though motionless and footless, nourish and uphold a variety of offspring having foot and movement. Like parents holding a child on their bosom, O Earth and Heaven protect us from evil! I call for boundless Aditi's favour, bounteous, divine, perfect, inviolable, worthy of reverence. O ye Twain Worlds, procure it for him who worships you. O Heaven and Earth, protect us from evil! May we be close to both these worlds who know no suffering, parents of the Gods, who grant favours. Both are divine, with day and night alternate. O Heaven and Earth protect us from evil! These Twin Sisters, lying together in their parents bosom, kiss the centre of the world. O Heaven and Earth protect us from the evil! These two far spread realms, the parents of the Gods, I call with reverence for their protection. May they, beautiful to look upon, grant us life. O Heaven and Earth, protect us from evil.

This reverent pair, vast, far flung, variegated, I address at this our sacrifice. May this blessed pair come to our aid. O Heaven and Earth protect us from evil! Whatever sin as we might have committed any time against the Gods, a friend, or a chief, of this may our this hymn be expiation. O Heaven and Earth protect us from evil! May Heaven and Earth, blesss and preserve me with their aids and favour. May they grant riches to the men more liberal than the godless. May we, ye Gods be strong with plenty of nourishing food! With great understanding I have uttered the truth, for all to hear on Earth and Heaven. Protect us from every evil, be near unto us and preserve us. Ye Father and Mother! Fulfil, ye Earth and Heaven, this my prayer, wherewith, Father and Mother I address you! Be nearest of all Gods with your protection. May we have wholesome food in abundance.

Now my song will glorify Food, giver of strength through whom the Keeper of nectar smother the Demon dead. O Savoury Food, Food so sweet, thee we have chosen as our own, be our kind protector! Come to us, O delightful food and bring pleasant refreshment. Be thou our friend, health-giving and guileless! Your flavours, O Food, throughout the atmosphere are spread, like winds they are scattered. O Food, you are the sweetest and the best, and all these gifts are thine. Your juices create energy and delight in all the creatures. In you, O Food, abides all that the greatest Gods desire. Brave deeds were done under your flag, he slew the Demon under it. If you have gone into the splendour of high mountains, even from there, O sweet Food, return to us for our enjoyment.

By righteous path lead us to riches, Agni, lead us, O Lord, you know every duty. Deliver to us from the Sun that leads astray. We shall hymn ye with ample praise. Lead us afresh, O Lord, to bliss, lead us across the dangers and pitfalls. Be thou unto us, a high, broad and powerful tower, bless and grant peace and wellbeing to our children. Sweep away from us, Agni, all diseases, let them strike those who do not have Agni to their aid. May our dwellings be full of blessings, with all the Gods present, O Holy.

Consign us not as a prey to the wicked and the enemy, O Lord. Give us not over to the fanged that bites, nor to the toothless. Give us up not, thou conqueror, to the spoiler. A God like you, born after law, O Agni, giveth protection when lauded, preserving him against harm and reproach, for you O Lord, rescuest him from all ambush. To this Lord, we have addressed these words, I son of Man, have lauded Agni, the mighty. May we acquire wealth with the aid of seers, and be enriched with nourishing food in full abundance!

Book Second

O Agni, thou shinest with thy radiance through the days. Thou art generated pure, worthy of reverence, from out of the waters and stones, and forest trees, herbs and plants that grown on earth. Thou art our protector and ruler. One who acts according to the holy Law, you become his brother. Those who worship you, thou art a Son to them, and as a dear friend you guard them from every attack. The generous worshippers, who send liberal gifts of kine and steeds, to them who laud thee, O Agni, thou lead both these men and us to abiding happiness. May we in the assembly of the learned speak the truth!

Now laud Agni, as a charioteer, in race praises his own car, so now praise yoking of Agni's car, the bounteous, the most splendid. He who guides his worshipper aright and withers the foe, without being himself, withered by the age, Agni, the God fair to look upon when offered oblation. He who is lauded, in our homes, whose splendour is magnified at evening and morning, whose law is inviolate. Who shines like the Sun in his splendour, whose flames blaze ever, who sparkles with undecaying radiance. Him our songs of praise have waxed strong. Now he shines with all his glories. May we with the help of Agni, that of Indra and Soma, ye with the help of all the Gods unharmed dwell, and overthrow those who fight with us!

He, who by birth was chief of the Gods, the most wise, became the God's protector with his strength and power. Before whose great and mighty deeds the two realms shake, he, O men is Indra, the lord! He transfixed the earth that trembled, and set at rest the agitating mountains, who measured out the vast middle region in the space and propped the heaven, he, O men, is Indra, the Lord! He smother the Dragon dead, released the seven rivers and drove the kine out from the Demon's cave, brought forth the fire from between the two rocks, the hero ever victorious, O men, he is Indra! By whom this world can be made to shake, who humbling, swept away the enemy host, who, like a gambler collects his winnings from vanquished enemy, he, O men, is Indra! Many have an urge to know about him and ask where is he, the Terrible? Or some verily say, he is not, who like birds sweeps away the riches at stake, have faith in him, he, O men, is Indra! who inspires all, the poor, the humble and the strong alike to work, urging also the priest who sings his songs of praise, the fair-faced one, and him who presses out Soma juice with stones laid ready, he, O men, is Indra!

Under whose supreme control are steeds, cars, cattle and villages all, by whose power the Sun and Dawns come to birth, who leads and waters, he, O men is Indra! Who is called upon by both the enemies in the battle, the stronger and the weaker, by the twain in the same self chariot, each for himself threatened with danger, he, O men, is Indra! Without whose aid one never conquers the battle, whom the fighting warriors continously implore for help, who moves the immovable, he, O men, is Indra! Who smote long before they knew it, with his arrows, the wicked foemen, who pardons not the sinner, who strikes the demons dead, he, O men, is Indra! Who once discovered in the fortieth autumn Shambara dwelling in the mountains, and slew him putting forth his vigour, the demon lying down, there, he, O men, is Indra!

Who, the seven-reined bull, most mighty, freed the seven floods to flow at will, and shattered to pieces with his thunderbolt Rauhina, while he scaled the heavens, he, O men, is Indra. To whom Earth and Heaven make obeisance, before whose very breath the mountains tremble, the famed Soma lover, thunder-armed, he, O men, is Indra! Who with his aid helps the Soma presser, and him who brews it and him who chants his praise or offers libations. Whom our prayers exalt and the flowing forth of Soma and these our gifts, he, O men, is Indra. Thou Indra, who grants boons to men who press out and pour forth Soma in libation, art terrible and true. May we be evermore your dear friends and speak loudly in the assembly with our heroes!

For him, who scores victory overall, the Lord of truth, of wealth, horses and kine, for him who is Lord of waters and other resources, for Indra, the holy, shed Soma juice. For him who smashes and destroys the enemy, the ever winner, never conquered, the protector from enemy onslaught, worthy to rule over all, for heroic Indra, sing your sacred prayer. O Indra, grant us the best of boons, a pondering mind and fortune, increase of wealth, protection to our bodies, the sweet winsome speech, and days that are pleasant and fair.

At the Trikadrukeshu ceremony, the mighty Indra has drunk Soma blended with barley meal. With Vishnu, he hath drunk the juice to his fill, and it has waxed him strong to perform his mighty deeds. So, may Indra attain the other God, Soma, the true. He, who is resplendent and mighty, overcame the demon Krivi in the battle by his strength. He waxes strong with his might and fills both the worlds with his majesty. One share of libation he has devoured and the other he has left. So, may God attain the other God.

This hymn to Aditya, the wise and self-effulgent, shall be supreme above all for ever! I beg Varuna, the mighty for fame, the God who is exceedingly gracious to all those who worship him. May we possess ample wealth through these hymns of ours, sung in thy service with great care and reverence, O Varuna! We laud thee like the fires that are kindled each morning with their promise of kine and wealth. May we be ever under thy protection, O Lord of heroes, the king of vast kingdom. O Sons of boundless Aditi, God's ever faithful, forgive our sins, and admit us unto thy friendship. He, the God Varuna, made the rivers flow. They flow on at his command, their sustainer. They stop not flowing, nor get tired and they run swift like birds in flight in the air. Loose me from sin as from bond that binds, may our life swell your river of Law, O Varuna! Let not the thread of my life be severed while I weave the web of song, nor my work be cut short before its time, O Lord!

Sweep far away from me, all dangers. O Varuna, accept me favourably you holy Lord! Release me from my troubles that enslave me, like a calf from its cords, I am powerless even to wink my eyes without your help. Strike us not with dreadful weapons which strike the wicked at the command. May we never pass into darkness from light. Scatter them for our comfort far away who would harm us. As of yore, we will sing your praise, O almighty God, now and hereafter. In thyself, O invincible, are fixed firmly thy statue, as on a mountain. Sweep far away from me the sins committed by me, let me not suffer for the sin of other. Many more mornings remain to shine on us. May we enjoy them as long as we live. O Varuna, protect us from the man, be he a friend or relation who has threatened my peace even in a dream, affrighting me, and the wolf or the thief who wish to harm us. Let me never be deprived of my rich and liberal dear friend. O Varuna, may I never lack well managed wealth. May we speak out our mind loudly in the assembly as heroes!

O Gods, truly ye are our kinsmen, be ye kind to me who now supplicates. May your car never come slowly to our rites, nor we be ever weary of kinsmen such as ye are. I alone have committed many a sin against you, and you chastised me as a sire his gambler son. Far removed be mine offences, and so be your snares. Swoop ye down not upon me as does a bird on its offspring. Come unto us now ye holy Gods, that we with awe may approach to win you over. Protect us, O Gods from the wolf who would devour us. Save us from falling into a pit.

O Father of winds, let your grace shine on us. Let us not be deprived of the light of the Sun. May the hero on his steed be kind to us, may we live forth in our progeny. O Rudra, with your efficacious medicines, which you administer to cure us, may I live for hundred years. Banish from us all hatred and trouble and maladies to four quarters. O mightiest among the mighty, most famed, ye thunderer, escort us across the troubles to our weal and remove all assaults of the wicked. May we never displease you, O Rudra, with worship, by ill-praise or scanty devotion. Restore our heroes to health with your best balms, for I know, thou art the best of physicians.

Where is thy gracious hand, O Rudra, whose benign touch I crave, which heals and grants comfort, which removes the punishments sent by Gods. O Mighty God, look upon me with a compassionate eye. To him, who is mighty, great, fair-complexioned, I sing a lofty song of praise. We serve him with lauds, we magnify the splendid name of Rudra. This God of firm limbs and of many forms, the mighty and tawny, decks himself with bright gold ornaments. The power divine of this sovereign Lord, the ruler over the world never diminishes, worthy are you of your bow and arrows, worthy of the multi-hued and splendid insignia. Worthy you are to meet and overthrow any fiend, for there is none more mighty than you. Praise him, the car-borne, far renowned, the ever young God, who slays like a fierce beast of the wild. O Rudra, praised and hymned, be gracious to your singers, let your hosts spare us and strike down some other. Just as a son makes obeisance to his sire with reverence, so I bow down to you, O God, as you approach. I praise you, the bounteous Lord, giver of riches. Grant us medicines as thou art praised. The remedies so efficacious and pure, which are so wholesome and health-giving, which our father Manu chose, I beg from Rudra for our wellbeing. May Rudra's missiles deflect and spare us, may great Rudra's wrath spare us. Turn your bow aside from our friends and wellwishers, O Rudra, and be gracious to our sons and their children! O mighty Bull, who never slumbers, slay us not. Here, listen to our invocation. May we speak out our mind in the assembly loudly like heroes.

Savitar, the God who lights up and sustains the world, has risen up to urge the priest to his sacrificial duty. He grants riches to the Gods, and beatitude to the man who invites Gods to the sacrifice. Having risen up, the God spreads his arms widely forth for the good of the world. The sacred waters flow in his service, and the winds blow in limitless space. Though borne on swift rays, he will yet unyoke them and stop the car from moving. He controls the haste of those who slink away like serpents. Night follows Savitar closely. Then the warrior, desiring victory, returns from the battle, all the living beings begin to long for their dwellings, and the artisans leave their work unfinished.

At sunset, when Varuna seeks his abode in haste, and birds their nests and beasts their shelters, God Savitar provides a nice dwelling to each creature. Him whose Law is inviolate for Indra, Varuna, Mitra, Aryaman, Rudra and the wicked foe men, the God Savitar, I call upon now for my welfare. He protects us mortals and the celestial Dames. May the Gods worthy of invocation, most wise, mighty, help us. May we attain bliss, wealth and favour of Savitar. May the riches come to us from heavens, and earth and waters, bestowed upon us by the Gods.

Soma and Pushan, the parents of riches, of the heaven and earth, the stetwain the guardian of the world, are the centre of eternal life. At their birth all the other Gods rejoice. With Soma, Pushan and other Gods, Indra causes to generate the fresh, warm milk in the new milch kine. O Soma and Pushan, come hither on your seven-wheeled car that move everywhere measuring out all the realms. This car of your, five-reined and yoked by thought, O Gods, moving everywhere, inspires only the chosen ones. Pushan, the divine dwells in the highest realm, and on the earth and in the mid-region dwells Soma. May ye grant us ample wealth, the source of nourishing food and enjoyment, craved so much and by so many men. One of ye Twain, is the Father of all the beings, the other travels forth inspecting all. May ye Gods protect our Yajna, may we overcome all our foemen with your aid. May Pushan urge our thoughts, may Soma grant us wealth. May Aditi the boundless help us. May we speak out our mind loudly in the assembly of the learned like heroes.

Book Third

Agni made both the earth and heaven light up by his birth, an admirable son of the two mothers, worthy to be implored. He is oblation bearer of Gods, undecaying, beneficent for food, affuent in radiance, ever youthful, and all-pervading. The Gods with their intelligence, preserving strength and powers, generated Agni. I being desirous of gaining strength, generate Agni who is like a horse, great and bright with radiance and so vigorous. We choose Agni, eager to acquire joy and strength, him who is praiseworthy and ever so friendly. He is highly desirable, shining with celestial splendour, waxing strong with the sages' laud. The sacrificers, having spread the sacred grass, establish radiant Agni before them in the Yajna and raise ladles to him for happiness. He, the resplendent, beloved of all the Gods, present at all sacred rites, accomplishes the Yajna.

The Agni has filled both heaven and earth and the spacious firmament with light, giving great delight to the Gods by his birth. He is led to the Yajna like a horse. Let the sages ever revere him to win us strength. O learned, honour and serve him, the oblation-bearer, the lord of house, the seer of truth, the friend. He is also the upholder of the law, evermost active and giver of knowledge of all that exists. The three radiant forms of circumambient Agni, which are indestructible, purify all. One of these divine forms has been given to men for their enjoyment. The other two pervade the sister realms and its objects. The people desiring the fulfilment of their wishes offer him oblations, him the lord of men, the Sage of human beings. He stirs with life when generated and creates a roar like a lion or a laud bellow like a bull. Agni, the beneficient to all, the immortal, bestows wealth and gifts on his devotees. He, the benevolent, ascends to the heaven and roams in his own way, as of old. He gives wealth to all, as of old, ever watchful and moving. We implore Agni for wealth and prosperity, him who is most radiant, gold-haired and bright. He is verily admirable because he makes us dwell in happy homes and upholds the law.

Agni, the wonderful envoy, goes between the earth and heaven and as the high hotar priest of men bears oblations. He adorns the lofty dwelling places with his radiant flames, sent forth by the deities and made strong with hymns. We, the learned men laud him with sincere praise, the symbol of Yajna. Through him, the noble sacrificers, in association with other wise men, attain happiness and bliss. Agni, the protector and symbol of all sacrifices, the great God of the learned and wise, the ordainer of the earth and other worlds, has pervaded heaven and earth giving joy to his worshippers in various ways, being present everywhere. He the effulgent whose chariot is radiant like the gold, possessing great powers pervades all the dwells in the floods. He, cherished by all, swift and wild, established by Gods, bestows happiness. He, borne on car, moves between the earth and heaven accomplishing many sacred rites, the swift lord of the household who removes curses. He fulfils desires, destroys diseases and promotes sacrifices in his different forms. O learned men, hymn Agni for good sons and long life. O God, grant us proper and nourishing food in plenty, satisfy the learned men thou ever watchful, desiring the company of other Gods.

For sacrificial act, an exalted priest has been appointed, and Agni, the taker of oblations to the higher realms, has been kindled. Through Yajna, the oblations offered, soar high to the firmament. The priest has been seated in the centre of the radiant hall and the sacred grass spread for the Gods to rest. May Night and Dawn, praised come hither, through different in forms but smiling. May Varuna and Mitra and Indra in association with the Maruts serve and gladden us. I crave the favour of Agni and Varuna, the two chiefs of heavens and propitiate them with seven kinds of oblations. They hold truth and ever admire the truth. They always observe their vows and uphold the law.

O lord of the forest, annointed with the sacred oil in sacrifice by the priests, grant us wealth when you stand upright or when you repose on another Earth's bosom. Set up to the East of the sacred fire, accept our prayer, never decaying. Driving away far from us poverty and want, hold yourself high to give us prosperity. Lord of the forest, lift yourself up on the highest spot of the earth, and give glory and splendour to one who brings a sacrifice, O fixed and measured one! Well clad and adorned, he comes, the youthful, and yet is fairer by far when sprung to new life. The sages, whose meditative mind is ever turned godwards rear him. Born anew, he is raised up on a day most fair, waxing great in wisdom in the assembly of men. Wise and skilful men consecrate him with hymns, approaching the Gods, the singers chant aloud. O Lord of the forest, whom religious men have so firmly planted, and the axe has fashioned, be gracious to give us riches along with children, O divine post of sacrifice.

May ye posts, filled and fixed in the ground, to which the sacrificial ladles have been raised, which mark the boundaries of the field, bring blessings from Gods full of precious things. The Gods, Adityas, Rudras, Vasus leading Earth and Heaven and earth's atmosphere shall bless our rites and raise the banner of our sacrifice high in the sky. Like swans that fly in a long drawn out line, the posts have come to us in various shining colours. Raised high by the learned in the East, they go forth as Gods to Gods' dwelling places. These posts, fixed in the ground and embellished with circles, appear to sight like horns of horned creatures. Raised by the priests in invocation, may these help us with their aids in the battle. O Lord of the forest, whom the axe has whetted, set in our midst, put forth a hundred branches, and so may we rise with a thousand branches.

O resplendent Agni, we the mortals, meditate upon and communicate with you, whom the sages kindle in sacrifice. You are Lord of men and other beings and giver of happiness. They worship you in their sacred rites as an accomplisher of sacrifice and all in all. Thou shine forth in thine on dwelling as upholder of the Law. One who worships you with fuel acquires knowledge of all the things. He attains strength and prospers from all sides. He, loftly like a banner, has come with Gods, accompanied by seven priests, to him who offers oblations and gifts. To Agni utter lofty speech and offer your best gifts, who purifies all and inspires hymns. May our hymns refurbish Agni, worthy of our praise, growing mighty in strength and spectacular as he multiplies. Thou, Agni, the best Priest, most venerable, bring the Gods here to the holy men. You are a giver of delight and your radiance drives away our foemen afar. O

Purifier, shine on us good wealth and glory. Be ever nigh to those who laud you for their wellbeing. O ever awake and watchful, versed in holy hymns, the sages kindle thee, oblation bearer, full of vigour, divine and deathless.

Be kind, O Agni, when we approach you, good as a friend to friend, or like parents to their child. Thou burn those up who are great oppressors among men, consume all the wicked who scheme against us. Burn up the unfriendly neighbour, and foe man's curses issuing forth from impious lips. Burn, thou all-seeing, the foolish, surround yourself with thy eternal lofty flames. This fuel and sacred oil, O Agni, I eagerly present for strength and victory. With this sacred hymn, as far as I have powers, worshipping, I crave a hundred blessings. Thou Son of Strength, grant with thy warmth, when worshipped and praised, great vitality and power to those who toil in your service. We have anointed thy body. O Liberal Lord, grant us great riches, as you possess, when enkindled, with your arms far extended, send it to the dwelling of your happy singer.

O Agni, repel hostile forces, and drive away our foemen. O insuperable, surpassing all the foes, give riches to the worshippers. O immortal God, lit up with libation, who calls Gods to banquet, be pleased and come to our sacrifice. Thou Son of Strength, resplendent, ever vigilant, invoked by men, come and sit here on this sacred grass. We sing songs of praise to exalt Agni and ail other Gods, and all those enlightened men who attend the wholly rites. Agni, kindly grant your favours and wealth in heroes and prosperity to all your devotees. Make us prosperous in noble and righteous progeny.

O all-knowing Agni, accept this our oblation of Purodasha (a cake with butter) at morning session of the sacrifice, rich in hymns. O Radiant, this cake with butter has been prepared and dressed for you, accept it, O ever youthful God! O Agni, accept this well cooked good food prepared in day time, and lovingly offered, O Son of Strength. Please accept this afternoon food offering of the sacrifice, O wise and learned Agni. The sages in sacrifices never diminish the offerings due to you, the most mighty. O mighty Son of Strength, accept this Purodasha in this third course of libation and enjoy. Bear this offering to the Gods, thou ever alert watchful immortal God. Thou knower of all objects, waxing strong, accept this oblation and well cooked cake, that has been prepared today.

Those who desire you offer Soma. They shed Soma and offer oblations. They bear patiently the calumny and violence of others. Protect them, Indra, as there is none wiser than you. O Lord of the fine steeds, come hither for even the remotest regions are not distant for thee. These libations are meant for the steadfast and strong. The stones are laid ready and the fire is kindled. Where are now those your heroic powers with which thou alleviated sufferings and did marvellous deeds? Fair visaged art thou, O Indra, performer of great tasks, destroyer of enemies when roused to fight, lord of righteous fellow travellers. Thou alone movest forth to overthrow the unshakable, and goest forth to destroy Vritra. For the observer of your vows, the heaven and earth, stand firmly like a mountain. O Indra, much invoked, you speak the truth in the safety of your glories, thou demon and separate. They prop us the mighty Gods, but do not reel under their weight. The One is the lord of all things, fixed or moving, walking or flying this multiform creation. From afar I see the Ancient one, our mighty Father from of old and ponder over our kinship. By singing the laud of whom the Gods, established on their own spacious pathways, go about their jobs.

Mitra, the divine friend, brings men together. He sustains both earth and heaven, ever watching the mankind with eyes never closing. To him offer an oblation rich in butter. He is foremost among the men who brings you offerings, the one who abides by thy sacred law. On him whom thou help never falls the affliction, nor is he ever conquered or slain. May we the mortals enjoying ourselves, free from maladies, with our knees bent on earth in obeisance, and following divine Friend Mitra's statue, remain in his kind favour.

O Dawn, richly stored, endowed with wisdom, accept our songs of praise, O thou Lady of plentitude. O ancient yet ever youthful Goddess, thou movest in accordance with the Law, bearer of all the boons! Divine Dawn, shine forth thou with your rays, on the radiant car engendering pleasant sounds. May thy steeds, well guided, bring you hither, the golden-hued and powerful ones. Having arisen, thou Dawn, turn thy face on every creature, standing on high as the emblem of the immortal. To the same one goal you proceed each day like a wheel. O newly born, turn your chariot hither like one that lets fall from her a robe, she cometh, the generous Dame, encompassing both the slayer. The boundless heaven and earth are but a handful when thou grasp them.

O Indra, thou hast established firmly the unbound vast earth in her seat. Thou hast propped the other two regions as well. Let the floods engendered by you flow freely. The demon who held the kine secretly, yielded them before thy power. You make good paths for the travellers and travel by them yourself. The loud lauds waxed you strong, Indra, thou much invoked. O hero, you destroy your enemies and fulfil the Earth and Heaven, the Pair who clasp each other in love, full of riches. Come thou near us, and bring thy car of nourishing foods. The Sun never goes against the laws created by the lord of bay steeds. When his journey is over, he lets loose his steeds, and he is Indra. All people during the course of night would gladly look on the broad, bright front of the refulgent Dawn, and acknowledge the wondrous works of Indra, when she comes in her splendours. A mighty splendour is stored on her bosom; bearing the ripe milk, the unripe cow comes. A great sweetness lies in her, created for our joy by the God Indra.

The all-seeing and omniscient Sun, the Sage, who looks upon human beings has seen the Earth and Heaven enjoying in their places ordained by the Law. They create a home as does a bird, the nest, though parted and yet together. Though parted, but partners, they stand ever alert on one firm place and being young lovers address each other. All creatures they unite Heaven and the Earth and bringing forth light to. Hail the Goddess Dawn and offer her your songs of praise. Exaltantly set in heaven, beautiful to look on, she pours forth sweetness and lavishes her splendour all around. Our hymns have awakened the Daughter of Heaven. She, the Dame generous, comes with her rich light into the two worlds. O Agni, when she approaches shining forth, thou go towards her, eager to share her treasures. The mighty Sun, firm based on the Law, the Bull speeds after the Dawns and enters the earth and heaven. Great is the wisdom, Varuna and Mitra, which in her brightness spreads splendour in every direction.

O nourishing, divine Pushan, this our newest and the best laud is sung forth to thee. Be gracious and accept my hymn, as a bridegroom does his bride. May he who sees all beings together at a glance, may he, may Pushan be our protector. May we meditate upon the excellent glory of the divine Savitar. May he himself illumine our minds! Knowing through our minds the God Savitar we beg of him our portion of the prosperity. Urged by their impulses, the learned men, worship and laud God Savitar in sacred rites. The God Soma, the giver of success ascends to the heaven, to the dwellings of Gods to seat at the seat of Law. May Soma grant us and our cattle the nourishing food, to biped and to quadruped. May he, granting us long life, and removing our foe-like diseases, be established in our assembly. May Varuna and Mitra, dear to us like our own life, shower on us sweetness and fat on our pasturage.

Book Fourth

Agni, the Gods' envoy hath been sent down here with one accord. O thou eternal learned, devoted to Gods, Agni, they have kindled thee, the immortal among the mortals. O Agni, bring hither your dear and brother-like Varuna, who loves sacrifice, Aditya, the effulgent, upholder of Law and guardian of mankind, and the King, supporter of human beings. O Friend, turn hither our friend and wellwisher like a wheel or as a swift steed, and O thou remover of afflictions be nigh unto us. O Agni, find favour for us with Varuna and with Maruts, who illumine the world like the Sun. Bless us, thou effulgent, with progeny and happiness. O banisher of ignorance. Thou knower of Varuna, sweep far away from us the Gods displeasure. Thou the best conveyor of oblations, the brightest and most refulgent, remove from us all those who are wicked and malicious. Be thou Agni nearest to us with thy aids now while the Usha dawns. Reconcile us to Varuna, be gracious unto us and grant your boons to us, the best callers on thee.

Fashion forth a vast net from your body and fare, forward like a mighty king with his attendants. Entangling the wicked in the net, transfix the foemen with your fierce burning darts. Chase the demons with your whirling weapons, follow them closeby, O effulgent Lord, in thy wrath. Shoot with your tongues, the winged flames from all sides, O Agni, spread thy firebrands all around, unfettered as you are! Send your spies forward, the most swift in speed, be our never failing guardian. Let none bent upon doing evil to us, from far or from near, venture to cross you. Rise up Agni, spread your fierce flames, burn down our enemies to ashes with your sharp arrows. Let the blazing fire that we kindle consume like dry stubble those who would do us evil. Rise O Lord, send them far away from us, who are hostile to us, manifest us thou thine celestial powers. Slacken the bows of the wicked ones, annihilate them, whether they be kinsmen or stranger. He attains your favours, O ever youthful God, who walks the path of high devotion. Shine thou on him, O lord, riches, magnificence and splendour, fling open for him the floodgates of opulence.

May he be blessed and loaded with your gifts. O Agni, who in his dwelling place offers you regularly oblations and prayers to please you, all his life. Listen, now I hymn your bounteous favours. May you receive this my song like a lover. May we adorn you, O Lord of steeds and chariots, that you may grant us dominion, we desire to serve of our own choice, the radiant one, shining day and night. So we pay you our homage and feel rejoiced in our hearts. Aid us that we may surpass all others in glory. The man who approaches thee with steeds and gold, and comes nigh in a car loaded with treasure, him thou grant favour and protection, and he enjoys your grace thereafter. I, your kinsman, destroy the foe with these words and the power that I have inherited from my father Gotama. Mark you these my words, ever youthful, most wise, the Lord of the hearth. May all the protecting forces, ever watchful, eager, speedy, ever friendly and never wearied gather here to preserve us, O God Agni, never failing! O God, your guardian rays preserved the blind Rishi from affliction in days of yore, he in his turn preserved the noble ones, O all-knowing God, from them who fain would harm the noble souls. With you, aided by you and guided by you we shall be strong and win riches. Fulfil both our prayers O God of truth, grant this thou whom power emboldens. Accept this fuel with which we serve you and the song we sing in your praise to win your favour. Reduce now the demons to ashes and preserve us from evil, from deceit and from shame, O friend great as God Mitra!

May Agni with his strong jaws and with fierce blazing flames consume them who violate the Law of Varuna and the commandments of Mitra, the best, most dear friend. They are like sinning young women who deceive their husbands. They, sinful, are false and faithless, they have produced this absymal region. O effulgent and purifying God, you have given me, as it were, a heavy burden in the form of this Saman hymn, solemn, great and mighty of seven elements, to me who is meek and weak. What is our wisdom and what is our wealth? Tell us, Agni, for thou knowest. What place is to be obtained and what thing to be doubled in the course of our journey? What is our limit, what is the Law? Why do we speed to the fray like a swift courser? When will the Sun, the lord of immortal Ushas, pour forth his splendour on us? Tell us why they, unsatisfied with a speech lacking conviction, uninteresting and frivolous, address you here? O Agni, let those who are without arms suffer sorrow here in this world. He, who is the most beautiful to look upon, worthy of acceptance by all, rich in splendour, mighty, has appeared in the home. He enrobed in radiance shines most brilliantly, as a house with opulence.

The auspicious presence of mighty Agni, ever victorious, beams brightly even at night with splendour, he makes the fair food look more fair by his light. O God of power, in response to our prayer, disclose for your singer, who sings with fervour, a source of inspiration, the chain of his thought. Give us that mighty hymn, O resplendent Lord, which you and all the other Gods approve. From you issue forth, O Agni, the mighty wisdom, the poetic inspiration and chants most beautiful. From you spring riches, adorned with heroes, for the devotees true and faithful who offer oblation. From you come the hero who wins the spoil, insuperable strength, spirit and help. From you come the joy-giving wealth, sent by Gods, and the swift, impetuous courser.

Agni has gazed benevolently on the wealth giving radiant Dawn. Come, Ashvins to your devotees' dwellings, the Sun has risen in splendour. The Sun god has spread his radiance far and wide, unfurling his banner in the heaven like a hero bent on winning spoil. The Gods Varuna and Mitra go their appointed path, lords of constant domains, sending forth the Sun on his unchanged course. Him, who drives away darkness, him whose eye beholding all the objects, is borne onward by seven strong steeds. Spreading like a spider's web, with his mighty steeds, rending the Night's black rob, comes the Sun. The beams of the Sun god shining tremulously push down under the waters, the darkness, like a hide. How marvellous, the Sun, unbound, unpropped, he hangs in the space, without ever falling. By what self power is he propelled? Who has seen it? He guards the vault of heaven, the sky's pillar.

The God has come to meet the radiant Dawns many a time, the ladies of resplendent glories. Come on your cars, ye far travelling Gods, come to our sacrifice. Effusing light for all the creatures of the world, God Savitar, the inspirer has risen. He has filled the heaven and earth with radiance, revealing his presence. Rosy Dawn has come, decked in brightness she moves onward. Mounted on her well harnessed chariot, she wends her way awakening men to joy and happiness. Come hither Ashvins, now at dawn, borne on your mighty chariots. Here is your honeyed Soma draught, offered by us for your delight. How is it that unbound and unpropped, he falls not down? By what self power is he propelled? Who has seen it? He guards the vault of heaven, a pillar of sky.

Lo, yonder goes up the light, and the chariot is being yoked in the high heavens. The chariot is laden with triple pairs of delightful foods, and the fourth, a skin is filled with honey that overflows. Forth come the delightful honey, cars and horses in the wide shining of the Dawn, rolling aside the stole of darkness that surrounded, and spreading glorious radiance through the atmosphere like the Sun. Drink of the sweet with your mouths accustomed to the draught, for the sake of the sweet draught yoke your beloved car. Refresh the path and its journey with the juice, full sweet is the skin, O Ashvins, that you carry. Friendly are the swans that bear you, gold-winged, sweet, strong, who wake with the Dawn. They rain the floods that cheer, full of rapture, exultant, they come to our Soma libations like bees. Well versed in sacred rites, full of honey, the fires sing to Ashvins at dawn in sacrifice, when the learned priests with pure hands have pressed out with stones the sweet Soma juice. The rays coming nigh chase away the gloom with day and spread shining through the sky like the luminous Sun while drinking the juice. The Sun too goes riding his car and you impelled by your nature, let his paths be known. I have declared, O Ashvins, holding the devout thoughts in me, your car, that decays not, is drawn by perfect steeds, wherewith you move speedily all over the realms to a devotee who brings rich offerings.

Do thou enjoy our oblations never tasted yet even as a bard enjoys the spoil. O Vayu, come in thy car of radiant light to the drinking of Soma draught. Put aside all your denials, and drawn by steeds come with Indra for thy charioteer. O Vayu, in thy car of radiant light, come to the drinking of Soma draught. The two dark ones, that hold all treasures and in whom are all forms, wait upon thee. O Vayu, in thy car of radiant light come to drink the Soma. Let ninetynine harnessed steeds bear thee, they are yoked by thy mere thought. O Vayu, in thy car of radiant light come to the drinking of Soma draught. Yoke, O Vayu, thy thousand bright steeds to thy car and let it carry thee unto us.

He who hath established with his might the extremities of the earth Brihaspati, the Lord of the triple world of our fulfilment, him of rapturous tongue, the ancient sages set before them to meditate on. The sages in their perfected consciousness, rejoicing created the world from which the being was born. O Brihaspati, preserve thou this being. O Brihaspati, for thee they have dug the wells that drain the mountains and which murmuring overflow on every side with their sweetness. Brihaspati, bom of vast splendour in the highest heaven, with his seven faces, with his seven rays, with his many births, first drove away the darkness that encompasses us, with his cry. With his cry he broke Vala into pieces and drove upward the Agni that bears oblations. He cried aloud as he led thee, and bellowing they replied.

To Brihaspati, the Father, the universal Godhead, the Bull! we offer our oblations and gifts. O Brihaspati, may we acquire riches in progeny and fine steeds. Verily he is the King who with his might conquers, by his heroic strength he made himself the lord of all that in the world exists. The man who cherishes Brihaspati, worships him as foremost and offers him the first fruits of his enjoyment. Verily, he dwells in his own house in peace and to him the Earth ever offers rich food, to him all the people submit themselves, the King, with whom the Brahman goes in front. Resistless he conquers all the riches, both that of his subjects and that of the people who are hostile to him. He, cherished and upheld by the Gods, the King, rules supreme. O Brihaspati and Indra, drink ye of this Soma draught and rejoice in the sacrifice, lavishers of wealth. Let the joy sink deep into ye, grant us riches in steeds and happiness. O Brihaspati and Indra make us prosper together, may you be ever benevolent to us. Foster our pious thoughts, woke up our intellectual powers, destroy the wicked who bring hatred.

From Savitar, the God, the wise supreme Spirit, we crave that boon which is most worthy to be sought, wherewith he guards his worshipper. His rays may grant us the Great God's boon. Sustainer of the heaven. Lord of the entire world, the Sage puts on his golden-coloured mail. Clear-sighted, far spreading, filling the vast heavens, Savitar hath brought us bliss that our lips must laud. He, the God, with his arms outstretched fosters all living beings, urging, lulling all that moves, with his rays. He fills the Earth and Heaven and for his own delight sings a song. He lights up all living things, guards each sacred law. The great, lustrous God, has stretched out his arms to all the beings of Earth, observing his own laws he runs his mighty course.

With his own greatness Savitar has filled the three domains, three realms, and the three worlds. He revolves the threefold Heavens and the threefold Earth. He protects us with his threefold laws. Most gracious God, he stirs life and lulls to rest, the lord of all. that moves and moves not. May Savitar, the God, grant us shelter and security, with triple bars against distress. Savitar, the God, comes nigh with the change of seasons. May he multiply our sons and store of food. May he grant us vigour through the days and nights to follow, and may he send us riches with progeny.

We through the Lord of the field, as through our friend and helper, obtain nourishing food in abundance for our cattle and steeds. May he be good enough to grant us his favour. Just as a cow yields milk, so pour forth for us floods that bear sweetness dropping honey, pure enough as ghee. May the Lords of the law be gracious. Sweet be the plants for us, sweet be the heavens, sweet be the waters, and sweet be for us the air. May the lord of the field be full of sweetness for us. May we follow him unharmed! May happily men and oxen both plough the furrow, happily the yoke be securely harnessed, happily may the ploughman ply the God! We welcome the plough and ploughshare with this laud that they may shower the milk on earth which they have made in heaven. Auspicious Furrow, we venerate you, come unto us to prosper, bless and bring us harvests in plenty. May Indra draw the furrow! May Pushan guide right its course, may she yield us milk in each succeeding year! May happily the ploughshare turn up the land, happily the ploughman follow the oxen. May celestial rain pour down fat and milk. May the plough and ploughshare grant us happiness!

Book Fifth

O Agni, most ancient, the ancient men who observed the law, enkindled thee for their help, the bright God, the adorable, nourisher of mankind, worship worthy, Lord of the hearth and home. Of old have men established thee as their foremost guest, the lord of their household, high bannered, of many forms, benevolent helper, the winner of stakes and devourer of ancient forests. The races of men praise you, him who knows well the burnt offerings, discerner, liberal donor of riches, visible to all yet dwelling in secret, the most blessed one, loud roaring, skilled in sacrifice, glorified with the ghee. To thee, O mighty Agni, we mortals have ever approached with reverence, singing your laud. So now ye be pleased with our sacrifice and burst into flames, enkindled as a God by the hands of mortal man. O thou multiformed Agni, much praised, givest subsistence to every man as of yore. By thy might thou controleth all kinds of foods. That light of thine, when blazing forth may not be opposed. O most youthful God, the envoy and oblation bearer of Gods, they have made thee their shining Eye, ye of wide range, dwelling in sacrificial oil and nourished by oblations. Men through the ages have sought thee with holy oil and fuel easy to burn. Thus imbued with strength, thy size growing by the plants, ye spread yourself over all the realms of the earth.

To him, the Lord, the far famed, the wise Ordainer, ancient and glorious, I offer a song of praise. Anointed with oil is he the Lord, the mighty Agni, giver of bliss and protector of noble riches. By the power of the sacred sacrifice established in the highest heaven, they maintained the Cosmic Law. they our forefathers, though mortal men yet attained immortal seats, in the high heavens. The ancient men, avoiding sins, brought him, the irresistible God. May he rekindled conquer all the hostile forces. They stand around him as around a wrathful lion.

O Agni, draw nigh unto us in friendship to deliver and help us. Be gracious to us. Come thou nigh to us, O Lord, wondrous, most invoked, grant us most precious riches. Hear our call now, lend us your ear and protect us from the sinful man. To you, O mighty radiant God, we bring this prayer. Shine bliss on our friends.

By the supreme Law strict order is maintained where they unyoke the steeds of the Sun, there are the ten hundred stand together. That one the greatest of the Deities, I have beheld there. This is your greatness. O Mitra-Varuna! They (the sun beams) there milk out the floods by the day that stand there, ye twain swell the streams and your single wheel moves on its course. O Mitra and Varuna, ye twain Kings uphold the earth and heaven by your greatness, ye increase the milk in kine, nourish the plants and pour forth the swift rains in flood. May your well yoked steeds with their well managed reins bear you down to us. A veil of sacred cloud follows in your wake and the streams flow in your front.

With hands that spare not, protecting the man of holy rites, whom you deliver amidst oblations, O King, free from passion, together you uphold the kingdom propped on thousand pillars. Its form is of gold, its pillars of iron. In heaven it shines like a swift lightning, or shining established in a field. May we acquire of that sweet that is there in that home. Ascend ye Varuna and Mitra to that home whose form is of gold, whose pillars are of the iron, at break of Dawn, at the rising of the Sun, and from there you behold both infinity and limit, O Mitra and Varuna, your protection is most strong, vast and flawless. Help us by that. May we be victorious and attain peace.

O Guardians of the law, the law of the truth is yours in the highest heaven where you mount your car. O Mitra and Varuna, he whom you favour here, is the Lord of peace, for him pour forth the rain in sweetness from heaven. Emperors ye rule over this world of our, the seers of the realms of light. We pray you for rain, for felicious wealth, and immortality. The Maruts, the thunderer, roam abroad through heaven and on the earth.

Ye destroyer of the foe, Varuna and Mitra, we call you by this song, your arms encompass the realm of power as cast around pens of herds. Stretch out your arms with favour to this man who sings to you the praise, for through all the world is sung forth your friendliness. May I go by thy path of Mitra, the friend, that I may attain the goal of my journey. So men go protected under the charge of this beloved Friend in whom there is no harm. O Mitra and

Varuna, may I with my song, acquire that which you possess. That shall cause envy in the homes of the masters of wealth and those who praise you. O Mitra, come unto us with thy riches, and Varuna to our assembly so that the wealthy in their homes and your friends may thrive well in increase of riches. With those, among whom you rank supreme, you twain bring us the strength, and the vastness for the winning of our wealth, bliss and prosperity. At breaking of the Dawn when the sunrays flash, O Lords of sacrifice, in the force of the Gods come with speed on your trampling steeds to my pressed out Soma juice.

The man who has awakened to the knowledge, becomes perfect. Let him speak for us to the Gods. Varuna and Mitra take delight in the speech of such a man. They are the most glorious Kings, their fame is most widespread. They are the lords of all the beings, they increase the Truth in us, for the truth is theirs. I call on them, the first and foremost, the twain together, for help, we who travel on fine steeds. They perfect in knowledge, give us wealth. Even out of misery Mitra wins for us a dwelling for living at ease, for him who worships, lie has the grace of the hero ever fighting in the vain. May we abide in Mitra's protection which extends to utmost distance, so that we are free from harm and sin, guarded by Varuna as his sons. O Mitra, you set the men travelling on and lead them. Neglect ye not the rich, our lords and our seers of the truth. Be our protector while you enjoy the milk.

In truth, ye Gods possess the supreme sway. O Varuna, Mitra, Aryaman, you possess it most abundantly. When you sit in your dwelling of golden light, O Varuna, O Mitra, upholders of mankind, foe-slayers, reach them the bliss. All-knowing and universal are you, O Varuna and Mitra and Aryaman. You keep firm to the Law and follow it and guard mortal man from his enemy. They are true, they uphold the Truth and hold it in all the beings, perfect leaders in journey, perfect in delivering from distress, and perfect in giving bounteous gifts. Which of you, Varuna or Mitra is not affirmed and magnified by us? Wholly our thought turns to you, the traveller's thought turns to you.

Sing ye to Varuna and Mitra with a hymn that enlightens, they, the mighty Lords, theirs is the Law. All-powerful are they, ye, both of them, Mitra and Varuna, Gods magnified among the Gods. Therefore, put forth strength for our gaining riches, both celestial and earthly, for great is your sway among the Gods. By sticking to the Law with Law, you have attained great force, O Gods, ye grow and come not to hurt. With rain charged skies, and streaming floods, masters of the strength, you take possession of your lofty seat.

Three realms of light ye twain uphold, O Varuna, three heavens, three mid-regions. O Mitra ye waxing strong guard the warrior in the eternal laws of your working. Ye Varuna and Mitra have fostering cows yielding streams of honeyed milk. Your floods pour forth sweet rains. There stand the three luminous Bulls, who cast their seeds into thee three worlds. I call on boundless Aditi at dawn, in the mid-day and at the sunset I call on her. I desire of Mitra and Varuna the safety, riches and progeny in rest and movement. Ye who uphold the luminous regions of the mid-world and the bright sphere, O divine Adityas, O Mitra and Varuna. the immortal Gods never impair your laws, firm for ever.

Far and wide extends your grace, O Gods, ye Varuna and Mitra. May I have perfect wisdom. You are they who grant full security and sustenance, may we be they, O Rudras. Protect us, ye with your perfect deliverance. May we ourselves destroy the destroyers. O wondrous Gods, may be never suffer the control of any, nor our sons nor our progeny. O foe-slayers, come with your might, O Varuna, O Mitra, to this our delightful sacrifice. O Varuna and Mitra, ye sages govern every man. Fulfil and nourish our prayers. Come, O Varuna and Mitra to our sacrifice, that of the charitable giver to drink of this Soma juice.

O divine Dawn, come with all thy splendours, awaken us today to the great felicity, even as thou once awakened us, O high-born, delightful with thy steeds. O daughter of Heaven, thou break forth today, O high-born, delightful with thy steeds. Break forth today, O bearer of treasure, O daughter of Heaven, as once thou broke forth, O still mightier in thy strength, high-born, delightful with thy steeds. There are priests who sing thy praise, with their hymns they manifest thee, Bright One. They bear glorious and lavish gifts, O high-born, delightful with thy steeds. When these, thy bands seek to pleasure thee in hope of winning wealth, they set their desires all around, they lavish rich gifts, O high-born, delightful with thy steeds. Grant to these learned men, O Dawn, queen of plenty, fame, affluence and heroic sons. To these princes who shall lavish on us thy riches, O high-born, delightful with thy steeds.

O Dawn, Dame of plenty, bring to them high and resplendent fame, our rich princes, who shall give us enjoyment of the felicity of horses and kine, O high-born, delightful with thy steeds. Bring to us too, O Daughter of the Sky, subsistence in our herds of kine, together with the rays of the Sun, accompanied with the purity of bright and burning lights, O high-born, delightful with thy steeds. Break forth, shining, O daughter of Heaven, tarry not in thy task, for thee the Sun afflicts not with his burning rays as he does the thief and the robber. O high-born, delightful with thy steeds. So much, and more than this shouldest thou give, for to thy devotees thou breakest forth in thy fullest glories, O high-born, delightful with thy steeds.

The divine Dawn, of the glorious journey, of rosy limbs, by Law true to the Truth, who brings with her heaven of light, is worshipped by the sages. She has vision, awakens the man, makes the pathway smooth to travel and walks in front! How lofty is her car, how vast and all-pervading the Goddess, how brings she the splendour before the days! She harnesses her cows of rosy light, harming none, brings perennial riches. She lays down the paths to happiness, adored by all, she gives every boon. Behold her in the East, coming with changing colours, enrobed in Order, one who knows and reaches her quarters. See, how luminous is she bathed in light that we may see her. Driving away all darkness and enemies. Dawn, the Daughter of Heaven, has come with splendour. Dawn, the daughter of Heaven, like a woman full of happiness, moves to meet the Gods. Unveiling the boons for him who gives in sacrifice, the Goddess ever young, has again brought the light even as in the beginning.

The enlightened yoke their mind, ye, they yoke their thoughts to Savitar, the one knower of all, he alone assigns the work of sacrifice. Lofty is the praise of Savitar, the creating God, He, the Seer assumes all forms that he may bring forth good for the biped and quadruped. Savitar, the supreme God, lights our heavens and shines after the coming of Dawn. His going forth all the other Gods follow after his greatness. He is Savitar, the radiant God, who has by his great powers measured out our earthly realms. To the three shining spheres thou goest being manifested by the rays of the Sun. Thou encompasses on both sides of the Night, ye, thou art Mitra, O God, with thy established laws. Thou alone are the lord of creation and generation. Pushan thou art, by thy goings forth in thy paths, and thou art lord over all this world. O Savitar, the seer Syavasva has brought lauds to thee.

Savitar, God, drive far away from us, we prey all that is sorrowful and calamitous. Send us only what is good and lovely. May we be without sin in the eyes of Aditi through the gracious favour of God Savitar. May we have all good and lovely things. We, this day with our lauds, choose the general God, Lord of beatitude, Savitar whose laws are inviolate. It is Savitar, the wise God, who precedes both the Day and Night. It is Savitar, who gives glory to all the beings with the song, bringing them forth.

I invoke with these hymns the Mighty God, famed Parjanya, the bellowing Bull with speedy streams, loud roaring who deposits a seed in plants for germination. He flattens the trees and slays the demons; all living beings fear his mighty stroke. From his mighty strength even the innocent flee, when he, thundering strikes the wicked. Like a driver urging his car horses with a whip, he drives on the messengers of rain. From afar is heard the roaring of the lion when Parjanya fills the heaven with rain clouds. The winds burst forth, the lightnings flash, the plants shoot up, the heavens pour streams, the sap surges up in every stem, when Parjanya quickens the earth with a seed. You at whose command the earth bows in obeisance before thee, at whose command the hoofed beings scamper in fear, at whose bidding flowers wear different colours and shapes, O Parjanya, grant us protection!

Send down, O Maruts, rain for us from heaven, and let the Stallion pour forth his life-giving flow. Come here with your thundering, pour forth the floods, O our divine Lord and Father! Thunder and roar, deposit the seed. Circle round us in thy car heavy laden with rain. Tip downward your opened water skin and level the high places, fill in the hollows! Lift the great vessel up, let it spill over, let the waters pour down and flow forth. Saturate both the heaven and earth with fatness, and let there be thirst-quenching pools in plenty. When, O Parjanya, roaring in fury and thundering you strike the wicked down, then the whole universe shouts in exaltation, ye, everything that exists upon the earth. You have poured down the floods, now stop it, we pray. You have made the deserts fit for travel. You have made the plants flourish for our enjoyment. So, now receive the grateful praise in return!

You, mighty Earth, bear the burden of massive mountains on your shoulders, rich in torrents, you germinate the seed with quickening power. For you resound now our hymns of praise, O wanderer at will, bright one. Like a neighing mare you drive away abroad the swelling clouds. You hold fast the forests with your great strength, when rains and lightning from the clouds in heaven descend.

Sing thou the hymn sublime, profound and dear to renowned Varuna, the Lord of all, to him who tore away, even as one who skins a beast, that he might spread the earth before the Sun. On the tree tops he spread out the mid air, put milk in kine and strength in steeds, in hearts he put spirit, fire, in the waters, the Sun in heaven and Soma on the mountains. Varuna poured forth the waters on the earth, heaven and the mid air, the lord of waters whose windows open earthward. He, the lord of the universe, floods the earth as the rains flood a field of barley. He floods the vast earth and heaven, ye, when fain for milk, he pours it forth. Then the mountains are clothed with clouds, the Maruts put forth their strength and cast it down. I will declare the mysterious deeds of Varuna, renowned, the Lord immortal, who standing in the firmament has measured out the earth as it were, with a yard stick. Vast is his wisdom, the greatest of the Gods, and none has ever hindered or done violence against it. Therefore, all the rushing rivers pour themselves into one sea and yet cannot fill it. Whatever sin we might have committed against the man who loves us, have wronged a brother or a friend, or a companion, against a constant neighbour, or a stranger, remove this sin from us, O Varuna! If we have committed a sin like cunning gamesters who cheat at play, or have done wrong or sinned against the law in ignorance, cast away all these sins from us like loosened bonds, and let us be then your beloved ones, O Varuna.

Book Sixth

The half of the day is dark, the other bright. Both these revolve by their own intelligence. Vaishvanara, once born, the Sovereign Lord of the universe, has overthrown the darkness with his lustre. I discern neither warp nor woof, nor the pattern of those who weave in the contest. Whose son will speak here so well as to surpass his father without assistance from the Father before him? He who knows the warp and woof, he knows how to weave. He will speak what should be uttered in due course of time, Agni, the immortal God knows it and though moving below on earth, he sees beyond others. Behold him, the Hotar priest, first of all to perform the sacrifice. Among mortal men, he is the immortal light. He is born and is firm seated among us, the immortal, ever waxing strong in his body. A steadfast light has been set for mortal men to look on, of all the moving objects the mind is the swiftest. All Gods with one thought, with one intention, march on unobstructed towards that single Splendour. My ears grow weak, my eyes grow dim, but the light that dwells within me grows brighter. Far abroad roams my mind, its thoughts spreading wider. What shall I utter? What shall my mind imagine? All the Gods made obeisance before thee in fear, O Agni, while thou wast dwelling amidst darkness. O Vaishvanara, the universal God, grant us your grace, may the immortal now favour us!

May God Agni, kindled bright through Vedic hymns, served with oblations, fain for riches, strike the Demons dead. Agni, the Father of fathers, shining ever in his mother's side, removes all ignorance by revealing the Vedic knowledge, the source of all true learning. O ever active Jatvedas, the seer of all, grant us devotion that brings progeny. O Lord, that is illustrious. O Son of Strength, handsome to look on, we thy devotees, have poured forth oblations with our songs. O Agni! O Agni, who glitters like gold, we come to thee for shelter, as to the shade from fierce heat. Mighty as a hero who slays with shafts, or like a bull with sharpened horns. O Agni, thou breakest down the forts of bondage with thy darts of knowledge. O Agni, thou God, verily yoke thy steeds, the most excellent, to bring thee hither with speed. O God, reveal unto us fully by coming hither. Bring other Gods here to the sacrifice to enjoy the Soma drink. O Agni, sustainer of the universe, ever radiant, of unfading splendour, manifest thy lustrous glory and illumine the world, O immortal One!

The cows have come and brought good fortune. Let them stay here in our stalls and be happy near us. May they bring forth multicoloured calves for us. yielding milk each morning for Indra. Indra seeks to aid him who is liberal in gifts, he increases his possessions, and takes away nothing. Increasing his riches ever-more, he makes the pious dwell in an inviolate realm. These cows are never lost, nor robber shall ever harm them, no wicked foe ever dare to mislead them. The Lord of the cows, who offers to the Gods in sacrifice, lives long with them. The courser, raising the dust can never overtake them and never do they resort to the shambles. These cows of the devout man who performs Yajna, roam about the vast pasture where no danger lurks.

These cows are Bhaga, these cows are Indra, they are a first poured oblation of Soma. Verily these cows are my brother. Indra for whom I long with my heart and soul. O cows, ye fatten even the thin and weak, and give beauty to unlovely. Make my household prosper with your strength. Graze on our fine pastures and be prolific in calves, drink pure water at the springs. Let ye be owned neither by a thief nor by a robber, may ye be spared the shafts of Rudra! Let this portion mixed with the seed of the Bull and thy strength, O Indra, bring to these cows fertility!

Sing together the praise of the Hero, much invoked, to please him, a mighty Bull, when Soma juices flow. He, the all-pervading God, Indra, withholds not his bounteous gifts of riches in cows, when he hath listened to our songs. May he with his strength unclose for us the stall of kine, wherever it be to which we may go, led by Indra, the Demon-slayer. O Lord of opulent wealth, these songs of laud have been sung aloud to thee, like milch kine who low for their calves! It is hard to obtain thy love. You art a Bull to them who crave for cattle and kine. Be to them a Bull who crave for cattle. Enjoy thyself with the juice shed for your pleasure. Cast not away thy eulogiser to reproach. O God, lover of songs, these our hymns reach thee, sung with draughts we pour as milch kine speed to their calves.

We, thy worshippers and bards call on thee for strength to win us wealth. The valiant horsemen fighting in the battle call on thee for help, O Indra, when besieged by foemen. O wondrous God, thunder-armed, praised as mighty, adorable, shower on us wealth in kine and car horses, the hero's strength. We call upon him who ever active strikes the enemy dead. Thou Lord of the heroes, most mighty, aid us to prosper with thy thousand powers.

O Indra, whatever physical and spiritual strength there is in men and whatever glory there exists in the five People, grant us all these and all manly powers. O God, whatever manly strength in Triski lay and in Puru folk, grant us that in full that in the struggle we may defeat our enemy. O Indra, grant me and these devotees of thine, for their weal, the lustrous refuge that wards off triple afflictions and keep thy shafts far away from us.

Indra, the rescuer, God the saviour, almighty, whom we ever gladly adore, powerful lord, invoked by all people, may he, the bounteous, grant us his favours. May he, the God Indra, as Lord of riches and our sure protector grant his succour. Baffle thou O God, our enemies to give us rest and security. Let us have heroic strength and manly vigour. May we be ever in his benign grace, may we enjoy his favour. May Indra, our guardian sweep away from us, even from afar, the foemen, our songs, prayers and verses reach thee Indra, as the streams rush down a slope. O thou thunder-armed, kine, libations, water and Soma juice, all are thine like a vast bounty.

Hymn Agni with each song in every sacrifice to acquire strength. Come, let us laud him, the wise and immortal God, even as a well loved friend. Agni, the Son of Strength, is our gracious Lord. Let us laud him who bears our oblations to Gods. Let him be our aids and strength, ye, verily a saviour of our beings. O Agni, the resplendent God, most youthful, all purifier, with thy pure brilliancy, kindled by the Seer's hand, shine on us with thy glorious beams, O Agni, one of the eight Vasus, grant us your protection along with riches. O wondrous One, thou art the lord of earthy wealth, give rest and safety for our progeny. Prosper our sons and grandsons with thy protecting powers, never negligent but ever inviolate. Keep far from us, O God, all divine anger and wickedness of godless men! O friends, bring her here with songs who liberally pours forth her milk, unbound her who never turns away.

I call upon both Indra and Agni, whose deed in the form of creation of this universe has been renowned from the ancient times. Indra and Agni harm us not! We praise the twain, Indra and Agni, the destroyers of the terrible foe. May they be auspicious to one like me. May they both drive away all our enemies. May they slay our foemen, smite the enemy, the guardians of noble men, O Indra, O Agni, these our songs of praise have been sung for you, who bestow blessings. Come Indra, come Agni, with those teams invoked by many, O heroes, for your admirers and enjoy the juice. Ye heroes, Indra and Agni, come to drink Soma juice, we have poured the libation. O worshippers, glorify that Agni who encompasses all enjoyable things and makes everything without sin with his radiance. He who gains Indra's grace through enkindled fire in the sacrifice, finds a smooth passage across the floods to glorious riches. Give us ye twain, swift steeds to bring the Gods here and pour on us abundant food and wealth. O Indra, O Agni, ye twain I invoke to gain strength. Ye are giver of food and wealth. I call upon you both to gladden you with the gifts I offer. Come here to us with wealth in kine and steeds, we call you both, the Gods, as friends for friendship, giving bliss.

Savitar, the God has stretched his golden arms in mighty blessing towards the sacrifice. Like a young and most skilled priest, he lets the fatness drip from his hands over the realms. May we enjoy the vigorous force of Savitar, the God radiant, may he grant us wealth. He, the mighty One, sends to rest and awakens all life that moves on two feet or on four. Protect our home, O God today with thy never failing powers. O God of the golden tongue, keeps up on the righteous path let not the ill-wisher have us in his grasp. This God Savitar, friend of our home, gold-handed, has risen to meet the twilight. With cheeks of brass and honeyed tongue, the God, worthy of laud, gives rich gifts to every worshipper. Like a Hotar priest, Savitar has extended his golden arms so beautiful to look on. He has ascended the heights of heaven and earth and made each fiend speed away in haste. Give us, O God, fair wealth today and tomorrow and each day that is to follow, O ye the lord of ample riches. May this our song now favour us with your grace enriching us daily with life strengthening powers!

Great is your might, O Indra, O Soma! It were you who performed those first and powerful exploits. It were you who found the Sun, you found the light of heaven, you overthrew all the darkness and all the blashphemers. You Indra and Soma, make the morning radiant and cause the Sun on high to rise with all his splendour. You are a supporting pillar to prop the sky and spread out in all direction, the Mother Earth. You twain smote the serpent Vritra dead, who obstructed the waters. The heavens approved your deeds. You urged the streams to flow fast and filled many a sea. You filled within the unripe udders of the milch kine the sweet ripe milk. You have held the unimpeded stream within the many coloured moving creatures. O Indra, O Soma, ye great Ones, grant verily great riches, which victorious pass to our children's children. You both invest with manly powers the progeny of men, that they may carry the day in the battle.

O Soma, O Rudra, the mighty lords, may these our sacrifices reach ye with speed. Fill full our houses with your sevenfold treasures and pour forth blessings on all bipeds and quadrupeds. Let the sickness that may visit us be chased away to four quarters. Sweep away the forces of death and destruction, and grant us glorious fame. O Soma, O Rudra, provide us with all needed medicines for our bodies. Remove and loosen from us the sin we might have committed, which we have still within our persons. Armed with shafts and other weapons sharp, you kind loving Gods, be gracious unto us. Keep us away from the noose of Varuna, keep us safe from sorrow in your gracious protection.

Thou shaft, sharpened with our prayer, fly away shot from the bowstring, reach the enemy, strike him home and let none be left alive. There where the showers of arrows fall like boys whose tonsure have not been performed, even there may Aditi, the boundless, and Brahmanspati guard us well, protect us well all the days. Thy vital parts I cover with armour, O hero. May immortality clothe thee, O Soma, may the high Varuna give thee more than ample, and may Gods be delighted in thy victory over the wicked! Who wants to kill us, be he an unknown foe or one of our kinsmen, may all wise Gods torment him. May my prayer be my closest armour.

Book Seventh

Agni, the golden God, the Dawn's lover has spread forth his far reaching lustre. He, the golden hero, refulgent, pure, has aroused and inspired our eager thoughts. He, like the Sun shines forth while the Dawn breaks, and the priests sing the laud at sacrifice, revealing their prayful minds. Agni, the most bounteous, who knows well all the generations, visits the Gods as the swift envoy. To Agni are addressed our songs and sacred verses, seeking the God and asking his kind favours, to the beautiful to look on, of lovely visage, the mighty mediator who carries man's oblations. O Agni, bring here unto us Indra, along with Vasu, bring here the mighty Rudra with all his followers, Aditi gracious to all men, along with his sons and much invoked Brihaspati with the singers. Man prayfully worship Agni at sacrifice, the ever youthful God, the priest of joy. He is verily the God of all the riches, an untired envoy to the Gods at the Yajna.

Pour forth oblations in his mouth, the kind of God, worthy of reverence, our closest friend and kin. Agni, who has seated himself in every home for people's weal, lord of the house, seer, youthful. May this Agni guard us and our homes from all sides. May he protect us from woe! I will compose a new hymn of praise to Agni, the falcon, he is sure to give us riches. How fair are his glories to behold as he shines forth at the sacrifice, like one possessed of heroic sons. May he be pleased with our invocation, may our praise find favour with him, the best of worshippers! O, ye worthy of our invocations, lord of our homes, rich in wealth of heroes, may we set you down. Glow forth at night, shine forth at morn, your favour has kindled our homes, by your favour we shall be rich in heroes!

O Indra, the lowest earth is thine, thou cherishest the middle region, thou rulest the highest one. Thou art the lord of the whole world. None can resist thee in the world. Thou art the lord far famed for giving wealth to every one in the battle. O much invoked, all men on the earth call thee for protection. If I, O Indra, were the lord of riches ample as thine, I would give them, O King, to the singer who scattered wealth and never cast him to woe. Each day would I enrich the man who sang my laud, in whatever place he be. O Indra, no kinsman is better shelter than thee, no father is better guardian than thee. The active man with skill will win the spoil. O Indra, much invoked, I bow unto you with my song, just as a carpenter bends the wheel of wood for smooth motion. They who bestow great riches love not paltry praise, wealth comes not to a niggard churl. Light is the task to give all things that are worth giving, O Indra, to one like me on this day. Like cows unmilked we call to thee. O Indra, and sing thy laud. Thou all-knowing, lord of the animate and inanimate creation, we bow unto thee. None other divine like thee has ever been, nor ever shall be. None like thee has ever been born on this earth nor ever shall be. We longing for horses and kine, O Maghvan, call on thee. O Mighty Indra, bring thou all this unto us, as thou art rich in treasures from of old and worthy of being invoked in each fray! O Indra, grant us wisdom like a sire to his sons. Guide us, on our path, O much invoked, let us live long and look upon the Sun. Grant us that no foe, whoever mighty, unknown and malevolent, tread us to the ground. O heroic Indra, may we through thy aids accomplish all our deeds without any hindrance!

May the God Savitar, chariot borne, rich in treasures celestial, filling the heavens, come hither, dispensing that which makes man happy, lulling to slumber and then arousing all the living beings. His arms, mighty, golden, sublime, far extended, reach the limits of heaven. Now his greatness is to be highly lauded, even the Sun submits to him his active service. Now, may this God Savitar, strong and mighty the Lord of riches, grant us his wealth. May he, extending his wide-spread radiance, bestow on us the food that nourishes human beings. These our songs laud Savitar of gentle tongue, whose arms are full and hands lovely. May he grant us strength. Preserve us evermore, ye Gods, with blessings!

Without rest they flow from the depths, pure, ever active, the Waters, the Ocean, their Chief, through the channels ordained by Indra, the thunderer. Now may those divine waters, protect me! They may pour forth from heaven, or run through channels made by men, or flow freely, pure and sparkling, rushing to the Ocean. Now may these divine Waters protect me! In the midst of these waters, moves Varuna, the sovereign lord, he who discriminates man's truth from falsehood. Exceedingly sweet, bright, purifying and clear are these waters. Now may these divine Waters protect me! From them, Varuna the King, Soma and all the other Gods drink strength and vitality. Into them Agni, Vaishvanara has entered. Now may these divine Waters protect me!

O Sun, today arising blameless, thou hast spoken the truth to Varuna and Mitra. May the boundless Aditi, Aryaman and all the Gods, love us while we sing these songs of praise. O Mitra and Varuna, he is the Sun, the all-seeing, who ascends over earth and heaven in the pervading wide and guards all things that moves and moves not, for the seer goodness and crookedness in mortals. Seven shining gold hued horses has he yoked and they bear him dropping nourishment. He surveys the worlds of Varuna and Mitra like a herdsman who watches over his herds. Your steeds rich in sweetness have risen high, the Sun has ascended to the ocean of pure light and for him the Adityas make pathways ready, even Aryaman, Mitra and Varuna in harmony do so. These Gods, Aryaman, Varuna and Mitra discern falsehood in us and chastise. These mighty sons of Aditi grow in the house of Law eternal. These lords of love, purity and wisdom who none can repress, give discerning knowledge to him who has none. They impart to him right vision and lead him along the smooth paths beyond grief and evil.

They are ever watchful with eyes that close not in slumber and lead the ignorant. They carry him in his forward march across the fathomless pit in the river to safety on the other side. The boundless Mother Aditi and Varuna and Mitra, like guardians give peace, protection and happiness to their devotees engaged in sacrifice, in them let us seek all our creation and lineal succession, let us do no violence to or anger these Gods, O ye bold ones! He whom Varuna upholds, removes away from his altar the stains, Aryaman, save us from all who would hurt us, O givers of plentitude. A shining power and a realm of illumination signify their coming together. By their wondrous power they hold dominion. O Gods, we tremble with fear of you, have mercy on us, sit us at ease by your greatness. He who wins favour through his prayer and worship, that he may acquire felicity, strength and riches, has his home filled with comforts. For you, O Varuna, O Mitra, this priestly task has been performed in our sacrifices. Lead us safely through all the perils. Keep us safe, evermore, with your blessings.

The Sun, beneficent to mankind, whose gaze rests on all, auspicious God, is coming here. The God, the eye of Varuna and Mitra, has rolled up darkness like a scroll of leather. The Sun, the inspirer of men, unfurling his mighty shimmering banner, is advancing. Now he will roll his chariot wheel again, which harnessed to the shaft, the steeds pull. Emerging radiant from the bosom of the Mornings, he, in whom the singers take delight, ascends. This Sun-God, I hail as my chief joy, who never breaks the harmony of universal laws. This shining jewel of the heavens, far seeing is rising. Far is his goal, he hastens on resplendent. The people inspired by him, speed about their assigned work and perform their duties. He follows the pathways, prepared by the Gods, like an eagle in his unswerving flight. O Mitra, O Varuna, we long to serve you with worship and oblations, the Sun has already risen. Now Varuna, Mitra and Aryaman, grant us release and room enough for us and for our children. May we find fair pathways, good to travel. Preserve us evermore, O Gods with blessings.

When the Sun has risen today, may Mitra, Aryaman, Bhaga and Savitar, the Gods free from sin, bestow happiness on us. May they the sinless protect well our homes and carry us safely over all the distress! These great Kings and boundless Aditi are verily the sovereigns of vast domains, and their laws are inviolate. Early at sunrise I hymn to Mitra, Varuna and Aryaman, the foe-slayers. May this hymn of praise bring wealth in gold and nonviolent strength. May the Sages obtain sacrifice! May we be thine O Mitra, and thine Varuna with our princes. May supreme joy and fine food be ours!

So, when the Sun rises, we invoke you with hymns now, O ye charioteers of law, Varuna, Mitra and Aryaman! Adhering to law, bom in law, the strength of law, fierce, hater of the false, in their guardianship which provides the best security may we mortals and our friends dwell. May we see the rising for a hundred autumns that Eye of light, ordained by the Gods, ye, may we live for a hundred autumns! O Varuna, O Mitra, come here to Soma draught, the infallible Gods in wisdom. Come here as ordained by the laws of Heaven, free from guile, Varuna and Mitra, come close, ye Gods and drink the Soma draught. Come ye heroes, come Mitra and Varuna, accept our oblations, drink the juice, the strengtheners of the law!

From her birthplace in heavens, the Dawn hath flushed revealing herself as ordained by the Law. She hath swept away friends and scornful gloom. She lights up the pathways most auspicious, most noble! Arouse us today to success and lofty fortune, to loftier felicity, promote us, O Dawn! Grant us riches of every kind, O Goddess far famed among mortal men, friend of mankind! Behold, the Morning's splendours approach us, everlasting, bright with varied colours. Filling the region of midair, they ascend high, producing the holy rites and worship. The Daughter of Heaven, the world's regal queen, yoking her car goes far away and swiftly. She visits the lands where dwells the five tribes, surveying the deeds of the mortal men.

Rich in wealth beyond telling, the consort of the Sun, rules over all riches. She steels our youthfulness, the sages praise her, and the priests chant the lauds of the effulgent Dawn! She approaches her steeds of varied hues, the red steeds draw the resplendent Morning. On her fair car the beautiful Goddess comes, bringing treasures for her faithful servant. True with the true, mighty with the mighty, divine with the divine, holy with the holy, she has broken down all the barriers to release the rays of the Sun, and they greet her with shouts of joy! O Dawn, now give us riches in kine, horses and heroes full of manifold joys. Protect our sacred grass from trampling feet. Preserve us, ye Gods, evermore with blessings!

Dawn hath come shining like a youthful lady of light, stirring to life every living being. Now it is time to kindle Agni, for she, the resplendent Dawn hath scattered the shadows. The fair lady, beautiful to look on, with her face turned towards the world, hath risen, enrobed in bright raiments. Decked with gold and bright rays, she sends the world on its daily course. Bringing the Eye of the Gods, the lady of light, comes riding her beautiful white courser. Distinguished by her radiance. Dawn shines apparent, bestowing marvellous wealth on all the world. O opulent lady, come unto us with your bounty, chase away the foe men, grant us safe and rich pastures. Scatter those who hate us. O liberal one, pour boons on your singer! Send thy excellent beams to guide and sustain us, providing us prolonged days, O Dawn, O Goddess, grant us food and riches in cattle, kine, chariots and horses! O high born, Daughter of Heaven prayed by many an illustrious seers, grant us vast and glorious wealth. Preserve us ever more with your blessings!

Behold once again the beams of Dawn approaching. Her splendours diffuse their lustre on high in the sky. O Usha, refulgent, riding thy sublime chariot, grant us wealth that makes us happy. The well kindled fire rings aloud thy praise, the chanters sing thy lauds. Goddess Dawn approaches in her radiance, sweeping away all darkness and danger. There in the east the Morning has appeared, sending forth light, increasing the lustre, and bringing on the Sun, sacrifice and Agni, while detested darkness flees in the west. Affluent Daughter of the Sky has appeared once more, and all mortals look on her as she advances. Her car, which she has mounted, moves self harnessed and drawn onward by its team of fine yoked steeds. Urged with loving minds, we and our nobles greet thee this day. Show yourselves favourable, O Dawns, as you arise and preserve us evermore with your blessings!

Rousing the lands where dwell the five peoples, Dawn has revealed the pathways of the people. The fine clouds of dawn convey her radiance. The Sun with his light has disclosed earth and heaven. The Dawns approach like tribes arrayed for battle, their bright beams paint the distant limits of the sky as the Sun extends his arms. They give forth their light imprisoning darkness. The Goddess Dawn has arisen, endowed with great riches, getting homage that assures our weal. This Daughter of Heaven, the noblest of the noble, gives varied treasures to her worshippers. Bestow on us, Goddess Dawn, that ample bounty which thou grant to those who sing thy laud. Aloud, they acclaim you, like mighty bulls bellowing as you unbar the doors of the firm set mountains. May your appearance grant us the charm of pleasant voices and thoughts for our upliftment as thou arises. Preserve us evermore, with thy blessings!

Behold, the effulgent Daughter of Heaven comes, dispelling the gloom of night that we may see. The friendly lady spreads the light. The rising Sun, the refulgent Star of heaven, pours forth his rays together with the Dawn. O Dawn, O Sun, at your arising may we attain our portion in your light. O Dawn, Daughter of the high Sky, promptly we rise and come to greet you. You most bounteous one, granter of all that we seek, to thy worshippers you give both blessings and wealth. O resplendent one, you light up the earth that we may see it, and also the high vault of heaven. We long to be your own, sharing in your boons. Accept our love like a Mother from her children. Bring us your most wondrous bounty, that shall be famed far and wide. Give us to enjoy the nourishment you possess, O Daughter of Heaven. Grant to our princes riches and immortal fame, and to us herds of kine in contests. May you, O shining Dawn, who urges the wealthy, Lady of fair charms, drive our foes away!

The beings are verily wise because of the greatness of Varuna, who has fixed in their stations the spacious earth and heaven, who has propped up on high the mighty vault of sky and the stars, who has spread out the earth in front of him. I ponder in my own heart and contemplate the question how again I may be united with Varuna? Would he accept my offerings without anger? When may I have his mercy? Fain to know my sin I ask myself, O Varuna, I seek the wise to ask them, all the sages give me the same one answer, "Surely the great God Varuna is displeased with you". Then O Varuna, what has been my greatest transgression, that you would destroy your singer and friend? Tell me, O all-knowing God and possessing everything, that I sinless may quickly approach thee begging your forgiveness.

Free us from the sins of our fathers, and also from those we ourselves might have committed. O King, release us, as a thief is set free or a calf is loosed from its cord. The evil deed was done not deliberately, but it was wine, dice or anger that betrayed us, or the thoughtlessness, or the elder led the younger astray. Even in sleep evil doing is not wholly removed. I am willing to serve you like a slave, you, the God, free from sin, inclined to anger. This most noble lord gives wisdom to the simple and leads on the learned to riches. O God Varuna, may these songs of praise reach you and lie within your heart. May it be well with us in peace and strife! Ever guard us, ye Gods, with your blessings!

Let me not pass yet, O king Varuna, to the house of clay, the grave have mercy, forgive me, mighty Lord! When I totter like wind-blown skin, O Thunderer, have mercy, forgive me, mighty lord! If through want of wits by ill-chance, I went astray, have mercy, forgive me, mighty lord! Thirst plagues thy worshipper, even when he stands amidst floods, have mercy, forgive me, mighty Lord! O Varuna, whatever offence we mortal men commit against the immortal Gods, or in thoughtlessness violate your laws, Oh, punish us not!

O Indra, O Agni, this noblest praise, of your comes out of my contemplative heart, as rain from the cloud. O Indra and Agni, listen to the singer's call, enjoy his songs, fulfil, ye mighty Lords, his desires! O Agni, ye heroes, induce us not to sin, nor to slander and violence! O Indra and Agni, we bow in reverence with hymns of praise. All the holy singers beg the twain for help and aid, and priests implore them to win strength. We learned men, eagerly laud you both, and offer sacred food, longing for wealth and success in sacrifice. O Indra, O Agni, come unto us with your favours, ye Gods, who conquer men. May not the wicked ever control us. Let not harm come unto us from any hostile man. O Gods, evermore potect us. O Indra and Agni, let us acquire whatever wealth in gold, in cattle or horses we beg of you.

Vishnu, the God of hundred splendours, strode three times over the earth in his high majesty, He, the foremost of the Gods, stronger than the strongest, most illustrious in fame, lives for ever. With mighty steps strode Vishnu over the earth, being desirous give it to mankind for a home. In him the lowly and humble seek safety, he, the great God has given them this whole world, O all-pervading God, clothed in rays of light, I a skilled devotee, ever extol thee with his oblation today. Yes, I the poor and weak, laud thee, the Mighty, who dwellest in the realm beyond this region. O God, whom thou proclaimest thyself as all-pervading, with what words can I speak of thy nature? Hide not this from us, nor keep it secret, since thou didst wear another guise in the battle. O God Vishnu, I accept thee with my lips as the fulfiller of all desires, be pleased to accept this my offering. May these my songs exalt thee. Do ye, preserve us, evermore with blessings!

O Indra, O Soma, plunge into the abyss the wicked, into bottomless darkness hurl them, that none of them ever comes back! May your fierce might prevail and conquer them. Fling your deadly thunderbolt on the evil-doers from the heaven and from the earth, ye Indra and Soma. Forge out your fatal dart out of the mountain and therewith burn down to ashes the growing race of the fiends. Cast ye twain your fierce darts of stone burning with flames from the heaven, the scorching darts, never perishing. Plunge ye the wicked in the bottomless depths and let them sink without sound. Listen ye both to our prayers, and strike swiftly the wicked never prosper, whoever harms us with malign power! Whoever accuses me falsely, a man who pursues his righteous path, may he the speaker of falsehood, be, O Indra, like water which the hallowed hand compresses. The wicked who harm, as is their habit, the pure, and with their evil deeds injure the righteous, may Soma send them to the serpent or consign them to the lap of Death. The demon, desirous to harm our nourishing food, kine horses or our bodies, may he, the foeman, thief and robber sink to bottomless destruction with his progeny! May he be destroyed, himself and his children. Let him be consigned beneath the three earths. May his fair fame who day and night seeks to harm us, O ye Gods, be for ever blighted! The wise find it easy to discriminate between true and false for these oppose each other. O these twain which is true, the God Soma preserves, and brings the false to nothingness. Soma never helps or guides him who is wicked or falsely proclaims himself a hero. He destroys the wicked and him who speaks untruth. Indra, entangle these in his noose.

Slay, Indra, the male demon! Slay the witch who joying triumphs in her magic. Let the idolaters fall with broken necks. May they not see any more the rising of the Sun. O Indra, O Soma, watch ye well, look here, look around. Hurl your weapons at the wicked, against the witch fling your thunderbolt!

Book Eighth

Cast us not as a prey to the hateful or the proud, O Indra. Help us thou mighty with thy power and strength, O King Indra, we thy devoted friends implore thee and sing thy praise. The learned also praise thee with their hymns. O Thunderer, I praise none except thee in the skilled singer's eulogy. On thy praise only have I thought. The Gods seek out an active man, who presses out Soma, they like not a dreamer. They chastise idleness unweariedly. O God, come into us with wealth, do not deprive us of food and strength. Thou art venerable like a grandfather before a grandson. May he not in anger spend the evening far from us today, like some unpleasant son-in-law.

Priests blend Soma juice for Indra and press out each draught most excellent, for him, the hero, the brave, for his enjoyment. The Virtra slayer drinks the juice. May Indra, who helps us in hundred ways, approach unto us, and not stay afar. The two strong courses yoked by our prayer, shall being our friend Indra here, the song lover, he stays not far away from us. Come here, blend the Soma juice, come the sweet juice is ready, thou Seer-like, strong, fair of visage, come fast to our feast! Our lauds, which we sing for bounty and vigour, wax thee strong. Come and exalt thee, O Indra, God of many a glorious deed! O Song lover, these our songs are verses addressed to thee, these confirm thy renowned might.

O Indra, drink of the sweet savoury juice, enjoy our draught and be kind to us. Grant us wisdom, may your favours ever more guard us well. Be thou our friend and may our feast cheer thee up! In thy kind grace and favour may we still be powerful, cast us not into the net of enemy violence. Guard us, succour us with your manifold protections, establish us well in happiness! May these our hymns exalt thee, thou lord of opulent wealth! The holy sages, skilled in sacrifice, ever pure, sing thy praise in the presence of Agni. This God, to whom thousands of Seers resort for spiritual strength has spread like an ocean. True is his greatness and majesty. I admire his powers at solemn rites where his singers rule. O Indra, all the worshippers invoke thee alone in sacrifice. They call thee for acquiring spoil in the battle, in the mortal struggle we invoke thee. With his powers Indra hath spread out heaven and earth, with his strength hath lightened up the Sun. In him abide all the beings, in him reside the purifying Soma juice. Thy devotees are urging thee, Indra, to drink of the Soma draught first. The Gods of Seasons have raised their voices up and the Rudras have hymned thee as the foremost of the Gods, The mortal men even today as of old praise Indra at sacrifice, where he waxes strong on manly strength in the ecstasy of the Soma juice.

Just as chariots racing in the field of battle, displaying their strength, conquering foes, bring us wealth, so do these songs full of sweetness, rise unto thee, O Indra, from our hearts. The Seers and Sages like the rays of the Sun gain every thing they desire and enjoy that. The learned men sings verses of praise to exalt Indra. O Indra, the best slayer of the Demons, harness thy bay steeds and come from far off realm to us with the Gods to drink of this Soma draught. The poets and bards have called on thee with their hymns at the sacrifice. O Indra, thou Song lover, as such thou listen to my call! Thou hurled headlong down Vritra from the high heaven and drove away the cows of the deceitful and wicked demons who have hidden them in the mountain caves.

O Indra, thou art called by men in the east, and in the west, in the north and in the south. Thou art worshipped like a lord by all men, living beings and chiefly by Seers. O God, though thou shinest alike on beautiful and ugly, and on all affluent men, yet the seers and learned men of the Vedas, seeking after thee, attain unto thee with songs of praise. Just as a thirsty bull goes to a pool of water, so do thou come here quickly at evening and morning and with the seers enjoy divine juice to thy fill. May these drops gladden thee, God Indra that he who sheds the juice may acquire bounty. Thou stole the juice when pressed out and enjoyed its pleasure and waxed mightly strong. With that strength he won more strength and with energy he crushed the demons. O mighty Indra, ever youthful, all thy enemies who fought battle with you, bent down before you like the trees. The man who has won thy favour roams about as if surrounded by a thousand warriors. He begets heroic sons serving you well with prayers. In the friendship of almighty Indra, we have no fear nor feel any exhaustion. May we enjoy bliss and joy through thy favour and glorify your mighty deeds, O hero! On his left side he hath reclined himself. The offered oblations offend him not. The Soma juice blended with honey of the bee is ready. Quickly come here, hasten and drink the juice. O Indra, when thy friend grows strong in might, fair of form, and rich in chariots, horses and cows, he then with his rich qualities becomes fit to join the company of learned men. Come O Indra, like a thirsty stag to our sacrifice and drink the juice to thy fill. Pouring it down day after day, O Maghavan, thou grows surpassing strong in might. O Adhvarus, let the Soma juice flow because Indra longs to drink thereof. He hath yoked his mighty Steeds, the Virtra slayer hath come nigh.

Like Parjanya rich in rain, Indra is great in his might. He has been glorified with hymns sung by the seers. When the learned men magnify Indra, they offer him gifts and sing hymns of praise of sacrifice. When the learned singers of praise pronounce Indra as an instrument of completing the sacrifice, they declare all other instruments as useless. Before Indra's displeasure all the men and beings bend down as rivers bow down themselves before the ocean. Indra's strength shone brilliantly when he brought together the heaven and earth like a skin. He severed mighty Vritra's head with his powerful knotted thunderbolt.

Verily I have obtained deep knowledge from my father, and therefore, have become illustrious like the Sun. After the ancient manner, I, like a seer adorn my songs, whereby Indra gains strength. O Indra, only the Godless do not praise thee. The Sages praise thee. Wax strong indeed when lauded by me! When Indra thundered and rent the Vritra to pieces limb by limb, he sent the waters to the sea. Indra of hero's strength, hurled his mighty bolt on the demons, he, the dreaded one. Neither the sky, nor the heavens, nor the regions of the earth can contain Indra, the mighty Thunderer!

Laud him, the Lord of Light, the Son of Strength, the messenger who bears oblations to Gods. Agni, the lustrous God, the liberal giver, is wise and worthy of adoration through songs. He is the Lord of sacred food blended with Soma, and has first claim to oblation. We have chosen thee, the most skilled in sacrifice among the Gods, as our Hotar priest, immortal, wise accomplisher of ever holy rite. May Agni, the Water's son, the ever shining and blessed, whose light is most excellent, win favour for us through sacrifice to Mitra, Varuna and waters in heaven.

O Agni, the Son of Strength, glorious friend, whom we praise, bring us bliss. O Agni, reveal to us the mind that wins success in battles with fiends, wherewith thou conquerest in war! Dash to the ground the firm hopes of the foe men and let us overthrow them with your aids. I laud with hymn the friend of mortal men, made envoy and oblation-bearer by the Gods, the best messenger and conveyor of gifts. O Son of Strength, if you were the mortal, and I the immortal, I would not deliver you to evil tongues, O Bounteous One, to calumnies. My devotee would not be in distress, Agni, or in sin, or be in hunger! Like a son loved in his sire's house, let our burnt offerings reach unto the Gods. O Agni, may I, a mortal, with an immortal to help, thou excellent, with thy immediate aid attain my desires. May I collect wealth by thy grace, by thy leading me. O excellent one, thou art my Providence, be pleased to be generous. O Agni, he whom thou choose as your friend, conquers with thine aid, possessing many heroic sons and great deeds.

O matchless one, we call on thee, desiring our protection, possessing nothing of our own, O thunder armed, O Indra, for protection in all our actions, we call on thee in sacrifice. Thou art bold, terrible, mighty and subduer of the foe. We, thy friends, therefore, have chosen thee as our succour and aid. Come here Indra, the juice is effused, thou lord of corn, lord of steeds and lord of kine, and drink of Soma, Soma's lord! We pray thee in our most reverential words. Then, why art thou pondering yet awhile? Here are our desires, here present are our prayers, O generous lord of the bay steeds. It is not that in recent times alone we have obtained thy aid, but in olden times also we had thy opulent riches, O thunderer. We had thy riches and friendship. These we now crave anew of thee, O hero! O Vasu, for the wealth in kine, increase and sharpen our strength, fair, visored one. I praise him, the same God who of old has been granting us this aid and that blessing, him I praise unto you, even Indra, O friends, for protection. Borne on car, drawn by bay steeds, the lord of men and horses, it is he who gives delight. May he, Indra Maghavan, grant us, his devotees, thousands of cattle and steeds. May we, O hero, with thee for friend, resist one who frets against us in anger. May we win the fight with them rich in kine. May we be victorious in song contests and challenge the fiend, O much invoked! May we strike the foe with our heroes putting forth their strength. O Maghavan, further thou our desires. O Indra, since thy birth, thou art foeless ever, independent, all alone without a companion, yet thou longest for a friend in a war. Thou findest not the wealthy to be thy friend for thy flused with the wine of wealth destroy even their friends, when thou thunderest and gatherest, then thou art invoked by men as a father!

Come here Indra, come chariot-borne to the nice eulogy of the Sage. Ye have gone to heaven, by commands of Father Heaven, the God shining by day. O God, may the pressing stones, bring here, the Soma stones with ringing sound. Ye have gone to heaven, by command of Father Heaven, the God shining by day. Just as a wolf shakes a sheep with terror, so do the stones shake the Soma here. Ye have gone to heaven by command of Father Heaven, the God shining by day! The Sages call thee here, O Indra, for help and to win the spoil. Here is set for thee the first draught of Soma expressed, as for the mighty. Come here with your plenteous blessings and perfect care to help us. Come, God of lofty mind, of abundant wealth and numerous aids. Agni, the Hotar priest of men, the adorable God among Gods shall bring thee here. Just as an eagle is borne on its wings, so will ye be borne here on ear drawn by speedy steeds. Come here to our sacrifice and Soma juice. Come from the enemy, with thine ear ready to hear our prayer and take delight in our lauds.

May Indra, listen to our these prayers uttered in praise and supplication. May the almighty Maghavan with his thought favouring come unto us to drink of this Soma draught. For him, the refulgent God, the sovereign, heaven and earth have been fashioned forth with power and strength. Thou long for the Soma draught. Thou art the foremost and peerless amongst the Gods, the art present in their assembly. Drink to thy fill, O Indra, lord of wealth, the expressed juice. Thou art famed far and wide, as lord of bay steeds, victor in the fray, conquering even the unconquerable! O Indra, lord of infinite strength, assist us with all thy aids to gain us renown. May we verily follow thee, the hero, the giver of wealth. O God, thou art the increaser of our steeds and multiplier of our kine. Thou art a golden well for none can impair thy gifts. Give me whatever thing I ask for! Come thou Indra, to thy devotee to make him rich. Fill thyself full with the juice, O Indra, Maghavan and grant us kine and steeds. Thou, as thy boon bestowest many hundred kinds of riches, ye, many thousand kinds of riches. We the learned singers have brought our hymns of praise for acquiring your grace, O Indra, the dismantler of the forts!

O !ndra, make us fearless from that whereof we are afraid! Help us, O Maghavan, for thou art competent to protect us. Drive away our foes and enemies! For thou, O generous God, art verily the Lord of prosperity and home. So we with our Soma shed, call on thee, the song lover. Thou, the Vritra-slayer, art our guard and the best defence against the enemy. May he guard us from all sides, protect us from behind and before, preserve our last and middle most. Guard us from behind, below, above, in front, on all sides, protect us well. Hold away from us the terror sent from heaven, and fatal weapons. Protect us, Indra, each today, each tomorrow, and each following day! Thou lord of the heroes, preserve us, thy singers, through all the days, both by day and by night! O God, thy arms, exceedingly strong, wield the thunderbolt. Thou art passing rich, a matchless hero, endowed with all manly powers.

Though, O Indra, thou art called by men from all sides, they invoke thee from east and west, from north and south, yet come here quickly borne forth by fleet steeds. Thou takest delight in effluence of heaven, rich in light or in the Soma juice shed by thy devotees. With songs I invoke thee, O Indra, most rich in wealth as a cow to benefit us, for the enjoyment of Soma draught. O God! Thou, Maghavan would be praised in songs as great, strong and of mighty deeds, come here to drink of the Soma draught. Come, sit on our sacred grass, the Soma is shed, the feast is ready, we, thy devotees are calling thee. O Indra, thou are the life of men, come to us, O lord of plentitude. We call on thee now. The men have milked out the Soma juice with stones, the nectareous drink. Drink of it and be pleased. Neglect all other pious men skilled in hymns. Come here quickly to grant us high fame. May our King, who gives me spotted kine decked in gold ornaments, rest in peace unharmed. He has given me a gift of gold, pure, shining and of great value besides a thousand kine.

I eulogise Indra; sovereign lord of men, who moves about in his car unrestrained, the Vritra-slayer, most illustrious and winner of the fighting hosts. Honour that Indra, ye learned men for obtaining his aid, in whose sustaining hands of old the mighty thunderbolt was placed as the great Sun was established in heaven. None can attain Indra by deeds, him who works and strengthens evermore. Not even by sacrifice, him, praised by all, unconquerable by might, daring and strong. I praise him, the powerful conqueror, invincible in war, at whose birth the mighty ones bowed in obeisance, the learned and ordinary persons of the world also bent down before him in respect. O Indra, not even a hundred heavens, or a hundred earths can match thee. O Thunderer, not even a thousand suns and both the worlds can match thee. O Indra, thou hast performed many a heroic deed with thy might, ye, with strength, O mightiest. O Maghavan, help us to obtain a stable full of kine with thy wondrous aids! The godless mortal gaineth not his desired goal, O thou immortal Indra, but only he who yokes his bright steeds with prayers. Indra harnesses his bay steeds. Urge ye learned men Indra, the conqueror, to give him to be greatly praised, to be called in shallow water and in depths, to be invoked in all deeds requiring strength.

Call ye, O learned men, Indra with your song of praise to drink of your draught of Soma juice, the subduer of the foe, most munificent, giver of wealth to his subjects! O men know and tell forth, his name is Indra, lauded much and invoked by many, the song-lover, renowned of old! Indra alone is the giver of might and abundant wealth. May he, the almighty give it us knee-deep! Indra, the handsome to look on hast drunken the rapturous draught, the Soma drink with barley brew. Call him aloud with your songs of praise to drink the Soma draught, for it waxeth him strong. When he hast consumed this gladdening juice, the God of Soma God, with vigour surpasseth all things that exist.

Indra, the warrior whom none may harm, the Soma drinker never to be overthrown, is the chieftain of resistless might. Indra, thou all-knowing, worthy of our praise, send us riches, help us in this decisive struggle! Hence, O Indra, come unto us with food that gives a hundred, ye a thousand powers, come even from heaven your dwelling place. O Indra, how rejoice with thy joy of carouse, which is most glorious of all! Indra, the best slayer of demon Vritra, far famed, is the best bestower of might and strength. For that which is thy gift, thou art well known amongst the people, O thou Soma-lover, thunder-armed! For Indra, lover of carouse, loud be our songs about Soma juice, let poets sing the song of his praise. We invoke Indra to the drink, in whom all glories reside, in whom all the seven presiding priests rejoice. At Trikadrukeshu rite, God expands the sacrifice which inspires thoughts. Let our hymns aid and prosper it. Let the Soma juice pass within thee, as the rivers flow into the sea. O Indra, naught excelleth thee! O thou watchful hero, by thy might hast taken in the juice, which is now within thee, O Indra! O Indra, Vritra-slayer, let Soma be expressed for your drink, the juice be prepared for the Gods in your company. Sing well the praise of Indra that the kine and cattle may come. Sing adequately that Indra may come!

O Indra, Lord of light, whatever joyous things thou hast broughtest from the wicked, prosper therewith thy devotees who laud thy deed, and then whose grass is spread for thee, O Indra, grant to thy devotees, who press out Soma juice and give gifts, their share of kine and steeds, which thou hast brought in spoil. Give them and not unto the ill-bred fellow. May he, the godless and riteless man who enjoys his unbroken slumber, O Maghavan, die by following his own device. Show him not the nourishing wealth. Whether O Shakra, thou be far or near at hand, thy worshipper who hath expressed Soma invites thee with his heaven-reaching hymns. O Vritra-slayer, lord of long maned bay steeds! Whether thou be in heaven's shining realm or in the basin of an ocean or in some other place on the earth or in the sky, come unto us to drink of the Soma draft, O lord of strength and gladden us by granting abundant wealth and thy favours. O God, turn us not away. Be present in our banquet with us for thou art our only refuge, yea, thou art our kin. O Indra, turn us not away! Sit ye down with us, sit beside the draught to enjoy the sweet. Sit beside us to drink the juice and shower your favours on thy singer! O Thunderer, neither Gods nor mortals can attain thee. Thou in strength surpasseth all that hath been created. The Gods have not attained thee. All the heroes collectively have made Indra their King, one who is subduer of the foe, firm in his seat of power, the great destroyer, fierce, exceedingly mighty, stalwart and full of vigour. The Bards in unison sing the praise of Indra that he might drink the juice, the lord of light whose laws are inviolate, that he might help with his aids. The sages form a ring, bow into him and sing his praise. Ye also, full of brilliance, free from guile, quick in action, should praise and worship him.

Sing ye a Sama song to Indra, sing a great hymn to the lofty and wise God, who is worthy of adoration and loves praise. O Indra, thou art the conqueror, thou givest splendour to the Sun, thou art the creator of all things, the God of Gods and almighty. O illuminator of the world with thy radiance, thou wentest to the luminous region of the space. The Gods strive to win thy friendship and love. Come unto us, O God Indra, ever conquering but never conquered, vast as a mountain spread in all directions, lord of the heaven. O truthful Soma drinker, mightier than the heaven and earth, Thou lendest strength to him who offers oblations, O lord of heaven! O Indra, thou upholdeth all our forts, thou art verily he who sustains mankind and slays the wicked, lord of heaven. O Indra, lover of song, we draw nigh to thee with a longing. We have streamed to thee as waters follow waters! Just as the rivers swell the ocean, so do our hymns increase thy strength, O almighty hero, thunder-armed day by day. The sages yoke the steeds to thy spacious car with their sacred songs, they yoke the bearers of Indra by a song. O Indra, give us manly strength, bring vigour, thou doer of manifold deeds, grant us a hero conquering in war! Thou hast been unto us mother and a sire. So now for bliss we pray to thee, O gracious Indra. To thee, strong, much invoked, the source of all strength, do I pray, grant thou us heroic power!

O Thunder, thy devoted laud-singers gave thee Soma drink before. So listen to them, Indra, who offer thee praise, come nigh our dwelling place! O Indra! lord of bay steeds, meet for praise, rejoice thee for thee we seek. Thy majesty is the loftiest, O Indra, lover of the song. Just as a son inherits his wealth from his father, so do we enjoy all good things from Indra, just as the rays of the Sun receive light from him. O men, laud him who gives us wealth, prompt with his generous gifts. Good are these things that come from Indra. He goads himself to give and satisfies the desires of all the devotees. O Indra, in our struggle against our foe, thou art the conqueror of all hostile people. Thou art father, all conquering, the dispeller of infamy, the victor of the violent. The earth and heaven cling close to thy victorious might, as do sire and mother to their child. When thou attackest the Demons, all the enemies shrink and faint at thy wrath, O Indra!

Book Ninth

O sacred Soma, conqueror of high renown, flowing on thy way, make the better than we are. Bring to us light, the light divine, and all pure felicities, make us better than we are. Strengthen our skills and mental powers, drive away all our foes, O Soma, and make us better than we are. O purifier, make this Drink, a draught for Indra to drink. Make us better than we are. Give us our share in the Sun through your wisdom and grace. Long may we see on the Sun! Make us better than we are.

O almighty Soma, pour upon us a double share of riches and grace. Make us better than we are. O God, ever victorious, never subdued in battle, pour forth on us your riches. Make us better than we are. O Pavaman Soma, strengthened by man's worship, you shower boons. Make us better than we are. O Purifier, grant us wealth in seeds manifold, life-quickener. Make us better than we are.

The divine Sage, wise of heart, when placed between both hands and pressed, gives pleasant, delightful powers with a roar. Thou flow forth, O Soma Pavaman, enjoying our laud, to a splendid home, free from guile and dear to men. The bestower of joy like a son, pure and mighty, great son, strengthens law, when born, he illumines his parents the Earth and Heaven. Inspired by intense devotion he has gladdened the seven guileless rivers which have magnified the Single Eye, Soma the Moon.

O men, worship ye Soma, him who is now purified, fain to serve the Gods. The learned priest have blended the sweet and divine Soma juice with milk for Gods. May thou grant happiness to our cattle, happiness to our people, happiness to steeds and happiness to growing planets, O King with thy flow! Sing ye learned priests a song of praise to Soma, brown-hued, independent in might, radiant, reaching up to heaven! Purifying Soma when shed with stones which are moved rapidly by the skilled hands, and then blend the milk with the sweet juice. With humble homage draw ye nigh, blend Soma with curds and offer Indu to Indra. O God Soma, foe-queller, fulfilling the desires, pour forth prosperity on our kine! O God, sovereign of the heart, thou heart knower, thou art expressed that Indra drink thee and be delighted. O God, give us riches and heroic strength, O Indu, through Indra, our ally.

Effused through the fleecy filter in thousand streams flows forth purified Soma Pavaman to the meeting place of Indra and Vayu. Sing ye men for help to Soma, the Sage, shed for the enjoyment of Gods. The Soma juice of thousand powers is clarified to gain strength, and praised to become the feast of Gods. O God, as thou flowest grant us mighty powers and abundant food, Indu, give us excellent manly strength. Just as the horses are urged by their riders, so are poured forth Soma drops to win us strength, fast through the fleecy filter. May these drops grant us riches in thousands and manly strength, these god-like Soma drops expressed. They flow forth roaring like milch kine lowing to their calves. They have raced on from both the hands. Thou purified, beloved of Indra, full of joy, roaring, drive away all our foes! O Pavaman, sit in the place of Yajna and sweep away the godless, looking on the light!

The sage Soma has enrobed himself with sheep's wool for the feast of Gods, the subduer of the foe. He grants riches in thousandfold in cattle and comforts! O Soma thou purifiest all with thy knowledge, and graspest all things with thy mind. O Soma, grant us renown! Being purified, O Soma, the wondrous courser, thou has entered into the hymns, like a pious sovereign. He, sparkling, invincible like a courser in the floods, pressed out with hands, is resting under the press. Soma flows on to the woollen sieve like a liberal chief, strengthening the laud.

While being cleansed, the Soma drops flow on. Before blended they are rinsed with water. The milk has rushed forward like a river in flood down a precipice to meet these drops. They come and attain Indra, the God. O Soma, thou Indra's joy, flow on seized and led by the learned men. Pressed out with stones, thou Pavaman, runnest to the sieve, ready for Indra's high decree. Triumphant to be hailed with cheers, O God, flow for man's delight as the sustainer of mankind! O pure, wondrous purifier, flow on, thou best Vritra slayer, worthy to be hailed with shouts of joy. Beloved of Gods, pure, purifier of others, sweet and effused, slayer of sinners, he is called Soma.

Flows forth the Soma juices, pure, benevolent, granting riches visible to all of us. O thou Indu, increase for us the splendour from earth and heaven. Be thou the Lord of all the might! For ye the winds blow full of love, for you the rivers flow increasing thy greatness, O Soma Pavaman. Surge and wax great, O Soma. May vigorous strength gather within you from all sides! Be the nucleus of all the power. For thee, O brown-hued Soma, the kine have yielded undecaying milk and fatness on the sublime heights. O Lord of all, thou noble armed, we long for thy friendship, O Soma, potent defender!

The streams of Soma like waves skilled in song, speed forward, they march onward buffaloes to the woods. The brown-hued, bright juices have flowed with strength in store of kine into the sacred vessels of wood. Let the Soma juices, pressed out with stones, flow for Indra, Vayu, Varuna, Vishnu and for the Maruts. The three several forces urge us, as milch-kine low for their calves. Soma, the brown-hued flows bellowing on. The young and sacred mothers of holy rites, the milch kine, have uttered praise, embellishing Soma, the Son of Heaven. O Soma, for our weal, give us from every side, the four seas, filled full of thousandfold riches.

Like a car horse, flows on with speed the Soma juice from the press, through the sieve, and spurts into the wooden vat. The winner of the race has now attained the goal. This Soma, pure, watchful bearing with dignity, call on the Gods, flows through the sieve to the honey dropping receptacle. Excellent Purifier, let your lights shine brightly on us now, urging us to mental powers and skill of the hand. He, embellished by the hands of faithful to law and holy men, he is cleansed as he flows in the wooden strainer. May Soma pour all the riches of the heavens, of the earth and those of the airy realms upon his charitable worshippers! To the heights of heaven you soar, O Soma, O Lord of strength, seeking horses and cattle, and in search of heroes!

This Soma, the giver of happiness, the strong, shed for drinking, flows on to the cleansing filter, slaying the fiends and loving the Gods. Far-seeing, tawny-hued, flows Soma through the sieve bellowing to attain his seat of rest. This powerful God Pavaman, speeds forth to the luminous realm of heaven, the fiend-slayer, through its woolen filter. This Soma high above on the place of sacrifice, has made the Sun, together with his Sisters, the Dawns, shine. This Soma, espressed, still the best slayer of Vritra, invincible, the room-giver, has gone eagerly as it were to the battlefield to win the spoil. This God, urged by the sages on his way, speeds on to the vats, Indu to Indra, showering boons.

Come unto us flowing swiftly, O God, in thy beloved form, saying, I am there where dwell the Gods. Consecrating that which is unconsecrated, and bringing store of food to man, make thou the rain pour from heaven! This Soma, swift of course, hath flowed down like a river's wave from heaven upon the straining cloth. Through his strength, infusing lustre, the drops enter the purifying wool, all-seeing, sending forth his light. Inviting the juice from the distant world and even from near at hand, the sweet Soma is shed for Indra to drink. The learned priests together have sung the song, with stones they urge the golden-hued Soma, for the pleasure of Indra to drink.

Engendering the luminous heaven, engendering the Sun in the waters, the brilliant Soma clothes himself with the waters and the milk. He, according to the ancient plan, flows forth pressed out in a stream, a God among the Gods. For him increasing and speedily advancing there flow the juices with their thousand powers for his winning. Milked out, the ancient fluid, he is poured into the strainer that purifies. He, roaring, has brought forth the Gods. Soma, while being purified, gives all desirable boons, to the Gods who strengthen the Law. O Sorna, stream on us wealth in cows, heroes, steeds, spoil and the plenty of food, when thou art pressed out.

O Soma, flow on, be pure and ever more pure, winning cattle, steeds and all that which is delightful. Bring here riches with progeny! O you inviolable, flow forth from the waters, flow on from the plants. Flow forth thou from the pressing stones. O Soma Pavaman, flow on surmounting all troubles and distress, and sit, O Sage, on the sacred grass! O Purifier Pavaman, thou foundest the divine light, thou, once born, grewest great, O sacred One, surpassing all!

Established in delight he flows forth on his way to the dear names in which the youthful one increases great. The great and wise now ascends his chariot of the mighty Sun, the car of a universal motion. The speaker of the Truth, the tongue of sacrifice, a pleasant meat, invincible, the lord of this hymn, the Son places the third hidden name of the Parents, the Heaven and Earth, in the lustrous world of heavens. Breaking forth into flashes he hath bellowed into the jars, guided by men into the golden vat. To him the milky streams of sacrifice have sung, he shines brightly on triple heights of the Dawns. Pressed out by the stones, placed in delightful hymns, illuminating the parents, the Earth and Heaven, he flows on evenly through the fleece, a stream of honey ever increasing day by day. Flow forth everywhere, O Soma, flow on for our prosperity, purified by the men, clothe thyself with the milky draught. With thy rapturous drinks that are strong and smiting, impel Indra to give us wealth!

Widespread for thee is the purifying sieve. O Lord, as Prince thou pervadest the limbs of the being. The unripe whose body has not suffered the heat of fire, he gains not that delight. They alone are able to enjoy it who have been prepared by the fire. High above in the seat of heaven is spread the strainer. Its threads shining with light stand extended. His swift juices protect him who purifies. He ascends the height of heaven by the conscious heart. This foremost dappled Bull hath made the Dawn to shine out and cherishing strength sustains all things that exist. The Sages by his lofty wisdom have wrought, the Fathers, strong of vision, set him within as a child to be born. The Gandharva protects his seat, as the supreme and wondrous one, he guards the Gods. Lord of the snare, he seizes the enemy with the same. Those who are most perfect in rites have enjoyed a share of his honeyed meat. Thou rich in food, enrobed in clouds, thou art vast, the mighty seat of Gods, thou encompassest the sacrifice. O King, thou goest up to the war riding thy chariot sieve, and with thy thousand brilliant weapons conquerest the vast renown!

Like embellishments striving for the neck of a victor, like the cries of men striving for light, our hymns strive for Soma, who as a Sage is cleansed with waters. His wisdom is like a stall where kine may prosper. All worlds have expanded for him who found the light and revealed the home of immortality. Our swelling songs, like kine in the pasture call aloud on Soma in deep devotion.

Like a chariot, bearing all his wisdom, the Hero, the Seer, moves about all the world, seeking glory among the Gods for the mortal men, rewards for the skilled, and new things worth praise amidst the divine beings. Born for glory and life to his singers, he, enrobed in glory, has gone to immortality. He, measuring his course, makes the encounter a success. Stream for us food, nourishment, steeds and cattle. Shed light abroad and fill the Gods with joy. All these are easy to achieve for thee, for thou. Soma Pavaman, quellest all enemies!

Be seated, O friends and sing aloud for him who purifies himself. Array him alike a child in festive raiment and bring him offering. Unite with his worshippers even as a calf to its mother cow, this doubly potent, the God, giver of property, producer of happiness, the God-gladdening juice. Purify him who gives power, that he, most blessed one, be a feast for Varuna, Mitra and their attendants. Our songs have lauded you like lowing cows, as producer of wealth for us. We cover the hue thou wearest with a robe of flowing milk. Thou Soma art the Lord of raptures, gladdening drink of the immortal Gods, as friend to friend, show us the path as the best guide. Drive far away from us the rapacious demon, the godless and the false, whoever he may be. Sweep away all sorrow!

Ye learned, sprinkle forth the Soma shed, the best of holy gifts, the friend of man, who hath run among the water streams, pressed out with stones. More adorous and purified, he flows through the woolen filter, the invincible. We take great delight when thou art shed, mixing thee still with juice and milk. Expressed for all to see, the seer, gladdening the Gods, Soma is verily the mental power. O Soma, purifying all, thou manifests thyself flowing in a watery robe, giver of treasures, thou art the root of Law. O God, a fountain of gold.

When they purify thee, O dear Indu, ever watchful in the sieve of long fleece, thou becomest a singer, thou made the Sun ascend the heaven. Thou best furtherer, generous, sage and singer, clear of vision, floweth forth. Thou art a Sage most loved of the Gods, thou made the Sun ascend the heaven. Extracted by the pressers with stones, Soma goes over the tleecy back of the sheep, goes even as with a mare in a tawny coloured stream, in a sweet singing stream. Down with the water, Soma hath flowed, he hath flowed with kine which have been milked. The gladdening Soma juices go to the wooden vat as water flow to the ocean, the cheerer flows for the carouse. Pressed out with stones, O Soma, and filtered through the fleecy sieve, thou enterest the vat even as a man enters a city having conquered a fort, gold-hued. He like a racing horse beautifies himself through the sieve of long fine wool the munificent. He, the

Soma Pavaman, becomes the joy of the sages and the holy bards. The delightful Soma hath flowed river-like for the feast of Gods, sweet with the liquor he hath flowed into the vat that drops with honey. Like a dear son he must be cleansed and embellished. He, the glorious one, hath clothed himself in a bright robe. The men skilled in their craft drive him forth, like a chariot driven to the battlefield by a clever driver.

O Soma, full of sweetness, most divine, great gladdening juice, flow thou for Indra! Thou of whom realizing the rapture, Indra, the Bull exhibits his manly strength, having deep drunk that divine juice. He, the giver of happiness and light, most wise, hath come nigh to food and booty as a steed comes to the battle. O Pavaman, thou pure, God, divine, full of brightest splendour, givest all beings a message of immortality. By whom the Priest opened the closed portals, by whom the Sages attained their desires, through whose support they won the renown of splendid Amrita at the place of sacrifice in the felicity of Gods.

Press him out and pour into the vat, praiseworthy speeding like a horse through the flood, him who swims in water and dwells in the woods. The Steer with thousand streams pours about like rain, beloved of the Gods and true in essence. Born in law, he hath grown strong by the law, sovereign Lord, and the lofty law in itself. O God, Lord of food, make high and splendid glory shine all around us. Unclose the covering of the middle region! Roll forth out of the press, O potent God, like a king, supporting his subjects. Pour forth rain on us from heaven, send us the goods for developing our intellects to win the spoil. Strain him, even this steer who milks the heavens, him with a thousand streams, bringing rapturous joys, him who showers all marvellous things! The potent one, born immortal, who lends life, and lights up the darkness with his shine. The Sages have praised him well, who by his wondrous might enrobes himself in threefold attire. Soma, who bestows on us riches, milch kine, food, houses to dwell in, fine children, is effused by the priests. He whom Indra, the Maruts, Bhaga and Aryaman drink for their felicity, by whom we bring Mitra, Varuna and Indra to our sacrifice for our great defence, he is our sound refuge!

Flow on thou sweet Soma, flow forth meat to Gods' taste. Thou divine and bright, flow forth, flow to the vast dwelling place of immortal Gods. Let Indra drink of thy juice of joy for wisdom, let all the Gods drink it for strength! Flow on as a mighty ocean, O Soma, as Father of the Gods to every form. O God flow on, resplendent to the Gods, blissful to the heaven and earth and all living beings! Flow forth thou divine, sustainer of the Sun, flow, mighty One, in accordance to the Law! Flow thou splendid, through the woolen sieve with thy many streams, O Soma! Let Soma the light finder, joyous and cleansed, expressed and led by men, make all happiness flow. He, while cleansed, makes all happiness flow. He, while cleansed, protects the people, shall grant us all treasures for our own.

Flow forth to battle to win Vritras. Thou speedest to quell the enemy like a hero exacting debts. We all rejoice ourselves in thee, O effused Soma, for attaining supremacy in fight. Thou Soma Pavaman, enterest into mighty deeds. Thou Soma, didest engender the Sun with thy might and rain in the high sky, hasting to us with plenty vivified with milk! Thou didest beget the Sun, the immortal one, for mortal beings, for upholding Law and sweet Amrita. Thou evermore makes the wealth to flow to us. Thou hast with thy might pierced for us, as it were a never drying well for men to drink, led on thy path in fragments from the presser's arms. Then resplendent Gods proclaim their kinship with him as they look upon him and God Savitar open us, as it were the folds of heaven. Some men of old whose sacred grass was spread, addressed the song to thee, O Soma, for gaining strength and fame. So thou hero inspire us now to manly strength. Some priests of old have drained forth from the great depth of the sky the ancient primeval divine milk that deserves the laud. They sang aloud to Indra at his birth. O Pavaman, thou art the lord of heaven and earth and all that exists. Thou shinest like a sovereign Bull among the herd.

We all possess various thoughts and plans and diverse are the callings of men. The carpenter seeks out that which is cracked, the physician the ailing, the priest the worshipper. Flow, Soma flow for Indra's sake! The smith with his seasoned plants, with his feathers of the birds of the air, and stones for the tips, and with enkindled flames seeks him, who has a store of gold. Flow, Soma flow, for Indra's sake!

I am a bard, my father is a physician, my mother's job is to grind the corn. Our callings are different, but we all aim at wealth. We follow in its wake like a cow herd after his kine. Flow, Soma flow for Indra's sake! A horse wants to draw a light car, gay hosts like to evoke a laugh and a jest, the male desires his mate's approach, a trog wants a flood to plunge within. Flow, Soma, flow for Indra's sake.

Let Indra, the Vritra slayer drink Soma juice by the Lake, gathering strength in his heart for doing heroic deeds. Flow, Soma flow on for Indra's sake. Flow thou Soma, the lord of heavenly regions, a boon to men, through the land, shed with vigour and devotion and a sacrificial song. Flow, Soma flow for Indra's sake! Hither has she brought the mighty Soma plant, nursed by God Parjanya. The Gandharvas have caught hold of him. Flow, Soma flow thou, for Indra's sake! By law splendid, upholding law truthful and speaking the truth, Soma, the King, is embellished by the pressers. Flow, Soma flow thou, for Indra's sake! He flows on in streams, the great and truly mighty. The Soma juices, cleansed with prayer, mingle with one another, the golden-hued. Flow, Soma flow thou, for Indra's sake!

O Pavaman Soma, where the priest recites the meterical hymn, moving the pressing stones, exults in juices, through Soma bringing for delight, flow, Soma flow thou, for Indra's sake. Where the celestial light ever shines, where the Sun is ever present, in that deathless and undecaying world place me, O Pavaman, beyond any harm's reach. Flow, Soma flow thou, for Indra's sake! Make me immortal in that world where the King Vivasvat's son rules supreme, where is the shrine of heaven, where the waters are ever fresh and young. Flow, Soma thou flow, for Indra's sake! Make me immortal in that radiant realm where they move about as they will, in the threefold region, in third inmost heaven, where realms are full of light. Flow, Soma thou flow, for Indra's sake! Make me immortal where vows and eager longings are fulfilled, the realm of the golden Sun, the kingdom of oblation, and joyous felicities. Flow, Soma thou flow, for Indra's sake!

Book Tenth

O ye Waters, source of joy, help us to gain strength that we may have great delight. Grant us the propitious sap. You art like loving mothers ever longing to give to dear children. To you we willingly come. O Waters, to aid him, to whose abode you send us on. Waters you are the source of our life and being. The Waters be to us for drink, divine for our help and happiness. May they flow to us health and strength! We beg these Waters to grant us healing balm, who rule over precious things and have supreme control of men.

Within these Waters, Soma has told me, dwell balms that heal, and Agni who blesses all. O Waters full with healing balms, keep my body safe from harm, that I may see long the Sun. Whatever sin is found in me, whatever evil I have done, if I have lied or falsely sworn, Waters, remove it from me. This day I seek the Waters, this day we mingle with their sap. Come thou Agni, rich in milk, come and bestow on me your splendour!

Worship the King with oblations, Yama who has climbed up the lofty heights, the Son of Vivasvat, the gatherer of men together, who shows the path to men. He was the first to show us the way, the pasture which none can take away from us. Men born once tread their own path, the path that our ancient Fathers walked. Matali dwells there with the ancient Bard, and Yama with the Agni's sons, and Brihaspati, singers of laud, both exalters of Gods and by Gods exalted. Some take delight in praise, and others in offering oblation. Come and sit ye on this sacred grass, accompanied with the ancient Priests and the Fathers. May the hymns recited by the sages bring you here. O King, may this oblation make thee rejoice! Come, O Yama, with ancient holy priests. Rejoice ye here with Virupas children. I call also on Vivasvat, your father to sit on our sacred sacrificial grass! May our Fathers, the ancient Priests, the Navagavas, Atharvans, Bhrigus all observing Soma, may all these look on us with kindness, may they ever regard us with their grace and favour!

Go forth, proceed along the ancient pathways whereon our forefathers have gone before us. There you shall find both the Sovereigns enjoying their oblations, God Yama and God Varuna! Meet Yama, meet the Fathers with all your oblations and pious actions in the highest heaven, leaving sin and evil, seek again your dwelling and wear another body bright with glory. Depart hence, off with ye spirits, flee from here, for him the Fathers have provided this place. Yama grants him a place to rest in, where days and nights rotate and waters flow. Be quick on your happy pathway, and outspeed the brindled two dogs, Sama's offspring, the four-eyed. Then come nigh the gracious Fathers who rejoice there in the company of Yama.

Entrust this man, O King, to the protection of your two dogs, four-eyed watchful, the guardians, the keepers of the pathway. Give him happiness and wellbeing. May the Yama's two envoys, dark-hued, broad-nosed, insatiate, who roam about among the men, restore to us today a happy existence, that we may live long to see the Sun! For Yama pour the Soma draught, bring sacred sacrifice for Yama. To Yama goes oblation prepared and heralded by Agni. Offer to Yama, an offering rich and sweet, and come nigh that he may grant us long days of life amidst Gods. Offer to Yama, to the King, an oblation rich and sweet. We offer our humble homage to Seers of old, to the pioneers who made this path in the days of yore.

May they, our Fathers who in their skill belong to the lowest order, attain higher one, those of midmost may attain the highest, they who deserve a share in Soma. May they who have attained a life of spirit, the knower of sacrifice, the guileless, help us when called upon. Now this oblation is for Fathers who passed of old and those who followed, those who are established in high position on the earth and for those who dwell among the learned and the best subjects. May I attain the experienced and lofty minded Fathers. I have got fine son and progeny from Vishnu, the eternal. May they who enjoy the expressed Soma juice with libation, seated on the sacred grass, come to our sacrifice. May the learned Fathers who sit on the sacred grass, come to your aid. These oblations are for them, may they accept these. Come Fathers to us and grant us health and vigour without trouble and sin. May they, the Fathers, worthy of the juices, invited to the sacrifice, come here and listen to our speech. May they favour us with their grace and bless us! O ye Fathers, seated southward with your knees bent, accept our offerings with favour in this sacrifice. Chastize us not for a sin which might have been committed out of human weakness! O Fathers, seated on the altar the seat of leaping flames, grant riches to the charitable man. Grant to his sons and grandsons clothes, wealth etc. to those who offer oblations in the sacrifice!

Don't burn him up or completely consume him, O Agni, let not his body or skin be scattered. Perfect him, O ye Jatavedas, the all-seeing and send him on to the dwelling of the Fathers, when you have perfected him, O Jatavedas, then consign him over to the Fathers. When he reaches the realm of spirits, he will be a controller of the Gods. The Sun receives your eye, the Wind your spirit, go as your merit is to earth and heaven, or if that be your lot go to the waters, making your home in the herbs of the field. Your portion is the goat, consume him with your heat, let your blazing flames and splendour consume him! By these your auspicious forms, O Agni, carry this man to the realm of the saints. O Agni, convey him again to the Fathers, him who offered to you oblations, now follows his destiny. Let him unite with a new body, putting on a new life, let him multiply his progeny. O all-knowing Jatavedas!

Whatever wound the blackbirds, or the ant, the snake, or the jackal has caused you, may Agni, the all-devourer, heal it, and Soma who has entered into the priests. Shield thee against fire with the hide of the cow, smear thy body with fat and oil, that the bold Agni, eager to consume thee, may not encompass thee with his fierce blaze. Forebear, O Agni to overturn this cup, dear to Gods and to them who merit Soma. This chalice which serves to quench the thirst of Gods, in it the immortals find delight. May flesh-consuming Agni go away afar, removing all sins, may he go to Yama's abode. But may the other forms of the Jatavedas, the all-knowing, bear this oblation to the Gods, for he is skilled. I have chosen Agni as my God, for worship of the Fathers, he the flesh-consumer, who dwells in your house. May he light flames in the assembly of the learned.

Tvastar prepares his daughter for her marriage. The whole world has assembled on hearing the tidings, but Yama's Mother, consort of great Vivasvat, vanished while being conveyed to her house. From mortal men they did this immortal woman, and fashioning another like her, they gave her to Vivasvat. She, Saranyu bore him the twain Ashvins and then deserted the twins. May the all-knowing Pushan, the guardian of the world, whose cattle are never harmed, convey thee to the Father's keeping, may Agni escort thee to the Gods, who is ever gracious. May Pushan escort and protect you on your distant path. May Savitar lead you thither where go and dwell the pious and doers of good deeds, who went before you! May Pushan, the knower of all these pathways, conduct us by the ways that are free from fear and danger, going before us the wise, watchful, giver of blessings, glowing, the hero. On distant pathways was Pushan born on the road that lies far from heaven and far from earth. He travels on his way with perfect knowledge to both the realms, most dear to men. During the sacrifice, the holy ones call on Saraswati. Saraswati they worship. May Saraswati grant us bliss, Saraswati adored by pious aforetime.

O Goddess Saraswati, whom the Fathers invoke, thou be seated on the sacred grass, taking delight in our sacrifice. O Goddess Saraswati called on by the Fathers, who come to join our sacrifice, grant food and wealth to him who now offers sacrifice, a portion worth as much as a thousand of an offering! The Mother Waters which cleansed the sacred oil, shall cleanse us of stain with the self same oil. They remove all defilement. I rise up from them cleansed and purified.

Go away, O Death, pursue the distant path, not travelled by the Gods. I tell you, one who can see and hear. Do not harm our children, touch not our heroes, when you efface Mrityu's footsteps to further time, to prolong your existence, may you be rich in offspring and wealth, live splendid lives, performing sacrifices in honour of Gods! Apart from the dead are these, the living. Our prayer to the Gods have been granted. We now resort to dancing and laughter, returning to further our span of existence. Here I make a barrier around the living, that none of them this barrier may cross. May they live a span of hundred autumns, burying the Death beneath this mound! As days follow days in close succession, as do the seasons one another, as successors fail not their predecessors, so shape the life of these, O ordainer! Attain your prime, then find old age delightful, striving by turns for one behind the other. May he, the ordainer, Tvastar, maker of good things be pleased to grant you lengthened span of days!

May these ladies, unwidowed, with their noble husbands, anoint and embellish themselves with fragrant balms, adorned with nice jewels, tearless, free from sorrow, mount the place where lies he in rest. Rise, O lady, come to the world of living, come, for he is dead by whose side you are lying your wifehood is over with this your husband, who wooed you earnestly by holding your hand. From the dead hand of him, I take this bow that he carried so that it may bring us power, prestige and glory. There you are, and here we are with heroes to frustrate all the snares and attacks of the enemy hosts. Subside thee into the lap of Mother Earth, far spreading, kind and gracious lady, young and soft like wool to the generous giver! May she preserve you from the lap of nothingness. O Earth, heaving thyself make a vault, do not press down much on him, grant him easy access, afford him tender refuge, cover him up with your skirt, just does a mother to her child, O Earth! May earth, like a vault over him, propped upon to thousand pillars, lie lightly. May it be his home dripping with fatness, a place of refuge to him for ever. I raise a mound of earth around you. May I be free from harm. May the Fathers support this pillar for you, may Yama give you this as your dwelling place!

Pay homage to the Eye of Mitra and Varuna, offer to the mighty God this worship, to the far seeing Ensign, born of the Gods. Sing praise to the Sun, the son of Heaven. May this speech of truth guard me on all sides, wherever the Heaven and Earth and days are spread. All else that moves finds rest, but never cease the Waters flowing or the Sun rising. From ancient times no godless man can obstruct your chariot when you drive the winged tawny steeds. One of your sides is dark and turned eastward while with the other, the lustrous one, you rise, O Sun. By the light, whereby you scatter the gloom, by your rays which arouse every moving thing, dispel from us worthless worship, drive away all disease and evil dreams. Sent forth as a guardian of the law, you watch the weal of every being, and rise day by day without any wrath. May the Gods favour us with our desires and purpose through this our prayer today. May this prayer of our Heaven and Earth, Waters and Indra, and the Maruts hear. May we never lack the Sunshine, may we live happily and attain old age. Keen of sight and sharp of mind, free from disease and without any sin, with a store of children, may we live long, O Surya, to look on you, rising day by day thou Mitra, our great friend!

O far seeing Sun, may we live long and look upon thee ever, flooding the world with your glorious radiance, the source of joy of every eye. With your lustre all the living world comes to life and with your setting again returns to reset. O Sun, golden haired God, arise each day for us better than the last bringing innocence. Bless us with your beams, bless us with radiance and shining. Bless us in cold and intense heat. Grant us, O Sun, blessings at home and when we are travelling abroad, give us your wondrous treasure. Grant protection to both our bipeds and quadrupeds. Grant food and water that their wants are adequately met. Grant us health and strength and protection against harm, O Gods! If by some grave offence we have provoked the Gods, O Deities, by our speech or by thoughtlessness of mind, lay upon this sin on one who ever plans evils, on him, O Vasus, who led us into distress.

I hymn the fame of Maghavan, who with his greatness protected the Gods, transfixed the enemy when both the Heaven and Earth cried for help in terror. When thou roamed abroad, O Indra, waxing strong in body, telling thy strength among the people, that might was sufficient for thy battles which they tell, but today thou hast no foe or knewest one before. Who were the sages before us who comprehend the limits of thy greatness? Didst thou not generate thy father and mother together out of thine own body? Verily, thou possessest four supreme mightiness while dwelling in vastness. All these thou surely knowest and wherewith thou hast performed thy great deeds, O Maghavan! Thou possessest all the treasures, those made manifest and those lying hidden in the secret. Strike not asunder my desire, O Maghavan, thou art he who commands it and thou art he who giveth! To him who established light in the heart of other light and united sweetness to sweetness, to him, to that Indra this hymn was sung by Brihaduktha, when he fulfilled in himself the Brahman.

May this life be now renewed and earned further, as by two car-borne charioteers, on their course. May he, like Chyavana, attain his goal. Let Goddess Nirriti depart to distant places! Here is a song for wealth, for food in abundance. Let us do many noble deeds to achieve glory. May all our deeds rejoice the singer. Let Nirriti, the Goddess of Doom depart to distant places. May we subdue our foes with our deeds of valour, as heaven spreads over the earth and mountains over the plains. All these our deeds the bard has acclaimed. Let the Goddess of Doom depart to distant places. Consign us not as prey to Death, O Soma, still may we look upon the rising Sun! May the full span of life granted by the Gods be ours, may the Goddess of Doom move to distant places! O Yama, the guide of spirits, keep the soul within us and lengthen the span of our life, allow us that we may still enjoy the vision of the Sun. Wax strong in body with the fat we offer you!

Give us, O Guide of the Spirits, our sight again, give us our breath again and powers of enjoyment. Long may we see the Sun rising. O Gracious one, grant us your favour and blessings. May the Earth restore us our vital breath, may the Goddess Heaven and mid-air restore it. May Soma once again return our body, and Pushan guide us on the path of peace and prosperity. May with the worlds bless Subandhu they the Mothers of Eternal Law. May Heaven and Earth sweep away all evil and shame. May neither sin nor sorrow trouble you! May health giving medicines descend on us from Heaven in twos and threes or singly roam about the Earth, May both Heaven and Earth uproot and sweep away all evil and shame. May sorrow never trouble you! Restore the wagon-ox, O Indra, that brought hither the chariot-borne wife of Ushinara. May both Heaven and Earth uproot and sweep away all evil and shame. May sorrow never trouble you!

When the seers began to name objects, then Brihaspati, the Lord of the Holy world, sent forth Speech, the first and earliest utterances, that which was best and purest, hidden in their hearts, was revealed through their affection. The sages fashioned the speech by means of their mind as corn is shifted with the sieves. Friends see and recognize each other's friendship, their speech bears the blessed seal imprinted. With sacrifice they traced the path of speech and found her entered in the heart of the Seers. They brought her forth and dealt her among many. In unison the Seven Singers chant her. Yet one hath never seen her though seeing, and the other though hearing, never heard her. But to some she reveals herself in beauty like a fond embellished bride surrendering to her husband. One man they call dull, unbending in friendship, they never urge him to contests. He wanders on his way of illusion, his efforts fruitless, the speech he hears yield not either fruit or flowers. No longer does he possess a portion in the speech who has abandoned his own dear genuine friend. Verily vain in his hearing, whatsoever he listens, for he knows not the righteous path.

The friends though endowed alike with eyes and ears, may yet be unequal in quickness of mind. Some look like ponds that reach the mouth or shoulder, others resemble lakes deep enough for bathing. When friendly Brahmins sacrifice together, with impulses from the spirit within, they leave one behind in their achievements, while some others though counted as Brahmins, stray away. Those who fare not forward in the direction, or know not the Brahmins or preparers of sacrifice, they have attained the speech in sinful fashion, being ignorant, they weave their threads in faulty fashion. All friends rejoice when their friend returns in triumph, being declared conquered in the assembly. He removes their sins, provides them with food. Ready is he for a dead of valour. One with perfection composes the verses, another sings a song in metrical measures. The third, the Brahmin, tells the wisdom of being, while still fourth lays down the rules of sacrifice.

Let us with our skills proclaim the birth and generation of Gods in hymns so that men to come in future know the truth of the past. Brahmanaspati, the Lord of the Holy World, with a blast smelted them together like a smith, in earlier times of Gods, and then Existence sprang from non-existence. In the earliest times of Gods' Existence from non-existence was born, thereafter came to being the realms from the Creating Power. Earth was born from this creating Power, and from her sprang the cardinal points. Daksha was born of Aditi and Aditi was Daksha's child. Aditi did issue forth first, the Daksha's daughter. After her followed the Gods, the blessed ones, sharers of life immortal. When ye, O Gods were found in yonder waters close ciosping one another, then from you a thick cloud of dust arose as from many dancing feet.

When ye. O Gods, like wonder workers, caused all the worlds that exist to spring, then brought forth the Sun lying hidden in ocean. Bight are the sons of boundless Aditi, who sprang forth from her body, with seven she joined the ranks of the Gods, the eighth, the Sun, she cast aside, so with her seven sons Aditi went to meet the earlier age. She brought the Sun to earth that he might generate life and die again.

Once our Father, the Seer, sat down as Hotar priest and offered all the existing worlds in oblation in order to achieve riches, and then he entered into later creations as archetypal. What was the place, what the substance? What supported him? How was it created? From what matter did Vishwakarman, seeing all made the Earth and shaped the Heavens? He has countless eyes on all sides, and has as many faces, arms and feet untold in all directions, he the sole God created the Heavens and Earth and welded them together with his arms and wings. What was the wood, and what was the thee from which the Heavens and also the Earth were fashioned forth? Ponder, ye wise men, inquire in your hearts, on what did he stand when he created all these worlds?

Your haunts where you dwell, O Viswakarman, ever true to the law, your highest and lowest, thy mid-most and the lowest depths, reveal to your friends at sacrifice. Come ye blessed to our sacrifice and thus exalt it. O Maker of all, bring thou thyself here, growing strong with each oblation, come with Earth and Heaven. Let other men loiter here and there in folly, let us have here a liberal portion! Let us now invoke the Lord of Speech for our help, Viswakarman, the designer of all things that exist, may he kindly listen to all our prayers, and grant us all his blessings, whose work is ever righteous!

The Father of vision, the wise, in spirit created in the manner of a ritual both the worlds. When the eastern ends there firmly fastened, then the earth and heavens in their turn were far extended. Most wise and exceedingly strong is Vishwakarman, the designer, the creator, the most high presence. Men rejoice that their offsprings, rich in juice are accepted by one who is beyond the seven Seers. Me is our Father who made us, he is the Disposer, who knows all things and every creature. It was he alone who gave the Gods their names. To him come all beings seeking information, to him the Seers of old offered their sacrifice, and also sang in multitude groups as singers. It is he who fashioned this whole world when the distant, the near, and the lower spheres were set in their places.

That which is earlier than the heavens, this earth and both the Gods and demons, say what was that, the first primeral germ which the waters received when all the Gods together, they alone were watching? He was the primeral germ received by the waters, wherein all the Gods were gathered together. It rested upon the navel of the unborn the one and only one in whom all created things abide. You have no knowledge of him who created all these worlds and things for some other thing has come between you. The singers of hymns who ravish life in their rites go on chanting enwrapped in confusion and ignorance.

He born anew is ever fresh, the emblem of days, he follows the Dawns. Arising he provides the Gods their portion. May the Moon lengthen the span of our existence. Mount, O Sun, this gold-hued chariot shaped from many forms of Kimsuka planks and Salmali -wood, strong wheeled, easy rolling. Forth to the world of life immortal, make a happy bridal journey for your lord. Get up from hence, this maiden has a husband. Go, seek another in her father's home and get the portion from of old assigned you. Rise up from here, Viswarasu, we entreat you with due reverence. Seek you another willing maid leaving the lady alone with her husband. Straight be the paths and thornless whereupon our friends travel to the wooing. Let Aryaman and Bhaga lead us, let there be a stable union of the wife and husband, O Gods! Now I free you from the noose of Varuna, wherewith the kindly Savitar hath bound thee. Unharmed I give thee up with thy consort to the law, in the world of goodness. May bounteous Indra lead you by the hand that you may live blessed in fortune with your sons, may the Ashvins escort you on their car so that you may enter your husband's house as the mistress. May authority be ever yours in speech. Happy be thou and prosper with your children there, be ever watchful as mistress to rule over the household. Unite yourself wholly with this man your husband. So authority will be yours in speech till fair old age. Dark blue and red is the Magic sign which clings so closely, now driven off. May the kinsman of the bride thrive well, the husband is bound fast in bonds. Throw you away the dirty woollen robe, give wealth to the Brahmin priests. This female fiend, now assuming feet attends her husband as a wife.

I anoit with fat the mighty demon-slayer, to the renowned Friend. I come for refuge to him who enkindled and boldened by our rites may protect us from evil day and night. O Agni, assail the demons with thy iron teeth and blazing flames. With thy tongue seize the foolish worshippers, rend to pieces and devour the raw, flesh eaters, O God Agni, use thy both upper and lower teeth, enkindled and annihilating. Roam about in the air, O God, around us and with thy mighty jaws attack the evil spirits. Bend thy darts through sacrifice, O Agni, whet their points with song as if with a whetstone and therewith pierce the hearts of the devils and tear their arms away raised to attack thee. Destroy annihilate with your heat the workers of magic, destroy the evil spirits with your blazing flame. O Agni, destroy with fire the foolish adorers, blaze and destroy this day the evil-doer, may each blazing curse of his return and consume him. May arrows pierce the liar in his vitals and Vishwa's net enclose the Rakshashas, The wicked who anoints himself with flesh and blood of cattle, with flesh of steeds and of human beings, who steals the milk away, O Agni, tear off the heads of such fiends with fiery fury. Guard us, O Agni, from above and from below, from behind and before. May you flames most fierce, ever blazing wholly consume the sinful man.

A thousand heads has Purusha a thousand eyes, a thousand feet. Encompassing the Earth from all sides, he exceeds it by ten fingers breadth. This Purusha is all that has been and what is to be. This Lord of immortality waxes ever greater by food. So vast is the measure of his greatness, and still greater is Purusha. All creatures are a fourth of him, three-fourths are in eternal heaven. Three-fourths of him ascended high, one-fourth remained here down on the earth. From this he spread to every side over living and non-living things. From him Virat, the shining was born and from this again Purusha was born. As soon as he took birth he spread himself over the entire Earth both before and behind. The Gods prepared the sacrifice with this Purusha as their oblation. The spring was the clarified butter, summer the fuel, and autumn the offering.

This Purusha, born in the earliest time, the Gods embalmed on the grass as sacrifice and performed their holy rites, so also did the Seers and Sages. From that universal sacrifice the curd dripping with butter was collected. Thence came the creatures of the air, and beasts both domestic and wild. From this universal sacrifice were born the Vedic Richas and Saman hymns, from this came the various meters, and from this were born spells and sacred formulas. From this were born horses, all creature such as have two rows of teeth. From it sprang kine, from it the sheep and goats were born.

When they divided up Purusha, in how many parts did they divide him? What did his mouth become? What his arm? What were his legs called? What his feet? The Brahmin was his mouth, his arms the heroic prince, his thighs became the Vaishya, from his feet came the humble Shudra. The Moon was born from his mind, the Sun was born from his eye. Indra and Agni were born from his mouth, and the Wind from his breath. From his navel came forth the air, the heaven was formed from his head, the Earth from his feet, the four directions from his ear. Thus were formed the worlds. Seven were the fencing sticks, thrice seven the sticks of fuel were fonned, when the Gods performing sacrifice, bound Purusha as their victim. Thus the Gods in the sacrifice sacrificed the victim. They were the earliest established rites. The Mighty ones ascended up the heaven, where dwell the Gods and other celestial beings.

These stones, who have like race horses ten sets of rein and iron bits well fixed in their jaws, and travel round and round. They were the first to taste the flowing Soma, they were the first to enjoy the milky fluid of Soma stalks. These Soma tasters kiss the bay steeds of Indra, they are placed on the ox-hide for their task of Soma pressing. Having drunk the sweet Soma draught drawn by them, Indra growing in might waxes great like a Bull. Strong is your stalk, you shall never be harmed, you are full of sap, ever satisfied, fair like wealth of a rich, in whose sacrifice. O stones, you find delight. Bored deep, but not pierced through, are these Stones, never tired and ever free from death. Immortal, free from sickness, old age and suffering, slim looking, free from the thirst of craving.

Arise, my friends with one mind, enkindle Agni, my numerous companions. I call on you Agni, Sun and the Goddess Dawn, come ye down to aid us. Spin out your songs of praise, be pleasant in your thoughts, make a boat equipped with oars to cross the waters, get ready the implements and let the sacrifice now proceed further, my friends. Fix well the ploughshares, lay on the yokes. The furrows are made, sow now the seed. If your speech is heard with attention, the richer the harvest for our scythes. The learned make the ploughshares ready for ploughing and lay the yokes well on either side. These men possessed of the wisdom gain favour of Gods. Arrange the buckets well in their places, and fasten securely on the straps. We shall draw from a copious well, rich in stream, fair flowing and inexhaustible.

The fool acquires food with fruitless labour, that food, I tell the truth, shall be his doom. Me feeds neither a friend nor a man who loves him. Alone he eats, alone he bears the guilt. The ploughshare that ploughs the soil grows the food that satisfies hunger. The traveller, on his legs, reaches his goal, the eloquent priest surpasses that who is mute, a friend who gives is better than a miser one. The

Sun with one foot outruns the two-footed man, and the two-footed man overtakes the old man with three. Quadrupeds like dogs come when called by the biped men. They stand and keep watch where five men meet together. The hands are both alike but differ in their work. So do two cows, or offspring of the same mother. The sister milch cows may differ in their yield of milk, even twins differ in their strength, or kinsmen in charity.

In the beginning arose Hiranyagarbha, the Golden Germ, born only Lord of all created beings. He did fix and hold up the Earth and Heaven. What God shall we adore with our oblation? He who gives vital breath and manly vigour, whose commands even the Gods obey, whose shade is life eternal, the lord of death. What God shall we adore with our oblation? Who by his grandeur has emerged the sovereign of every living thing that breathes and slumbers, he who is lord of two-footed man and four-footed creatures. What God shall we worship with our oblation? By right the snow capped mountains, the world stream and the sea belong to him. By his own might they are his possession. The four directions and these heavenly regions are his extended arms. What God shall we adore with our oblation?

By him the mighty Heaven and the Earth are upheld steadfast, by him are propped the vast vault on high and light's realm. By him were measured out the regions of the mid-air. What God shall we adore with our oblation? Towards him the embattled armies look while trembling with fear. Through him the Sun rises to shed forth his light. What God shall we adore with our oblation? When did the mighty Waters come, bringing the universal germ, whence sprang Agni. Then sprang the God's one spirit into being. What God shall we adore with our oblation? He with his great might surveyed the Waters pregnant with creative force and generating sacrifice. He is the God of Gods and none beside him. What God shall we adore with our oblation? O Father, thou Creator of Heaven and Earth, by eternal law ruling, pray protect us, O Father of the great and lucid Waters. What God shall we adore with our oblation? O Prajapati, the Lord of beings, you alone pervade all the created beings. Grant us our heart's desire when we call on thee. May we possess a store of many riches.

I move with the Rudras and the Vasus, with the Adityas and with all the Gods I travel. I uphold Varuna and Mitra, Indra and

Agni and the Ashvins twain. I cherish the exuberant Soma and Tvastar. I support Pushan and Bhaga. I shower wealth on him who offers oblation and pours forth the Soma juice in sacrifice. I am the sovereign Queen, the amasser of wealth, most wise, foremost of those deserving worship. The Gods have set me in many places. I enter many homes and abide there in various forms. Every human being who breathes, who sees, who hears the words uttered, attains his nourishment through me alone. They know me not, yet they abide in me. Listen ye all, who know, what I declare is the truth and worthy of attention.

I myself announce and utter the tidings that both Gods and men alike rejoice to hear. I make the man whom I love, a sage, a seer, a priest and make him grow in might. I make the bow of mighty Rudra bend, so that his dart slay the hater of the Holy word. I rouse battle among the people and I have penetrated Earth and Heaven. On the summit of the world, I bring forth the Father Heaven My home is in the Waters and in the ocean. Thence I have spread over all the world and even touch the yonder sky with my forehead. I breathe a strong breath like a wind and tempest. Within myself I hold all the world and the things that exist. I lord over the earth and the heavens, so powerful I am in strength and grandeur.

Here approaches the Night, with her twinkling eyes that Goddess has lit many a spot, embellished with all her glories. The immortal Goddess has encompassed the whole world, she has filled the valleys and covered the high peaks. She conquers darkness with her light. Approaching quietly the Goddess has once again set her sister Dawn in her seat, and now the shadows will also vanish. Let this Night be gracious to us as we repair to our homes like birds to their nests.

The villagers all have reached their homes, and all that walks and all that flies have gone to rest. Even the falcons fain for prey have gone to rest. Keep off the wolf, the wild beasts, keep off the thief, O Night undulating. Let thou be easy our passage to the other side! Verily she has now come and enfolds me in her black apparel. O Dawn banish them like debts? O Daughter of Heaven, I have brought for thee, my song of praise like a rich offering. O Night, accept this laud as for a victor.

The sacrifice is like loom with yarn stretched on every side, consisting of hundreds of rituals. See now the Fathers weaving at the loom, seated beside the wrap and shouting, weave forth, weave back. Here is the man who stretches it and then unwinds the yarn. These are the pegs, fastened to the place of worship, the Saman hymns are the weaving shuttles. What was the design and the model, what the order? What were the wooden fender, what was the butter? What were the hymn, the meter and the chant when all the Gods sacrificed Purusha in worship? The Gayatri meter conjoined Agni, Savitar combined with meter Ushnish. Soma, the one lauded in hymns, joined Anushtup and Brishaspati was aided by Brihati. Varuna and Mitra took to Viraj. The Trishtup was Indra's companion day by day, while the meter Jagati joined all the Gods together. So to this arrangement the seers conformed. This same arrangement was followed by the Seers and our Fathers. With my mind's eye, I think I can see them all who first of all performed the sacrifice. They who were well versed in rites, meters, and hymns, were the Seven Godlike Seers of old. Now the sages follow the path traced out by the ancient Seers, they have taken up the reins like charioteers.

Near the tree decked in fine leaves where Yama drinks with Gods, he, the Father Yama, the lord of the home, attends with affection our ancient forefathers. I looked reluctantly on him who tended our ancient sires, on him who treads the path of evil and then longed to see him again.

Without seeing it you mounted, O child, the new, wheelless car, shaped by your mind. It is one-poled yet it goes in every direction. This car which you have made to roll away from the priests, O child, was followed by a Saman chant, conveyed on a boat from here to there. Who was the father of the child? Who made the car roll away? Who can tell this to us today how the funeral gift was made? At the placing of the funeral gift, a flame at once appeared. It spread first in the front, and later a passage was contrived behind. Such is the seat of Yama, which is also called the home of Gods. Here ministrels play on flute for Yama, here he is magnified with songs.

The Sun with long loose of hair supports Agni, he upholds moisture, earth and heaven. He is verily light himself, the long-haired Muni. Girdled with the wind, the Munis wear garment soiled in ocher hue. They, the ascetics follow the swift wind's course and walk the path the Gods have troden before. Possessed they declare, with our austerities we ride the winds as steeds. You mortal men below see our bodies alone. The Muni aids each God in his work as a friend and associate. He flies through the realm of air, viewing the various forms of things. Ridden by the wind, friend of Vayu, urged by the Gods, the Muni is at home in both the seas, the eastern and western oceans. He walks the path of all the spirits, of Gandharvas. Apsaras and sylvan beasts. He knows their desires, he is their fair friend, he the long-haired Muni. The Vayu has churned and prepared a drink for him, for him he pounds things most hard in their nature, the long-haired Muni has drunk with Rudra. from the cup.

Goddess of the forest. Goddess of the wild, slipping away from the sight, how is it that you avoid the human habitation. Are you not afraid alone? When the grasshopper replies the cicada's shrill call, it is the Goddess of wild they welcome with their praise as with tinkling of the bells. Cows seem to graze yonder in a pasture, which looks like a dwelling place. Is that a cart with creaking wheels? Or else the Goddess of the wild passes. Hark, there is a man calling his cows, another there is felling a tree. At evening the dweller in the forest fancies he hears someone screamed. The Goddess of the woods slay never, unless one comes bent on murder. One may eat her luscious fruits and take rest, even as he wills under a shade. O Goddess of the woods, embellished with fragrance and sweet smelling balms, thou Mother of all wild beasts, you need not toil for food, now I bow to you.

By faith is fire kindled, by Faith is oblation offered. We sing to Faith now, the height of joy. O Faith, bless him who gives, bless him who fain would give, but has not. Bless thou the liberal sacrificer, bless the song I sing now. Even as the Gods evoked Faith from the mighty Asuras, so let my prayer for the liberal worshippers be accepted. Led by Vayu, Gods and men rever Faith at their sacrifice. Faith is made of the yearnings of the heart and opulence comes through it. Faith at Dawn, Faith at noon and at the sunset we invocate. O Faith, grant us faith!

May the Sun in the highest sky guard us, may the Wind protect us from the airy spaces, and may Agni be our guardian in terrestrial places! May Savitar, whose flames deserve a thousand sacred offerings, be pleased with us! May he preserve us from falling lightnings. May he, the God of Light grant us light, and may the celestial Summits also give us light! May the Creator grant us sight! Grant sight to our eyes, sight to our bodies so that we may see. May we see the world and survey the things at a single glance! Thus, O Sun, may we look on you, most beautiful to look on. May we see clearly with the eyes of men!

Oh, the Wind chariot, its strength and glory! It goes crashing with a voice of thunder. The regions are red, so are the heavens, the earth is covered with dust, the Wind passes. The Wind hosts hurry along the path of Vayu, and follow him like dames to an assembly. Car-borne, he speeds forth attended by his hosts, the Sovereign of the world. He neither rests nor slumber even for a single day but travels on the pathways of the air.

O Almighty Agni, who gathers up all that is precious for thy devotee. Kindled on the altar of sacrifice, give us all your treasures. Come together, converse with one another in the assembly. Let your minds be of one accord. Just as Gods in ancient times sat down in perfect harmony to receive their appointed share of the sacrifice. United be your assembly, united the minds, and so be your thoughts and counsel. A common plan I propose before you, a single sacrifice I lay. One and the same be your resolve, and your minds in harmony, united be your thought that you may long together a dwell in happy accord.

Yajur Veda

Book One

To thee, O lord, we resort for food and vigour. May Savitar, the God of creation, bliss and knowledge inspire us to perform the most noble deeds. May the kine, never to be killed, be healthy and strong, swelling with calves and free from disease. May a thief and an evil-minded man be never born amidst us rich in progeny, free from pain and sickness. May the lord of land and cattle be in constant possession of these. May God guard the progeny, kine and wealth of the Yajman (Sacrificer)!

Thou art the purifier of the sacrifice, thou art heavens, thou art earth. Heat art thou of the being. Thou art sustainer of the universe. May thou increase and stand secure and firm by the help of God and never stumble, nor be the lord of thy sacrifice unsteady!

Thou, the thousand-streamed, art the puri fier of the Vasus; thou art, indeed the thousand-streamed purifier of the Vasus. May the all-purifying, thousand streamed God Savitar, cleansing, purify thee with that with which he purifies the Vasus. Which cow didst thou milk?

Here is a wishfulfilling cow Vishvayushya of the full span of life. Here is another, Vishvakarman. and here is still another, Vishvadhaya. Thee, as Indra's portion, I do increase and prosper with Soma. O Vishnu, be thou protector of this oblation!

O Agni, the lord of vows, I will observe the vow. May I have strength for that. May I be successful in this my vow. Now I enter into the truth and renounce the untruth!

Who is it that impels thee to perform noble deeds? He inspires thee. Why does he guide thee? For performance of noble deeds he guides thee, he inspires thee two for doing good deeds, ye two for the completion of the home.

Scorched are the devils, scorched are the niggards. Burnt down are the fiends and the evil ones. Now, I roam at will in the vast spaces.

Thou art destroyer, destroy him who injures us. Harm him who harms us. Destroy him whom we wish to destroy. Thou art Gods best conveyor, the best purifier, filled fullest, the most desirable, and the best invoker of Gods.

By the impulse of Savitar, the creator of all. I hold thee with arms of Ashvins, with the hands of God Pushan. I take thee, dear to Asni, dear to Soma!

I have generated thee for abundance, not for niggardliness. May mine eye look upon the light of self, may the doors remain safe and secure. I travel at will through the vast spaces; upon the lap of the boundless Aditi, on the navel of the earth I place thee. O God Agni. protect this oblation!

Ye two born of Vishnu's powers, are the source of purification. By creator Savitar's impulse, with his flawless strainer, with the rays of the Sun, I purify ye completely. O bright waters, ever flowing forth, thou art first purifiers, promote now this sacrifice and lead forward the Yajman the God-devoted Sacrificer, the noble and liberal donor.

Indra elected you in destroying Vritra, and you elected Indra in fighting with Vritra. You art sanctified. I consecrate thee, dear to Agni; I purify thee, dear to both Agni and Soma. Be thou pure for divine work, pure and holy for sacrificial rites to Gods. Because some of you have been defiled by the impure touch, hereby I make you pure from all this pollution.

Thou art a source of bliss. The fiends have been swept away and so have been the niggards. Aditi's skin art thou, may thou be well received by Aditi. A wooded hill art thou. Thou art a firmly founded stone. May the skin of Aditi receive thee!

Thou art the body of Agni, the releaser of speech. I accept thee for the enjoyment of Gods. Thou art a great stone formed out of wood. Make thou ready the joy-giving oblation for Gods, carefully make it ready. O maker of oblation, come. O Havishkrit come. Havishkrit come!

Thou art a speaker with the tongue sweet as honey, tell us about manly vigour and sap. May we be victorious over our foes with thy help, O thou ever increasing knowledge! May knowledge receive thee. Swept away are fiends, swept away are niggards.

Destroyed are devils. May Vayu purify thee. May Savitar, the golden-handed God. receive you with his flawless arms.

Dauntless art thou. Remove the raw flesh eater away. O Agni, drive off the fire that consumes corpses. Bring here the devotee of Gods. Steadfast art thou. Make the earth firm. I bring thee close for the slaying of the foe, thou devoted to the priests, warriors and the kinsmen.

O Agni, accept our oblations, thou art sustainer, keep the heavens firm. I set thee close for the enemy's ruin, thou devoted to the priests, warriors and kinsmen. Thou art sustainer, keep the heavens firm. I set thee close for the sake of all directions. Be thou heated with the tapas of Bhrigus and Angirases.

For progeny I unite with thee. This is Agni's. this is Agni's and Soma's I joined thee for food. Thou art heat, thou art full span of life, vast art thou, spread thou forth widely. May the Sacrificer be far famed. May Agni harm not thy skin, may the God Savitar perfect thee in the highest heaven!

I hold thee by the impulse of God Savitar, with the arms of Ashvins, with the hands of Pushan, thee, who performs sacrifice to Gods, I hold. Thou art Indra's right arm. Thou art destroyer of thousands of enemies, armed with thousand sharp spikes. Thou art foe-slaying keen-edged wind!

O Earth, whereupon men perform the sacrifice for Gods, may I not harm the roots of the plants that grow here. Go thou to the kine stall. May heaven rain for thee. O Savitar, creator of all bind him on the earth with hundred fetters, him who hates us and whom we hate. Do thou never release him.

Scorched art the fiends, scorched are the niggards. Burnt down art the devils, burnt down art wicked ones. I travel at will in the vast space. Unsharpened, still thou art slayer of the foemen! Thou art mighty, for might I cleanse thee.

A girdle for Aditi thou art. Thou art an abode for all-pervading Vishnu. I take thee for food and great might. I look upon thee with an unblinking eye. Thou art the tongue of Agni. Be thou a good invoker of Gods at every sacrifice, in every home!

By Savitar's impulsion, with flawless strainer, with the rays of the sun, I hereby purify thee. Thou art effulgence, thou art manly strength. Thou art amrit. Thou, verily, art sacrifice and God's abode. Thou art beloved of Gods and Gods' inviolable sacrifice!

Book Two

O Yajna, you are being performed in a well prepared place. You attract all. I consecrate you devoted to Agni. You are the yajna and its altar. I cleanse you for sacrifice. I purify you loying the sacrificial ladles!

You give moisture to Aditi; you are a special creation of all-pervading God. I spreadyou, soft like wool, the best seat for Gods to sit on. Praise be to the lord of the earth, to the lord of the world, and to the lord of all beings!

For the weal of the world the Yajna is performed. For the purification of speech Agni is adored. May Vishvavasu Gandharva lay you round as a protection. You are the protector of the sacrifices To protect the world Agni is being lauded in the sacrifice. You are sacrificer's protector and Indra's right arm. May Mitra and Varuna preserve you all around by their firm law!

O sage Agni, the giver of bliss and opulence to all! We enkindle you in the sacrifice till you shine brightly.

You are a kindler. May the Sun preserve you from the front from every curse. You are Savitar's arm. I spread you soil as the wool, the best seal for Gods to sit on. May Vasu, Rudra and Aditya, the three Gods sit on you!

You are giver of ghee. You are called Juhu (ladle). Set you down on this pleasant seat with the dear home. You are giver of ghee. You are called Upabhrit. Sit you down on this pleasant seat with the dear home. You are giver of ghee. You are called Dhruva. Sit you down on this pleasant seat with the dear home. They have sat down at the place of sacrifice in safety. Protect these. O Vishnu, protect the yajna, protect the sacrificer, protect me the hotar priest.

O Agni, winner of corn, giver of food, hastening to the corn. I purify you. Salutations to the Gods, libations to fathers, be both of you an aid to me!

Today have I brought for oblation the unspoilt ghee. Let me not transgress the sanctity of the sacrifice with my foot, O Vishnu. O Agni, may I abide in your shelter abounding in store of riches. You are Yajna's home, Indra began his deeds of valour from here and so the sacrifice became highly elevated.

O Agni, be the hotar priest, be an envoy of Gods. May earth and heaven protect you. May you guard the earth and heaven. May Indra be, by this offering, maker of good oblation to Gods. Svaha! May light unite with light!

May Indra grant me the Indra might. May wealth in abundance gather round us all. May all our desires be fulfilled, our blessings come true. Svaha! I have worshipped the mother Earth. May the mother Earth make me shine like fire, I being the kindler of fire.

I have rendered homage to the father Heaven. May father Heaven accept my homage. I feed upon the corn with the mouth of Agni. I feed on you by the impulse of Savitar, with the arms of Ashvins and with both the hands of Pushan I consume you with the mouth of Agni!

O God Savitar, this yajna of yours, they say, is performed for Brihaspati, the Brahmin priest. Therefore, protect the sacrifice, guard the sacrificer, therefore, protect me.

May your rapid mind enjoy the ghee. May Brihaspati extend this Yajna. May he preserve it from harm. Let all the Gods enjoy here. Let it be so. Om, fare forward!

O Agni, this fuel is for you. Increase by means of it and grow mighty. May we also increase and grow in might. O Agni, you are winner of com. you produce corn. I cleanse you!

May I have the victory like the victory of Agni and Soma. May I fare forward by the impulse of sacrificial food. May Agni and Soma drive him away who hates us, drive off the man whom we detest.

We offer you for the Vasus, for the Rudras, for the Adityas. May Heaven and Earth bring you to light. May Mitra and Varuna nourish you with rain. May the birds fly licking what is drenched. Go with the speed of the spotted mares of the Maruts. Go to heaven, having become a spotted cow thyself, and from there bring the rain for us. O Agni, you are the guardian of eye, guard my eye!

Protect the two yoke fellows, you rich in fatness. You are in grace and conduct me unto grace. Glory to you Yajna and increase. Be auspicious to me. steadfast for my weal!

O all-devouring, unfeebled Agni, protect me against weapons, protect from the lightning, protect me from snare and ruin, from harmful food, render our food free from poison. Let me abide happily in my house praying to you and performing noble deeds. Svaha! This is our prayer to God of close embracements Agni, and to Sarasvati, the sister of Fame!

O Veda, you are the knower of all. May you become knowledge-giving Veda for me just as you have become for gods their Veda. O path-showing Gods, knowing the pathway of truth, walk on it. O God, lord of mind, this sacrifice is for you, fix it rightfully like a world in the air!

May Indra with the Adityas, the Vasus, the Maruts and the Vishvadevas bless the sacred grass with ghee. Svaha! May all these oblations reach the heaven.

Who liberates you from the bonds? He, the sustainer of subjects, liberates you. Why does he liberate you? He does it for him, for happiness of all. This is the allotted portion of the fiends.

We are united with glory, vigour, bodies, we are united with the best mind. May Tvashtar, the bounteous giver, grant us riches of many kinds. May he purge each and every fault and blemish from our body.

O God, you are self-existent, self-effulgent and most exalted! You are bestower of splendour. Grant me splendour! I follow the path that Surya treads.

O Agni, lord of the home, may I become a good householder through you, living with you, O Agni, master of the home. May you be the excellent householder through my prayers, O Agni. May the household affairs of both of us, the husband and wife be well managed through hundred years. I follow the path that Surya treads.

O Agni, the lord of vows, I have observed the vow. I was successful in the vow I had taken, full power was mine. Still am I he who observed the vow, I am verily he, and no other.

To you Agni, hail, who bears oblations to father. To you Soma hail, accompanied by fathers. The fiends and demons who occupied the same altar have now been destroyed.

May Agni drive these demons away who being nourished by the oblations offered to fathers, roam about freely in various guises, whether they be disguised in thin or fat bodies.

O fathers, enjoy yourselves here, be nourished like bulls with each of the allotted portions. The fathers have enjoyed themselves, and here like bulls have grown healthy and strong with their allotted portions.

Salutations to you, O fathers, and to your genial sap. Fathers, obeisance to you for your ardour. Fathers, salutation to you for your longevity. Salutations to you for your life, O fathers, for your righteous passion, obeisance to you, O fathers! O fathers, grant us homes. Fathers, we offer you ever what we possess. O fathers, we offer this raiment, clothe yourselves in it,

O fathers, grant us a baby son, a boy garlanded with a wealth of lotuses, so that there may be a heroic man.

O waters, you are the bearers of ghee, corn, milk and dripping saps. You are the best and immortal drink. You increase the sustaining vigour. Satisfy my fathers.

Book Three

Serve Agni with the fuel, with oblations of ghee, awake the guest and then pay offerings to the Gods.

Offer rich oblations of ghee to Agni, the well kindled Jatavedas.

O Angiras, we increase you with fuel sticks and sacred ghee, O youthful Agni, grow brilliant with great flames!

O Agni, rich oblations, dripping with ghee may go unto you along with fuel. Accept these my oblations with favour!

You are power, knowledge and bliss. I lay upon the back of the Earth, the place of sacrifice to gods, this food-consuming Agni, for obtaining food. May I become like heaven in plenty and like earth in compass.

The Sun, the spotted Bull has come and sat before the mother Dawn and is now advancing to his father Heaven.

His lustre penetrates within the space like inhalation and exhalation. The Sun shines throughout the heavens.

The Sun rules supreme over the thirty worlds, all the days at break of dawn. Hymns are showered on the Bird.

Agni is light and light Agni. Svaha! Surya is light and light Surya. Svaha! Agni is brilliance and brilliance Agni. Svaha! Surya is brilliance and brilliance Surya. Svaha! Light is Surya and Surya light. Svaha!

May this oblation reach unto Agni, who lives with effulgent God Savitar and Night with Indra besides her. May Surya, living with Indra with Dawn beside him, accept this oblation.

Performing yajna, may we pronounce the vedic texts in praise of Agni who hears us even when afar from us.

Agni, the height and head of heaven, the lord of the earth, quickens the vitality of waters.

I invoke you both Indra and Agni and please you both together with oblation of corn. You both are bestowers of corn and riches. You twain I call for obtaining food.

O Agni, this is your ordained place of origin whence born you shine forth. Knowing this, O Agni, rise up making our riches grow.

The learned priests made Agni the first invoker, the first to be worshipped in sacrifice, and praise in rites. The seers Bhrigu and Apanavana kindled the all-pervading Agni first in the forests for the weal of mankind.

They, the learned priests, knowing his ancient splendour, have drawn this milk from this cow-like Sage.

O Agni, you are our protector, protect my body. You are giver of life, give me full span of life, O Agni! You are giver of splendour, give me splendour. O Agni! All that is lacking in my body, Agni, grant me that!

O uninjured, effulgent, mighty, foe-slaying Agni, we. well nourished with food and strong, shall enkindle you through hundred years. O Goddess Night, rich in shining lights, may I attain your end in safety.

O Agni, you have attained the glory of Surya, the praise of Seers, and the abode dear to you. May I attain likewise to long life, to glory, to offspring and to abundant wealth!

O kine. you are food, may I enjoy your nourishing food.

You are strength, may I have your strength. You are energy, may I have your energy. You are abundant wealth, may I have your abundant wealth!

O wealthy kine, sport hero in these places, in this stall, in this region, in this house. Remain here and go not away.

O cow, you are made of many forms and colours. May I attain the ownership of such power-giving kine. To you, remover of the gloom, O Agni, we approach with prayers, day by day, with reverence do we come.

We do come to Agni, who is splendid, protector of holy rites, illuminator of truth, effulgent One, increasing in his own abode.

Just as a sire is to his son, so be you to us easy of access, O Agni, be ever with us for our weal.

O Agni, be our close friend, our protector and our wellwisher, dwelling with us. O effulgent one, come, dwell with us and grant us glorious wealth.

O most radiant Agni, we approach you with prayers for happiness and weal for our friends. So listen our prayers, be friend and guard us against all wicked men.

O cow Ida, come, O cow Aditi, come here, O cows so much desired by all, come here. May I obtain all my heart's desire through you.

O Brahmanaspate, the lord of knowledge, make him glorious who presses out Soma juice, even as you made Kakshivan, the son of the seer Ushik.

Let him dwell ever with us who is rich, removes disease, increases wealth, and is prompt in actions.

O Brahmanaspate, protect us, Jet not the foeman's curse, let not his treachery approach us.

May we attain the divine, unassailable and great protection of the three Gods—Mitra, Aryaman and Varuna.

Neither in home nor on pathways nor in places perilous, has the wicked foe power over these Gods.

They the sons of Aditi, grant light for ever to a mortal man so that he may live long.

O Indra, you are never fruitless, you are ever gracious to your devotee. O Maghavan, your bounty as a liberal God is boundless.

We meditate on the excellent radiance of God Savitar, the generator of all. May he inspire our minds!

May your unassailable chariot wherewith you protect your devotees, be ever near us on every side!

O God, may I be rich in subjects, well manned with excellent heroes and well nourished with best food. O friend of man, protect my subjects. O adorable, guard my cattle. O God, increasing all, protect my food!

O effulgent Lord, giver of excellent wealth, all-knowing, we approach you alone. O Agni, grant us splendour with strength, O imperial God!

This Agni, the Grihapatya, is the lord of the home, is the giver of wealth to the subjects. O Lord of the home, O Agni, grant us splendour with wealth. This Agni dwells on the earth, increases riches and strength. O earth-dwelling Agni, grant us splendour with wealth.

O house-dwelling man, fear not, nor tremble. I bearer of strength come to you. I bearing strength, excellent wisdom and happy mind, come to you, rejoicing in spirit.

The home on which the traveller ponders, staying far from it, there dwell happiness and joy. We call that home to welcome us. May it know us well who know it well.

Here in this our house may we have cows, goats, sheeps and rich food in abundance. I come to you for safety, and quietude. May we possess mundane and divine joys and felicity!

We invocate the foe-slaying, the voracious, the loving Maruts who take delight in their mess of meal.

We do expiate each sinful act that we have committed either in village or the wild, in company or corporeal sense. Svaha!

O ever moving, purifying Bath, you move slowly on your path. I wash out the sins that I have committed with my sense organs, and the sins done with men against mankind. O God, preserve me from the foe who inflicts much injury.

Well have they feasted and rejoiced, the friends have risen and gone away. The sages, effulgent in themselves have lauded thee with their latest hymn. Now, Indra, yoke your two bay steeds!

O Maghavan, so fair to look upon, we reverence you. Thus lauded, come to us as desired with richly laden car. Now, Indra, yoke your two bay steeds!

O Rudra, this is your allotted share. Please take it with your sister Ambika. Svaha! This is your allotted position, Rudra, the rat is thy victim.

We have contented Rudra, who makes the foetnen weep, the three-eyed God, so that we may grow wealthier, be more prosperous, our dwellings better and may achieve greater success in our jobs.

We worship the three-eyed God Tryambaka who augments our prosperity. As a ripe cucumber is released from its stem, so may I be released from bonds of death by his grace and not be bereft of immortality. We worship him, Tryambaka, the bestower of husband, full of sweet fragrance. Like a ripe cucumber from its steam, may we be released from the bonds of death, and not be bereft of immortality.

This, Rudra, is thy allotted oblation, with it depart beyond the Mujavans with your bow unstrung and muffled in a clothe. Depart, O God, wearing skin garments, with auspicious mind and without harming us.

May we attain the triple life, the triple life of Jamdagni, the triple life of the sage Kashyapa and triple life of the gods. May the same threefold life be ours!

Shiva, the gracious, is your name, the thunder is your sire, salutations be to you, harm me not. I approach you for longevity, for good food, for progeny, for wealth in abundance, for noble children and for heroic strength.

Book Four

We have reached the earth's sacrificing spot wherein all Gods take delight. May we crossing by Rik, by Saman, and by Yajus the miseries, rejoice in food and the growth of the wealth. May these divine Waters be gracious to me. May these herbs protect me. O weapon, forbear to harm the worshipper!

May these waters purify us like mothers. May the purifiers of ghee cleanse us with ghee. The divine waters remove all our physical defilements. I emerge from them cleansed and purified. You are embodiment of tapas and diksha. I bear you, gracious and blissful ones, maintaining shining and happy appearance.

You are splendour-giving milk of kine. Grant me splendour. You are pupil of Vritra's eye. You are giver of eyes. Give me the sense of sight.

Purify me the lord of knowledge. Purify me the lord of speech. Purify me, O lord Savitar, with flawless strainer and with the rays of Surya! O lord God of the purified souls, may I with your grace accomplish my lofty desire to purify myself.

O Gods, we approach you for happy wealth, as the yajna proceeds. O Gods, we invoke you for blessings during this sacrifice.

We perform the sacrifice with steadfast mind, Svaha! We perform the yajna with the aid of heavens. Svaha! We perform the sacrifice for the good of Heaven and Earth. Svaha! We perform it with the grace of wind. Svaha! We perform it with full dedication.

For resolute and inspiring Agni is this offering, it is for that Agni who develops intellect, the consecration bestowing Agni. This is for Purban, Sarasvati and Agni. O divine, shining, great and all beneficial Waters, O Heaven and Earth, O vast mid region between them, we perform this sacrifice with oblations for Brihaspati. Svaha! May all mortal men seek the friendship of the all-guiding God Savitar. All pray to him for happy wealth. May all acquire wealth and prosper thereby!

You are the art of Rik and Saman. I commence the yajna with this art. May Rik and Saman protect me during the sacrifice. You are refuge of all, grant me refuge. Salutations to you, forbear to harm me you Angirases vigour. You, soft like wool, grant me vigour. You are the garment knot of Soma. You are the all-pervading bliss obtained from God. Give sacrificer this bliss. You are the source of Indra's might. Make the crops abundant. O Tree, stand erect, and guard me against sins till the sacrifice is over!

Observe the vow. Agni is Brahman, Agni is sacrifice, the fuel is pure and fit for yajna. We meditate on divine intelligence for aid. May that intelligence be within my control. May the gods, mind born, endowed with intellect and wisdom, prompt in action, protect us. Svaha! This oblation is for them.

May the waters that we have drunk become strength giving, become auspicious drink within our stomach. May they be pleasant to our taste, free from disease, sin, sickness, remover of the fear of death, full of divine qualities and strengtheners of eternal laws.

This earth is your sacrificial body. Waters I foresake but not the offspring. Freed from sin and sanctified by Svaha, may the waters enter the earth. May they unite with the earth.

O Agni. keep the vigil, we shall enjoy the most refreshing sleep. Guard us with watchful care. Awaken us again from sleep!

After rebirth I have regained my mind, I have regained my life, breath and soul, eyes and ears. May Vaishvanara, the guardian of our body, the unassailed Agni, protect us from sin and distress!

O radiant Agni, you are the guardian of sacred vows among men, you are adorable in holy rites. O Soma, give us this much wealth now and yet more later. Savitar, the God of creation, who gives wealth has given us riches.

O Shukra, this is your body, this is your radiance. Unite with this your form and gain splendour. You are active and impetuous, sustained by mind and loved by Vishnu.

For your truth-oriented progress use this form as an instrument. Svaha! You are pure and blissful, you are immortal and united with the powers of Gods!

You are knowledge, mind you are, intelligence, skill, imperial power, adorable and double headed Aditi. Be our aid in going forth or in retreating back. May Mttra fasten you by the foot, may Pushan guard your pathways for Indra, whose eye is over all!

May your mother permit you to go, your father and brother, and your friend living in the same herd allow you to depart. O goddess, go you to the God, to Soma, go for Indra's sake. May Rudra send you back. Return in safety with Soma as your friend.

You are Vasu's might, you are boundless Aditi, you are Adiiya, you are Rudra. Chandra you are. May Brihaspati grant you bliss and rest. May Rudra with the Vasus look upon you auspiciously!

On boundless Aditi's head, on the sacrificial sacred place I sprinkle you. Rich in ghee you are Indra's footstep. Svaha! Rejoice in us, we are your kinsmen. There are riches in you. May I possess riches. May I never be bereft of riches and nourishment. Yours are the riches.

I adore him, the God Savitar, shining brightly between heaven and earth, embodiment of truth, wealth-giving, beloved of all, thoughtful, poet, and sage, to him whose effulgent self shines high in the sky, the golden-handed, the most wise, creator of heaven. May all living beings enjoy life in you. May you grant breath to all living creatures!

I buy the splendid with splendid, the immortal with immortal and you who are pure with what is pure. Let the cow be with the sacrificer and these gold pieces with us. You are embodiment of fervour and Prajapati's nature. With the best animal you are bought. May I grow rich with thousandfold riches.

O friend, come unto us increasing the number of our friends. Be you seated on the right of Indra desiring your own increase and happiness of others. Eloquence, brilliance, enmity to evil, dynamism, dexterity, and friendship with the weak, these seven are your gold pieces for the purchase of Soma. Preserve these, let them never fail you.

O Agni, establish me firmly in righteousness, keeping me away from sin and unrighteousness. May I attain beatitude and long life by following a virtuous path of living!

Now we have attained the path which is free from sin and is full of bliss, the path on which a man overcomes his foes and gathers wealth.

O lord of the world, be my gracious aid, move forward on your path to all the places. Let not thieves, let not robbers and malignant wolves waiting your coming not find you. Fly away like a falcon, go to the houses of sacrificer. That is the place specially cleansed and purified.

Homage be unto Varuna and Mitra's eye, the great god, far-sighted, omniscient and the ensign of Gods. Sing hymns of praise to Surya, to the son of heavens.

You are both seat and support of Varuna. You are Varuna's sacrificial seat where he sits, Varuna's place of sacrifice. Sit you down on Varuna's seat!

May you, O Soma, come to all those houses where you are honoured with worship and poured oblations. O wealth-giver, advancer of heroes, slayer of the foes, sparing the brave, come to our houses!

Book Five

O Soma, you are body of Agni. I accept you for the completion of the yajna. You are the body of the Soma juice, I accept you for Vishnu. O Soma, you are the source of reception of the guests, you are for Vishnu, you are fast in speed like falcon, therefore, I accept you for Vishnu. I accept you as bestower of abundant wealth. I take you for Vishnu.

You are the birth place of Agni. You are the cause of manly strength. You are Urvashi, you are Ayu. You are Pururavas. I churn you with the Gayatri metre. I churn you with the Trishtup metre, and with Jagati metre.

Be you both of the same one mind for us, of one thought, free from sin and blemish. Harm not the sacrifice, harm not the sacrifice's lord and be kind to us this day!

Protector from the curse, son of the seers, this Agni is active having entered the invoked Agni. Here is this sacrifice for us, offer oblations to the Gods without slackness and a happy mind.

O Agni, protector of the vow, may we be able to fulfil our vows under you. May your form be ever with me and my form be with you. O guardian of the vows, let our vows be united and one. May the lord of consecration inspire me for initiation, may the lord of fervour impell me to take a vow of fervour!

O Agni, your form which is present in iron, in the lowest depths, has driven away the awful speech. Svaha! That same form is present in silver, in gold and in every object. Svaha!

O Agni for me you are an abode for the afflicted. For me you are a gathering place of wealth. Protect me from the state of destitution. Protect me from fear. I call you Nabhas, the space-born. Approach us, O Agni, with the names of Angira and Ayu. You whom this earth contains, I lay you down with each inviolate holy name which you bear. I lay you down for gods delight!

You are like foe-subduing lioness, be ready for Gods' weal. You are foe-subduing lioness, be sanctified for gods. You are foe-slaying lioness, beautify yourself for Gods!

May Indra with the eight Vasus guard you in the east. May Varuna with the eleven Rudras protect you from the rear, and the swift like thought guard you on the right with Fathers. May Vishvakarma protect you on the left with the Adityas! I throw away this heated water from this place of sacrifice.

The sages, skilled well in knowledge concentrate their soul, yea, concentrate their mind and intellect in yoga. He, the only knower of all functions, assigns their priestly tasks. Great is praise of the God Savitar. Svaha!

The all-pervading God sustains this world. He has created the three worlds of earth, heaven and the mid region. In his feet abides the whole world. We offer this oblation to him.

O earth, you are rich in sweet food, rich in good milch kine, rich in fertile pastures, and engaged in rendering service to mankind; Vishnu has kept both Heaven and Earth apart and has firmly established the latter with pegs around it.

Now I will describe the mighty deeds of Vishnu who measured out the earthly realms and propped the heavens above, taking three mighty strides during this course.

O Vishnu, fill both of your hands full with riches from heaven, from earth and from the vast wide air's mid region and grant us these riches from the right and the left hands. We worship you through this sacrifice.

For his mighty deeds is Vishnu acclaimed. He dwells in the mountains like a wild beast, roaming at will. In his three mighty strides are set all the realms.

By impulse of Savitar I take you with arms of Ashvins and hands of Pushan. You are woman to aid us. Hereby I cut the necks of demons as under. You are mighty and great, and mighty is the sound that you utter. Utter your mighty sounding prayer to Indra.

You are self-effulgent and foe-conquering. You are king and subduer of the enemies. Men's lord are you and the slayer of the fiends. All ruler are you and the killer of the foe men!

Prop the heaven, fill the air full, make the earth firm. May the effulgent Maruts establish you and Mitra Varuna protect you. I guard you with valour, knowledge and wealth. Strengthen the Brahminhood. increase the nobles, increase the life span and strengthen the offspring.

O wife of Sacrificer, firm established you are. Firm be your husband the Sacrifices with offspring and cattle in this house. O Heaven and Earth, be you rich in fatness. You are like Indra's shadow and the refuge of all people.

O Indra, worthy of adoration with lauds, may these our songs of praise reach unto you. May they, wise like the aged, ever increasing be dear to you.

You are vast like ocean, all-pervading and unborn. The entire universe is within one part of your energy. You are eternal and source of the universe. You are speech and the shed of sacrifice, full of splendour. You two doors of the sacrifice do not distress me. O lord and ruler of the pathways lead me forth. May I be happy on this God-reaching path!

Look you upon me with the eye of a friend. O adorable mighty Agni's, receiver of oblations, guard me with your blazing army. Fill me with wealth, Agnis, be my guardians. My salutations to you, harm me not!

O Soma, you are a light that wears all forms and figures and serves the Gods as illuminator. You withdraw your generous protection from body-wounding enemies and those who practice hatred. May this oblation reach you easily, O mighty one. May God Soma graciously enjoy this my oblation of ghee.

May you, O Agni, grant us ample abode and comfort for our living and go in front of us attacking the enemy. May you win spoil for us. May you subdue our foes on your triumphant march!

O Vishnu, step forth thou widely in order to give us ample place for our dwelling. O increaser with ghee, drink this ghee and grant increase to the sacrificer. This offering is for you.

This Soma is for you, god Savitar, guard him well, let not demons harm you. O Soma, now you have joined Gods as a God. I have joined here my, fellow men through abundant wealth. Offer this oblation to Varuna and be free from Varuna's noose.

Book Six

By impulse of God Savitar I accept you with the arms of Ashvins and with the hands of Pushan. You are woman and I your husband cut the necks of the fiends. You are the remover of our foes, therefore, remove our haters and enemies. May the worlds where dwell our fathers be pure. You are the abode of the fathers.

You are our leader. You establish on the path of rectitude even the leaders of high caliber. Know this well. May God Savitar, who rules over you anoint you with sweet juices. You have touched the sky with your top, has filled the air with your middle and has strengthened the earth with your base.

Your abodes which we desire to visit are full of bright rays of light. In those very places we imprinted the loftiest step of the wide-striding Vishnu. I know you as the winner of riches, the winner of Brahmins and the warrior class. Strengthen the Brahmins, strengthen the Nobles, strengthen the life of the subjects, strengthen the subjects!

O men, look you upon the mighty deeds of Vishnu whereby he, the friend of Indra, has let his holy ways be known.

The learned evermore behold the loftiest seat of Vishnu in the form of heaven's splendour. Behold you ever that!

You are omnipresent. The learned people know as such. May the Sacrificer obtain riches from all sides. O Sacrificer, you are lustrous son of the heaven. May all these people living on this earth be your friends and all the beasts of the forest be under your control!

You are protector and remover of distress of your subjects. May you possess virtuous subjects and glorious, able and learned men. May you be creative and as such enjoy all the pleasurable riches!

O wealthy subjects, enjoy. May Brihaspati protect our wealth. I release you, O prince, from bondage of ignorance. Be bold and struggle against ignorance to acquire knowledge.

May you both balmed with ghee preserve the cattle. O fortunate woman be one thoughted with the Sacrificer and treat him lovingly. Protect him well as does the vast space the air. Perform yourself the sacrifice with all the materials. Be united with his body to obtain a son. O giver of happiness, help him in this great and vast sacrifice, and thereby establish him in the sacrifice. Welcome the learned visitors who come first and also those who come next in the yajna.

Be not crooked like a serpent, be not poisonous like a viper or violent like a wild beast. Obeisance be to you, O performer of yajna. Progress you unhindered and accept the stream of water for purification and follow the path of truth and righteousness.

O Waters, convey this offering to Gods, you pure, divine and well provided waters. May we providers be well provided.

I cleanse your speech. I cleanse your breath, your eyes, your navel, your sexual organ, your rump and your whole conduct.

May your mind grow full, your breath grow in strength, your eyes become fuller, your ears grow stronger. Whatever in you is short-tempered, may that be removed, your desire be fulfilled and your conduct be purified. Blessed be your days. O herb, guard him and do not harm. Weapons, you also protect him.

O evil one, you are the devil's share, be expelled from here. Hereby I sweep away and repel the demons. I send the fiends to the nether most dark region. I invest the heaven and earth with yajna-sanctified sap. Let Agni enjoy the oblation of ghee, let Vayu enjoy the offerings. Svaha! May consecrated Earth and Surya go to Vayu, the offspring of the Maruts.

O Waters, wash away all my malicious deeds, sinful taints and stains, any wrong that I have done to others, the lies I have uttered and the curse of mine. May these Waters and Pavaman free me from that sin!

May your mind be strengthened and your breath united with life force. You are the slayer of foes. May Agni mature you, waters impel you. May you be possessed of Vayu's speed and Surya's heat so that the enemy reel and stumble under your pressure.

O you enjoyers of ghee, drink it, enjoy the gravy you drinkers of gravy. You are heaven's oblation. We offer oblations to all the directions, to fore-regions, the high regions, the lower and middle ones, to all the regions.

Sail on the oceans in the best ship, fly in the aeroplanes, go to God Savitar. Svaha! Go to Mitra and Varuna, know day and night, know the Vedas, Rig, Yajur, Soma and Atharva with their constituent parts. Possess the knowledge of heaven and earth, know the rites of sacrifice, obtain knowledge of herbs, go to the divine ether. Know Vaishvanara through science, grant me good mind and heart. May the smoke of your sacrifice ascend to the sky, and your radiance to heaven.May you fill the vast earth with the ashes of the yajna.

Harm not the waters, injure not the herbs, guard us at every place. O Varuna, we take the vow not to kill the kine, unworthy to be slain. Let waters be our best friends. Let the herbs be unfriendly like foes to them whom we detest and who hate us.

These waters are full of saps and good food, rich in that food, one desires to have. May the sacrifice be rich in oblations and rich be Surya in giving Sacrificer the abundant gift.

I set you down in the assembly of wise. You are Indra Agni's share, you are Varuna-Mitra's share. You are the share of all the Gods. May the waters collected around the Sun, and those wherewith the Sun has joined come hither to our yajna with speed.

O Soma, approach your people like a father and let people come to you like sons. May Agni with his fuel hear my invocation. May divine waters hear it, and you learned and steadfast people. May God Savitar hear my prayers. Svaha!

O god Agni, whom you protect in the battle or urge to the fight, he is the lord of abundant food.

By impulse of god Savitar, with the arms of Ashvins and with the hands of Pushan I accept you. You are the best giver of gifts. Perform this great yajna for Indra with most excellent sacrificial things.

Satisfy my mind, satisfy my speech, satisfy my breath, my eyes, my ears, my soul, satisfy my progeny, satisfy my kine, elephants, horses and cattle, satisfy my men and followers, let my bands of men never be sad!

We appoint you for Indra accompanied by the Vasus and the Rudras, for Indra with the Adityas. For foe-slaying Indra, for Soma bringing and falcon-like foe-attacking Indra. You for splendour-giving Agni!

O Soma, your light that extends in heaven, on the earth, that in mid region's vast space, with that help the Sacrificer in his enrichment, bless you the giver!

O you immortal consorts, possessed of great might, foe-slaying, bestowing wealth, devoted to your divine husband's grant success to this sacrifice and enjoy Soma at our request!

O ladies, be not afraid, tremble not in fear, take courage. You twain being firm, stay resolute taking courage so that your shortcomings are removed and you be happy like the moon.

O Mother, let from the east, west, north, south, from every direction the regions rush to meet you. O Mother, let noble meet, noble!

O Mightiest, O Maghavan, bless the mortal man. There is none but you to bless with happiness. I repeat your words!

Book Seven

O man purify yourself for the lord of speech. Becoming pure by the hands of the Sun, yourself a divine one, be pure for the Gods whose share you are.

O Soma, sweeten our foods and drinks. Whatever divine name you have, life-giving, victorious, to that I pour out this libation of Soma. Svaha!

Self born you are from the powers that are in heaven and on earth, for the good of senses, for the weal of learned and for ail the beings. I appoint you for divine beings who guard the light. May you be of pure mind to win the Sun. I laud you for your virtuous conduct. May your enemy who transgresses the law be ruined. I appoint you for exhalation and breath diffused!

You are lord of yamas and niyamas. Therefore, control your vital internal powers, guard your own splendour emanating from within. Destroy all your distress with your yoga so that you may be rich in all sorts of food and wealth.

I place within you the spacious heaven and earth and also the vast mid-region of air. The whole of boundless space is within you. Living and rejoicing in the company of Gods, gladden all your subjects.

O Vayu, devourer of the pure, adorn us with thousands of virtues. To you I pour out this rapturous juice, whose first draught, God, you take as your portion.

These pressed and poured out pleasant juices long for you both, O Indra and Vayu. This is your home. This is for you both Vayu-Indra.

This Soma has been shed forth for your order-strengthening Varana and Mitra. Listen you to my invocation, O Soma, I offer you to Mitra and Varuna in this vessel.

May we be delighted in much wealth just as Gods are in oblation and kine in pasture. O Indra. O Varuna, give us for ever that milch cow who shrinks not from milking. This is your home. I welcome you twain, the righteous ones!

O Ashvins, with your honeyed speech and pleasant tongue fulfil this sacrifice. We have accepted you for your Yama and Niyama. This is your abode. This Soma is for you the sweet ones!

You, well manned with heroes, beget heroes with abundant wealth surrounding the sacrificer. Be thus adorned with glory conjoined with heaven and earth. Let Sanda be expelled. You are the abode of manliness and heroism!

O sparkling Soma, may we be possessed of your chivalrous strength and never ending wealth. This is the first all bounteous consecration. He is the first king, guard, friend and leader.

He is the first sage and lord of speech. Offer you the Soma juice to that effulgent Indra. May the sacrificers satisfy him with sweet oblations, those who become pleased having gained their due offerings and are engaged in the sacrifice. May they approach Agni.

May all the eleven majestic Gods residing in heaven, the eleven ones who dwell upon the earth, and those eleven dwelling in waters, accept this our sacrifice, and be pleased.

This Soma is pressed out for the priest, for the nobles, this is pressed out for the sacrifices for increase of food and obtaining of power, for the satisfaction of earth and heaven, for excellent life. I accept Soma for all the Gods. This is your home and refuge. You are for all the Gods!

You are bound with righteous laws. I take, you for lord Indra of the Brihat, O mighty one, lover of invocation. I take you for Indra, the lord of might and vigour, for Vishnu, your home. I take you for Gods' protection and for long life of the sacrifice.

I accept you for Mitra and Varuna, for the protection of Gods, for the long life of sacrifice, you for the learned men, for yajna. I take you as the protector of Indra, Agni and sacrifice you for Indra and Brihaspati, for Indra and Vishnu.

The Gods have generated Agni, the envoy of earth, head of the Sun, the sage, the guest, the lord of men, a pure receptacle fit for their mouths, the effulgent, born in holy order, the Vaishvanara.

Bound by laws you are firm, firmly established, the firmest of the firm, the most steadfast of those who never have been shaken. This is your home. I with a firm mind, with firm speech take you as the leader of humanity. So now may Indra make our men of one heart, one mind and free from enemies.

Who are you? Who amongst us all are you? Whose son are you? What is your name? We want to know your name so that to delight you with our Soma juice. May I be possessed of the majesty of the earth, the space and the sun, the lord of my subjects. May I be possessed of heroic men to nourish the country to strength with the help of these heroic warriors.

Come, Indra and Agni, unto us being pleased with our lauds, come to the precious Soma drink. Drink of this draught, impelled by our songs. I take you for Indra, for Agni. This is your home. I place you here for Indra and Agni.

Come here the learned men who kindle the sacred fire and offer oblation with firm mind, whose friend is Indra, the ever youthful. I take you for Indra and Agni. This is your dwelling. Having accepted you we offer oblation to Indra and Agni through you.

O you all the Gods, protector, bestower, cherishers of mankind, come here to your devotee's offering. This is your dwelling. I offer you to all the gods.

O Indra, accompanied by the Maruts, come here, guard and drink the Soma as you did the juice in the yajna performed by Saryati. O hero, the learned singers serve you ever under your guidance and keeping in the sacrifice. You are the strengthener of the law. I accept you for the love of Indra, girt by the Maruts. This is your home. I take you for Indra's sake.

The sages call Indra to secure new protection, him who is the lord of men, the mighty, whom the Maruts accompany, who is the best bestower, remover of sorrows, the divine ruler, the subduer of the foe and the winner of battles. You are the strengthener of the law. This is your dwelling. I accept you for Indra accompanied by the Maruts, for the strength of the Maruts.

Surya's bright beams bear him high, the God who knows all that breathes, so that all may behold him. Svaha!

Surya is the might of Gods, the eye of Mitra, Varuna and Agni, the sustainer of heaven, earth and space, the soul of all that moves and moves not. This oblation is for him.

O divine Agni, through righteousness lead us to riches, you the knower of all the pathways. Remove from us the sin causing us go astray and wander from the right path. We offer you rich adoration and this oblation.

May Agni grant us ample room and comfort. May he march forth before us to the battlefield destroying the foes. May he win spoils for us, and subdue the foemen. This is for him.

May I today honour a Brahmin sprung from illustrious father and grandfather, born of Rishis, is himself a Rishi, the fit recipient of priestly guerdon. May this guerdon go to the learned priests established by the gods and satisfy them and enter into him who gives.

Who bestows? Upon whom is it bestowed? Desire bestows, for Desire it is bestowed. Desire is the bestower and Desire is the bestowed. O Desire, to you, I give this all!

Book Eight

The sacrifice is for Gods' happiness. O Adityas, be gracious to us. Send your favours here and be our kind liberator from distress. I accept you for the love of Adityas.

O Adityas, this is your Soma draught, enjoy it. O you men, believe my speech, the wife and husband, the householders, achieve their good by following the righteous path of duty and a manly son is born to them who earn riches and leads a happy sinless life.

O Savitar, grant us bliss today, tomorrow, grant us happiness each day of the life. May we, through our excellent wisdom, gain splendour with happy and spacious dwelling, O God creator!

Bound by laws, you are Savitar's worshipper and giver of happiness and food. Grant me joy and food, promote the sacrifice and bestow riches on the Sacrificer. I take you for Savitar, the lord of all riches!

Bound by law you are. Firmly established abode of bliss you are. Homage be to you, O doer of great deeds. I appoint you for all the gods. This is your home. You are for the universal Gods.

Bound by yama and niyama you are. O God Soma, radiant, pleasure-giving full of sustaining power, protector of wise speech, impelled by the sages I strengthen all my body for you. May I ever prosper whether far or near. May the heaven protect me.

May I behold the sun on both sides and also that resides in the inmost heart of the sages, the absolute truth.

O Agni, full of affection for all, bestower of bliss, drink this Soma juice produced by the learned, truthful in speech. You are Prajapati, strong manly impregner. May I obtain a heroic son, in connection with you, the mighty impregnate, the lord of valour and the protector of progeny!

You are atonement of sins committed against the Gods. You are atonement of sins done against mankind. You atone the sins done against the fathers, done against oneself. You are atonement of sins of every kind. You are atonement of all the sins, of those I have knowingly committed, and also of those done unawares.

May we all be ever united with radiance, fine body, refreshing sap and cheerful spirit. Let Tvashtar grant us wealth and remove our bodily deficiency.

O Indra, lead us with the nobility of your mind to wealth, kine and the sages, O Maghavan, to princes, lead us to divine deeds inspired by the learned, and to devotion of Gods who deserve our adoration.

May this oblation of our please Savitar, the generous Dhatr, Prajapati, Agni, Tvashtar and Vishnu. May these Gods grant the Sacrificer the abundant wealth with offspring!

O Gods, we have made your seats smooth and comfortable, who pleased with us, have come to this yajna. Enjoying and bearing oblations, O Gods, grant us abundant wealth!

O God Agni, the willing Gods whom you have brought here in this sacrifice send them to their respective abodes. As you all have enjoyed food offerings and libations, approach the air, the heat, the light of the Sun. Svaha!

O Agni, at this place, in this sacrifice, we have elected you as our presiding priest. You performed the sacrifice with your special efforts, removing all the obstacles. Now the sacrifice being over you may please go to your place. Svaha!

O Gods, knower of the righteous paths, go along the righteous one when you have discovered it. O God, lord of the mind and thought, perform this sacrifice in the right spirit. Svaha!

O sacrifice, approach the sacrifice, seek the Sacrificer, seek your own dwelling. Svaha! O Sacrificer, this your sacrifice has been performed by many sages, uttering aloud the vedic hymns. Accept it with Svaha!

Never be a serpent, never be a viper. God Varuna has made a spacious pathway for Surya to travel. He has made the path smooth and for easy walk where no path was. He has warned away the fiends who distress the spirit. Homage be to such sin-removing god Varuna. His fetters beneath our feet are crushed!

Your heart is in waters, in the oceans. May herbs and waters be co-mingled with you. We worship the lord of Sacrifice with vedic songs of praise and sacrificial offerings.

O divine Waters, this is your offspring. Protect him carefully, dearly loved and so well nurtured. O Soma, this is your home, obtain bliss therein and protect us by warding off all our distress.

Definitely he is possessed of the best protectors in whose place of yajna the Maruts, the resplendent lords of the sky has drunk the Soma juice.

May the vast Heaven and Earth, the mighty couple, shower riches and ample food on this our sacrifice, and protect it from the foes.

Mount your car, O Vritra-slayer Indra, your bay steeds have been harnessed by saying. May you, bound with yama and niyama, be attracted to this sacrifice by the utterance of hymns. This is your house. We establish you in this place of sixteen aspects and full of splendour.

O Soma drinker Indra, yoke your pair of bay steeds of long mane, strong in body and fast to conduct you to the desired place, and then come to listen to our lauds.

Both Indra and Varuna are chief lord and sovereign. They, the first and foremost have made this draught. I drink after them. May she, the Goddess of Speech, seated with Soma, rejoice herself.

Just as the bright rays of this Sun are beheld by all the human beings, so are you bound by the laws of yama and niyama. I take you for the resplendent Surya. This is your dwelling. I accept you for Surya. the resplendent one. O Surya, you are the brightest of the gods. May I be the brightest among men with your grace!

O mighty cow, smell this jar of Soma. May this Soma juice pass into you. Then return to us with a rich store of milk. Pour forth riches for us thousandfold in floods of your milk. May I grow rich in milch kine.

Adorable, delightful, loveable, splendid, full of milk and ghee, most glorious, inviolable, the mighty one, these are your names O cow. Teach me the righteous deeds of Gods to follow.

O Indra, subdue or foremen, humble them who would challenge us in battle. Cast him down to the gloom of the nether world who seeks to harm us. We accept you for you are bound by the yamas and niyamas, for Indra, the foe-dispeller. This is your dwelling. I take you for Indra who dispels our foes.

Let us invoke today, to help us, the lord of speech, the doer of noble deeds, Vishvakarman, the knower of our thoughts. May he kindly hear all our invocations, who grants us bliss and whose deeds are righteous.

O Vishvakarman, the doer of noble deeds, you have made Indra unassailable with your strength-giving oblations. The people make obeisance to him because the Mighty one is specially adorable.

I stir you for the shower from rain-bearing clouds. I stir you for the shower from rain-bearing thunder-clouds. I stir you for the shower from rain-bearing clouds that are pleasing to behold. I stir you for rain from the happy clouds. I stir you pure, in the form of pure water. I stir you in the form of day, in the form of the rays of Surya.

O virtuous and radiant Soma, eagerly go to Agni's cherished food, go willingly to Indra's well loved food. Go as our friend to all the gods, O virtuous and radiant Soma.

Dwell here in all delight, here is surety, live here with performance of your virtuous acts. Produce a child suckling his mother. May he maintain the increase of abundant wealth living among us.

You are the growth and promotion of the sacrifice. May we obtain, with your aid, the light of wisdom and immortality. May we ascend the heaven from earth. May we attain bliss, enlightenment and heaven.

O Indra, O Parvata, slay with your fatal weapons the man, who fain would war with us, O champions who march forward in the battle. If the foemen approach us, drive them away without fail, slay them with the bolt. O you Render, render our foes on all sides, tear them to pieces, O hero, in all the ways, so that we may grow rich in offspring, rich in heroic sons, rich in food to feed with everywhere, on the earth, in ether and in the sky!

Here is Soma, brought with reverence on the choicest chariot. Varuna is seated on his seat, Agni is seated on the sacrificial platform and Indra on the sacrificial barrow, and there is nigh Atharvan ever ready to guard.

The sacrifice has gone to heaven, to Gods, may riches thence come to me. The sacrifice has gone to men, to clouds, may riches thence come to me. To fathers, to earth, the sacrifice has gone, may riches thence come to me! Whatever sphere the sacrifice reaches, may bliss come thence tome.

May the four and thirty threads of the sacrifice made up of the eight Vasus, eleven Rudras, twelve Adityas, Indra, Prajapati andNature, establish this our yajna with Svadha. I unify together of these that is broken. Svaha! May this sacrifice reach all the Gods!

The fruit of sacrifice has spread far and wide. It has extended in eight directions in the sky. O sacrifice, pour down on my offspring abundant wealth and prosperity. May I attain the full span of life through righteous conduct.

O Soma, grant us gold, steeds and heroes. Svaha! Make us rich in kine, corn and knowledge.

Book Nine

O God Savitar, promote well our sacrifice, increase the yajman's portion of wealth. May the divine Gandharva, purifier of our wisdom and will, cleanse our mind and puipose. May Vachaspati, the lord of speech sweeten our speech.

I take the life-infusing essence of waters, that are gathered in the Sun and spread in all directions. The essence of waters, the essence so excellent for us, I accept for you.

You are foe-slayer like Indra's thunderbolt. May this man win the war with your aid, you so experienced in war. In gaining wealth we laud the boundless mother Aditi on whom this whole world of life has settled. May Savitar, sustain and establish it.

Immortality lies in waters, in them the healing medicine. O steeds, grow you strong and fleet, having realized the qualities of waters. O celestial waters, food-giving, whatever high and swift moving waves are yours, therewith may this man attain the desired riches.

It were the wind, mind and twenty seven Gandharvas who at first harnessed the swift steeds. May they grant this man that speed.

O steed, you grow swift like wind and add to Indra's splendour when harnessed at right in the chariot. May the enlightened Mamts harness you, may Tvastar render your feet swift.

O steed, what swiftness was laid in you in secret that resembles the swiftness granted to the falcon, and the speed found in the air. With that same swiftness be strong for us. O horse, wealth winning and victorious in war. Become you our winner of riches and saviour in the war. O steeds, winner of foods, going for food, smell you Brihaspati's portion of food offerings!

May I rise to Brihaspati's loftiest heaven by getting Savitar's inspiration, the true impeller. May I attain Indra's highest heaven by Savitar's inspiration, the true impeller. I have attained the loftiest heaven of Brihaspati by Savitar's inviolable inspiration. I have reached Indra's loftiest heaven by God Savitar's inviolable inspiration.

O Brihaspati, win the battle. O men, lift up your songs of praise to Brihaspati, make him win the prize. O Indra, win you the battle. O learned men raise your lauds to Indra to make him win the prize.

May I win the battle under the control and inspiration of Savitar, the giver of true knowledge. O war-winning swift steeds, reach you all that goal beyond, blocking the enemy's path and winning the quarters with your speed.

This vigorous courser bound in the mouth, bound by the neck and bound at the flanks, gathers new speed, passes by the milestones along the winding paths and its rider hero hurls with speed his weapons on the enemy.

He alone can conquer the foes who like a fleeting horse or a falcon flying fast onward to its aim, marches forth speedily with firm determination and valour fully equipped to the battle.

O fleet courser be auspicious unto us, while they steadily go to the Gods' assembly. May they crush the serpent, the wolf and the wicked and quickly remove all distress!

May the heroes, riding the coursers, known for performing sacrifices, the mighty ones, unassailable warriors, listen to my call. They content thousands of people, perform yajna, and obtain food in abundance. Such heroes win great spoil and splendour in the battle.

O courser, intelligent, immortal, truth-knowing, make us rich in wealth and food. Drink this sweet juice and be satisfied and then follow the path walked by the Gods.

May food in abundance come to me. May both Heaven and Earth approach me, the form of the universe. Let father and mother come to me, may Soma with immortality approach me. You heroes, winners of the battle, purified in heart, obey the behest of your commander.

May our life increase through sacrifice, may our life breath thrive through sacrifice, may our eyes be strengthened through sacrifice, may our ears grow strong through sacrifice. May our back be strengthened through yajna. May sacrifice increase through sacrifice. May we ever live as subjects of the Prajapati. May we be victorious, divine, virtuous and lead a happy and long life.

O mother Earth, may we possess your might and manly strength, may we have all your splendour and working strength. Salutations to the mother Earth, homage be to her. This is your sovereignty. You are controller, you are firm and unshaken. I accept you for agriculture, for our welfare, for the good of the world, for increase of wealth in the nation, for peace and calm, and for nourishment of the subjects.

Let us worship Soma, the king, Agni, the twelve Adityas, Vishnu, Surya the creator of all, Brahma, Brihaspati and above all the Prajapati, who has generated all these Gods for our protection. Svaha!

Urge the mighty Gods Aryaman, Brihaspati, Indra, Sarasvati, the Goddess of speech, Vishnu and Vak to grant us riches. Svaha!

O Agni, be auspicious to us and teach us good things in this sacrifice! O winner of thousands, you being the giver of wealth, give us wealth. Here is our oblation.

May Aryaman grant us wealth, God Pushan and Brihaspati. Let goddess of speech Sarasvati grant us our desires. Here is the oblation.

With penta syllabic metre Pushan won the five directions, may I also win them. God Savitar won the six seasons with six syllabic metre, may I also win them. With hepta syllabic metre the Maruts won the seven domestic animals, may I also win them. With octo-syllabic metre Brihaspati won the Gayatri, may I also win that!

With nine syllabic metre Mitra won Trivrit Stoma, may I also win that. With deca-syllabic metre Varuna won proud god Viraj, may I also win him. Indra won Trishtup with hendeca syllabic metre, may I also win that. And all the gods won Jagati with dodeca-syllabic metre, may I also win that.

O Agni, overthrow the opposing forces and cleave into pieces the enemy. O invincible God, driving away the foemen, grant riches to this sacrificer.

By Savitar's impulsion, with Ashvins arms and hands of Pushan, with the strength of the nearest, I offer you this best oblation for the destruction of the demons. As you have slain the demons so may we also slaughter them. Just as we have slain them so may we slaughter others!

May Savitar impel you for sacrifice. Let Agni of the householders, Soma of the herbs, Brihaspati the lord of speech, Indra for lordship, Rudra for cattle, Mitra for uttering truth, Varuna for the obeying of the Law, urge you to sacrifice.

May Gods anoint this mighty man to be without a rival, for mighty rule, for mighty dominion and for great splendour. This man, son of such a person, such a woman, of such a clan, is anointed king, O you subjects. O you so and so kings, he is your lord, he is joy- giving like Soma. He is also sovereign of our learned Brahmins!

Book Ten

The Gods drew water lull of sweetness, refreshing sap, strength- giving and sovereignty-bestowing. Therewith they anointed Varuna and Mitra, therewith they sprinkled Indra who drives away foemen.

These waters are majestic and joy-giving, inviolate, industrious and investing. In these waters dwells Varuna making his home, he, the son of waters, the best of mothers.

O king, you are the main stay of regal power, you are the strength of princely power. You are the womb and navel of princely power. You are the foe-slaying arm of Indra, you are Mitra's mighty weapon. You are Varuna's possession. With your help may this man subdue his foes. You are the render of forts, you are afflictor of the foe like an arrow. You are the protector of the Law. O brave warriors, protect this king from front, protect him from the rear, protect him in the flanks, guard him from all sides.

Let all men protect him. Let Agni, the master of home, know him. Let famed Indra know him, let Mitra and Varuna, the all-knowing God Pushan know him. May Earth and Heaven know him and also the boundless Aditi, the giver of vast shelter.

The biting creatures who torment others are destroyed. You ascend the east. May the Gayatri metre guard you. May the psalm Rathantra, the triple song of praise, the spring season and the riches of knowledge protect you,

O king, march towards the south. May the Trishtup verse, the Brihat Sam, the fifteenfold praise, song, the summer season, riches and power of the princes guard you.

Advance towards the west. May Jagti verse guard you, the psalm Vairapa, the seventeen-fold praise song, the rainy season, the store of riches and the people.

Advance towards the north. May Anushtup be your guard and so be the Viraja psalm, the twentyone fold praise song, the autumn season and riches, the fruitage of sacrifice.

O king, ascend the zenith. May Pankti verse be your guard, the twain psalms of Shahvan and Revati, the thirtythreefold praise song, the season autumn, three divisions of time, both Winter and Dew seasons and splendour. Cast away the head of the wicked.

You are Soma's brilliance, may my brilliance also shine like yours. Preserve me from death. You are vigour, victory and life.

O Varuna, O Mitra, you rise on high with your golden bodies at the flush of\dawn and then mount your car to view the infinity and limitation. Mitra, you are friend to all, and you Varuna. the mighty enough to ward off the enemy.

O king, I anoint you with the brillance of the moon, lustre of the fire, splendour of the sun and power of Indra. Be the lord of princes and guard your subjects.

O Prajapati, you only comprehended all these created forms and none besides. Give us our heart's desire when we invoke you. He is father of so and so, he is son to so and so. Likewise we accept you as our father. May we become the lord of splendour through righteous ways. O Rudra, your excellent name and form relieve us from miseries, we worship you at home with oblation. All hail!

You are Indra's thunderbolt. I yoke you at the direction of Varuna and Mitra, the great directors and appoint you for alleviating the sufferings of the people and for providing food. May you be unassailable and victorious over the enemy with great might. May we be united with you with mind and might.

O Indra, conqueror of the mighty foes, may we never fail to obtain you through lack of devotion, may we never be without enlightenment. O hero, mount your car. You control the reins and the noble steeds with hands that bear thunder.

All hail to Agni, the lord of household! All hail to Soma, the lord of herbs! All hail to the valiant Maruts! All hail the might of Indra! O mother Earth, never harm me, and may I never harm you.

O Surya, throned in space, the Vasu in mid region, the priest at the sacrifice, the guest of the householder, you are adorable at all the places. You are ubiquitous, present in space, in truth, creator of waters and earth, mountains, trees and kine. You are mighty law in yourself.

You are so great, you are life, give me life, you yoke all with righteous deeds, you are splendours, give me splendour. You are strength, give me strength. O Mitra and Varuna, you both are two arms of mighty Indra, I draw you near him.

You are handsome, good to sit on, the source of regal power. Sit you down on this pleasant seat, be seated on that which offers comfort, sit you on this seat, the womb of royal power.

Varuna has sat down among his subjects, to administer law and justice, the most wise for universal sway.

You are the subduer of the foes. May these five regions be prosperous for you. You are greatly mighty, master of spiritual wisdom, and the example of righteous conduct. You are Varuna whose might is real. You are Indra whose might is of the people. You are auspicious and kind Rudra. doer of much, giver of wealth and comforts. You, the source of abundant rich, are bolt of Indra. Therewith grant me success.

As the spacious Agni, servicable and devoted to duty, reverently receives the oblation of ghee and diffuses them through the rays of the sun, so should a king maintain sovereignty over his subjects.

I go forward urged onward by Savitar the giver of all splendour, by Sarasvatrs speech, by Tvashtars created forms, by Pushan's cattle, by Indra, by Brihaspati, by Varuna's might, by Agni's radiance, by king Soma, by Vishnu the tenth.

Be you good preachers and teachers like the sun and moon, be mature for Sarasvati, exert your best for protection through your sovereign. Be pure like air, full of virtues to lead a righteous life. Be friend unto him by practising yoga.

Like a farmer whose fields are full of barley, reap the ripe corn, removing the chaff in order to offer food to the aged who deserve respect. O wise king, full of splendour, we accept you for the Ashvins, you for Sarasvati and for Indra, the excellent protector.

You Ashvins, lords of riches, drank full draughts of Soma juice and helped Indra in his mighty deeds and killed Namuchi of demon birth.

As the parents help a son, so helped the twain Ashvins, Indra in distress, with their wonderful might and wisdom. O Maghavan, you drank the draught that pleases Sarasvati and refreshed yourself having slain the demon Namuchi.

Book Eleven

God Savitar first of all having harnessed his mind and thought, spread the light from Agni on the earth and in the heaven.

Under the inspiration of God Savitar, having harnessed our mind, we strive to acquire heavenly light for our bliss.

The all-creating and bliss-bestowing God Savitar harnessed the Gods, possessed of celestial light and thought, and impelled them on their way.

The learned priests, well versed in vedic knowledge harness their mind, harness their holy thoughts. He alone, the all-knowing lord of the law, assigns them their sacred tasks. Lofty is the praise of God, the creator of all.

I yoke your mind to God with prayer and meditation. May the hymns of both of you rise high and pervade the heaven. May all the Gods, sons of eternal Prajapati hear it, who dwell in heavenly abodes.

He, the creator of all, the generator of all the worlds, is followed by all the Gods according to their might. He who pervades all and has measured out the entire universe, is Savitar.

O all-creating Savitar, promote and advance our sacrifice, increase the sacrificers portion of splendour. O guardian of divine knowledge, lord of speech, creator of all, cleanser of thoughts and will, sweeten our speech.

You are the excellent woman. May we possess the power by your grace to increase Agni in his dwelling, as did Angiras with Jagti verse.

Let Savitar, with a gold implement in his hand, raise Agni high from the earth with Anustup verse as did Angiras.

O steed, the heaven is our loftiest place of birth, your navel is in the mid region of the space, your shelter is on the earth. Come you running here, impelled to speed, O steed, along the vast space.

O horse, come running and trampling upon the wicked ones, come, spreading gladness all around, come to Rudra. Speed along the vast air with Pushan as your guardian.

The first and foremost Jatavedas illuminates the days before dawn and also illuminates the rays of the sun. He alone illuminates both earth and heaven.

Just as a fleet horse having started on his course, causes fear in the enemy, and just as a householder longs to see with reverent eye Agni kindled in a fine place, so should you.

O steed, having approached the earth, seek Agni with a deep desire and trample on the ground and then instruct us where can we search that learned and effulgent one.

Sky is your back, the earth your seat, the air your spirit, the ocean your place of birth. Assail and trample down the enemy looking around you.

O wealth-giving Courser, rise high from this place for increase of splendour. May we be established in excellent thought while kindling Agni on the earth.

The wealth-giving and fleet Courser has come down on the earth. He has rendered the world beautiful and sacred. May we kindle Agni here on the earth, beautiful to look at, in order to ascend the lofty heaven, the place of happiness.

O Agni, I kindle you reverently with ghee, you dwelling in all the worlds, vast in splendour, of great age, the most widespread, mighty with food, conspicuous and moving transversely.

O Agni, spread you fully in all directions. I enkindle you with ghee. Accept this my ghee oblation with grace. Agni, the adorable, effulgent, moving in all directions, is not to be disrespected!

The lord of food, the wise, farsighted has walked round the oblation, granting the sacrificer the splendid boons.

O mighty Agni, of various forms, learned, victorious, heroic and ever foe-slaying, we adore you from all sides.

O Agni, sovereign lord of men, being pure, you are generated from waters, from stones, from forests, from medicinal herbs and in the house of the sacrificer.

By impulsion of Savitar, the all-creating God, I kindle the all-pervading Agni on the earth as did Angiras in ancient days, with the arms of Ashvins and the hands of Pushan. O Agni, luminous, beautiful to look on, every radiant, engaged in the weal of the subjects, peaceful, never injuring, splenderous I produce you from the womb of the earth as Angiras was to do.

O Agni, you are nourisher and support of the whole world. Atharvan was the first to kindle you by rubbing the sticks well and then he brought you forth by rubbing the lotus and finally the sacrificers of the world rubbed you to life reverently.

Dadhyach, the son of Atharvan, kindled you, O Agni, the slayer of foes, the breaker of their forts.

Agni, the promoter of law, has seated himself well in the seat of Hotar priest. He is invoker of the Gods, splendid, dynamic, resplendent, passing mighty, pure-tongued, and nourisher of thousands.

O mighty Agni, beloved of the Gods, adored by all, sit you down here, be kindled with sacred oblations and then emit the smoke, bright and beautiful to look on.

O pure, heavenly and sweet Waters, pour you down here so that medicinal herbs with their goodly berries spring forth for the cure of diseases like consumption.

O Agni, nobly born with splendour, reside in comfortable nice abode, and robe yourself in many-hued attire!

Arise erect like the lustrous Sun for our protection. You are lofty and bestower of food. We invoke you with oblation-bearing bright rays.

O Agni, you are a fair child of Earth and Heaven and dwell among the herbs to nourish them. O brilliant child, you remove the gloom of night and come forth roaring aloud from your mothers.

O courser, be steady and firm of limbs. Be strong and fleet of foot and broad to bear all that which Agni needs to please himself.

O Agni, be you gracious to creatures of human race. Scorch not heaven and earth, nor air's mid realm nor the plants and herbs.

We kindle and feed Agni, in himself the law and truth, as Angiras was wont to do. O herbs all, accord a warm welcome to Agni, the gracious one who comes to see you here and be happy. O Agni, you remove all our distress, diseases and evil tendencies by dwelling here near us.

O herbs, laden with beautiful flowers and goodly fruit, welcome you well this Agni. This seasonable child Agni has been here since ancient times.

O mighty and resplendent Agni, remove all the sorrows, sufferings and the demons who detest us with your vast lustre. May I be happy to engage myself in pleasing Agni, him who is invocable in all holy rites.

May the Vasus form and kindle you with Gayatri verse like Angiras. You are firm and steadfast, you are earth. Grant me, the sacrificer, progeny, ownership of kine, riches, happy heroism and kinsmen. May the Rudras like Angiras form and kindle you with Trishtup. You are firm and steadfast, you are earth. Grant me, the sacrificer, progeny, ownership of kine, riches, happy heroism and kinsmen. May the twelve Adityas form and kindle you like Angiras with Jagati verse. You are steadfast and firm, you are the Heaven. May all the Gods form and kindle you like Angiras with Anushtup verse. You are steadfast and firm, you are Quarters. Grant me, the sacrificer, progeny, ownership of kine, riches, happy heroism and kinsmen.

Let the Vasus narrate you like Angiras with Gayatri metre. Let the Rudras narrate you like Angiras with Trishtup metre. Let the Adityas narrate you like Angiras with Jagati verse. May all the gods, beloved of all men, narrate you like Angiras with Anushtup verse. May Indra describe you, may Varuna describe you. May Vishnu narrate you.

May all mortals seek your friendship, the guide of all. May all solicit him for glory, riches and fame. May all of us prosper just as you do.

O mother, wean us not from learning, injure us not. Accomplish with firm mind the task undertaken. May you and vour son Agni finish this work with determination.

O Goddess Earth, be steadfast for weal. May your sustaining power and the power of life increase. May this oblation be acceptable to Gods. Emerge from this sacrifice unharmed!

Fed with wood and ghee, the ancient, the invoker of Gods of strength, wonderful in virtues, is Agni.

O Agni, in the fight with the foe men, help us close to you, guard the men with whom I stand.

O Agni, come here from the farthest place, O lord of the red coursers. Come hither and subdue our enemies, O beloved of many, renowned and lustrous!

O mighty Agni, whatever fuel we offer you, may that be like ghee to you. Accept that most graciously, O youthful one.

The wood that termites have eaten away, from which emmet comes out, may that all be like ghee to you. O youthful God, accept that lovingly.

Just as we feed carefully day after day a stable steed with fodder, so may we enjoy food and our wealth ever increasing, unharmed, your neighbours, offer you every fuel, O Agni.

Having enkindled Agni on earth's navel, we invoke Agni, ever victor, conquering the battle, pleased with oblation, adorable and much lauded, for increase in wealth.

Whatever, enemy hosts there are, attacking fiercely, charging all around with weapons, drawn up in order with arms, whatever, thieves and robbers there are, all these I consign to your mouth, O Agni!

Devour the burglars with both of your tusks, consume the robbers with your teeth, with both your jaws, eat up the thieves and cheats. Turn him to ashes who would seek to harm us, the man who detests us, and the man who slanders and cheats us.

O lord of food, grant us a share of food, that would invigorate us and cause no sickness. Onward, still onward lead the giver. Grant us maintenance both for our quadrupeds and bipeds.

Book Twelve

We ever adore Agni who has shone far effulgent, beaming, immortal, of great manly might, remover of distress, bestower of longevity and fame to the sages, him who exhibits diverse things on this earth.

Night and Dawn, different in visage, accordant, meeting together, suckle the same babe, the sun, which beaming shines between the heaven and earth. The mighty and divine forces support the sun.

Savitar, worship-worthy, at dawn shapes and exhibits all objects with his radiance. He is the bringer of weal both for bipeds and quadrupeds and removes their distress.

O Agni, you are goodly pinioned eagle. Trivit-stoma is your head and Gayatri your eye, Brihat and Rathantar your two wings. The yajna is your soul, all the verses your limbs and the formulas your names. Vamdevya Soma is your body, Yajna Yajniya Sama your tail and the sacrificial altars your claws. Thus, O Agni, you are like a goodly pinioned eagle, soar into the sky, reach the heaven!

O Agni, come back again with power, return again with food and life and protect us from sins.

Return Agni, with abundant wealth and drench us with your flowing stream that nourishes all.

O Varuna, free us from the upmost bond, let down the lowest, remove the midmost, so that we may be without sin in your holy law and belong to boundless mother Aditi, O Surya!

The mighty Sun has risen high in the sky before the dawns, removing away darkness with his radiance and light. The fair formed Agni with lustre has filled at birth with splendour all the world.

He, the embodiment of purity, all-pervading, dwelling in mid air, the hotar priest, the guest and lord of home, imbiber of truth, omnipresent, invoker of Gods, present in the minds of the people, creator of prana, kine, the holy law, floods, earth and mountains, to the great Agni, we offer our prayers.

O Agni, knower of all the deeds, be seated in the lap of this your mother. Do not scorch her with your heat nor bum her with your flame. Shine with your pure lustre in her lap!

First Agni was born from out of heaven, then secondly from us was born Jatavedas. Thirdly he, the most manly souled appeared in the waters whom the pious and learned sacrificers ever laud and kindle.

O Agni, we know your three powers in three stages and also, your diverse forms in many places. We know your most secret and supreme name, we know the source from which you have emerged.

Varuna kindled you in the waters, Prajapati lit you amidst the heavens. There as you stood in the third high region, the mighty Maruts increased you amidst the floods.

The giver of splendour, source of glories, giver of wisdom, guardian of Soma, refuge of all, the son of strength, a king in the floods, he shines enkindled in forefront of the dawns.

Germ of creation, ensign of the world sprang to life and pervaded the heaven and earth with radiance. Even the dense clouds he cut as under when passing over, as such he is offered sacrifice by the five clans in unity.

Thus among mortal men immortal Agni was established, the effulgent, purifier, wise, remover of the evil ones and envoy to the Gods. He emits the ruddy smoke above him and reaches the heaven with his brilliance, the sustainer of the world.

The most adorable, man's best friend, the Soma's guard Agni, is praised by the sages. We call gracious heaven and benign Earth to grant us hero sons and abundant wealth.

Nurse Agni, your guest with fuel, enkindle him with oblations of ghee and pour into it your sacred offerings.

O divine Water, accept the ashes and lay them safe in a fragrant place. Just as the wedded ladies of noble minds bow down to their husbands so do you before this Agni. Bear the ashes on waters as does a mother her son.

O Agni, your home is in floods, into the herbs you force your way and are born anew through the rubbing of fuel sticks.

Agni. you are the womb of herbs, you are the womb of the trees, you are the womb of all created beings and of all the waters.

O Agni, mark you well my speech, O divine and most youthful God, one detests you and the other sings your laud.

Germ of creation, ensign of the world sprang to life and pervaded the heaven and earth with radiance. Even the dense clouds he cut as under when passing over, as such he is offered sacrifice by the five clans in unity.

Thus among mortal men immortal Agni was established, the effulgent, purifier, wise, remover of the evil ones and envoy to the Gods. He emits the ruddy smoke above him and reaches the heaven with his brilliance, the sustainer of the world.

The most adorable, man's best friend, the Soma's guard Agni, is praised by the sages. We call gracious heaven and benign Earth to grant us hero sons and abundant wealth.

Nurse Agni, your guest with fuel, enkindle him with oblations of ghee and pour into it your sacred offerings.

O divine Water, accept the ashes and lay them safe in a fragrant place. Just as the wedded ladies of noble minds bow down to their husbands so do you before this Agni. Bear the ashes on waters as does a mother her son.

O Agni, your home is in floods, into the herbs you force your way and are born anew through the rubbing of fuel sticks.

Agni, you are the womb of herbs, you are the womb of the trees, you are the womb of all created beings and of all the waters.

O Agni, mark you well my speech, O divine and most youthful god, one detests you and the other sings your laudly, your devotees, make my obeisance unto your form.

O lord of wealth, O Agni, you are the generous giver. Drive away our foemen. May you accept this our oblation graciously, O best performer. Svaha!

Agni, let the Rudras, Adityas and the Vasus again kindle you, may the priests rekindle you with their oblations, O bestower of riches. Increase your form with the offered ghee and with it may the sacrificer's wishes be fulfilled.

May all the ancient guards and new protector depart and go away. Yama has ordained this place of earth for the sacrificer. This place for him the Fathers have given.

Agni, you are giver of the best knowledge, may your desires be mine. In me be the fulfilment of your desires. You are the form of Agni, you are the ashes.

Agni, your splendour which is in heaven, in earth, over all the mid air's vast space. in the form of lightning, that is dynamic, the seer of all the good and evil acts of mankind and is your own radiance.

Agni, you reach the floods of heaven, you invoke the Gods who inspire thoughts. You are in the waters which are beyond the resplendent sun, and those which are beneath the earth here.

This is your ordained source of being, O Agni, whence born you shone forth. Knowing this, Agni, ascend high and make our riches grow more.

Be you steady and firm, fill up the room, fill up the hole. Indra, Agni, and Brihaspati have established you here in this place.

All the vedic hymns, the Rik, Yajus and Sama have magnified Indra, vast as the ocean, the car-borne, best of the heroes, the lord of corn, the lord of might.

Be you both Jatavedas Agni one-minded, one thoughted for us, free from guile. Destroy not our yajna, injure not the sacrificer, be auspicious to us today, you all-knowing ones.

Just as the mother bears her son in the womb so has Earth Ukha has borne in her womb Agni. May Prajapati, the creator of all, accordant with all the Gods and seasons release her from the bonds.

Nirriti, follow him who performs not the sacrifice, offers no oblation, follow the thief, the robber. Seek the irreligious, to you be our obeisance!

I unfasten the binding noose which Nirriti, the Goddess of destruction, has fastened on your neck that none may loose. The same I loose for you. Now eat this food which I offer you. Obeisance be to that Goddess by whose grace this has been possible.

Establisher of the sacrificer, protector of truth, gatherer of wealth, Agni, reveals every form and figure with his might, and like

Savitar the God of inviolate laws, like Indra faces the enemy warriors in the battlefield.

Happily may the ploughshares turn up the land, happily follow the farmers their oxen! May Vayu and Aditya being pleased with our oblation cause our herbs and plants bear abundant fruit.

Let our furrows be moistened with sweet sap, approved by the Visvadevas and the Maruts. Be you furrows, succulent, full of corn, milk, ghee, etc. for us.

The keen-shared plough, the bringer of bliss, producer of the Soma drink, shear out for me a fine cow, a sheep, a speedy drawer of the car, and a blooming woman stout and plump.

The year together with its fortnights and other parts, the dawn with its ruddy kine, the Ashvins with their wondrous attainments, Surya with his dappled courser, the Vaishvanara with corn and ghee. Svaha!

O Herbs, nourishing like mother, you are thousand-named, thousand are your growths. You are possessed of thousand powers, release this Yajman of mine from disease.

Herbs that sprang up in the beginning, at the time of creation, earlier than the Gods, of these, which are brown and capable of nourishing the world will I proclaim the hundred and seven.

O Herbs, be gracious to us, both bearing blossom and fruit and also those which would lead us to success with speed like fleet- footed mares.

O Herbs, comforting like mothers, by this name I speak to you. O God, may I gain a horse, a cow, clothes and a body free from disease with your favour!

This holy fig tree is your abode, you have made Prana tree your home. Winners of cattle shall you be if you regain this sacrificer for me.

He who goes to places where there are herbs as the kings go to the battlefield, Physician is his name, the slayer of fiendish diseases and chaser of ailments.

Herbs rich in Soma juice, rich in steeds, rich in nourishment, rich in bestowing strength, all these I know that this may be freed from the disease.

Let fruitful herbs and those fruitless, those that blossom and the blossomless, created by Brihaspati, relieve us from disease and distress.

Relieve me from curse's evil, and the vow arising from Varuna, release me from Yama's noose, from sin and violation done against the sages.

The herbs descending from the heaven said, "no disease shall assail the man, whom, while he lives, we pervade".

May unharmed be he who digs you up, unharmed the man for whom I dig. May our bipeds and quadrupeds be free from disease by its use and application.

The Gandharvas dug you out from the earth, Indra and Brihaspati did. King Soma knowing you, made himself free from consumption by your use.

Long-lived be he who digs you out, and he for whom I dig you out. May you also live long for hundred years and grow up with hundred shoots.

O immortal Agni, bestow on us abundant wealth being enkindled by us. Your brilliant form is beautiful to look on, you promote our sacrifice.

First of all they established you, O Agni, for sacrifice, truthful, mighty, visible to all, so radiant friend of the Gods, with ear to hear prayers, most known and magnified by songs of praise.

O Soma, may many nourishing juices be with you, may you wax mighty from every side to subdue the foe men. May you, thus progressing, win immortality and highest fame in heaven.

Increase you most pleasing Soma, grow strong through various means like the sun with its rays. Be you our friend for giving us prosperity and vast happiness.

O Agni, your devotee, the sacrificer draws your mind away, even from the highest abode of yours, with reverent speech and songs of praise.

O Agni, all turn to you with prayers of diverse kinds for the fulfilment of their wishes, as did Angiras.

You alone shine forth with brilliance, you royal lord Agni, in your dear dwellings to fulfil the wishes of all that are and are to be in future.

Book Thirteen

I, the sacrificer, first of all establish Agni within my home for increase of wealth, good progeny and manly strength. May Gods aid me in this!

You are support of waters, the source of fire, and enveloper of ocean as it swells and suges, the loftiest, resting on the lotus, spreading out in amplitude in space and its own measure.

The famed Aditya at first appeared in the East and then filled the worlds with his radiance, the womb of both creation and non-creation.

Hiranyagarbha, the golden germ, sprang up first of all, the only lord of all created beings. He was also there before the creation of things. He sustains this earth and heaven. Let us worship him, the Prajapati with our oblation.

Surya sprang forth through this earth and heaven along this space and that which existed before. I offer my seven oblations to Aditya who travels to his own dwelling.

Homage be to all enemies, like serpent in nature, who dwell on earth, those dwelling in the air, and also to those dwelling in the sky.

Homage be to those that are demons' darts, to those who dwell in the trees like serpents, and to all of them who lie low in holes be homage paid.

Homage be to all the serpents, to them that are in heaven's bright realm, to them that abide in the sun's rays. Adoration be to them that have their home in waters!

Increase and put on your vigour like a widespread net, attack the foemen like a mighty king with your aids. Strengthening yourself, shoot deadly arrows to transfix the demons and subdue them all.

O Agni, let your rapid flames riding the wind follow the fiends with all their blazing fury and flaming weapons. Let the demons be scorched with your tongues of flying flames, Agni, let your fire brands rain all over the foe.

O unassailable Agni, send forth the army to destroy our enemy, be he far or near. Be yourself the guardian of our people. May you be ever unharmed and safe from the trouble sent by the foemen.

Rise and sweep away those who take up arms against us, O Agni, burn down the enemy, you possessed of sharpened darts. Humiliate and consume completely like dried-up stubble, him who creates mischief by encouraging our foe!

Rise up, punish them all who fight against us, manifest your own divine strength. Blunt the weapons of the fiends, slay the enemy whether related to us or be he a stranger. I settle you with fire's ardour!

Agni is lofty like the head of heaven, he, the sustainer of earth, quickens the waters' seed. I settle you with mighty Indra's strength.

You are the lord of the sacrifice and the heaven. With your oblation bearing flaming tongue, you sustain the Adityas in the sky and attend the auspicious rites with your benign teams.

Firm you are, sustainer, established in your place by Visvakarma, O Earth. Let not ocean harm you, let not air injure you, O you steadfast, unshakable earth!

May Prajapati settle you on the waters, on the ocean's surface, you so spacious and vast. O vast one spread yourself wide.

You are bliss-giving Earth, god mother Aditi, sustainer and nourisher of all the beings of the world. Steady her, do you no harm to her and look on her with an affectionate eye.

O Agni, your light which spreads out in the sky in the form of the beams of the sun, therewith help us and our children today to gain splendour,

O Indra, Agni, Brihaspati, O Gods, whatever your light is there in the sun, or that in the kine and horses, with all that glorify us!

May honeyed Madhu (Chaitra) and Madhava (Baisakh), the two spring months, sprung of heat, increase my prosperity. May heaven and earth, the waters and the herbs, may Agni help me, the sacrificer in my progress. May all the Agni between heaven and earth one-minded, in accord, attend these two spring months as the Gods attend Indra. Be seated with this God firm in your seat like Angiras.

You are invincible by the foes, O conqueror, conquer our foemen, subdue them who fain would oppose us, you are possessed of a thousand manly powers, so do you help and be gracious to me.

In spring the winds blow sweetly, the streams flow sweetly for him who performs sacrifice, So may the herbs be sweet for us!

The nights are sweet, sweet are the days, sweet is the terrestrial atmosphere. May sweet be the Heaven to us like our fathers.

May trees be full of sweet fruits for us, and full sweet the sun. So may our milch kine be sweet for us.

Seat yourself firm in the deepness of waters, lest sun, lest heat burning within, scorch you. Let the well formed subjects be surveyed. May the goodly rain that pours, aid you.

Steadfast you are, and sustainer of the world. So sprang forth he, Jatavedas from these wombs, the all-knowing one. May this Agni, who knows his rights, convey to the gods these our oblations offered with Gayatri, with Trishtup and with Anushtup verses!

O Agni, abide here in pleasure for long for granting us food, wealth, power, fame, milk, ghee, saps and offspring. You are the lord of earth and self effulgent. May both the mind and speech of Sarasvati protect you!

O radiant Agni, yoke your most excellent steeds, that bear you with speed to the sacrifice.

Anoint Agni with milk, of diverse forms, the womb of Gods, the sustainer of animals, the creator of thousands, the lighter of the world. Remove all the diseases with kindled Agni, obtain the boon of living for hundred years and always avoid the pride!

O Agni, harm not the wind's impetuous rush, Varuna's navel, the cloud, the stream's tawny child and, the steed sprung out from waters, dwelling in the highest heaven, that can crush even stones to powder by trampling.

The ruddy, unwasting, eager, pressing forward, sustainer of all, adorable by the sages, Agni, I worship with lauds. Harm you not the cow, so rich in milk.

O Agni, you dwell in the loftiest realms, you are of diverse forms, Varuna's navel and Tvashtar's guardian. Harm her not, the great, protector of the beings and the source of weal for thousands.

O Agni, may your fierce displeasure spare the sacrificer. You have your being from Agni or heat of the earth, or from the heat of the sun, whereby the omnific lord has engendered creatures.

The Sun, the wondrous strength of the Gods, has risen, the eye of Mitra, Varuna and Agni. The spirit of all, the moving and unmovmg things. He has filled the heaven, earth and the air with his splendour.

O Agni, injure not these biped and quadruped brought for the sake of sacrifice. Be gracious to these corn-producing beasts, and guard them. Therewith build your form and be well nourished. Let your wrath be upon violent wild beast. Let the foe, whom we hate, be put to grief.

Injure not this one-hoofed animal, the beautiful horse, neighing in the midst of horses. I offer to you the harmful forest deer, fair in colour. Building your flames up with him be steadfast. May that deer be your victim. Let your flame reach him. May he be injured whom we hate.

Book Fourteen

Drive O Agni, our known foemen, drive from us the unborn ones, O Jatavedas, graciously minded; without anger bless us so that we may live happily in the thrice guarded home.

Drive away our enemies, O Agni, with your might, our known foes, ward off those who would attack us secretly. O benevolent in thought and spirit, bless us. May we live long, drive away our foes!

Stoma, the lady of sixteen arts, grants strength and wealth. The Stoma of forty-four skills also grants splendour and riches. You are complement of Agni. As such may all the Gods greet you with lauds. Enriched with songs of praise and butter, stay here and grant us wealth and store of children.

This Agni is the head and height of heaven, he is the lord of the earth. This same Agni quickens the waters' seed.

This Agni is the lord of thousandfold pleasures, the master of hundredfold food and wealth, the sapient one.

Atharvan, the best of priests, brought you forth from the lotus by rubbing, the head of the priest.

Leader of the sacrifice, you are end of the region to which with your auspicious company you attend. You bear the light-giving Aditya in the sky, making your tongue the conveyor of oblations to Gods.

People kindle Agni with their fuel. As a calf is delighted to meet its mother cow so are people gladdened by seeing the Dawn appear. Just as the branches of the young trees shoot up high so do Agni's flames rising high in the sky.

We offer our songs of praise to Agni, the adorable sage, pure, virtuous and strong. The sage has raised his hymn of praise to Agni far reaching as the Sun in the sky.

Agni was ordained to be the first invoker, the best in sacrifice, to be lauded at rites. Him the Bhrigus with their offspring made to kindle in splendour in the forest, spreading to every home.

Agni, the watchful guardian of the created beings has been born, ever active, strong for fresh prosperity. Increasing with ghee, his flames reaching high in the heaven, he shines radiantly enkindled by the priests of sacrifice.

O Agni, dear to Angiras, they caused you to appear when you remained hidden, fleeing back from wood to wood and plant to plant. You are generated by attrition as conquering strength. People call you the son of highly powerful strength.

O men, offer to Agni seemly oblations and your songs of praise to him who is supreme, highly mighty, the son of strength.

O mighty Agni, the lord of all, you bestow all the fruits of the sacrifice on the sacrificer, your friend. Bring us the riches as you are kindled at the place of yajna.

O Agni, beloved of many, people invoke you in their homes as most famed and wondrous one. They call on you, the bearer of oblations whose hair is flames.

I invoke Agni for you with this my reverent song, the son of strength, beloved, the wisest envoy, immortal, adored with oblations, the messenger of all.

We call on Agni, the immortal messenger, envoy and representative of all. He yokes his two ruddy steeds, all cherishing. He comes riding fast when invoked properly and reverently.

Let Agni be invoked and worshipped well. Let him be invited reverently. Then has the sacrifice proper end and happy performance and rich boon for the sacrificer.

O Agni, son of strength, all-knowing, lord of kine and wealth, grant us great riches, O Jatavedas.

O Agni, brilliant, wise, good, worthy of laud with our hymns, shine on us, O of many forms, shine on us wealth.

O radiant one, shining by day, by night and morning, burn the wicked with your blazing flames, you whose teeth are sharp like the bolt.

O adorable Agni, bring us bliss, may the sacrifice and the gifts bring us bliss, may our songs of praise bring us bliss, O invoked Agni!

The determined mind wherewith you subdue the foes in the war, show us that, that with which you conquer the enemy. May our prayers bring us bliss.

O Agni, wherewith you conquer the foe in the battle, therewith slacken the strings and destroy the bows of the mighty enemy. May we vanquish the foes with your aid.

I recognize Agni, the good lord of home, the fire to which the kine return, whom the coursers seek as their home. Grant abundant food to those who are your devotees.

I laud God Agni, to whom the milch kine return in herds, to whom the princes of royal birth come, to whom the fleet-footed coursers come. Grant abundant food to your devotees.

O pleasurable God Agni, you pour ghee within your mouth with both the ladles. So fill us also full with riches, O lord of might. Grant abundant food to your devotees.

Today we bring to offer you, O Agni, the things dear to you like a disciplined horse with reverence.

O Agni, you have ever been a great charioteer, full of pleasurable intellectual and physical strength, high sacrifice and proper judgement. So may we certainly be!

Being pleased with our hymns of praise come you unto us, O Agni, well disposed with your various aspects as does the Sun in the morning with all his rays.

I hold Agni, the son of strength, as learned Brahmin who knows all the Vedas, the knower of all created beings, lord of sacrifice, a God with erect form, envoy of the Gods, charitably disposed and the drinker of the sacred ghee offered in sacrifice.

O Agni, be our closest friend, our guard, liberator and a gracious friend. Come unto us, O God, with bliss and weal for our household, give us renowned wealth and splendid riches. We approach you, O effulgent one, most radiant, with lauds for bliss and wealth.

With whatever fervour the sages came obtaining knowledge and kindled Agni at the place of sacrifice for bliss and true happiness, with that I establish Agni in heaven whom the learned and thoughtful men call as pervader of the atmosphere.

O Gods, let us adore Agni with our wives, sons, brothers, relatives and wearing gold ornaments so that we may attain the blissful, luminous realm of virtues, the world of heaven, high on the third height.

May this Agni, knower of the essence of the Vedic speech, lord of the heroes, protector of the virtuous, established on the earth, ever active, the effulgent one, cast under foot those who would fight against us.

May this Agni, most manly, bearer of oblations, doer of thousands of noble deeds, shining with never failing light, resplendent in the midst of heaven, shine and attain the divine dwellings.

O you all men, come near this Agni from all sides and attend him well. O Agni, light the pathways of godward travel and then rejuvenating the Fathers with life's vigour, extend fully through the sacrifice.

O Agni, wake up and then keep the sacrifice! Awake and watchful. May his desires meet fruition with your grace. All the Gods and this Sacrifices in connection with you, may occupy the highest place here and hereafter in the loftiest realm.

O Agni, bear our oblations and give them to the Gods in heaven. Wherewith you carry a thousand, wherewith, O Agni, carry this our offering to heaven among the Gods.

O Agni, this is your ordained home of birth, whence born you shone forth. Knowing this, Agni, rise up and make our wealth to grow in all the ways.

Just as a horse desiring food neighs for fodder, so does Agni roar having sprung out from the fuel sticks. Then the winds blow in his wake. Black is the path that this splendrous Agni travels.

You illumine the heaven, the earth and the broad realm between them. You are luminous, I set you in Ayu's seat, in the shadow of the protector and in the heart, deep like the ocean.

O Agni, you are the measure of thousands of powers, you are the embodiment of thousands of splendours. You are equivalent of thousands of might. You are far better than the thousands. You are the lord of the thousands. I set you on the thousands!

Book Fifteen

Salutations be to the Rudra's wrath, salutations to your arrows, homage be to your twain arms.

With your gracious form, O gentle Rudra, pleasant to look on, with that most benign form look you on us, O Mountain dweller!

O Mountain dweller, whatever shaft you have in your hand to shoot, render that auspicious, Mountain god, harm not man nor injure the moving things!

O Mountain dweller, we salute you with our graceful hymns so that all our world be free from disease and well satisfied!

The first divine physician and advocate, Rudra has saved us by crushing deadly serpents and by driving away the fiends.

He, the most auspicious one, of coppery, red and brown hue, is surrounded by thousands of Rudras. May the wrath of these Rudras stationed on all sides be ever far removed from us.

May Rudra, who travels in the form of the Sun, whose throat is blue, whose hue is coppery red, whom the herdsmen and maidens carrying water have seen, may he be auspicious to us when beheld.

Salutations be to him. the blue-throated, the thousand-eyed, the beautiful to look on, and also to his ministers, to them be our homage!

Loosen your bow string, slacken it at both the extremities of the bow, put away the arrows that you hold in your hand, O lord of the matted locks!

O Lord of braided hair, let your bow be stringless, your quiver hold no sharp arrows. May arrows be driven away and your sheath that contained your sword be empty.

O blissful Rudra, protect us well on all sides with your weapon, with the bow that you hold in your hand, the bow harmless to us.

O thousand eyed, thousand-quivered Rudra, having blunted the points of your arrows, be benign and auspicious to us.

Obeisance be to your unstrung bow, homage be to your weapon. Salutations be to your two arms, and to your bow homage be!

Harm not, O Rudra, our elders and young ones, injure not our growing youths, harm not our children in the womb. Slay not our rearing sires, slay not the mothers, and harm not our own dear bodies.

Harm not our seed in embryo and our offspring, harm us not, our kine and steeds. Kill not our heroes in the fury of your wrath. We with oblations ever call on you.

Salutations to Rudra, the commander of the hosts, whose arms are gold-ornamented. Salutations to him who is the lord of entire world. Homage be to him whose hair is green trees, whose sheen is like green grass, the lord of beasts. Salutations be to the brilliant lord of pathways, to the golden haired wearer of the sacred thread, homage be lo the ageless lord of the healthy people.

Salutations be to brown hued-Rudra, the piercer of the foes, to the lord of food, to the lord protector of the world. Salutation to Rudra's weapons, salutation to him whose bow is bent in readiness, to the protector of the regions. Salutations to charioteer Rudra who harms none, to the lord of forests be salutations!

Salutations to the red architect, to the protector of the trees. Salutations to Rudra, who expands the earth and giver of riches and splendour. Salutation to the lord of riches and splendour. Salutation to the lord of herbs and plants, to the sagacious tradesmen. Salutations to the lord of the bushes of the forest, to him who makes the wicked weep, to the shouting lord of hosts!

Salutations to Rudra, who rushes at the foe with the drawn bow for our protection, to the lord of all believers. Salutations to the foe-conquering and enemy slaying Rudra, to him who protects the heroic army. Salutations to the sword bearer against the fiends, to the lord of persons serving in secret saluations be. Salutations to the wandering robbers and the roamers, to the protector of forests be salutations!

Homage to lord of assemblies and to the assemblies, homage to horses, and to you masters of the horses. Homage to the warrior hosts that pierce and slay the foe, to you killing armies with fine bands be homage!

Salutation to the bringer of weal, to the guard of the beings. Salutation be to the fierce and awe-inspiring. Salutations to him who slays the foe in front, to him who slays the foe at a distance. Salutations to the slayer and frequent slayer of the wicked. Salutations to the green tressed trees, to the deliverer from distress be salutation.

Salutations to him who causes happiness, and to him who causes light. Salutations to the source of bliss and the source of joy, salutations to the auspicious one and to the most auspicious be salutations!

Salutations to him who is beyond suffering, and to one who is struggling for release. Salutations to him who crosses over and to him who crosses back. Salutations to him who is in the ford, to him who dwells on the banks of rivers and shores of seas, to him who is in the grass and to him who is in the foam.

O distresser of the foe, the lord of corn, you cleaver, blue and red Rudra, slay none of these our people and children, none of these our cattle, nor make them diseased. Let none of us be sick!

We offer to the mighty Rudra of matted locks, these our songs of praise, the lord of heroes so that all our people and the cattle be happy, well fed, healthy and free from distress and disease.

O Rudra, with that your auspicious aspect which heals and causes weal be gracious to us that we may be happy.

O Rudra, spare us and keep away your weapons from us, save us from your great fury of wrath. Turn aside your mighty bow from us, O Bounteous lord, and be auspicious to seeds and progeny.

O most bounteous, most gracious Rudra, be you gracious and well disposed towards us. Approach us here skin robbed, bearing your bow, and having laid down your weapon on some remotest tree.

O harm-remover, splendid and holy Rudra to you be salutations. May all those of your thousand weapons strike dead another than from us.

O lord of the splendour and the world, thousands and thousands are the weapons ready in your hands, turn their points away from us.

Countless, thousands are the Rudras on the face of this earth. Of these Rudras we send the weapons to places thousand leagues away.

Homage to Rudras whose abode is the heaven, whose arrows are floods of rain. To them ten eastward, southward ten, ten to the south, ten to the north, ten to the realm uppermost! To them be homage. May they protect and spare us. Within their jaws we put the man who dislikes us and whom we dislike.

Book Sixteen

O Maruts, so charitably disposed, grant us food and strength contained in stone and mountain and saps obtained from waters, herbs, plants and trees, that food and strength. O all-devouring Agni, in the stone is your hunger, in me your food. Let that wrath of yours strike the man whom we detest!

O Agni, may these brick be my milch kine, one and ten, and ten tens, a hundred, and ten hundred, a thousand and ten thousand and a hundred thousand, a lac and ten lacs, a million, and ten millions, a crore, ten crores, hundred crores, thousand crores, it is ten times Mahapadma, it is ten times shankh, it is ten times samudra, it is ten times madhya, it is ten times prardh. O Agni, may these bricks of this altar be a source of bliss in this and the next world.

You are law-strengthening pleasant Spring season, set in the cycle of seasons. You fortify truth and are ghee giving, bestowing sweet sap, full of splendour, glorified, fulfiller of our desires and imperishable.

With ocean's cool mantling we robe you, Agni, be our purifier and auspicious to us.

We wrap you with snow's investing garb, Agni, be our purifier and auspicious to us.

Come you down on the earth, take the support of reeds, take abode in the rivers, because you are the essence of the waters. You also come here with them, female frog, and make this sacrifice of ours splendid and successful.

This place of Agni is the waters' meeting point, here meet the floods. Let your flames burn others than us, be our purifier and propitious to us!

O excellent cleanser, Agni, radiant one, bring here to our yajna and adore the Gods, O pleasant tongued!

O pure, purifying, splendid God Agni, bring the Gods to this our sacrifice, to our offerings bring the Gods!

He who with purifying radiance has shone up on this earth like dawns with sunlight, who comes speeding like fleet coursers in the battle, ageless, who in the heat of battle tolerates thirst.

O Agni, salutations to your flame that attracts all the saps, salutations to your blazing fire. Let your flame bum others than us, be you our purifier and propitious to us!

To Agni who abides in man, Hail! To him who abides in waters, Hail! To Agni who abides in the holy sacrificial grass, Hail! To him who abides in the trees, Hail. And this Agni who is known as the Sun, to him, Hail!

O Agni, you are the giver of vital breath, of our breath and diffusive breath. You are giver of wealth and power. Let your weapons distress others than us. Be you our purifier and propitious to us!

May Agni destroy all the devouring fiends with his sharp blazing flames. May Agni grant us riches and splendour.

He who protects all, dissolves all the worlds at the time of final dissolution, sat down as Hotar priest, our Father, the sage, is ever present. With his grace he fulfils all our wishes, pervades the subtle primordial matter and the world created therefrom.

What was the support before this creation? What was it that propped him? What was its nature? Whence Vishvakarma, the seer of all, creating the earth, with boundless power produced the heavens?

He has eyes in all directions, mouths on all sides, arms and feet on all sides. He, the only one, has produced heaven and earth with the might of his arms and put them in motion.

Let the learned men enquire within their soul what was the cause, what the resultant creation? From what the heaven and earth were created? Whereupon he stood when he shaped all the objects?

Whatever your highest, lowest, midmost deeds and places are, O Vishvakarma, the creator of the universe, reveal them all to us, your friends at sacrifice and come yourself to our yajama.

O Vishvakarma, be pleased with my oblation and come to the sacrifice with heaven and earth, come to our worship. May our enemies be ever in confusion and here may we have a rich and generous portion!

When the father Vishvakarma created both heaven and earth, and extended far both of them fastening securely their eastern ends, then he, the lord of eye and light, submerged these in saps.

Vishvakarman, the creator of the whole universe, is all-seeing; most excellent, full of deep knowledge, mighty, creator, disposer and without second In him the souls, controlling their seven senses including mind and intellect live in enjoyment according to their desires. Let us all worship him.

He is our father, he created us. He as the sustainer knows all races and all things existing. He is the name giver of all the Gods. He is one, him alone all seek for knowledge.

The ancient seers and rishis offered him their treasures with their songs of praise sung in groups, him who in the highest, lowest and the mid region created all things that have existence.

He was there before this earth and heaven, and before gods and demons came into being. What was the first germ that waters received, where the Gods beheld that primeval element?

The waters received that primeval germ where the Gods lived together. Indeed there in the navel of the unborn is that supreme primeval element from which all things spring up and in which they exist.

O men, you know not him who has created all creatures and worlds, he is different and another and yet pervades you all. You are enwrapped in mist of ignorance, engaged in fruitless discussions and controversies, preoccupied with fulfilment of carnal wishes, hymn-singers, wandering, confused and discontent.

First of all came the God, Vishvakarma, then secondly was the Sun created, who sustains the kine and the earth. Thirdly was born the cloud in succession, that quickened the germ in waters and preserves the herbs.

Terrific like the bull, swift in striking the foes, who keeps his weapons sharpened, who does not even wink, causer of distress to the enemy, the sole hero, Indra subdued at once the hundred armies, the arouser of the people.

O warriors, with him as helper, the loud-roaring, alert, invincible, ever victorious, rouser of battles, Indra, the mighty, bearer of arrows, now win the opposing army.

Indra, the master of his passions, girt with arrow and quiver-bearing warriors, foe-subduing, keeper of stores of arms and weapons, strong in arms, the Soma enjoyer, fond of battle with sharp shafts, rulers over all.

O Brihaspate, you are the slayer of demons. Guard you our chariots, O chariot-borne, destroyer, victor, breacher of enemy forces!

O Indra, master commander of the forces, experienced hero, lord of all, passing mighty, conqueror of the foes, fierce in battle, accompanied by the heroes, far famed for strength, kine winner, mount your conquering chariot!

O Indra, O Brihaspati, you are the warder and commander of these foe-destroying, battle-winning divine armies. Let Soma and the Maruts, the leaders of big bands, march in front of these heavenly hosts that destroy and demolish.

Ours is the powerful army of mighty Indra, king Varuna, the Maruts and the Adityas. The soaring roar of the winning Gods, the highly learned ones, has caused the worlds to quake.

O Maghavan, excite the spirit of our warring heroes, make their weapons flourish, urge to speed the strong steeds, O Vritra-slayer, and let the din of conquering cars soar skyward!

May Indra aid us when our flags flutter high in the battle, may the arrows of our army be victorious. May our heroes enjoy triumph. May all the Gods protect us everywhere during the war!

The forces of our enemy that is coming against us with its full might, O Maruts, meet and enwrap it in thick darkness so that they may not recognise one another.

O Agni, well satisfied with ghee, lead this man to high position, grant him increase in riches and multiply his progeny!

Indra, lead this man to prominence. May he possess control over his foes. Grant him glory, let him offer their due share to the Gods!

May Indra prosper him in whose house we perform sacrifice. May the Gods and Brahmanaspati bless and comfort him.

O Agni, all the Gods bear and uplift you high according to their wisdom. May you so famed, rich in splendour, be auspicious to us.

Surya, the golden-hued, flame-haired, preserver of all, the bright fire, has appeared high in the east. He, the guardian of the righteous, nourishing and knowing his own virtues travels surveying all the worlds.

He sits in the midst of heaven, the measurer, flooding the earth, sky and air's mid region with light. He looks upon the far extending fertile pastures between the eastern and western limits.

The same Sun who pours down the rain, is red when rising in the east, pervades the heaven, marches through the sky, is set amidst the space, lord of the innumerable rays, measurer of the sky, has attained the abode of the Primeval Father.

All the sages glorify Indra, vast as the space, the best of car-borne heroes, the lord, the very lord of strength.

May Indra, the lord of food and riches lift me up through elevation, and with his subjugating might keep my foemen down!

May the Gods increase our powers of uprising and knowledge and also the power of foe's depression and punishment. May Indra, may Agni drive away my foemen in every direction.

I have ascended the heaven from the earth, and from mid region I have mounted up the heaven. From heaven's high and happy region I have attained the world of eternal light.

The sages attain God, the sustainer of the world, through the sacrifice. On their march to heaven they look not round, but rise to salvation that releases them from the cycle of birth and death.

O Agni, you are thousand-eyed and hundred-headed. You are possessed of hundred breaths and thousand through breaths. To you, the lord of thousand-fold riches, we offer our oblations of power.

You are a bird of fine wings and so well seated on the earth. Fill the space with your light, and fill the sky with your glow. Flood the quarters with your sheen.

I solicit god Savitar's wondrous wisdom desired by all, good for all mankind and cause of this world's creation. The sages like Kanva milked this mighty thousand-streamed milch cow of Savitar.

We worship Agni of the loftiest birth and offer him oblation with hymns of praise in his lower station. I worship the place whence you have sprung out, and offer oblations having enkindled you well.

O most youthful Agni, first enkindled with reverence, shine in front of us constantly, never fading out and we shall offer you sacred oblations without stop.

I offer the oblation of ghee with a contemplative mind so that the Gods may arrive who love oblations, the strengthners of truth. I pour oblation day after day to Vishvakarma, the lord creator of all.

O Agni, you have seven kinds of fuel, seven tongues of flame, the seven rishis have envisioned you, you have seven beloved mansions of verse and seven priests in sevenfold sacrifice pay you homage. Seven are your places of birth, fill these full with ghee, Svaha!

Forth from the ocean sprung the watery waves of sweetness with the stalk, it turned into Amrita, that which is ghee's secret title, which is truly Gods' tongue and Amrit's navel.

We utter the name of ghee aloud in this yajna and bear the sacrifice with oblation. So let the four hotar priests hear this praise of ghee that expresses the fruit of sacrifice through oblation.

Udgatar, Hotar, Adhvaryu and Brahman, the four priests are the four horns of this sacrifice, Rik, Yajur and Sama are his three feet, his heads are two and his seven heads are the seven verses. Bound in triple bond the Bull roars loudly. The most adorable God has entered the world of mortals.

These many kinds of ghee streams flow forth from the innermost reservoir of heart which the foe does not behold. I look upon the golden Agni amidst these streams.

Like streams flow together unceasingly our oblations, purifying themselves in the innermost reservoir of heart. These streams of oblations flow swiftly to the sacrifice as do the wild beasts fly before a hunter.

Just as the high-born ladies at a fair look on and gently smiling, incline towards their husbands, so do these streams of holy ghee reach the sacrificial fuel and Jatavedas happily receive them.

Just as maidens adorn themselves with gay ornaments to join the bridal feast, so do the streams of sacred ghee flow down where Soma is poured and sacrifice is performed.

O Gods, send to our lands riches and cattle, and convey our oblations of streaming ghee, pure and sweet to heaven.

Oh Agni, this universe depends on your sustaining power. Whatever your loftiest form is there within the ocean, within the heart, within life and within sacrifice, that sweet, enlightening and blissful wave of yours may we obtain!

Book Seventeen

May my corn and my wealth, my best efforts and my mind, my thought and power of action, may my speech and my praise, my power of hearing, and my light, my spiritual power prosper by this sacrifice.

May my inhalation and exhalation, my through-breathing and my other breaths, my thought power and my knowledge, my speech and my mind, my eye and my ear, my skill and my strength prosper by this sacrifice.

May my energy and my tolerance, my soul power and my body, my happiness and my armour, my limbs and my bones, my joints and my members, my health and long life prosper by this sacrifice.

May my pre-eminence, and my ownership, my courage and my wrath against the wicked, my seriousness and my life force, my victorious power and my importance, my dignity and my breadth, my long life and my greatness, my old age and progress prosper by this sacrifice.

May my truth and my faith, my cattle and my wealth, my portion and my greatness, my play and my pleasure, my son and my future son, my hymn and my rites prosper by this sacrifice.

May my simple acts and my immortality, my freedom from consumption and my health, my medicine and my long life, my freedom from enemy and my fearlessness, my joys and my rest, my fair dawn and fair evening and my fair day prosper by this sacrifice.

May my leader and my supporter, my security and my patience, my goods and my capability, my knowledge and discretion, my command and my propagation, my plough and my harrow prosper through this sacrifice.

May my Agni and my Indra, my Soma and my Indra, my Savitar and my Indra, my Sarasvati and my Indra, my Pushan and my Indra, my Brihaspati and my Indra's favour prosper by this sacrifice.

May my Mitra and my Indra, and my Varuna and my Indra, and my Dhatar and my Indra, and my Tvashtar and my Indra, and my Maruts and my Indra, and my Vishvadevas and my Indra prosper by this sacrifice.

May my vows and my seasons, and my fervour and my year, and my day and night and my thighs and knees and Rathantara Soma prosper by this sacrifice.

May all the Maruts come unto us today. Let all guardian Gods come to our sacrifice to protect us. Let all the Agnis be kindled well. May we gain all wealth and riches.

O Agni, with the milk of the earth and such other saps I unite me, unite myself with waters and herbs. As such I gain nourishment from herbs and waters.

The protector of all the subjects, creator of all the beings, mind is the Gandharva. May he guard our Brahmins, and Nobles, Svaha! The wish-fulfilling Richas and Samans, his Apsaras may protect us, Svaha!

O Prajapati, lord of the world, you are the prop of the homes above and here, grant protection to these our Brahmins and Nobles.

O Maruts, you are deep and vapoury like the sea, you are the source of rain pouring down on the earth and the blessing arising therefrom. You are the heaven-wandering Maruts, blow on me food, riches, weal and release from bonds. May I attain you from all sides. Svaha!

O Agni, grant glory to our Brahmins, set lustre in our Kshatriyas. lustre in our Vaishyas, and in our Shudras, and in me establish lustre.

O Varuna, with my songs of praise I beg this of you, your devotee begs this of you with oblation. Abide with us and set not angry. Do not decrease our age, O vast one!

I unite Agni with ghee, the possessor of divine virtues, fair of speed, great and mighty. Through him we shall reach the world of

Aditya and then ascend to the loftiest realm of heaven.

O Agni, both of these your wings are never wasting, wherewith you fly ever and destroy the fiends. Through them may we fly to the realms of the pious souls where have gone the first-borne Sages.

O Agni, fill the earth full with sap, fill the herbs with sap. fill the heaven with sap, fill the space with sap, full with milk make all the regions for me.

By the impulse of Savitar, with arms of Ashvins, with the hands of Pushan, with the speech of Goddess Sarasvati, with the law of Prajapati and with Agni's sole dominion I anoint you.

Agni is maintainer of law, practiser of truth, the sustainer of earth, destroyer of the foe, protector of priest and warrior classes. For his pleasure we offer this oblation, may he accept it graciously. May these herbs the Apsaras of Gandharva Agni protect and guard us. Svaha!

The Sun who conjoins day and night, lauded by the Saman, sustainer of the earth, may protect our priest and warrior classes. This oblation is for him. May his rays, the uniting and life-giving Apsaras guard as well. Svaha!

The high-minded Moon, who receives light from the Sun, is the Gandharva. May he protect our Brahmins and Kshatriyas. The bright stars of constellation Asterism are his Apsaras. May they protect us. All hail to them!

All-pervading and quick-reaching Wind is the Gandharva. The Waters and Saps which sustain life, are his Apsaras. May they guard us. All hail to them!

O Agni, you are pleasurable like the moon, you were like falcon in speed, righteous in conduct, fair pinioned, mighty, firm, settled, established in sacrifice and nourisher of all. Homage be to you. Harm us not!

O Agni, you are head and height of heaven, naval of the earth, essence of the waters and of the herbs. Life of all the beings you are, bliss-giving, and omnipresent. Homage be to you, the path and destination of all.

O omnipresent you are placed at the head of the world, your

heart is in the sea, your life is in the waters. Guard us by giving waters. Pour rain by cleaving the clouds.

May Agni, satisfied with oblations, fulfil all our desires. May this oblation quickly reach the Gods.

The knowledge which has arisen either from exertion or from judgement, or obtained from soul force, or from the meditation, or from mind, eyes or ears, hold fast to it so that you may follow the path of salvation along which have gone the first born ancient sages.

O Gods, dwelling in the loftiest heaven, to you I trust this sacrifices I offer you the fruit of this sacrifice. After you will the Sacrificer follow. Here know him in this vast and loftiest heaven.

Recognize this Sacrificer, O Gods, dwelling in the loftiest heaven. Know him well and his form. When he follows the Gods' pathway, reveal to him the fruits of righteous action!

May Agni, Vishvakarma's own, establish us among the Gods in heaven, where the streams of honey, milk and ghee flow unceasing.

Agni I am, the knower of all the created things, adorable in the form of sacrifice, immortal. My eye is ghee, in my mouth is nectar. I am the Rik, Yaju and Sama, the creator of the three realms, immortal heat I am and conveyor of burnt offerings.

I am triple vidya of the vedas in name. You are the best of the five Agnis found among the five races of men for their weal. Speed us on lengthened life.

O Indra, the slayer of the foe, conqueror of the armies, we call on you again and again for power and strength.

Like a dreadful wild beast roaming in the mountains, you have come unto us, O Indra, from the farthest land. Now encircle our foes and crush the enemies, whetting your sharp thunderbolt, and scatter all those who detest us!

Come, O Agni, come to guard us from the distant land. Come Vaishvanara, to listen to our beautiful hymns of praise!

Agni has entered all, he has entered the sky, the earth, the air and the sun. All herbs he has entered. May that Agni, pervading all, preserve us all day and night from harm.

O Agni, help us that we may have our desire fulfilled, obtain hero sons and the best riches, O wealthy one! Waging war with the enemy may we be victorious and enriched. O Ageless, may we attain your eternal glory!

O Agni, approaching you with folded and raised hands, we have this day fulfilled your longing. With contemplative mind and devoted spirit, with no unfriendly thought, O Agni, worship the Gods!

Book Eighteen

Sweet with the sweet, I mix you with Soma, strong with the strong, Amrit with Amrit, the honeyed sap with sap that is sweet as honey. O Sura, you are Soma. Dress up yourself for the Ashvins, dress up for Sarasvati, dress up for Indra, the protector!

Soma is the best sacrificial food. Pour you forth the flowing one, the friend of human beings, cleansed with the waters, and expressed with stones.

Purified by Vayu's strainer, the swift flowing Soma is Indra's intimate friend. Purified by Vayu's strainer, the Soma that has passed away backward is Indra's intimate friend.

O Soma, you are attainable through yamas and niyamas, this my heart is your place. You possess Ashvin's splendour, Sarasvati's vigour and Indra's might. I take you for enjoyment, I take you for delight and take you for greatness.

You are lustre, give me lustre. You are manly vigour, give me manly vigour. You are strength, give me strength, you are energy, give me energy. You are righteous wrath, give me righteous wrath. You are foe-conquering strength, give me foe-conquering strength.

I bruised my mother in delight when as a boy I sucked her breast. With that debt I become free from my mother. May my parents be unharmed and happy be me. You are all my associates, as such unite me with bliss, you are free from sin, let me be free from sin.

The divine physicians, the twain Ashvins, stretched out the healing sacrifice, and Sarasvati the physician with speech invested Indra with all hero-powers.

The twain Ashvins are the Soma store, Sarasvati the sacred hearth. For Indra there is his seat the spacious hall, the Sacrificer's house.

The morning sacrifice is performed with the Ashvins, the midday libation with Indra, the evening one with Sarasvati with oblations very dear to the Vishvadevas.

The Gods and the Brahmins have explained the form of sacrifice so for. All that one gains in the Sautramani rite when Soma is shed and expressed.

The learned priests promote the sacrificial rite with food, sacred grass, Soma juice, and host of heroes. May we also be happy, doing righteous deeds and offering libations to Indra with gods.

The Soma juice which the twain Ashvins brought from demon Namuchi and which Sarasvati prepared and poured out for Indra, that sweet, honeyed, brilliant juice I drink here in this sacrifice.

Whatever portion of this savoury juice is clinging here, what Indra drank with his powers, I drink and feed on that sparkling juice, with a pure mind.

O Agni, you prolong life, pour down on us food and vigorous strength. Drive you afar from us the gang of evil-doers.

O learned ones, cleanse me, make my mind, intellect and spirit clean. May all beings purify me. May Jatavedas, the all-knowing, purify me!

O Agni, effulgent one, purify me with your sacred bright fire and then purify our sacrifice!

May Pavamana, the all-knowing, ever pure and purifying others, cleanse us today, he who is purifier, render us pure.

O God Savitar, impeller of all, purify me from all sides with both of your forms and through this sacrifice.

I have heard the mention of two pathways of mortal men, the way of the Fathers and the way of Gods. One of these two paths each moving one travels, each being leaves its present parents and gets new ones.

May this my oblation cause the birth of the best progeny. May this bring ten brave sons, all fine things, physical strength, good children, cattle, fearlessness, peace and power for our weal. O Agni, confer on us food, milk and manly strength and render my progeny abundant.

Our reverend ancient Fathers Angirases, Navagvas, Atharvans, Bhrigus deserve Soma. May we follow the path of these adorable ancients, and enjoy their loving gracious favour!

Our ancient Fathers, deserving Soma, may come again and again to our sacrifice and with them let Yama happily enjoy our oblations at his will.

O Soma, you are pre-eminent for wisdom. With your wisdom you follow the straight path of gods as our leader. O Soma, our learned ancient Fathers by your wisdom and guidance obtained the best treasures among the Gods.

Associating with the Fathers, O Soma, spread out yourself abroad between heaven and earth. Therefore, let us serve you, O Indu, and let us be lord of the wealth.

O Fathers, sitting on best seats and the highest positions, these oblations we offer you, accept them and come here to help us. Come here unto us with auspicious favour, peace, happiness, and protection. Remove whatever sin and distress are within us.

I know the blissful Fathers, so knowledgeful and protector. I know the all-pervading God's immortal varied creation. May those visit this our place, who wholly dedicated to God, with their life force enjoy the nectar of self realization.

May the ancient Fathers, worthy of Soma, invited to their loved sacrifice, come here and listen our speech. May they enlighten us with their teachings and protect us.

O you all Fathers, harm us not for any sin which we might have committed through human frailty. Bowing down with the bent knees and seated on the right side we pay you homage. Accept our homage with favour.

O Fathers, grant riches to the charitably disposed men and your sons sitting beside their fair mothers. Give them a portion of your riches so that they may thereby gain energy.

O kvyahana Agni, bearer of best things to the wise, grant us that supreme wealth which you through praiseworthy speech consider fit to be granted to the wise.

Now let us offer oblations to the Fathers, to those advanced in age and wisdom and to those who followed them, to those who are engrossed in the wordly affairs and to those who dwell among the men of lofty character.

O Agni, as in the ancient days our Fathers, holy, devoted to truth, spreading knowledge, sang hymns of praise and acquired radiant wives and ground to live on, so should you remove ignorance and cast away the darkness.

Book Nineteen

You are the birth place of princely power, you are centre of royal power. Let none harm you, do not harm me!

By the impulse of God Savitar, with arms of Ashvins. with the hands of Pushan and with the healing powers of Ashvins, I anoint you for splendour, and the glory of a Brahmin. With the healing powers of Sarasvati, I anoint you for gaining food and might. I anoint you by might of Indra for gaining wealth, fame and physical strength.

Let my head be grace, my mouth be fame, my hair and beard full of brilliant sheen, my breath be light and deathlessness, my eye the king, my ear the prince.

May my tongue be bliss, my voice be power, my mind the righteous wrath, my intellect self-illumined. May joy be my fingers, delight my limbs and conquering strength my friend!

May my two arms be Indra's might, my hands be deeds of heroism, my soul and heart, a shield against attack.

May ribs be my government, my belly, shoulders, neck, hips, thighs, elbows, knees and all other members of the body my subjects.

I take my stand on princely power and kingship, on horses I am dependent, and on kine. On members I depend, on body I depend. On vital breath I am dependent, on welfare, on heaven, on earth and on sacrifice do I depend.

Whatever disrespect or fault of ours, those of others has caused your wrath, O gods, may Agni set me free from all that iniquity and fault.

If during the day or in the night I have done any act of sin, may Vayu set me free from that iniquity and fault.

If when awake or in our sleep we have committed acts of sin, may Surya set me free from that iniquity and fault.

Each fault done in a village or in forest, in society or mind, each sinful act that we have committed to Shudra or Vaishya or by preventing a religious act, even of that sin, you are the expiation!

May pure water cleanse me from my acts of sin just as one released from the stake, or a person is cleansed by bathing after toil, or as ghee is purified through a sieve.

May we be weaned away from darkness by looking upon the loftier light of the Sun, and that is among the Gods, the light that is most excellent.

O Agni, today I have sought waters and have united with their sap and thereafter have come to you. O Agni, grant me glory, wealth and progeny.

That society I regard as the perfect where work the Brahmins and the Nobles in ideal harmony, and where the gods and Agni together dwell.

Fain would I know the holy land where want and langour are not known, where in complete harmony do move Indra and Vayu side by side.

Let your soul be yoked with God, let each of your joints be frill of vigour. Let the imperishable joy be yours and let your noble nature be the Soma's guard.

Chant your lofty lauds to Indra, to Maruts, to him, the best Vritra-slayer, whereby the Gods created the Sun of radiant light that never fades.

He is the sovereign lord of all living beings upon whom the world depends. He is mighty, the mighty king. I accept you by his might and place you in my heart.

With the Sun kindled in forefront of the mornings, with forward light, ever active, growing strong, and with thirty-three gods, Indra, the thunder-wielder, passing mighty, may approach our sacrifice rejoicing.

May Indra, lord of bay steeds, full of rays, vast in extent, be sprinkled by the Adityas and the Vasus, full of expanse, occupy his seat in the east on earth and accept our burnt offerings.

Just as the child-bearing, goodly dames approach their heroic husband through open portals moving swiftly, so should the armies full of heroic warriors, yoked with might stand on all sides of Indra of manly strength and subdue the foemen.

The fair and lovely Dawn and Night, full of sap, rich-yielding, lofty ones, as they weave their long-extended thread of varied colour, adore Indra, the great, mighty, God of Gods.

May Indra lauded here, fearless and heroic come to us for our protection, and be our friend. May he whose powers are diverse, grow in strength, like the Sun to subdue the foes.

May Indra, come for protection from near or a far away place, fulfiller of desires, lord of the excellent might, guardian of mankind, thunderbolt-wielder, slayer of the foes in the battles.

May Indra come to us riding his bay steeds, the gracious one, to favour us with wealth and protection. May Maghavan abide by us in our sacrifice and in this performance of Prajapati.

I invoke Indra, Indra the protector I call in every sacrifice. Indra the mighty, worthy to be invoked reverently, Indra adored by many. May Indra come to us and bless with riches and prosperity.

May Indra, the best protector, accompanied by excellent heroes, lord of wealth, prosper us with food and happiness. May Indra, the king grant food and happiness. May Indra, the king render us all fearless and baffle the foemen and thereby may we be the lords of vigour.

The sage Vashishtha praised Indra with hymns, the mighty, the thunder-armed. May he, adored and prayed, protect our kine and heroes. O you Gods, preserve us evermore with your blessings.

O you both Ashvins, the bright and radiant Agni has been kindled, Soma has been pressed out and the milch cow Sarasvati, the bestower of the best things, has poured forth the sparkling juice, Indra's own.

Protect us by day O Ashvins, protect us by night, O you Sarasvati. O divine priests, O physicians, both of you guard Indra in accord when Soma is expressed.

The Ashvins and Sarasvati united together made Indra wax strong with oblations, who slew demon Vala with Namuchi of Asura birth.

Waxing him mighty with sacred oblations and burnt offerings, Sarasvati and the twain Ashvins sang Indra's songs of praise.

The great protector Indra snatched away by force power, strength and wealth from Namuchi, and Savitar and Varuna bestowed boons of strength and wealth on the liberal sacrificer.

May both the Ashvins, fair of form, the doer of righteous deeds, knowledge bestowing Sarasvati and the foe-slaying Indra, help us in our sacrifice.

O Agni, we pour sacred oblation into your mouth as Soma into a receptacle and ghee into a ladle. Vouchsafe us riches, strength winning, blessed with heroes, lofty wealth, full of glory lauded by men.

O twain Ashvins, wedded to truth, O Rudra, come to this house with kine and horses, the sure protectors of this sacrificer.

O longed-for Ashvins, lead us on to wealth full of shining gold and service.

May Sarasvati, pure and purifying, rich in food and wisdom, promote our sacrifice.

She, the inspirer of truthful speech, awakener of the best intellect, Sarasvati, protects our sacrifice.

Sarasvati, rich in knowledge, illuminates the vast ocean of learning and the pious thoughts.

O Indra, wondrously bright, come and enjoy these libations so enjoyable, prepared and purified by these fingers.

Well urged by the holy singer, sped by the sage, come here, O Indra, to the hymns of oblation-offering priest!

Book Twenty

O Varuna, hear this my prayer, be ever gracious unto us. Longing for help I yearn for you.

O all-knowing, most-adored, Agni, oblation-bearer, effulgent, put away far from us Varuna's displeasure, God, remove from us far away those who hate us.

Be you the closest unto us, O Agni, our bosom friend while now this rich dawn is breaking. Reconcile Varuna to us, be bounteous and grant us your compassion and listen our prayers quickly.

We call on Mother Aditi, the womb of those who steadfastly observe their vows, protector from various attacks, ageless, the promoter of truth, the form of happiness, we invoke the boundless Mother for our protection.

May we ascend this vessel for our weal, flawless, divine, rowed with fine oars, vast and all-accommodating, comfortable, never leaking and built by master builders.

O Varuna, O Mitra, you gracious pair, sprinkle our pasturage with rich sap, and with honey, the realms of the air.

O Mitra-Varuna, ever youthful, stretch your arms hearing my prayer and let our span of life be extended, sprinkle the pasture of our cattle with sap and make me glorious in the world.

May Agni, well kindled with fuel, bright, excellent, and adorable, and the Gayatri verse grant power, long life, kine and riches.

The two Dawns of great splendour, all the immortal gods, the Trishtup verse and the bull that carries burden on his back, here in this sacrifice, grant us strength and long life!

Agni and mid Air, the two divine Hotar priests, the twin Physicians, Indra's own friends, grant us strength and long life!

The Earth, Sarasvati and the three intellects, the Maruts, a milch cow, the metre Viraj and a bull grant us strength and long life!

The eight Vasus, praised with triple Stoma, and Rathantara along with Spring season and Gods, grant us long life and splendour in the light of Indra!

May Rudras with Summer season, and Gods, lauded in Panchadash Stoma of fifteen verse Brihat, grant us strength, long life and fame in Indra!

May the Adityas with the Rainy Season and Gods lauded in Saptadash Stoma of seventeen verses Virupa with folk, grant us manly strength, longevity, and sacrifice in Indra!

May the Maruts with Autumn Season and Gods, praised in a hymn of twenty-seven verses, the Sakvaris, grant us longevity, strength and sacrifice in Indra!

Sarasvati offered the seat of sacred grass to Indra, the divine and virtuous, the two Ashvins gave Indra splendour, like brilliance of the eyes, for gain of wealth, and performed sacrifice to honour Indra, so should you perform the sacrifice.

The celestial Doors, the twain Ashvins, the Physicians and Sarasvati gave breath into Indra's nostrils and manly strength for gain of wealth and performed the yajna, so should you perform the sacrifice.

Just as the beautiful Dawn and Night, the Goddesses, the two Ashvins and Sarasvati gave strength and speech in the mouth of Indra for gain of wealth and performed yajna, so should you perform the sacrifice.

Just as both the nursing Goddesses Morning and Evening, both the Ashvins and Goddess Sarasvati making Indra grow strong gave him fame and power for gain of wealth and performed yajna, so should you perform the sacrifice.

Just as the two Goddesses, well-yielding cows, divine Sarasvati, the healing Physicians, the two Ashvins formed Indra's guards and from their breasts through sacrifice gave him strength and brilliant light for gain of wealth, so should you by sacrifice.

Today this man, the Sacrificer cooking oblations, cooking sacrificial food, binding to the sacrificial post a goat for the Ashvins, a ram for the Sarasvati, a bull for Indra's love, pressing out Soma juice for the Ashvins, Sarasvati and Indra, the best protector, has chosen Agni as his Hotar priest.

Today the God of Herbs has rendered a good service to the Ashvins with a goat, to Sarasvati with a ram and to Indra with a bull. The Gods have accepted the sacrifice, they have accepted the cooked offerings and have grown strong with these oblations. They, Sarasvati, Ashvins and Indra have enjoyed the Soma juices.

O Seer, foremost of the Seers, descendant of the Seers, this Sacrificer has chosen you today, of all the gods assembled here together saying that you shall, O Agni, win for him by sacrifice the choice-worthy treasures among the Gods. O God Agni, whatever gifts the gods have given, kindly you do approve and grant. O Hotar Agni, you have been sent as a man, selected and sent for benediction, for good speech, speak good words!

Book Twenty-one

You are effulgence, you are splendour, immortal, and protector of life, therefore, protect my life. I accept you by impulse of God Savitar, with the arms of Ashvins and the hands of Pushan.

In this Soma sacrifice is present with us this girdle, which our ancient seers assumed in religious rites in the beginning, declaring the relation between the Primordial Cause and the created things.

O God, you are famous, you are the universe, you are the controller and sustainer of all the worlds. You, Sacrificer go and consecrate by Svaha to Agni Vaishvanara of vast fame.

We contemplate the divine virtues of God Savitar with our mind so that he may stimulate our thoughts.

I invoke for protection the effulgent, all creating god Savitar. He knows all, stimulates all and is refuge of all the Gods.

We invoke and praise the all-creating God Savitar, the all-seeing to obtain the lofty wisdom wherewith to discriminate truth from untruth.

Having eulogized Savitar, the creator of the universe, we seek his gifts in riches, who knows all our desires.

I invoke the liberal giver Savitar, protector of the men devoted to the vows, full of splendour on all sides, the God Savitar, the cheerer of the Gods feast.

The proximity of God Savitar cheers the company of the Gods, with prayer we desire riches from him.

Agni well kindled with hymns of praise conveys our oblations to the Gods. O Adhvaryu, awake Agni well, the deathless God!

The oblation-bearer, immortal, wise, messenger of the Gods and auspicious Agni, approaches us with the thought.

I place Agni in front, the oblation-bearer, envoy of Gods and him here I address. Here let him make the Gods sit.

O all-pervading and purifying Pavamana. you have verily generated the Sun and sustain waters with their strength and abundant vivifying milk in the kine.

O horse, you are mighty by your mother, eminent by your father. You are indeed a horse, you are a courser, giver of pleasure, slayer of the foe, you are a yoke horse, you are splendid, you are manly minded. You are called Vayu and Shishu. Follow the path of the Adityas. O Gods, possessed of divine virtues, O Guardians of the Quarters, protect this sacrificial, anointed horse for the Gods. Here is delight, here is pleasure, here is contentment and here is self-satisfaction.

Hail to Prajapati, hail to Prajapati the foremost, hail to Prajapati, the supreme, this is for Prajapati, this is for the Adityas who know our mind! Hail to Aditi, hail to bliss giving Aditi! Hail to Sarasvati! Hail to purifying Sarasvati! Hail to mighty Sarasvati! Hail to Pushan! Hail to Pushan of the excellent objects! Hail to Pushan the sustainer and nourisher of mankind! Hail to Tvashtar! Hail to Tvashtar, the guardian of speed! Hail to Tvashtar of many forms. Hail to Vishnu! Hail to Vishnu, ever protected and ever protecting! Hail to Vishnu who in subtle form pervades all!

O Brahman, let there be born Brahmins in the land, illustrious for their Vedic knowledge, let there be born the Princes, heroic, skilled archer, piercing the foemen with darts, mighty heroes, the kine rich in milk, the ox good at carrying burden, the fleet courser, the woman skilled in household work. Let Prajanya pour forth rain as we desire, let our fruit-bearing trees ripen, let acquisition and preservation of property be secured for us.

Hail to Madhu, the month of Chaitra! Hail to Madhava, the month of Vaisakh! Hail to Shukra, the month of purifying Jeystha! Hail to Nabhas, the month of Ashadha! Hail to Nabhashya, the month of Shravana! Hail to Isha, the month of Bhadrapada! Hail to Urja, the month of Kartika! Hail to Sahas, the month of Agahan! Hail to Sahashya, the month of Pausha! Hail to Tapas, the month of Magha! Hail to Tapasya, the month of Falgun! Hail to Amhasaspati, the intercalary or the thirteenth month!

May life increase by sacrifice, Hail! May breath improve by sacrifice, Hail! May downward breath, diffusive breath, upward breath and breath digestive thrive by sacrifice, Hail! May vision, hearing, speech, mind, soul, self-devotion, light heaven, hymns and sacrifice succeed, all Hail!

Hail to the only One! Hail to the Two, Purusha and Prahriti! Hail to Hundred! Hail to Hundred and one! Hail to Daybreak! Hail to Bliss!

Book Twenty-two

Who by his grandeur has become the sole Ruler and Sovereign of the moving world that breaths and slumbers, he, the God is Sovereign lord of these men and cattle. Let us adore with devotion, him, the embodiment of bliss!

You are realistic by efforts, I accept you, O Prajapati as protector, this is your place. The Moon is your greatness. Your majesty can be seen reflected in the night and the year. This majesty can be seen in the Earth and Agni, in the stars and the Moon. Hail to your majesty, O Prajapati, and to the Gods, all Hail!

They steadfast and free from anger, move about performing sacrifice and yoke their mighty sun-like souls to God. The lights shine in the sky.

Just as they yoke on both sides of the chariot two beautiful steeds, tawny, stout, bearer of the rider from one place to another, so do the sages yoke their sense organs, soul and the vital breath to God.

When the horse, swift like wind, has reached the beautiful form that Indra loves, and the waters, O singer of hymn, by this path bring you back our Steed here.

May the Vasus besprinkle you with Gayatri verse, may the Rudras anoint you with Trishtup Verse. May the Adityas besprinkle you with Jagati verse. Eat you this food cooked from barley, from cow's milk and its products, O Earth, Ether, Heaven and Gods, enjoy this food, O Prajapati!

Who moves singly and alone? Who is brought forth to life again? What is the cure of cold? What is the great field for growing?

The Sun moves singly and alone, the Moon is brought forth to life again. Fire is the cure of cold. Earth is that great field.

What was the thought in the beginning? What was the bird of the mighty size? Who was she, the slippery matron? Who absorbs light?

Heaven was the primary thought, the steed was the mighty bird. The Earth is the slippery matron. Night absorbs all light and forms.

Agni was all-seeing, with him they performed sacrifice. He won this world in which Agni is. This world shall be your place of refuge, this you shall win. Drink these saps for this. Vayu was all-seeing with him they performed sacrifice. He won this world in which Vayu is. This shall be your place of refuge, this you shall win. Breathe you these vayus. Surya was all-seeing, with him the Gods sacrificed. He won this world in which Surya is. This world shall be you refuge, this you shall win. Enjoy you, these beams of the Sun!

We invoke you, lord of troops. We invoke you the lord of the beloved ones. We call you the lord of treasures, the lord of wealth. O God, all beings abide in you. You are my precious wealth. I know you full well, the bearer of golden germ and sustainer of nature for you keep the world safe as in a womb, you generate all.

I have magnified with songs of praise the Purusha white as curd, ever winning, strong and fast like a steed, Dadhikravan. May he sweeten our mouth and prolong the life we have to live.

Who flays and dissects you? Who teaches you the various texts? Who comforts your organs? And who imparts you peace?

May the Spring season, etc. in due course of time, giver of peace, impart you necessary knowledge, and pacify you by means of the splendour of the year.

May the Half months, and the Months flay and dissect your age and limbs. May day and night, and the Maruts granting you felicity remove your evil thoughts in order to give you peace.

May the learned Adhvaryu impart you special teaching and thereby eradicate your faults. May they examine the joints of your limbs. May the ladies in your connection impart you similar teaching.

May the Sky, Earth, Space, Air, Sun and Moon with the Stars of the heaven remove each of your faults and failings, and prepare a nice, successful world for you.

Well be it with your upper organs, well be it with your lower organs. Well be it with your bones and marrow and with all your body.

What's the lustre like that of the Sun? What Lake is equal to the sea? What is more spacious than the Earth? What is that which is beyond measure?

Brahma is lustre like the Sun. Heaven is a flood to match the ocean. The Sun is vaster than the Earth. Beyond all measure is the cow.

O friend of the Gods, I enquire for information, if you in spirit has pervaded the universe? Is this whole universe contained in the three strides in which Vishnu is worshipped?

I pervade those three strides of Vishnu in which is contained this whole universe. The Earth and Heaven I circle in a moment with a part of my strength, even beyond Heaven am I.

What are the things which Purusha has entered into? What are the things which Purusha has contained within him? The riddle we propose to you, O Brahman. Pray tell and unravel the mystery.

Within five things has Purusha found entrance. These things has Purusha within himself established. This is the thought I return in answer and yet you are not superior to me in wisdom.

Who knows the central point of the world? Who knows the heaven and the earth and the vast mid region between these? Who knows the creator of the mighty Sun? Who knows the Moon and whence she was engendered?

I know the centre of this world, I know heaven and earth and the vast mid region between them. I know the creator of the mighty Surya. I know the Moon and whence she was engendered.

I ask you of the earth's most extreme limit. Where is the centre of the world, I question you? I ask you of the strength of the mighty Purusha? I ask of the loftiest heaven where Speech abides.

This altar is the earth's extremist limit This sacrifice is the centre and navel of the world. This Soma, the king of herbs, is the strength of the mighty Purusha. This Brahman is the loftiest abode where Speech abides.

God who has engendered the Sun, the mighty and self-existent One, the first within the mighty flood. He laid down the timely embryo from which Prajapati was born. You all should worship him.

Book Twenty-three

By whose might these snow-clad mountains are standing, and men call sea full of sap his possession? Whose are these stretched arms. Whose are these heavenly quarters? What God shall we adore with our oblation?

He who is the giver of vital breath, of strength and power, he whose commandments all the Gods obey, whose shade is life immortal, the lord of death. What God shall we adore with oblation?

May auspicious powers come to us from all directions, unhindered, ceaselessly and ever victorious. May thereby the Gods be with us, day by day, our guardians, for our weal with their constant care.

May their auspicious favour be ours. May the bounty of the righteous Gods fill us with virtues. May we seek the friendship of the Gods with devotion. May they grant us longevity that we may live.

We call the gods here with hymns composed by our ancient fathers. We invoke Bhaga, the friendly Daksh, Mitra, Aditi, Aryaman, Varuna, Soma and the Ashvins twain. May auspicious Sarasvati vouchsafe us weal.

May the Wind blow to us happy medicines. May the mother Earth and our father Heaven grant us these, and also the happy stones that press out Soma juice. May both Ashvins give us bliss on hearing this our prayer.

Him we call who reigns supreme, the lord of all that stands or moves, inspires of the spirit. May Pushan, the nourisher of all, our keeper and guardian, infallible promote the growth of our wealth for good.

May the mighty Indra, so illustrious and vast, give us prosperity, may Pushan, the lord of wealth grant us prosperity. May the vast, unassailable lord God prosper us. May Brihaspati grant us prosperity.

May the Maruts, strong and fast like steeds, pervading the heavens, the generator of the clouds, moving for the weal of the people, whose tongue is Agni, their eye the Sun, come here for our protection!

O Gods, may we listen with our ears and see with our eyes what is good! With limbs firm and bodies stout may we extolling you lead a life appointed by the gods.

O Gods, may we live in your company for full hundred years. Let not our bodies decay before that period, during which period our sons become fathers in their turn. Break you not in midst our course of fleeting life!

Aditi is heaven, Aditi is the atmosphere, Aditi is the Mother of all, the Sire and the Son. Aditi is Gods, Aditi is the five tribes of men. Aditi is all that has been born and all that shall be born.

May not Varuna, Aryaman, Mitra, Ribhukshan, Indra, Ayu and Mitra ever slight or desert us. We declare amid the congregations the divine virtues of the Gods, full of splendour, strong like flying steed and mighty ones.

When they lead thrice round the sacrificial steed, that is sent to Gods as proper oblation, a goat precedes him, the proper oblation of Pushan, announcing the sacrifice to the Gods.

Invoker, presiding Hotar-priest, atoner, Agni kindler, Soma expresser singer and sage, with freedom from sin may boundless Aditi grant us. May this noble Steed with our oblations gain us lordship!

With Indra and all these gods as our aid, we shall bring these worlds under our rule. May the twelve Adityas, forty-nine Maruts, Indra and all the gods grant us healing medicines. May Indra with the Adityas make our sacrifice, our bodies and our sons virtuous.

Book Twenty-four

O Brihaspati, grant us that which foe deserves not, which shines splendid among the people, give that, O son of Rita, you effulgent with strength, that treasure splendid grant us.

O Indra, come Vritra-slayer, drink of this Soma, lord of hundred sacrifices, pressed out with stones. I accept you for the love of Indra whose wealth is kine. This is your place. I accept you for him.

We pray to and Adore Vaishvanara, the immortal, the lord of light and sacrifice, truthful, effulgent, protector of beings, the lord of the world. You practise yama and niyama. I accept you for Vaishvanara as the lord of kine. This is your home. I establish you for the satisfaction of Vaishvanara.

May we ever enjoy the favour of Vaishvanara, the sovereign lord of all living things. He, the refuge of all the world, sprung from this earth he looks upon. He is engaged in the weal of the world along with the Sun.

Agni is Pavaman, Sage, Hotar-priest of all the five Races. To him of great riches we pray. You are imbued with yamas and niyamas.

May Indra, the mighty and thunder-armed protect us well and slay the wicked who detest us. You are the lord of yamas and niyamas. I accept you for Indra's satisfaction. This is your home. I establish you for the sake of Indra.

Just as the cows low in their stall for their calves so do we sing the lauds of Indra, our lord and king, who removes affliction, the checker of assault, who enjoys riches and food.

Honour Agni, the king, the effulgent, who carries oblation with speed. Like the chief queen of a king, riches and food stuffs proceed from him!

O Agni, the Seasons spread your sacrifice, the Months guard your offerings. May the Year strengthen your sacrifice and keep our children safe!

In the seclusion of mountain slopes and the confluence of the streams Indra manifests himself with a song.

O Soma, high is your birth, your seat is in heaven but you have obtained a home and great renown on this firm earth.

O Soma, finder of home and freedom flow for Indra whom we pray, flow for Varuna and the band of Maruts!

Struggling to win with Soma we obtain all the wealth from the unrighteous foe we win all the glories of mankind.

May we be rich in strong, heroic sons, stout kine, strong steeds, cattle, each of our desires and blessings, in quadrupeds, in men around us. May the Gods protect and guide our sacrifice in seasons.

O Agni, bring you here the longing wives of the gods to enjoy oblations and also Tvashtar to drink the Soma draught!

O Nestar, the priest, leading the sacrificer's wife, accept our sacrifice, enjoy Soma according to the season, you are the giver of wealth!

O Priest, being the river of wealth, drink the Soma draught according to the season and so should you prepare the draught, perform sacrifice and attain respect.

O Indra, come you here unto us. this Soma is for you, approach it. Protect it ever and drink of it without stop. Sit you down on this seat of sacred grass in the sacrifice, and take you down these draughts into your stomach, O Indra!

O invoked Dames of the Gods, come here and sit on the sacred grass to enjoy yourselves as at home. O god Tvashtar, enjoy yourself the joyful draught in the gladsome company of Gods and Goddesses.

O Soma, flow forth in most sweet and enjoyable stream. For you, O Indra, is this juice pressed out to drink!

O Soma, fiend-queller, friend of all, you have in the vat attained your iron formed home, safe and dignified!

Book Twenty-five

O Agni, may years, seasons, half years and the seers strengthen you. Shine forth with your divine effulgence and illumine all the four quarters of the heaven.

Shine you, O Agni, make this seeker after knowledge wake, rise up erect for grand and great fortune. Be them uninjured who worship you. Let your priests be glorious now beside them!

The priests present here elect you as their leader. Be you gracious to them in this election. Subdue our foes, O slayer of the rivals. Agni, be alert and watchful in your house and keep us also so with never-ceasing care.

Removing them who kill, removing the foemen, removing the thoughtless ones, remove those who detest us. Agni, sweep away all our woe and distress and grant us opulence with heroic men about us!

O Agni, invincible, effulgent, royal one, shine here unconquerable Jatavedas! Illumine all the regions, chase away all our griefs. Guard us well for prosperity!

O Brihaspati, O Savitar, give this man knowledge, sharpen his intellect more and more. Raise him to high felicity, in him let all the Gods rejoice in triumph.

O Brihaspati, release us from the fruit of sins in the birth to come, free us from the fear of Yamraj in this birth. May Agni, the two Ashvins, the Gods' physicians chase away the fear of death from this man.

Splendid are the fuel sticks, lofty and brilliant are the flames of Agni, splendid is Agni, so fair to look on.

Let Agni, the protector of bodies, all-possessing, the best among the Gods, sprinkle our paths with ghee and sweet sap through rain.

Extolling, the bearer of knowledge, ne, the Adhvaryu comes here. While the sacrifice progresses he offers oblations to Agni with ladles full of ghee.

Let this Adhvaryu pay homage to Agni's greatness, so daintily fed. He, truly, is the giver of pleasurable things, the best wealth-giver and the wisest protector.

May Night and Dawn, his heavenly consorts, protect in our home this sacrifice of ours.

May both the divine Hotars, Agni and Vayu, greet this our lofty sacrifice, the tongue of Agni. May they conduct this sacrifice well.

May the three mighty Goddesses, Ida, Sarasvati and Bharati, lauded with hymns, be seated here on this sacred grass.

May Tvashtar pour forth on us the wondrous and productive wealth full of strength, splendour and merits.

The God whom both the Heaven and Earth have brought forth for the acquisition of wealth, whom celestial Goddess has appointed for our wealth, his yoked horses wait on Vayu, the splendid lord of riches.

When the mighty waters containing the universal germ came into being, generating the Sun, there was one Spirit present in all the forces of nature. What God shall we adore with our oblation?

God with his might then surveyed the floods containing productive force and generative germ. He among the gods is one supreme God and none beside him. What God shall we adore with our oblation?

O Vayu, riding which teams of horses you seek him who offers sacrifice within his house, riding that come to our sacrifice to grant us pleasurable wealth, heroic son, and gifts of kine and horses.

Riding your harnessed teams in hundreds, in thousands come to our sacrifice and solemn rite, O Vayu, to gladden yourself with our oblation. O Gods, preserve us evermore with propitious blessings!

Come here car-borne, O Vayu, come to us for receiving sweet Soma juice offered in the sacrifice, visit you the house where Soma has been pressed out.

Come you, O Vayu, riding your thousand cars, come to us chariot borne, to enjoy the Soma-draught.

Come you by one or two, three or ten, twenty or thirty chariots to our sacrifice. Come unto us and unyoke your team of horses here.

O Vavy, lord of truth, Tvashtar's son-in-law, your means of protection we elect, O god wondrous!

Like unmilked kine, we sing your praise aloud, O Hero, the lord of animate and inanimate beings, and so beautiful to look on.

O Maghavan, none other like you in heaven or on earth has been, nor shall ever be. Desiring horses, kine and power we call you offering libations, O Indra, lord of splendour.

O Indra, we, the poets and sacrificers call you alone. In war men call on you the lord of heroes, in the race of the steeds we call on you.

O wondrous lord Indra, thunder-armed, lauded as mighty, wielder of thunderbolt, grant us kine, chariot horses, ever to be the conqueror.

O ever prosperous and wonderful friend, with that potent protection and with what mighty company will you come unto us?

O Indra, you are the guard of your friends who laud you, come unto us, your devotees with your hundred means of protection.

Sing at every sacrifice the glory of Agni, for obtaining strength. Come, let us praise with our hymns the wise and immortal Agni, him, the well beloved friend.

O Agni, lord of might, giver of the best home, protect us through the first hymn, protect us through the second one, protect us through the third hymn. Guard us through three hymns, protect us through your hymns, O God.

O Adhvaryu, let us adore Agni, the son of strength, our friend, with gifts of oblations. He is our wellwisher and aids us in battles, he is the saviour of our bodies.

O Agni, you are Samvatsara, you are Parivatsara, you are Idvatsara, Idatasa you are and Vatsara. Dawns may prosper you! May Day and Night prosper you. May Half months, Months, Seasons and the Years prosper you! You arrange their coming and going hence and send them forth on their ordered courses. You collect all·the sources of protection. With that divinity lie steady like Angiras.

Book Twenty-six

On the earth's centre, at the place of sacrifice, the Hotar worships Indra with kindled fuel sticks. Agni, the mighty lord is kindled on the height of heaven. May he enjoy oblation of ghee in Hotar s worship.

Him the Hotar worships, him the self born, the mighty lord, the guardian of our beings. Indra, ever invincible, the conqueror, knower of himself and the heaven, virtuous, full of delight. Let him enjoy oblation of ghee.

Let the Hotar worship Indra. the thunder-wielder, render of the enemy forts, mighty, immortal, lauded, and invoked by the gods. Let him enjoy the oblation of ghee.

Let Hotar worship him, Indra, the Bull among Gods who sits on the sacred grass, doer of many deeds. May he sit down on the sacred Grass with the eight Vasus. eleven Rudras and twelve Adityas as his friends. Let him enjoy the oblation of ghee.

The Hotar performed yajna to Night and Morning, the two milch cows of Indra, the mighty Mothers. They have strengthened their calf Indra with nourishment of lustre like two mother cows of a common calf. Let him enjoy oblation of ghee.

The learned priest performed yajna to Ashvins, the divine Physicians, friends of Indra, wise, the sages, far famed among the Gods who healed Indra with oblation and gave him the mighty strength.

The learned priest performed sacrifice to the three Goddesses Ida, Sarasvati and Bharti with oblation of ghee. May these three, the divine consorts of Indra enjoy oblation of ghee in this sacrifice.

The learned priest offered sacrifice to Tvashtar, full of opulence, remover of diseases, good performer of yajna, of many forms, handsome, mighty and lord of wealth. May Tvashtar who gave Indra wonderful strength, enjoy this offered sacrifice of ghee.

The learned priest sacrificed to the Lord of Forests, the bringer of peace, doer of many deeds, the wise and friend of Indra. May he enjoying oblation of ghee, sweeten our sacrifice with savoury butter and balm our paths in order to make them easy and smooth.

Morning and Night, the Goddesses called upon Indra as the sacrifice began. May they, well beloved, our wellwishers, make the divine subjects come here. May they enjoy oblation of ghee for enriching the Sacrificer in wealth and position.

Both the Goddesses who give wealth and are gracious, have increased radiant Indra's strength. One removes sin and distress, the other gives acceptable riches and wealth to the sacrificer. May they enjoy oblation for the gain of wealth and position to the Sacrificer.

Both the goddesses, giver of food and sap, the milch cows have nourished Indra with their milk. One gives food and energy, the other feast and sap. They bring strength-giving sacrifice and give many portions, blending old energy with the new and new with the old. They are the givers of cherished wealth. May they enjoy oblation for increasing the wealth and status of the Sacrificer.

Both the divine Hotars, increased radiant Indra's might. They have brought wealth and gifts freed from the sinful thieves for the Sacrifices. May they enjoy sacrifice for increasing the wealth and status of the Sacrificer.

The three Goddesses have increased lord Indra's strength. Bharati has touched the heaven, Sarasvati, the companion of the Rudras, has enriched the sacrifice with wealth, and Ida has touched the earth.

The God Vanaspati with golden leaves, with honeyed bows and with fine fruits has increased lord Indra's might. He has touched the sky with his top, with mid portion the firmament and with root has established the earth. May he enjoy this sacrifice for increase of the Sacrificer's wealth and his firm establishment.

Bright Agni, the fulfilller of the best wishes has increased radiant Indra's night. May he, also called Svishtakrit today, making fine offerings, perform the sacrifice for us. May he enjoy the sacrifice for Sacrificer's gain of wealth and promotion of his status.

The priest sarificed to Agni, and Indra well kindled, venerable, giver of excellent strength, increasing his might, lending him the

Gayatri verse, a cow of one and half years and vigour. May the Sacrificer with indra enjoy ghee. So should you also perform the sacrifice.

The priest sacrificed to him who rends forts, the germ that Aditi conceived in her womb, Indra, the pure who gives life and strength, lending him great strength, the Ushnish verse, a two year old ox and strength. May he enjoy butter. So should you also perform sacrifice with oblation of ghee.

The priest sacrificed to Soma and Indra, laudable, praised, Vritra-slayer, strength-giver, lending him strength, Anushtup verse, a cow of thirty months and vigour.

The priest performed sacrifice to Indra, deathless, who sits on the sacred grass, nourisher, strength-giver, immortal, dear, beautiful, lending him strength, Brihati verse and a cow of thee years.

The priest sacrificed to the Goddesses Night and Morning, beautiful to look on, adorned well, of varied hue, to Indra, life-bestowing, lending him strength, the Trishtup verse and a bullock four years old able to carry burden.

Divine Agni, who makes fair rites, has lended strength to Indra, the giver of strength. The God has strengthened the God giving him Atichhandas verse, might and sway. May he enjoy oblation of ghee for the sake of the Sacrificer's wealth.

Book Twenty-seven

O Agni, all-knowing, well-kindled, enjoying tasty and sweet butter, fast moving, decking the minds of the learned. O Jatavedas, convey to the Gods, what is dear to them.

Sprinkling the paths with ghee that lead to the Gods, may the Courser go to the Gods knowing their oblation. O Steed, may the quarters of heaven attend you! Bestow food on this sacrificer!

O Steed, you are worthy of adoration and obeisance. You are swift and sacred for the sacrifice. May Vasus and Agni in accord with gods, take you, the contended bearer, to the abode of Gods.

May Aditi, the boundless, vast, far-famed, seated on the wide-spread sacred grass, imbued with divine powers, bliss-giving, accordant, grant strength and happiness.

O priests, may these Doors of the hall of sacrifice, divine, full of splendour, auspicious, of varied forms, lofty and wide, unfolding, well fitted and sonorous, richly decorated, offer us easy entrance and exit.

The two Goddesses Dawn and Night, established between Varuna and Mitra, rich in varied hue and wealth, intimate with the force of Sacrificer, I establish here in this sacrifice, the home of Truth.

I have pleased both these divine Hotars, chariot-borne, fair-complexioned, who behold all the world. They, the ordainers of sacrificial rules, inspirer of noble acts, have spread the light in every direction.

May Goddess Bharati with the Adityas promote our sacrifice. Sarasvati with the Rudras be our aid, and Ida protect our yajna. O divine goddesses, establish our rite among the Gods.

May the Sun, balmed with ghee, go himself, seeking his abode among the Gods in seasons. May Vanaspati, the lord of herbs, convey our savoury oblation to Gods, tasted by Agni.

O Agni, increased with Prajapati's brilliant fervour and born immediately from the friction of fuel sticks, you protect our yajna. Precede you unto the gods and Sadhyas bearing consecrated offering so that they may enjoy our oblation.

O fleet Steed, when you sprang to life neighing from the ocean or from the vaporous atmosphere, you had limbs of the deer and wings of the eagle. O Courser, you deserve applause for your high birth.

The Steed with first harnessed by Trita and given by Yama and Indra was the first to mount. Gandharva held his briddle. The Sun fashioned forth the Courser.

O Courser, you are Yama, Aditya are you, Trita are you by three secret operations. You are specially united with Soma, and it is said that there are three bonds in heaven that hold you.

O Steed, it is said that Surya is your loftiest generator. Three bonds are said to be there in heaven to bind you, three in the waters and three in the atmosphere, O Courser of the loftiest birth.

O Courser, here I see the places where they groomed you, I behold here the prints of your winning hooves. Here are the auspicious reins that guide you. They guard you who protect this sacred rite.

O Steed, I recognized your soul from distance, a Bird soaring up from below. I saw your head soaring, striving upward by paths untouched by dust and pleasant to travel.

I behold here your beautiful, matchless form, eager to win the foe and the food produced from the earth. Whenever one brings you fodder, you swallow the herbs. O you most voracious eater!

O Steed, the car follows you, the bridegroom follows you and the fortune of maidens comes after you. The people in groups follow you seeking your friendship, the Gods dwell upon your pattern of strength.

Lustrous and golden are his horns, his feet are of iron. Even though swift Indra is less fleet than he, Gods came only to Indra's sacrifice who first of all rode the Steed.

Thin bellied, symmetrical, with rounded haunches, mighty of strength, the divine Steeds of Surya's chariot put forth their mettle like flying swans when they obtained the heavenly pathways.

O Courser, your body is formed for flight, your spirit is swift like the wind, your horns are spread wide on all sides, they move restlessly like wild fire.

The fleet and dexterous Steed has come forth for sacrifice, with a contemplative mind. He follows a goat, his kin, and the sages and the poets follow after.

He is come to the noblest abode, is come to his Parents. Today he shall reach the gods, most welcome. He bestows best gifts on liberal givers and sacrificers.

Agni, who preceded Gods, prepared the sacrifice as soon as he was born. May the Gods enjoy our oblations made sacred according to the law and guidance of the priest.

O men, giving light where no light was, and form where no form was, Agni was born together with the Dawns.

Then a warrior goes to battle with his mail on, he looks like a thunderous rain cloud. O hero, be you victorious with unharmed body. May the protection of your armour guard you.

The bow string, close to the bow's ear, fain to speak whispers like a woman holding her beloved in her close enbrace, this bow string that preserves us in the battle.

The bow and its string meeting together like a woman and her husband bear like parents upon their bosom the arrow, their son. May the two bow ends in accord scatter asunder swiftly the foemen we hate.

Our fathers who gave us birth, lived in harmony, patient and powerful in distress, untired, armed with wonderful army and sharp shafts, free, invincible and conquerors of the enemy hosts.

O Agni, this day enkindled in the house of man, invoke Gods. O Jatavedas, best observant, virtuous, envoy of Gods, high spirited and wise, bring the Gods here in sacrifice!

Called upon, praiseworthy, deserving worship, you are the invoker of Gods, best sacrificer, perform this sacrifice to the Gods, O Agni.

Let the vast Doors of the hail be widely opened, like virtuous wives who decorate themselves with ornaments for their noble husbands. O high, divine, all-inspiring Doors, admit all the Gods and provide them easy approach.

Let the Dawn and Night, respectively of bright and pale hue, close to each other, be seated on their seats, the divine dames, high-born, decked in gold, sacrifice-worthy, great, fair and of lustrous beauty.

May both the divine Hotars, sweet voiced, inducer of men in deeds of sacrifice come to our site, the singers, knower of the Vedas, the revealer of the light in the east with their direction.

May Bharti, Ida and Sarasvati come unto us speedily from all sides. May all these three Goddesses executors of fine deeds be seated on the sacred grass.

O learned and wise priest, bring here quickly, now God Tvashtar, who knows that God who created heaven and earth, the generator of various beings with their various forms.

May the learned Brahmins and the Fathers worthy for Soma draughts, auspicious ones, matchless both in heaven and earth, protect us against evil. May Pushan, strengthener of order, protect us. May the wicked never be our master.

Guard well in the battle where arrow and weapons are swift, let our bodies be strong like stone. May Soma kindly instruct us, and Aditi guard us well.

O lord of the wood, O Vanaspati, be strong, be a victorious hero bearing us. Show forth your mettle, yoked with brave and let your leader win all the booty of the battle.

Grant us the strength of the Sun and the Earth, the vitality of the forest trees, the force of the saps and waters. Fill your chariot with mighty weapons shining like the rays of the Sun.

O you Thunderbolt, Vanguard of the Marut hosts, yoked to Varuna and son of Mitra, accept these our gifts we offer, receive like god our oblations.

O you thundering Drum, send forth your roar through heaven and earth, throughout the world along its breadth, and drive away a foe, ye, very far, our enemies, accordant with Gods and Indra.

O War drum, thunder out strength and fill us full of vigour, drive away all dangers and misfortunes. O you, Fist of Indra, render us firm and steadfast, and make them weep who war against us.

O War drum, drive hence away the enemy troops and bring here back our troops safe and victorious. The thundering war drum signals the waging of the war. O Indra, let our warriors riding steeds and chariots return together in triumphs.

Book Twenty-eight

Purusha has a thousand heads, a thousand eyes, a thousand feet. Pervading the earth on every side he transgresses the universe.

Purusha in truth is all this, what has been and what yet shall be. He is the lord of all that which grows still greater by food.

The visible and the invisible worlds reveal his mighty grandeur, yet he is greater than all this. All the worlds are but one-fourth of him, three-fourths eternal lies within him.

With three-fourths of his grandeur Purusha sprang up. With one-fourth of it he created the universe, and then he moved forth to every side pervading all that is animate and inanimate.

He created Virat from himself and then Purusha from Virat. When born he spread out to west and east transgressing the boundaries of the earth.

From that great venerable Purusha were generated curd and ghee. He fashioned forth the animals and birds both wild and tame.

From that Purusha, unto whom people make sacrifice, were born the Richas and Sama hymns. Therefrom then sprang up the spells and formulas of Atharvaveda and the Yajus.

From Purusha were born horses, and from him were born all cattle with two rows of teeth. From him were born kine, from him were produced goats and sheep.

They embalmed the Virat Purusha as victim on the grass, him all the Gods, Sandhyas, and Rishis sacrificed.

When they sacrificed Purusha how many portions did they make? What was his mouth? What were his arms? What were the thighs and feet?

His mouth was the Brahmin, both of his arms was the Prince created. His thighs produced the Vaishyas, from his feet the Shudra was born.

From his mind came the Moon, and from his eyes came the Sun, from his ears were born Vayu and Prana, and from his mouth was Agni born.

Midair was born from his navel, the sky was fashioned forth from his head, the earth from his feet, and the quarters from his ears. Thus the world was formed.

When the Gods sacrificed Purusha as offering in the yajna, Spring was the ghee, Autumn the oblation, and Summer was the fuel.

The seven were the covering sticks and three times seven were the kindling ones, when Gods performing sacrifice, bound Purusha as their sacrificial victim.

These were the earliest holy ordinances when gods sacrificed Purusha as their offering. The mighty ones attained the highest heaven, these were the Sadhyas and Gods of old dwell.

In the beginning God created the world nourished by waters, earth and sun. Fixing the form thereof the Sun proceeds on his daily course. This was the beginning of the mortals.

I know this mighty Purusha, golden as the sun, beyond the reach of darkness. By knowing him a man even now becomes immortal leaving death behind. This is the path to attain him, there is none other.

Prajapati, the all-creator, pervades the being in the womb and the beings that are born. Being himself unborn, he reveals himself in various ways. The sages alone know his true nature. In him alone exist all creatures.

The Sun who imparts light and heat to Gods, stands first and foremost among the Gods, was born before the Gods. Homage be to him, the resplendent the holy One.

The Gods in the beginning, when they generated the bright and holy Sun said thus: The Brahman who thus knew you shall have the Gods in his control.

Grandeur and Fortune are your two wives, each side of you are day and night. The constellations are your form, the Ashvins are your open mouth. Wishing salvation, grant me yonder world so that the whole universe be mine with absorption into Brahman, the All.

Book Twenty-nine

Agni is That, the Sun is That, Vayu is That, the Moon is That, Shukra verily is That, Brahma is That, Apa is That, Prajapati is That.

All divisions of time including the twinklings of the eyelids sprang from the resplendent Purusha. No one has comprehended him from above, across or in the midst.

There is no second of him whose glory verily is great. In the beginning was generated Hiranyagarbha. May he not harm me. He the unborn deserves our worship.

This Purusha pervades all the regions; ye, born afore time, in the womb he dwells. He is born now, and shall be born hereafter to meet his offspring, facing all directions.

Before whom naught whatever sprang to being, who with his presence aids all beings. He, the Prajapati, rejoicing in his offspring, maintains the three great lustres. He verily is Shodashi.

By him stand the heavens strong and the earth stands firmly. He props the realm of light and the vault of sky. He is the measure of all the regions. We worship that blissful God with our oblation.

Whom, the Sun and the Earth, propped by his help, moving in their orbits, do look with a yearning, in whom the Sun shines in full. We worship that blissful God with our oblation.

The sage behold that mysterious Being in the inmost recesses of the heart, in whom all the worlds have found one only abode. In Him is united the whole universe and thence it comes forth. Ubiquitous That pervades all creatures like the wrap and woof.

The Gandharva, knowing the eternal, may describe Him, the abode of release, hidden in the heart. His three steps are hidden in mystery. He who knows them becomes the father's father.

He is our Brother, our Father and Begetter. He knows all

beings and all worlds. In him the Gods obtaining life immortal have risen up to the third high heaven.

God reveals himself pervading all the existing creatures, the worlds, all the Quarters and Mid quarters. The sages having understood the holy order enter into God, the embodiment of truth.

Having pervaded the earth, the heaven, the worlds, the sky and quarters, and having lengthened the thread of law, he views, and he becomes, and is That Being.

To the wondrous God, the splendid friend of the soul who bestows wisdom, I have come closer in worship.

That wisdom which the Gods and sages long for, even with that wisdom, O Agni, make me wise today, Svaha!

May Varuna grant me wisdom, may Agni and Prajapati grant it! May Indra and Vayu grant it! May the Creator bestow it on me. Svaha!

May these Brahmins and Kshatriyas enjoy the splendour and wealth of mine, May the gods grant me the best wealth and splendour. To you all that splendour. Svaha!

Book Thirty

That which, divine, goes far, when man is waking, that which returns to him when he is sleeping. That light is one light that goes to a distance, may that, my mind, be moved by right resolve.

Whereby the virtuous and wise in assemblies, and in sacrifices perform their duties, the unique spirit abiding in living beings, may that, my mind, be moved by right resolve.

That which is wisdom, intellect and firmness, eternal light, which beings have within, that without which man can do no single action, may that, my mind, be moved by right resolve.

Whereby all is comprehended, the past, present, future and immortal Gods, whereby spreads the sacrifice by seven Hotars, may that, my mind, be moved by right resolve.

Wherein the Richas, Sama, Yajur verses, like spokes within a cart's nave, are included, and all the thoughts of human beings are inwoven, may that, my mind, be moved with right resolve.

As a skilled charioteer controls and drives with reins the fleet horses, so does the mind control and guide men. It dwells within the heart, is agile, most quick, may that my mind, be moved by right intention.

Five rivers flowing forth speed onward to Sarasvati and then merge into Sarasvati, a fivefold river in the land.

O Agni, you are the earliest friend of Gods, the seer, effulgent, a god. After your holy law, the Maruts, sages, wise and active with their splendid weapons, were born.

O Agni, worthy of reverence, preserve our wealthy patrons and ourselves. O God, with your succours. O God, guard are you of our seed, offspring and kine, incessantly protecting in your holy law.

O learned priests, bring great offerings to Indra, the great one, and chant the Sama hymn for strength, by whom our fathers, singing lauds obtained the laud and kine.

O Indra, you are the source of all wisdom. The men who press out and offer you Soma and other oblations, your friends, bear unmoved, the cursing of others.

Not even distant places are far for you, O Indra. Come here, lord of steeds, riding your Bay Courses. Pressed out are these juices for the strong and steadfast. The press stones are set, the fire is ready.

To him who adores Soma, he gives a milch cow, a fleet steed, a brave son, active in duties, skilled in council, dignified in the court, the splendid reflection of his fathers.

These herbs, these milch kine, these flowing streams, all these, O Soma you have produced. You have expanded the spacious firmament and with the light has removed the darkness.

O God Soma, with your godly spirit, win for us a share of riches. You are the lord of valour, let none prevent you. Remove our impediments both here and in the next world.

God Savitar, the radiant one, comes bestowing choice treasures on his devotees. He has illumined the earth's eight directions, the three regions and the seven rivers.

Savitar, the golden handed, fast moving travels between the heaven and the earth, driving away diseases, and by setting he fills the atmosphere with dark night.

O Ashvins twain, grant us well protected homes, both of you, where you may enjoy our libations.

O Ashvins, make our wisdom and speech effectual, and this our hymn, O mighty ones. In lucky game I invoke you for help, strengthen also, both of you, in the sacrifice.

Guard us well on all sides by day and by night with your undiminished care, O Ashvins. May Varuna grant us this our prayer, and Mitra, Aditi, Sindhu, Earth and Heaven.

The great Night has pervaded the earth, the atmosphere and the mid region. She has spread out on high through the seats of heaven. Her terrific darkness has come.

O Dawn, enriched with ample wealth, grant us that wonderful boon wherewith we may support our sons and sons' sons.

We call on Bhaga, the mighty, triumphant son of boundless Aditi, the sustainer of the world. Thinking of whom the poor, impatient, even the king says, let me share his bounty.

O Bhaga, be our guide, give us wealth, favour our prayer and grant us forthful gifts. Make us rich in horses and kine, O Bhaga. May our store be full in men and cattle.

May the Dawns favour this our worship and come to our holy sacrifice. As mighty steeds draw a chariot may they bring here Bhaga, the giver of riches.

As the fine dames of heroic sons, possessed of steeds, milk the kine, so may the Dawns, streaming with plenty, preserve us ever more with their wealth and blessings.

O Pushan, living ever under your guardianship, may we never be ruined. Here we sing your praise.

I praise aloud god Pushan who protects all the pathways. He went to Surya, impelled by his love for him. May he establish our wisdom and make our prays fruitful.

Vishnu, the merciful, protector and pervader of all, took three strides and thenceforth established his sacred laws.

By Varuna's decree the Heaven and Earth, stand apart from each other, full of sap, encompassing all created things, vast, spacious, full of sweetness and beautiful in form.

May our enemies stand apart from us. With Indra and with Agni we will drive them afar. The Vasus, Rudras, Adityas have exalted me, made me pre-eminent, mighty, thinker and over lord.

Come, O Nastyas, come, O Ashvins, with the thrice eleven gods to enjoy the sweet Soma juice. Lengthen out our days of life wiping out all our sins, be with us ever more and drive away our foemen.

This gold ornament which the learned bind on the kings of hundred-fold army, with benevolent thought, I bind on me for long life of hundred years so that I may live till ripe old age overtakes me.

Seven Rishis are established in the body, these seven protect it with unceasing care. These seven enter into the soul of him who lies asleep. Then two sleepless Gods Prana and Apana, the guards of the soul, keep vigil.

Arise, O Brahmanaspati, we yearning for you pray to you. May those who give good gifts, the Maruts approach us. O Indra, be you quick with them.

Now Brahmanaspati does speak aloud the solemn hymn of praise, wherein Indra and Varuna, Mitra, Aryaman and gods have made their abode.

O Brahmanaspati, protector of the world, know our prayer and prosper our offspring. He whom the gods favour is ever blessed. May we, possessed of heroic sons, speak aloud in the assembly. God who is our guardian, may protect us well. O lord of the food, grant us a good share of food!

Book Thirty-one

Avaunt, hence away, you Pisachas, inimical to gods, rebellious! This is the place for those who effuse the Soma juice.

May Savitar grant a happy spot on this earth for your mortal remains. May radiant Sun prove helpful in this!

Let Vayu purify you, let Savitar purify you with fire's glitter and sun's lustre. Let the rays release you!

God established you in this ephemeral world and made your abode here ever changing like a leaf, therefore, worship the supreme God alone and serve the cows!

May Savitar lay down your remains on the lap of mother Earth. O Earth, be gracious to this mortal man.

Here I lay you down, O man, in Prajapati, near this lovely place full of water. May his light drive away sin from us.

Go hence, O Death, follow your special pathway apart from that which gods are wont to talk. To you who hears and sees, I say it. Touch not our children, harm not our heroes!

Pleasant be to you the wind and sun, and pleasant be to you the bricks. Pleasant be to you the terrestrial fires, let them not put you to grief.

May the regions, the waters and the seas be most propitious. Auspicious to you be the atmosphere. May all Quarters prosper well for you!

On flows the stony river hold each other fast to cross it, keep yourselves up and reach the other bank. Let us here abandon that which is useless for us. May we attain the excellent foods.

O God, drive away sin, drive away evil, impurity and sorcery. O Apamarga, drive the evil dreams away from us.

May the Waters and the medicinal herbs be friendly to us and unfriendly to him who hates us and whom we hate!

We touch for our weal the ox, the son of Surabhi. May he be bearer of Gods and our deliverer as Indra is to Gods.

May we ever looking upon the loftiest light, above the darkness, effulgent, divine, the most excellent light, the Sun attain the Gods.

Here I raise this wall for the living. Let none of these, none other cross this limit. May you following this law for a hundred lengthened autumns and may you keep Death beneath this mountain.

O Agni, you purify our life. Give us abundant strength and food and drive away distress and misfortune!

O Agni, balmed in ghee, with butter on your face, live long, strengthened with sacrifice.

All these men have led about the cow, have led Agni round. They have offered oblation to high gods. Then who will attack them with success?

I drive away the flesh-devouring Agni, sinful let them go to Yama's abode. Here, may this other Jatavedas, foreknowing, carry our oblation to the Gods.

O Jatavedas, carry the portion of sacrifice to the Fathers, where, far away, you know them established. May streams of sap flow there for them. May their desires, so truthful, be fulfilled. Svaha!

O Earth, be you without thorn and pleasant as our resting place. Grant us spacious room full of comfort and happiness. May your fire burn down all our sins.

O Agni, you have been kindled by this man, let him be again born from you. For Heaven this man I name! All hail!

Book Thirty-two

This whole world, all that lives and moves on earth, is enveloped by God. Seek joy in renouncing the transient. Do not covet another man's wealth.

Only one performing actions with detachment should desire to live a hundred years. This is the only way for you so that your actions do not cling to you.

There are infernal worlds, ever enveloped in the deepest gloom. There go those when life here is done, who slay the self.

Motionless, the One is swifter than the mind. The Gods fail to overtake that speeding forth before them. Standing still, he outstrips those who are running. Abiding in him life force acts through everything.

He moves and yet he moves not; he is far and yet near. He is within all this and yet is without.

The man who beholds all beings that are in the Self and the Self in all beings, is never a prey of doubt.

When a man who knows well all beings become one with the Self, when he further sees that One alone in every thing, then how can distress or delusion touch him?

God is radiant, all-pervading, incorporeal, sans scar or sinew, invulnerable, pure, unpierced by evil. He is sage, seer, omnipresent, self-existent, and has assigned to everything its due prosperity unto the everlasting time.

Into the depths of blinding darkness fall those who worship ignorance, and into still deeper darkness sink they who enjoy pleasures carnal.

One fruit, they declare, results from the knowledge, another from ignorance. This we have heard from the sages who have revealed it to us.

The man who knows simultaneously both knowledge and ignorance, overcoming death through knowledge attains life immortal.

Into blinding darkness fall those who follow Nescience or Avidya, into blinder still those who pride themselves of their knowledge.

Different are the results, they say, of Nescience and knowledge. Thus we have heard from the sages who have revealed it to us.

He who knows well both knowledge and Nescience simultaneously, overcoming death by knowledge attains life immortal.

Soul is immaterial and immortal, but this body will be reduced to ashes. O man, doer of actions, meditate and Universal Soul, the protector of all, remember your deeds, remember your deeds!

O God, lead us along the righteous path to riches and prosperity; O God, you know all our deeds. Remove from us our sin that leads us astray. To you then, we shall bring most ample and reverent adoration.

The face of Truth is hidden over by a golden vessel. The spirit yonder in the Sun, the spirit dwelling there, I myself am he! Om!

Sama Veda

Purvarchika/Part First

Agneya Kanda/Book One

Chapter One

I

O Agni come, praised with hymn, to feast and sacrificial offering, like a Hota in the Yajna. Thou hast been ordained Hota of every yajna, by Gods among men. Agni, we accept as Hota, the revealer of the Vedas, envoy of the Gods. All-knowing, giver of all wealth. Served with devotion, resplendent, pure, duly adored, remove our sins and afflictions. I praise Agni, dearest unto us all, like a beloved friend, like a war chariot grantor of our desires.

O Agni, do guard us against all malignity of our foe and the hate of mortal man. O Agni, come, I chant more songs of praise for thee; be more puissant with these sacrificial offerings. Agni, I long for thee with praise. I receive Thy knowledge upto my pulsating heart, like a devoted son. O Agni! Thou art realized by the learned men by churning of their hearts as fire is produced by rubbing together the sticks. O Agni, protect us full well with Thy bright radiance. Thou alone art our God to show us the right path.

Agni God is one but sages call it by various names. Here in the Vedas, Agni, Mitra, Varuna, etc. are used for God. These various names manifest the different aspects and attributes of the same and one Reality.

II

O God, our obeisance to Thee, the people sing reverent praise. Thee to gain strength. Smite thou the foe with thy full might. O

God, I sing thy praise, admirable messenger, grantor of fruit of our works, immortal, worthy of the highest praise. Omniscient! O adorable God, the hymns of the devotees sung in thy praise, come to thee on the wind, O God, the illuminer of night, may we worship Thee full of reverence, day by day, morning and evening. O Agni, knowable through hymns of praise, take abode in our hearts for our weal. We adore thee with our hymns, thou, the chastiser of the wicked ones.

We invoke thee, may thou manifest thyself with Maruts at the sacrificial altar of our hearts. I render homage with reverence, God, like a long-tailed steed, imperial lord of sacrificial rites. I invoke Thee, all radiant, residing in the hearts, as do the men of wisdom and action. Man enkindle thee, O God in his heart with songs to develop his mind, so do I, effulgent Lord, the Sun. on the yonder side of heaven, is seen by the people all the day, verily obtains light from the primeval refulgent Source.

III

Worship Agni reverently, the giver of prosperity, the mighty Lord, brother and friend in all our good deeds. Lustrous Agni, with his blazing splendour, defeats the ignoble foes, and bestows on us the wealth, etc. Agni, be gracious, thou art great, and accessible by the pious man. Thou comest to sit in our hearts. O God, protect us against disease and distress. O Eternal, consume our foes with thy blazing flames. O Resplendent Agni, harness thou, thy steeds, most excellent in speech, they carry you so fast.

O Refulgent Agni, worthy of reverence, we worship thee ever, invoked by all men, Lord Almighty. Agni is the head and height of all, like the Sun in heaven, the master of the earth and knower of the seeds of our actions is he. O Agni, thou so graciously preach the Gayatri mantra among us and carry our sacrificial offerings to Gods. O refulgent Lord, an austere devotee manifests thee through his speech of praise. O Agni, purifier and remover of sins, hear thou my call.

Agni, the Lord of strength and wisdom, giveth precious gifts to the pious men, is Omnipresent. Like the Sun in heaven looked upon by all, he, the creator of the Vedas, is known by his divine virtues of effulgence, purity, etc. Praise Agni, O man, in this sacrifice, the Lord whose sacred laws are ever true, who is Omniscient and endowed with divine virtues, and is remover of diseases and distress. May the divine powers of God grant us our heart's desires, and fulfilment. May they rain happiness all over us. O Lord, protector of the saints, thou fulfillest the desires of him who lauds thee to gain control over his senses.

IV

O men, sing the glories of Agni at every sacrifice, let us laud the Everlasting God. Creator of the Vedas, even as a well beloved friend. O Agni, preserve us by one Veda (Rig), protect us by the second (Yajur), preserve us by three Vedas. O Almighty Lord, preserve us well by the four Vedas (Rig, Yajur, Sama and Atharva). O Agni, Effulgent, most Youthful, pure Brilliance, kindled in the heart of a devotee, shine on us with Thy sparkling beams, Lord of charity. O Agni, who art worshipped well let the wise be dear unto Thee. Let the wealthy princes, and governors, who protect the kine, Vedic wisdom, etc. be beloved of all. O Agni, lord of the world, mighty art Thou, the Ever-present, Household-lord, Guardian of the sky. O God, Lord of men, Thou consumest the Demons.

O God, Thou, Effulgent gift of Dawn, bestows various pleasures and much wealth on us and on him who offers you oblations. O Immortal God, Creator of the Vedas, Thou givest sense-organs, which awaken with the rising Sun and receive knowledge. O gracious Lord, the refuge of all, Thou art Wonderful, send us Thy bounteous help. Thou the charioteer of the earthly wealth, find rest and protection for our progeny. Agni, Thou alone art Famed, far and wide, Righteous. Omniscient, Enkindled, Radiant Lord, the wise singers invoke Thee with the hymns. O holy One, grant us wealth bringing fame among men and prolonging life. Thou Lord of the Universe, bless us with wealth, earned through righteousness, which many crave, and brings much glory. Lord, the Giver of pleasures and rewards, grant us the wealth of wisdom. To Him, like the first vessels filled with honey, to Agni let the Vedic hymns go forth.

V

O Yajin, I say unto Ye with his stotra, "I am the Guardian of strength. Good unto all, Bestower of wisdom, Lord, Adorable, Eternal and the Giver of the fruit of actions".

O Lord Agni, Thou lies in the womb of logs, men kindle Thee. Ever alert Thou, rewardest the sacrificer, and shinest in material objects. O God, Thou appearth unto the heart of him who dedicates his acts to Thee. May our hymns of praise go nigh to Agni, who giveth strength to an Arya. At the sacrifice of speech, Agni is the Chief Priest, the lauds are the seat of grass and Maruts are the Ritvij. O God, Revealer of the Vedas, I crave with vedic hymn the help that is most excellent.

O Soul! Laud Agni of vast glory, with sacred songs, for help and wealth, Ye Jivatman! God is well sung in the Vedas, and is a dwelling for sure protection. Hear, O man, who hast ears to hear, early in the morning at Yajna, invoke Agni and other deities like Mitra, Aryaman, etc. the bearer of oblations.

O God, pervading the Earth and the high lucid realm of Heaven, Wax stronger with my hymn of praise, and fulfil all the creatures, O most intelligent. O Agni, Thou ascendth to the far off maternal waters of the heavens from where Thou hast come here. O effulgent Agni, I a contemplative man, always meditate for Thy acquisition. O, Immortal Entity, whom the people reverence, shed thy brilliance on me, a learned man, so that I may become great and be revered by the people through the Vedic wisdom.

Chapter Two

I

The God giveth wealth unto Ye. He wants full oblation, so pour it out in full and fill it again. Then will God grant Ye your desires. May God, the Author of Vedic knowledge come to our Yajna which gives us perfect powers, righteous and brave offspring, is beneficial to all, and is performed by five officiating priests. O God, stand up erect for our protection like the Sun. We laud Thee along with other wise men, therefore, being thus praised, be the Giver of strength and food to us, waging war against the unrighteous. O Omnipresent God, the man desirous of vast riches surrenders himself upto Thee, and begets a heroic son, skilled in the Vedas and protecting thousands of human beings. With Vedic hymns and holy eulogies, we supplicate Thee, Lord of all, whom others too worship.

This Agni is the Lord of great prosperity, good fortune, riches, noble progeny, herds of kine, and Remover of diseases and distress. O God, Thou art the Lord of our homes, our Hota at the Yajna, the Purifier, the Protector, the officiating Priest, and Giver of fruits of our actions. Thou art passing wise, and Bestower of boons. We human beings, Thy friends have chosen Thee as our Protector. Thou art most Mighty, Blessed, Peerless, Remover of sins and Doer of good deeds.

II

Ye mortals worship Him, the Lord of hearths and homes, constantly at sanctified altars, offer oblations of clarified butter, etc. propitiate Him with prayers. Honour the officiating priest and Hota with homage and gifts. Thus perform the sacrificial Yajna. Verily wondrous are the acts of Agni, who never sucks at His udderless mothers' breasts, who bore him, but grows instantly strong to carry out the great errand of bearing oblations to other Gods. O Agni, the material fire is Thy One manifestation. The Sun the second, the third the lightning which pervades the firmament. O Beautiful, Thou art beloved of all the liberated souls. O God, Knower of all, Worthy of homage, we send this laud to Thee with our pure intellect, like a car. May our intellect be ever pure. O Lord, let us never suffer harm in Thy company. The wise speak of Agni, as the Head of Heaven, the Messenger of Earth, the Guest of man, the Sovereign, the Mouth of Gods, and worthy of homage.

As does the waters spring from the mountain ridges, so do the Gods through lauds, from Thee. O Agni, may our hymns and eulogies speed to Thee, as does the swift horse to the battle bearing the warrior. O Ye men, before you lie dead struck by thunder-like death, win for your protection the Effulgent Lord, the Giver of fruits of our actions, Prince of Yoga, the Punisher of the wicked, the Ritvij between the Heaven and the Earth. Agni, the King, All-pervading, lauded by the Yogis, worshipped in the heart with devotion, the Creator of animate and inanimate things, may shed the light of wisdom on the hearts of His devotees at the flush of morning. Agni with His lofty flames pervades the Earth and the Heaven and bellows like the Bull. He hath come nigh to our hearts from the sky's farthest limit, and is higher than others. O mortals, generate Agni, the Lord of us all, from two fire sticks in hands and rubbed together. He, the Dweller of our homes, is far-seen with its flashing flames.

III

Just as fire is awakened by the people's fuel, a milch cow yields milk at each dawn, so is our soul awakened through Yoga. Just as birds fly high above the trees, and the Sun's rays pervade the vault of heaven, so emancipated souls attain God, the abode of bliss. O man, realize in your heart Him, who is the Conqueror of different worlds, the Destroyer of forts, the most Wise, Free from delusion, effulgent, knowable through the Vedas, the Guide of our intellect, and richly Armoured in the splendid rays of the Sun. O God, Thy one form is bright like Day and another dark like Night. Thou Nourisher of all, the Lord of life and food, Thou art like the Sun, let Thy bounty be auspicious here in this world. O gracious God, Granter of cattle wealth, right speech, knowledge of various noble actions, may Thy gracious will be ever upon us, so that we possess happiness and illustrious children. God, the Giver of fruits of our actions, Dweller in the heart of a devotee, Protector of bodies, Adorable, Pervading all, Omnipresent, Bestower of wealth, grains and desired objects, is seated in our hearts.

O man, learn, to know the mighty deeds of God, as you know the Sun who is effulgent, life-giving, mighty, worthy of praise, energetic, and attractive. Just as well cherished germ is preserved in pregnant woman, so is Agni preserved in the two kindling fire sticks. The awakened souls worship Him day by day with oblations. O Agni, from days of yore Thou hast been chastising the wicked; the forces of evil can never overcome Thee in the fight. Thou consume the raw flesh devourers, let none of them escape Thine divine weapons.

IV

O Agni, restless on Thy way, pave for us the path leading to glorious opulence and strength, and bring us most mighty splendour. The man who serves Thee, and offers sacred gifts, enjoys bliss and Thy protection and help. O Agni, the Purifying and Resplendent God, Thy brilliance pervades the heaven, like the Sun, Thou beamest with thy radiant glow.

O mortal men, worship Him at dawn, the Immortal one, who is much beloved by all, and to Whom all men offer their oblations. O most Radiant Agni, shine on high. Grant us Thou riches and strength, our most precious songs are for Thee. We worship Lord Agni and glorify Him with Vedic hymns. He is loved by all and is Omnipresent. Sing hymns of praise to Agni, the effulgent, whom men always keep foremost for their eulogies. May we realize Him, the noblest Agni. Friend of men, the remover of ills, and most brilliant. Agni, the cause and source of the Sun, is born in a Yajna by the reflective, truthful and intelligent co-sacrificers and Hota. They are like His father, and their faith the mother.

V

We place our complete trust in King Soma, Agni, Varuna, and in Aditya, Vishnu, Surya, and the Brahmin priest Brihaspati. Just as the conquerors of the world walk exalted and rise high in esteem, so do our oblations go up high to Gods. O Agni, we kindle Thee in

Yajna so that Thou mayest rain ample happiness and wealth. Both Heaven and Earth are great oblation. Pray Him, O awakened men, God is the goal, the aspirant recites the Veda in His praise. This is the prayer of Him. He holds all knowledge in His grasp even as the felly round the wheel. O Agni, shoot forth and destroy with Thy might the violent sinners on every side, break down the strength of the demons and evil-doers. O God, let the Vasus who have observed continence upto the age of 24, Rudras, who have observed it upto the age of 36, and Adityas who have done so upto the age of 48 years, and who therefore shine like the Sun, be your companions.

Book Two
Chapter One

I

O Bounteous One, I surrender myself unto Thee with many a laud, as a servant does to a mighty master, who chastises the wicked. O wise men, reach the lofty lore of the Vedas to virtuous man. Sing His glory who is Purifier, the Gurdian of true knowledge, Genius, and the Creator of all O God, Thou art lord of cows, Vedic knowledge, food material and strength. Thou art the embodiment of prowess and master of the Sun. O God, Thou art great Purifier, and most Venerable, bring the learned to a man who is virtuous in actions and temperament. O great Donor and Giver of delight, Thou drive away our foes and thus shinest. Born of seven mothers (seven fires or sparks), He is firm and sure for the glory of the wise, and hath set His mind on glorious wealth.

May the infinite, ever come nigh to help and protect us. May He, the Bestower of happiness and peace chase away our foes. O men, worship and pray Him, whose smokes wander at will and none may grasp his flames. No mortal foe can ever prevail on him by deceit, who has served well the God with oblations. O Agni, Lord of the virtuous, drive far away the wicked foe the evil-minded thief, and make our path easy. O brave God, Lord of virtuous, on hearing this new laud of mine reduce to ashes with thy flame the wicked and evil foes.

II

Sing forth ye worshippers, to Him, the most Munificent and Sublime with His Refulgent glow. O Agni, whom Thou choosest as friend, conquerers all impediments and does great deeds by Thine aid. Praise Him, the Lord of light, the Messenger of Gods, who bears oblations to them. Anger Him not, our worthy guest, the bright God Agni, praised by many learned men, an excellent Hota, skilled in Yajna. May Agni, duly worshipped bring us bliss, may our sacrifice, virtuous actions and eulogies sing in His praise bring bliss. O God, we have chosen Thee, immortal, Best among the Gods, and Fine Finishes of the holy sacrifice. Bring us that splendour, O Agni, which may overthrow each fiend and sinner in our house, who deserves the wrath of every man. Whenever, the God is friendly to us human beings, the race of Manu, all our evils, diseases and disasters are swept away.

Ayendra Kanda

III

O Worshippers, sing the praise of Lord Indra, invoked and praised by many, who would bless you, as He does the Earth like a King. O Indra, Possessor of hundreds of powers and wise designs, let me rejoice in Thy joy, which is most glorious of all. O speech, go unto Indra and tell Him your aim. The two mighty ones, that is Earth and Heaven may bless the sacrifice. Let both the ears of men be blessed with the recitation of holy hymns. O learned men, well versed in the Vedas, sing praises of Indra, so that He may come. We praise Indra for destroying the mighty forces of the demon Vritra. He is all-powerful and giver of happiness.

O Indra, Thou art embodiment of strength, power and victory. The mighty one, bestowest might indeed. The sacrifice made Indra strong and great when he unrolled the earth and gave strength to the sacrificer. O Indra, if I become also powerful and Lord of wealth as Thou art alone, my worshippers would become rich in kine etc. O men, blend Soma juice for Indra, each offering more excellent. He is our Hero, joy and inspiration. O good God, enjoy this Soma juice to Thy heart's content, the well pressed juice, Lord, we offer it to Thee.

IV

Sun, Thou soars high upto great Indra, who is well known for his wealth, heroism, knowledge and beneficence. He hurls the thunderbolt to subdue the foes for happiness of mankind O Surya, the slayer of demons, whatever is there in the world, has been caused by Thee, and is all in Thy power. Indra, the Youthful, is our friend, who with his wise guidance brings back on the right path the souls astrayed afar. O Indra, let not evils overpower us stealthily from any direction due to darkness of our ignorance. May we, with Thee as our Friend subdue that evil, O God, give ample wealth, the ever victorious wealth, that delights the brave, and is an excellent aid to face onslaughts.

Both in mighty and lesser fights, we invoke Lord Indra, our Friend, who hurls his bolt to subdue the foes. Indra drank Soma juice to His fill, and being thus inspired, subdued the foe with his manly might in the battle in thousand ways. O God faithful to Thee, we sing aloud Thy praise. O Lord, Indra, take note of this act of ours. Those who perform the sacrificial rites by seating on sacred Kusa grass, have the ever Youthful Indra as their Friend. O Indra sweep away all our foes, smite them down who torment us, and give us wealth for which we long.

When we talk together, we hear as if it were close at hand. It reflects that speech is in their hands, which works wonders. O Indra, these friends of us, equipped with Soma look to Thee, just as men with fodder look to the herd of cattle. Before Thy righteous displeasure, bow down all people and men, as the rivers bow them to the sea. We choose the protection of mighty Gods, that it may help and succour us. O God of wisdom, make my breath free and vigorous in motion, so that I may realize the true relation between speech and its meaning.

May the mighty Indra, the Destroyer of ignorance, the Embodiment of bliss, listen to our prayers, and grant us wisdom. O God, grant us this day ever prosperity and progeny, and drive afar poverty and distress. Where is that mighty and ever youthful Indra, the strong-necked never bending down? What Brahmin, the knower of the Vedas ministers to Him? There where the mountains stand, and streams meet at confluence, the Sage manifests himself and practices Yoga. Praise the Lord through songs, the Master of mankind, the sovereign and most liberal, who alone controlleth men.

Chapter Two

I

O Lord of ample wealth, these songs of praise have been sung aloud to Thee, as milch kine low to their calves. The wisemen know that in the mansion of the Moon, there is hidden light of the Sun, that is, the Moon borrows her lustre from the Sun. Similarly the light of God is there in our souls. When Indra brought the water in streams down on the Earth, the Sun then with His beams stood by his side.

The Earth, the streaming mother of liberal Maruts, united with Indra and Surya sustains life. Come, Indra of rapturous joys, to our sacrifice, and enjoy the flowing Soma juice. O men, offer rich oblations in this Yajna and then nicely finish the sacrifice to the end with the cleansing bath. May I receive deep knowledge of eternal law from God, my Father, and then grow resplendent like unto the Sun. May we be rich in strength and knowledge, obedient to the Lord, so that wealthy in food we may rejoice.

II

O men, praise the God, all-conquering, Guardian of our foods, most Munificent, the Omniscient, and adored by all wisemen. O friends, sing the praise of Lord God, the Embodiment of all virtues, the Protector of His devotees and ever cheerful. O God, wise men worship Thee, as Thy friend with Vedic hymns. We, Thy ardent devotees, longing for Thee, also worship Thee. Many sing the songs of praise to God. May we also sing aloud his praise. O Indra, here is thy Soma drink, pure and excellent, come hither and drink.

Just as a good milch cow calls him who milks her, so we invoke and glorify God day by day for the acquisition of knowledge and protection of our people. O Indra, I pour the Soma juice for Thee to drink. Sate Thee and enjoy to the full. O Indra, the Soma poured in cups and saucers is for Thy pleasure, drink that, for Thou art Lord thereof. On the occasion of every struggle and need, we as friends call upon Thee, Lord Almighty for our protection and succour. O friends, come ye hither and sit down, sing the glory of God and bring hymns of praise.

III

O Lord of affluence, this Soma drink hath been prepared with much exertion, drink of it, Thou worthy of praise. Great is our Indra, the upholder of the thunderbolt. Wide as heaven extends His Power, O Indra of mighty arms, gather with Thy dextrous right hand many kinds of nutritious food for us. O men, praise Indra, as he is famed, the Lord of the kine, the Son of Truth and the Lord of the brave. With what unique help, with what powerful army, the wonderful friend, will come?

Indra, the ever conquering Lord, rushes down to help us, drawn to our songs of praise. May I attain firm intellect by meditating upon the wondrous Lord, the Lovely friend, the giver of the fruit of good and bad actions, the Learned Lord of the assembly. May all the paths beneath the sky whereby Thou speedest winds on, let all spaces listen our voice. O Almighty Indra, Thou giveth us excellent food and strength, when kind towards us. Here is ready the Soma juice. The Maruts, the twin Ashvins and the self-luminous Sun drink of it.

IV

The intellect of the meditative man full of wisdom, and inclined to act, realizes the Lord in the heart. May we, Thy worshippers, O Lord, be ever non-violent, free from illusion and acting according to the commandments of the Vedas. O soul, the chanter of Brihad Saman, evening has descended, sing loudly the praise of the Self-effulgent God, the Creator of all. Dawn, the dear daughter of the Sky, now shines forth and scatters darkness. I extol the praise of high Ashvins. O Indra, Thou armed with indomitable might and the bones of dead Dadhicha, destroy the innumerable demons led by Vritra.

Come Lord, Mighty is strength, Protector of all of us, and delight Thyself with the Soma drink at our feasts. O Indra, Thou slayer of Vritra, come hither to our side, Mighty with Thy mighty aids. Indra's might shines forth, as he revolves Heaven and Earth like the blazing shields. As a pigeon approaches his mate, so does Indra drawest near us hearing our prayers. O God, May we have Thy health-giving, healing and blissful balm in our hearts. May Lord, prolong the days of our life.

V

Never is he harmed whom the excellently wise Gods Varuna, Mitra and Aryaman protect. Be gracious and help us Lord, in acquiring kine, seeds and chariots according to our wishes. These kine yield their milk and butter and thus help in Thy sacrifice. Indra, O much lauded, many named Lord, mayest Thou manifest Thyself at each of our Soma sacrifice. May Goddess Saraswati, endowed with plenteous wisdom, enriched with prayer grace our sacrifice with her presence.

Who among the mortals can sate the Indra with Soma juice? He shall make Him grant us precious things. Come Indra, we have made this divine juice for Thee, sit Thou here on the sacred kusa grass and drink of it. May great unassailable heavenly favour be showered on us by Gods Varuna, Mitra and Aryaman. O Indra, Lord of plenteous riches, the Supreme Guide, the Settler of many, we depend on one like Thee.

Book Three
Chapter One

I

Let our worship make Thee glad. Grant us Thy bounty, O thunder-upholder, sweep away the enemies of Vedic lore. O Lord, Worshipped and prayed through our Vedic hymns, protect Thy devotee amidst us, Thou with streams of bliss are bedecked. Friends, Indra ever thinks of you, and tends you with care. The Lord is no heroic and loving, why do you not worship Him. Let the intellect plunge in the Lord, as the rivers flow into the ocean. O Indra, nothing excels Thee! The Udgatha chanters glorify the Great God, with their Samavedic songs, the Rigvedic reciters also do so through their Mantras. The Adhvaryus glorify Him, with the Yajurvedic hymns.

May Indra grant us desired strength and handy wealth. May He, the Omniscient God give us wisdom and wealth. Trully, the all-conquering God, sweeps away afar mighty fear, for firm is he and swift to act. These songs of praise reach Thee, with every oblation offered, as milch kine fondly hasten to their calves. Indra, and Pushan we invoke for friendship, wealth and prosperity. O Indra, the slayer of Vritra, none is better, mightier than Thee. Verily naught is like Thee.

II

O men, praise Him, the common Lord of all, the Saviour of our folk, the Giver of might, wealth and kine. O God, I praise Thee with Vedic hymns. As a beloved wife goes to her husband, so do these hymns reach Thee, our Protector, Showerer of peace and bliss. Verily, the mortals have good guidance, whom Gods Aryaman, Mitras and Maruts, the Friends of all, free from guide, protect. O Indra, give us the wealth for which we long, which is concealed in some strong chest or well or hill. O men, worship the mighty Indra, the slayer of Vritra, the Champion of mankind, for the sake of munificence and fulfilment of desires.

Indra, O mighty Lord, may we continue praising, Thy fame, fame of one like Thee. O Hero, may we realize Thee in our meditations. O Indra, at day break accept our oblation of Soma mixed with roasted corn flour, with cake, curds, and eulogies. Indra, Thou overcomest all the demons and evil forces, with Thy all conquering might. Thine are all these pleasures of the Soma juice, Lord Indra. Enjoy them and be pleased, Lord of royal wealth. For Thee, Lord of Light, Soma juice is pressed, and sacred grass seat is spread. Indra, be gracious to Thy worshippers.

III

O men, seeking strength, please Indra with songs and sacrifice, just as the farmer waters his field with water drawn from the well. He is most liberal, Lord of limitless strength. O Indra come unto us, and grant us food that gives a hundred, ye, a thousand powers. The new-born Indra asked His mother Aditi, as He upheld his shaft, who are the fierce and worthy opponents? We call Him for help and protection who is long-armed, and being lauded fulfils our desires. Mitra, the friend of all, Varuna, the Omniscient, and Aryaman, the just lover of the learned, lead us straight on the path of Dharma, that is, righteousness and duty.

Just as the lustrous Dawn sheds light on all objects from afar, as if She was present here, so does God giveth His light of knowledge from every direction. O Gods, Varuna, Mitra and Indra, most intelligent, pour fatness on our pastures and sweet rains on the regions of the air. The winds that are in the firmament and are the cause and extension of speech, move as do the cows bending their knees when they bellow for their calves. God created this world in three ways, that is, the visible earth, the invisible subtle world, and shining solar world. His power is manifest in this world.

IV

O Indra, Thou shunnest the wrathful, and speedest to the devotee who offers libations of Soma. Enjoy the drink presented to

Thee. What is the word addressed to Him, the Great God, excellently wise? For the same exalteth Him. Does not He know the worship offered by a poor and ignorant man? Does not He know the recitation of Gayatri Sama? He does know. Indra is pleased by songs of praise, He is the Lord of steeds and armies, the Friend of devotees who offer libations. O Lord, come to our libations, don't be angry with us. Thou art like a grand father, ever venerable.

When doest Thou O Lord, impede the flow of rains to them who are well learned in Vedas? Thou grandest copious rains to them who are dear like sons unto you. Indra, accept the Soma drink, according to the seasons, from the people learned in divine knowledge. Thy friendship is invincible, O Indra, lover of the songs, we are the singers of thy praise; O Soma drinker, gratify us. O God, Thou grant us bodily strength, the ever conquering might. O Hero, Thou art mighty, and verily a friend to the brave. May Thy heart be won by us!

V

O Indra, Thou Lord of animate and inanimate things, Omnipresent, illuminator of the Sun, we call aloud and praise Thee like unmilked kine. Indra, the Lord of the brave, we call on thee to win wealth and power. People in war call Thee alone. In adversity and exertion, we Thy devotees, worship and contemplate Thee only. We sing praise to Thee, for wealth and gifts. Thou art Lord of wealth, rich in treasure, and giveth Thy singers wealth and thousandfold gifts. Just as cows low to their calves in stalls, so we praise Indra with songs, the wondrous God who checks our foes and delights in Soma juice. Loud we sing Brihat Sama and invoke at the sacred Yajna where Soma flows, so that Thou the Propitious and Protector may grant us wealth.

I make, Ye men bend with Vedic songs before Indra much invoked, as a wheel wright bends a wheel of wood for swift motion. Indra, enjoy Thyself with savoury Soma and cheer Thee with our milk draught. Be our friend, grant us wisdom, and guard us well for our weal. O Lord, come to the worshipper and enrich him with wealth and wisdom. O Master of infinite knowledge, give us strength to control our sense organs. May we have strength to perform Yoga. God never overlooks even the lowliest one of you all. So, O men, let all of us drink deep the divine knowledge and be fulfilled. O friends, glorify none else, but Him, the Bestower of Dharma and Artha. Be non-violent, sing together aloud His praise again and again.

Chapter Two

I

No man can harm him who by his sacrifices has pleased God, the Protector of devotees, worshipped by the whole world and the controller of all. Such a person performs his deeds without desire of their fruits. The God even without ligature, before blood is produced, joins the joints together of the neck, and He at his will deserves them. Many hundreds and thousands of steeds are yoked to Thy golden car, O God. Let these long maned steeds speed Thee to our sacrifice to enjoy Soma. Come hither, Lord, riding the horses, brilliant like peacock's plumes. Let none check Thy course, as a hunter does a bird. Thou overcome them, as an archer does an animal. O God, Thou art verily the Mightiest, Thou blessest the mortal man. There is none Comforter as Thee, I address my words to Thee.

O God, Thou art far renowned, the lord of power and might, the Guardian of mankind. Thou alone art unconquerable, and smitest down resistless foes. We call Thee Lord alone for and at the beginning of sacrifice. We call Thee at the completion of a Yajna and also amidst war. We invoke Thee for the acquisition of wealth. May these my songs of praise exalt Thee, God of abundant wealth! Men, learned in holy hymns and pure, also sing their lauds to Thee. These exceeding sweet songs of our, these songs of praise come to Thee like ever conquering chariots that display their strength, gain wealth and provide unfailing help. Even as a thirsty deer repairs to the desert's pool of water, so should Thou come to us speedily evening and morning to enjoy the drink to Thy fill.

II

O God, Lord of action and intelligence, help us in gaining fame, wealth and protection. May we ever follow Thee, the Embodiment of bliss, Giver of wealth and might. O Indra, Lord of Light, whatever joy Thou takest away from the wicked and evil persons, prosper therewith, O God those who praise Thee and perform sacrifices for Thee. O friends, sing songs of praise to Mitra and Aryaman. Sing, Ye pious men in Vedic verses, the glory of Varuna, the Protector of our homes, the King of kings. O Eternal, learned men, desirous of longevity for the sake of life's full enjoyments, laud Thee through Vedic hymns. O men, sing Vedic hymns to high Indra and Maruta. Indra, the Lord of hundreds of actions, the slayer of Vritra, slays the foes with his hundred knotted thunderbolt.

O learned Ritvij men, sing the hymns of Brihat Sama to the Great Lord, whereby the sacrificers realize in their hearts the ever Divine, Sin-remover and lustrous light. O Lord, give us wisdom and good deeds as a sire gives his son wealth and knowledge. Guide us on this divine path, O much invoked God, may we live long and behold Thy Light! O God, desert us not, be present with us at our divine sacrifices, Thou our sole Refuge. Thou alone art our Protection arid Brother. O Lord, turn us not away! O God, Remover of evils and sins, we who have purified their hearts, whose Soma juice is ready in the Yajna, we sit here in Thy worship, like silent waters encompassing a holy island. Whatever strength is found in men and subjects, whatever spiritual power and beauty there exist in the five Aryan clans, grant us all these and manly strength.

III

O mighty Indra, Thou art verily our Guardian, the Showerer of rains. Thou art famed as Vrisha, the Embodiment of Dharma, in the Vedas. Thou art called by the same title, O Rain showerer, far and near, O Lord, whether Thou be far, or near at hand, Thou art the slayer of our foes. The worshippers invoke Thee in the sacrifice, with their lofty lauds and pressed Soma drink. O men, for the sake of obtaining spiritual and physical strength, sing to Glorious and Great Indra, the songs of praise, as ordained in the Vedas. O Indra, grant me and these, Thine devotees, for their weal, a triple refuge, triply strong and dwelling places, secure from triple afflictions. O friends, all beings born and ye to be born, enjoy all good things from Him as their heritage, like the rays that inherit the light from the Sun.

O eternal soul, a godless mortal can never gain spiritual food, for a driver alone can yoke the steeds. Similarly a devotee alone can realize God through prayer and devotion. In every struggle and affliction let Him be invoked with songs of praise. He is the Slayer of foes, Remover of obstacles, worthy of praise, may our songs of praise, ordained by the Vedas, be ever sung in His glory. O God, the lower region, that is Earth, is Thine, Thou nourishes the middle one. Thou art sovereign of the highest, celestial region. Thus, Thou art verily the Lord of the whole universe. None in the universe, can resist Thee. O Omnipresent, creator of the universe, Liberator from bandage, where art Thou, whither art Thou gone? Thou, all-knowing God, art present everywhere, Thou pervadest all; the singer sings Thy praise. O friends, we the knower of Brahman, have been pressing God in our previous births, the Punisher of sinners. Now, today in this well known Yajna, let us glorify Him.

IV

I praise in song, the Great God, the sovereign Lord of men, accessible through Yoga, Pre-eminent, Vanquisher of fighting hosts and Chastiser of the wicked. O Lord, grant us security from that whereof we are scared. O Indra, Thou art mighty to protect us; drive away with Thy powers our foes and enemies. O Lord of the homes, Thou art the strong pillar and support, Guardian like armour. Thou art the Friend of the learned and Yogis and grant them liberation from human bondage. Verily Thou art Great, truly Thou art Great O Absorber of all. O most Praised for greatness of Thy might, O God, Creator of all, Thou art Great by Thy greatness. A man becomes fair of form, rich in kine, steeds and chariots when favoured by Thee. Only such a man, full of virtues, knowledge and excellent powers, is fit to join the company of learned men. Not even hundred heavens or hundred earths can match Thee. O chastizer of the wicked, not even innumerable Suns and universes created by Thee, can ever match Thee. O God, Thou art called by men eastward and westward, north and south. O Almighty Thou art with all everywhere. Omnipresent, invoked by many, Thou art there in all men. Omnipresent, who can ever be disrespectful unto Thee? The strong and learned with faith in Thee, offer oblations of Soma juice to Thee. This Mind being without feet, reaches earlier than those with feet. Leaving the place of deliberation and speaking loudly through his tongue, he enters the field of action with thirty steps. O God, Omnipresent, near to all, come close to us, with aids of firmly based resolves; come most Auspicious, with Thy most auspicious help. Good kinsman, to Thine kinsmen come!

V

O men, call to your aid, Eternal, All-pervading, Inspirer of all, the Best Lord, Victorious, Immortal, Formless God, the showerer of rains and the most Beautiful. O God, even the learned who are far from Thee, are disliked by us. O Omnipresent, come and reside by us. O Omnipresent, come and reside in our hearts, and listen to our prayers. O men, prepare the Soma drink for Indra, the Upholder of thunder. Make ready your feast, please Him to favour us. He, the Giver, blesses him who gives. We call upon the God, who ever destroys the foes, Protects the good, is the Seer of good and bad actions, Master of all knowledge, the most manly help and maketh us prosper in the fight! Ye rich in wealth and wisdom, grant us blessings day and night. Let not your gifts ever fail. May not our gifts of oblations ever fail!

Whenever a mortal worshipper sings praise of God, the Fulfiller of all desires, let him laud God, who protects the people and removes the sins. O reincarnating soul, preserve thou thy body's organs through the enjoyment of best food for it is through these organs of action and recognition that thou can realize God, the Remover of sins. May God, Almighty, ever Cheerful, listen both our mental and vocal prayers, and come unto us to enjoy the sacrifice. O God Thou can never be given away for a huge price, not for a hundred, nor for a thousand, nor for ten thousand, nor for still higher, Thou, upholder of thunderbolt, Chastiser of the wicked and the Master of ample wealth. O God, Thou art more to me than father or a niggard brother is. Thou and my mother, O Lord, are alike in rearing me to attain wealth and house.

Book Four
Chapter One

I

These Soma drinks mixed with curds have been prepared for thee Indra, the Thunderer. Come, drink and enjoy these. O Indra, these Soma juices with songs of praise have been prepared for Thy pleasure. Enjoy the pleasant drink, listen to our lauds and reward the worshipper, O Lover of songs! Now I call on Thee Indra, Who is like desire fulfilling cow, excellent in gait, yielding milk in abundant streams, loveable and beautiful in appearance. O Indra, the lofty and huge hills are powerless to bar Thy way. None can prevent the act of Thine when Thou wouldest fain give wealth to one like me, who sings Thy praise. Who knows what vital power he wins while drinking with other Gods? None knows how long he stays? Gratified with drinks, Indra breaks down the castles in his strength.

O Indra, control and punish the anti-Yajna men, remove riteless people from around our homes, and grow in strength and opulence, our Soma plant, desired by many a one. May God, the Creator of the universe, the Lord of Vedas and their knowers, lover of His devotees, protect our Vedic words. May He, the Invincible, protect us along with our sons and brothers and our vows difficult to fulfil. Never art Thou fruitless, never dost Thou desert Thy devotee O Lord. Thy bounty, O God, is poured forth ever more and more. The best Slayer of our foes, yoke our soul to yoga wandering here and there from Thee. Come here with Thy high virtues to us, O Mighty God, to enjoy the Soma juice? O Subduer of the wicked, O God, the ardent worshippers offered Thee libations in the past, and are offering today. Listen now, here to the lauds of the devotees and come near unto us.

II

See now coming, sending forth her rays, the shining daughter of Heaven, the mighty one dispels the gloom of night that we may see, the friendly lady ushers in the light. O Sun and Moon, the settlers of the world, the subjects longing for light want to attain Ye! I too want to gain you for self protection. Thou, giver of wealth and wisdom, visit and reach each and all of us. O Sun and Moon, please enjoy this sweet Soma juice prepared for you in day time, and bestow treasures, chariots, etc., upon him who offers it. O God, I pray Thee with Soma libation, let me the sacrificer not be angry at any sacrificial beast. Who would not beseech the Almighty One, who nourishes the universe?

O Adhavaryu, let Soma juice flow, for Indra longs to drink of it. He, the slayer of foes, hath yoked together His horses and hath come nigh. O Mighty, great God, fulfil the desire of great and small, for thou art rich in wealth and worthy of being called upon in every calamity. If I, O God who scatterest riches, were the lord of wealth ample as Thine own, I would give it to the saint and never to the sinner. Thou art, O God, subduer of all the wicked. Father art Thou, all-conquering, remover of sins, Thou art, O God, subduer of all the wicked. Father art Thou, all conquering, remover of sins, Thou Victor of the vanquisher. In thy might Thou stretchest beyond the mansions of the sky. The earthly region comprehends Thee not, O God. Thou, who hast waxed mighty over the whole universe, liberate us.

III

Prepared is the Soma drink, mixed with cow milk and best grains, whereto He has ever been accustomed. O divine Lord of the steeds, we invoke Thee with our sacrificial good deeds, forget not these our songs of praise in the ecstasies of Soma. O Lord, we have made a house for Thee to dwell. O much invoked One, dwell there with all Thy might to guard and increase us, and give us riches and jewels of learning, etc. O Lord, Thou cleavest clouds and settest free the arrested streams, controllest the clouds in the sky. Thou layest great mountains open while letting loose the torrents. O Lord, we laud Thee on the occasion of pressing Soma and dividing grains; O Almighty, give us ample wealth and prosperity, and under Thy mighty protection, may we be victorious. O Lord of ample wealth, we deserving wealth have grasped Thee by the right hand, knowing that Thou art the Lord of the earth, cattle and valour, vouchsafe us wish-fulfilling riches of many kinds.

Men call on the God through their lauds in strifes to tilt the decision in their favour. O Valiant One, grant us fame, and stalls full of cattle. Like birds of shining plumage, the learned seeking more knowledge, the sacrifice fond sages, approach God and implore Him to dispell the darkness of ignorance, Lord fulfil their vision, and liberate them from the snares which entangle them. We gaze at Thee, O Lord, with intense longing in our hearts as on a mighty, golden winged bird, soaring higher and higher, possessing wondrous resources, the envoy of God. In the beginning of creation, God created the Sun, the womb of the present and future creations, and other similar shining worlds in the space. The wise use many matchless words for this Great Hero, most Mighty, Auspicious, Energetic, Wise God, the Wielder of thunder.

IV

The innumerable Demons of darkness engulf the Moon on the night of Amavasya, but the mighty Lord lays down His weapons only after liberating the engulfed Moon and subduing the demons. Flying in fear from the threat of Demons of darkness, all the deities who were Thy friends deserted Thee, but Thou conquered all the foes. Now, behold God's high wisdom and greatness, how he who died yesterday is revived today. The vanished Moon is reborn and runs her course through the stars of lunar mansion. O Indra, at Thy birth, Thou wast the only conqueror of the seven demons. Thou founded the hidden earth and heaven, and gave pleasure to the worlds. O God, Thou thunderer, I laud Thee with Vedic hymns, O Almighty, Eternal, most Wise, Excellent and Subduer of seven foes.

O men, gain favour of the Lord, the Great God through offerings and devotions. O Lord, the Sustainer of the subjects, go forth to noble and learned men. We invoke Thee, Auspicious, Omniscient, the best Leader of men, Mighty, Slayer of foes in this fight for protection, the Bestower of riches, victory and Listener of our supplications. O wise men, pray and sing Vedic hymns to God to obtain wealth and knowledge. Invoke Him, who is the Creator of all the world, and listens to the prayers, which I, His faithful servant utter! God pours copious rain from the clouds in the firmament, fastened over the earth, and fills the kine with milk and the herbs with sap.

V

We call on God, Omniscient, the Conquerer of all, the Mighty One, the Wielder of thunderbolt. Giver of riches. Praised by deities, Pervading all, the most Agile, and present in the hearts of His devotees, for our weal. I invoke the God. invoked by many, the Rescuer, God the Helper easily invoked, the Hero who listens. May He accept our devotions. We worship Indra, the upholder of the thunderbolt in his right hand. Remover of calamities, the Mighty and Terrible to foes and Lord of bay steeds. We worship Indra, the Lord of thunderbolt, Bounteous, Giver of blessings, the slayer of Vritra, the Great, Limitless, Mighty and the most Excellent. The man who fights against, with a desire to destroy us, deeming himself a hero or a giant, may be overthrown by us in the battle, O Lord, helped and strengthened by Thee.

He is Indra, whom men call upon when engaged in strife with the foe, whom poets praise. He is remembered by His subjects and lauded by the learned. O Indra, grant us nice viands and heroic progeny. O God. accept and enjoy our gifts, wax strong by our hymns and rejoice in our oblation! Let us sing His praise in a ceaseless flow, Who rains waters from the firmament. It is He who revolves the Earth and Heaven, like two wheels, fixed on either side of a car with an axle. May I incite Thee, O Friend towards friendship, far though Thou mayest beyond the rivers. May the Disposer grant grandchildren for his father, radiant in this mansion with special lustre! Who yokes the vigorous and strong steeds of turbulant spirit into the pole of Order, bearing in their mouth no fodder? He who does so, shall enjoy his life for long.

Chapter Two

I

O Lord, the possessor of knowledge and power of action, the Sama singers hymns Thy praise. The chanters of the psalms laud Thee. The knowers of all the four Vedas extol Thee with reverence that men have for the head of their family. All the hymns extol the Lord, who is diffused in every direction like the ocean, the Supreme Charioteer, the Master of heroes, the Lord of Strength and Protector of the Righteous. O Indra, drink this excellent, divine, exhilarating Soma juice. Here flow the streams of nourishing Soma to Thee at the place of sacrifice. O Indra, wondrous God, what wealth Thou hast not given us here in this world, give us that bounty filling full both Thy hands!

O Indra, the Mightiest, the Giver of prosperity, this Soma juice has been prepared for Thee. O Potent humbler of the foe, may it fill Thee with vigour as the Sun fills the world with his rays. O Indra come hither, with Thy knowledge, accept our lauds! O Indra, lover of the Vedic hymns, the prayers come to Thee fast like a charioteer. These Vedic prayers call upon Thee just as mother cows go unto their calves. Come men, let us praise Pure and Mighty Indra, with pure Sama songs! May milk blend with Soma juice and praise gladden Him and He be gracious unto us. O most Wealthy, Rich in splendours and illustrious, Soma is ready, Thy favoured drink, O Indra, Libation's Lord!

II

O men, bring forth oblations to Indra, the God, Who is Knower of all, Who fain would drink, never lagging behind, swift moving and the hero. May the great God, the mighty, residing in the inmost recess of the heart, the Sustainer of life, drive away the awful word from our mind. O Mighty God, the Lord of mighty deeds, the Subduer of the wicked. Protector of the learned, we approach Thee again and again for favour and help even as we apprach a car for aid. The learned men, amongst the respectable people, ranks the first for he acts like a wise father and through him God urges the people to contemplate and acquire knowledge. Where the man riding the chariots, drawn by swift and shining horses, reach and take delight in sweet Soma juice, there sacred rites are performed.

I glorify the Lord for your sake, who wrongs none, is the Leader of men, all-conquering, the Mightiest, the Wisest and the Best. We laud the lord, the Almighty, Pervading all. May He sweeten our lives and prolong the days we have to live! He is much lauded by many people, the Lord, the Shatterer of forts, ever Young, the Wise, of Unmeasured strength, Sustainer of life and the Wielder of thunder.

III

O learned men, offer Indra, worshipped by the heroes, the Showerer of rains, the sacred Soma mixed with oblations and accompanied by Sama hymns. Indra invites you, complete the rites. Sing, sing your lauds, O men of learning, sing your songs of praise to God, our Sustainer and Stronghold. Let young children sing His glories, Ye, let them laud Him. We should laud the Omnipotent God, who being kind gives to the soul, that longs to get prosperity and the teaching which makes it grow and admirable. O men, I call upon the Lord, the Ruler of all, the Master of unbending might, that He, as He is wont, may protect you and the chariots.

O man, even Indra, who is thine friend, he with the grace of God comes safe through strifes offered by the enemy, as he does overcome sins! O God of ample grace, widespread is Thy bounty, so good and liberal Giver, the Knower of all, Doer of many great deeds, give us splendid wealth. When bright Dawn, with her light appears, all living beings start to stir, both four footed and two, and round about flock the feathery birds from all the directions of heaven. The worlds which are there in the luminous realm of heaven, are there Vedas in vogue? Are Yajnas performed there? Is old rites of Yajna prevalent there? We perform Yajna and offer lauds to the Gods through Sama hymns. The Vedic hymns occupy an important place in society and sacred observances, thy bear sacrifices to Gods.

IV

Men in accord, select Indra as their King and Lord, who Conquers all armies, is Fierce, Firm in the battle. Great destroyer. All-powerful, Stalwart and full of Vigour, I trust Thee, O Almighty God, Most Brilliant, for Thou has destroyed the demon Vritra for the weal of mankind. Both Heaven and Earth fled unto Thee for refuge, and Earth even trembled at Thy strength, Thunderer! Come ye all men, seek refuge unto Him, the Lord of Heaven, the only One, worshipped by all men and beings. He is the First and only One to whom all pathways lead. O Lord of ample wealth, lauded by many, we all are Thine, and having faith in Thy help, draw to Thee. None but Thou, O Song lover, shall receive our prayers, as Earth loves all her creatures, so welcome this our song! May our high praise sound forth the glory of Him, who is the Supporter of mankind, the Lord of ample wealth, Who hath waxed mighty, much invoked with hymns, Immortal on whose laud is sung aloud every day!

O men, let your bliss-seeking minds, in unison, offer laud unto Him, the God, just as the wives embrace their beautiful wealthy and strong lords. O men, gladden with your songs the Gods, Ocean of wealth, Showerer of happiness, Invoked by many in Vedic verses, whose good deeds spread like the rays of the Sun for the weal of mankind, Most Mighty and Intelligent, Bestower of wealth and Destroyer of foes. O learned man, honour well God, the showerer of happiness, the Pure, Cause of all, under whom hundreds of planets and stars revolve. I as a devotee worship Him again and again and recite the lauds, the all-pervading, moving everywhere with horse like speed and propitiated through hymns, for my safety and protection. Filled with water, encompassing all things that be wide, spacious, pleasant and beautiful in their form, the Heaven and the Earth by His decree, undecaying and rich in germs, stand from each other apart. O Lord, like the Dawn, Thou hast filled both Earth and Heaven with light. Thou art Mightier than the mighty. Great king of men, the Mother goddess brought Thee forth, the divine mother gave Thee life. Sing praise for God, who gladdens all and dispels the darkness of ignorance. Let us, desiring help and protection, call upon Him for friendship, the Mighty and Mainstay of His subjects.

V

O Lord, when Soma flows, Thou makest the sacrifice pure and grantest us evergrowing strength. Indeed great art Thou. Sing forth to Him whom many men invoke, to Him whom many men laud. Worship the Mighty God with songs of praise! O Lord of the clouds, mountains, we sing for Thy delight, which conquers all struggles. Thou art the Creator of this universe, all-pervading the most beautiful and lauded by us all. O Omnipresent God, whatever immortality giving nectar exists either in Thee, or in the Yogis or in the Ida, Pingla and Shusmana, Thou art verily the source of all that. Come sacrificer and pour forth yet more libation, the highly gladdening drink. So praised He, the Hero, ever prospers us.

O learned men, pour out Soma, the sweet juice, for Him to drink. None but He gives bounteous gifts through His majesty. O men, come let us sing praise for Indra, the Hero who deserves the laud. He, with none to aid, overcomes all foes! O men, sing you a song of praise for God, the Giver of knowledge, the Great, Omniscient, the Creator of the Vedas. Sing a high song for Him, who is worthy of our adulations. He who alone bestoweth wealth on man, who giveth gifts, is God only, the potent Lord, whom none resist. Friends, let us sing a Vedic hymn for Him, the conqueror of all but never conquered, the chastiser of the wicked, the companion of men.

Book Five
Chapter One

I

O Indra, thou slayest Vritra, I praise O God, Thy most high might for the sacrifice. O Indra, this Soma hath been pressed for Thee, drink of it. Thou showerer of rain and remover of obstacles of Thy devotees, come unto us. O Indra, ever Conquering, Unconquerable, Dear, spread on all sides like a mountain, all-pervading, Lord of Heavens! O mighty Indra, Thou perceivest the great joy arising from Soma drink, whereby Thou smitest down the demons that joy we crave! O Gods, so mighty and learned, grant our sons and grandsons the lengthened terms of life that they may live long days!

O Indra, the Thunderer, Thou knowest how to avoid evil powers, just as he who knows the pitfalls and returns safe. Drive ye Gods, disease and strife away, drive ye away malignity! Keep us far removed from evils and sins. O Indra, Lord of steeds, may this Soma drink gladden Thee, just as a well trained steed driven away by an expert driver reaches the desired destination.

II

O Indra, from times immemorial, Thou art ever Rivelless and Leaderless. Thou seekest companionship through war! O friends, He who hath brought for us the best gifts, Him I praise for you, for protection and help. O learned men, come hither, fail not, stay not while marching onward, in a fit of rage Ye can tame even that which is firm! O Lord of horses. Lord of cows. Lord of Com, Lord and Protector of Soma, come hither and drink of the juice of Soma.

Learned persons, full of amity are akin by common ancestry, just as the rays of the Sun are to one another. O Indra, fetch us strength, fetch valour. All-knowing, Thou ever active, fetch us a hero conquering in war! O Lord, worthy of praise, just as water is united with water, so we draw nigh unto Thee with longing and are satisfied. Just as the birds are drawn to nourishing food, so we come unto Thee desiring bliss and sing Thy laud aloud. O Thunderer, ever youthful, Wondrous, we call on Thee seeking help and protection.

III

Just as the bright rays moving along the Sun, suck up the savoury essences diffused in space, and cause the rejoicing and happiness among the creatures, so does the company of the Lord to the soul and its sense organs. O Mighty, Sovereign Lord, just as the Sun dispels the clouds by his rays, so dost Thou drive away evil forces so that learned persons well versed in Vedas, may live in peace and by their spiritual powers drive advantage and help to others to do likewise. We invoke Indra, our joy and strength, Destroyer of all the wicked, alongwith his subjects. We invoke Him alone for protection and help in battles whether great or small. O Indra, the thunderer, Thine alone is unconquered strength. Thou with Thy surpassing strength smitest to death, the wile enemy, which act lauds Thine glory alone! O Indra. go forward and be bold, Thy strength of conquering the enemy is unchecked. Like the Sun that shatters clouds and controls the waters, do Thou slay the foe, establishing Thine own sovereignty!

O Indra, when wars are on foot, Thou destroys the enemy and givest booty to Thy friends and other brave men. Yoke Thy powerful bay steeds, humble the foe and make us affluent. O Indra, yoke quickly for us Thy bay steeds. Learned men, resplendent like the Sun, have praised Thee with their Vedic hymns. O learned men, may ye enjoy all the pleasures and be popular among the people. O Indra, listen to our requests and be not hostile to us. When wilt Thou lead us to prosperity? Make the learned happy and prosper! Now, quickly yoke Thy steeds! The Moon, the giver of delight speeds along the airs in the sky. The lightnings of the bright golden rays cannot be appreciated by the ignorant. O King and subjects who are like the heaven and the earth mark this my hymn! O Ashvins, lover of sweet Soma, the Seer is ready to laud Thee with Vedic hymns. O Lovers of sweetness, listen to my song!

IV

O Agni, Refulgent and Immortal God, we kindle Thee. This glorious lustre of Thine shines in heaven. Give food and bliss to those who are thy devotees and sing Thy laud. O Agni, we choose Thee as our Hota or officiating priest. Thou art Pure, Lustrous, present everywhere and waxeth great with oblations. O heavenly, high-born and glorious Dawn awaken us today to ample opulence even as thou didest awaken us before! O Great God, grant us mind full of delight, energy and mental powers. Let man joy, in Thy love, O God, as kine do in pasturage! Great Indra, Lord of shining bay steeds. Handsome, being fierce to the wicked and formidable to the foes, Learned, Mighty, who waxeth strong with His acts of wisdom and taking of nourishing food. He grasps the iron thunderbolt in His hand for our prosperity.

O Indra, he alone who knows full well how to yoke the steeds would mount the mighty car containing all material of war and other things. Now, Indra, yoke your fine steeds in the chariot! I praise that Agni, whom as their home all resort. The kine seek Agni as their stall, the swift footed steeds as their stable, and the learned men as their refuge. O Agni, give food to those who sing Thy praise. O learned men, no distress and sin affect the mortal man, whom Aryaman, and Mitra guide, and Varuna, through deep love, leads beyond his foes!

V

O God of tranquillity, shower bliss upon a friendly, mighty and opulent man! O Tranquil Lord, for the attainment of power, knowledge and wealth, rain thy blessing through Thy forbearance. O Discharger of obligations remove our foes like lust etc., which hinder our path! O God, Thou art the mighty ocean in which all beings take delight. O Sire of all the deities, purify all the hearts! O God, ever Pure and Mighty, Thou purify our conduct for obtaining power and wealth! May the Benign, Opulent, Wise God, purify us in the lap of actions, for the acquisition of wealth and happiness.

O God, in Thy Righteous Sovereignty, all are equal, following in Thy wake we realize Thee in the heart and enjoy bliss and happiness. O Purifier, grant us riches! Who are such blessed, moral and kind hearted men as living in unity and dwelling together? They are men dedicated to sacrificial acts and contemplation. O Effulgent Agni, we adore Thee with our humble deeds and prayers. Thou art our bearer of oblations to the Gods like a horse and mind, O Auspicious! O God, the Primordial cause, Pre-eminent, Great and mighty Protector, Thou purify us!

Chapter Two

I

O Giver from all sides, nourish us from all sides, Thou whom as the strongest we entreat! This Brahaman, benign in all seasons, renowned and named as Indra, I praise. The knowers of the Vedas, exalting Indra increase His strength so that He might kill the serpent of sin. Man use Thou, O God, as a vehicle to attain speedy liberation. O God, invoked by many, a man enlightened with knowledge uses Thee as lustrous protection! A man not devoted to charity acquires not wealth nor the cherished desires. He who long for wealth to be given in charity, attains riches and fame.

The Vedic verses are ever pure and all-supporting, the Gods ever free from stain and blemish. Dawn, with all thy beauty come! The kine with udders full of milk, follow thy path. O God, may we, dwelling in spirtually rich place, increase our wealth and meditate on Thee! The learned Ritvij men, chant the praise for God, who is Mighty, Famed in the Vedas and supports them. Chant aloud the song the praise of God, the Subduer of lust, etc. the song that He accepteth!

II

Agni, the Resplendent, who bears our oblation, hath come in His lustrous car. O God Agni, all-pervading, be Thou our nearest Friend, ye, our Protector, our kind liberator and worthy of our adoration! Of all the Gods, the Great God, lustrous like the Sun, giveth us wondrous wealth of knowledge. O the Best Worshipped God, Thou settles all and so settle me as well! The Dawn drives away the darkness of her sister Night, and maketh her retrace her steps. Similarly, Thou God, remove the darkness of our ignorance!

O God, may our souls and sense organs obtain pleasure from all these existing worlds! Just as the streams flow on their way, so let bounties flow from Thee! May we with this prayer obtain God given strength and enjoy happiness for hundred winters with heroic sons! May thou Indra along with Sun and Varuna, grant us nourishing and rich harvests! God is King of all the world.

III

The Mighty and Great Indra enjoyed Soma juices and barley brew at the Trikadrukehu Yajna performed in three days, with Vishnu. Nourished and exulted by it, He did many a mighty work. So this true and divine Soma served this true God Indra. This Brilliant God, Light of the learned, the Seer, sends forth His rays, spotless, lustrous and pure and thereby causes day light in various worlds. O Indra, come near to us who astrayed from Thee, just as the King, the protector of his righteous subjects goes to his seat of judgement, or just as the Sun, the protector of the earth reaches the Yajnas. We invoke Thee as sons do their sire, with gifts and Soma drink, that we may acquire wealth and power, O most Adorable. I call on Thee aloud through songs. O Mighty, Resistless, Opulent and Possessing many virtues. Thou art most Liberal, Thunder-armed, Worship-worthy and Omnipresent; make our pathways easy and full of riches and knowledge. Let my prayers be heard. Mentally I place the omniscient God in my heart and pray for the divine strength. I also invoke the soul and the vital breath (Prana). They both help in attainment of the Divine Light. All our thoughts, actions and holy hymns go forward on their way unto Him. O men, well versed in Vedas, let your praises born in hymns go forth to the God, the Mighty, the Holiest, the Master of all, the Omniscient just as lightnings flash for the clouds. Just as the Sun destroys darkness with his lustrous rays, so does the hero subdue all his foes with the help of his allies. God, the Almighty, all-pervading encompasses all things existing in seven airs of atmosphere; I praise this God, Creator of Heaven and Earth, most Wise, Almighty, Beloved of all. Giver of the riches, whose splendour is sublime, whose light shines brilliantly in creation. Who is Handsome and golden-handed.

Agni I regard as the Munificent, Liberal donor, Acceptor of what is offered with love and reverence, who knows all that exists like a sage, endowed with wisdom. The Refulgent God, who performs Yajna with high knowledge and reverential devotion, who shines like the clarified butter (ghee) when put in the blazing fire. O Almighty God, the Revolver of the sun, Thou art praised by the ancient learned men for Thy noble deeds. All the human efforts are centred on Thy brilliance, and it is Thou who bestows gifts of Prana, and strength. With Thy power Thou gets through all the substances and conquers all. Thou art the Master of unlimited powers, wisdom, bravery and foodgrains. May Thy blessings fall on you!

Pavamana Kanda

IV

O Soma, the pleasure arising out of foodgrains, etc. created by Thee, is obtained by the men of the entire earth. Thou art the source of happiness and Thy great renown is spread in the heavens. O Soma, flow in streams with Thy most sweet and gladdening power, pressed for the use of Indra. O Mighty, nourishing and satisfying flow in streams! Flow onward Soma, Thou slayer of the wicked, protector the Gods and delightful to all. Milch kine are lowing, the three Vedas are being recited, the Soma flows making a loud noise.

O Soma, Thou extremely sweet, flow and manifest Thyself to seat at the place of sacrifice. O Mighty, mountain-born residing in the clouds, nourished by the rains, Thou hath been pressed for rapturous delight! O Gold-hued, embodiment of delight, bestower of strength, flow on in streams for Vayu and other Gods to drink. Soma, the Mountain dweller, pressed through a sieve in pure vessel, in joyful and bounteous to all. Soma, the Sage of heaven, the wise, pressed between the hands by the priests, giveth joy and strength.

V

The rapture-giving Soma, pressed to flow, bestows wealth and fame upon the assembled people. Just as the waves of ocean, skilled in song, flow forward; just as the buffalo go to woods, so does the Soma juice flow in streams. O Soma flow on, fulfiller of our desires, mighty, glorify us among the folk, drive away all our foes away! O Purifier, bestower of happiness, Thou resplendent, we call on Thee, the fill filler of our desires. Soma, the beloved of the learned, enlightener, flows in streams as do the steeds of a chariot.

Potent, brilliant and swift Soma is offered in libation with a desire to possess kine, horses and heroic sons. God, flow Thou, working with mankind, may Thy gladdening juice reach Indra, and Vayu, as Thy Law ordains! The Pure Soma, has generated the wondrous light in the firmament, like the thunder, common to all human beings. The gladdening and sweet Soma flows on in streams with Vedic hymns and reaches Gods! Reposing on the wave of the mind, loved by many, and bearing the soul, the Soma flows on in streams around.

Book Six
Chapter One

I

The Gods resort to Soma, the slayer of the foes, the beautiful, inspirer of action, the best descended. Soma, the ever active, the giver of wisdom, hath overthrown all the foes. The learned adorn the Sage with holy hymns. Pressed and filtered Soma hath been poured into the jar. Soma is offered to Indra. Just as a powerful steed, yoked in a chariot, goes forward in the battle, so flows the Soma juice from two pressboards to a sieve. Just as the impetuous, brilliant, unwearied rays of the Sun come forth and drive away the dark covering of night, so does Soma sweep away the wicked.

Soma, Thou flowest in streams of happiness, chasing away the foes. Giver of wisdom and joy, drive Thou the Goddess folk away! O Soma. flow forth with that stream wherewith Thou hath illumined the Sun and urged the actions of men. Flow forth Soma, Thou who helped Indra in slaying Vritra who encompassed and hampered the mighty waters. O Soma, flow forth with that stream wherewith revelling in Thy wild delights, the Sun destroyed the 108 castles of the demons of drought. O Divine flow forth, speed through the sieve, who giveth wealth and food from all sides!

II

The greenish yellow mighty Soma, beautiful as Mitra in looks, gleams and flashes with the Sun, and flows roaring. O Divine we choose today in this Yajna, Him, who giveth protection, happiness, the Mighty one who is inspired by many. O Adhvaryu! Filter the Soma juice, pressed with stones, purify it for the enjoyment of Indra. The pressed, purified and invoked Soma, that which flows with speed in streams, giveth bliss and removeth sins. Soma, give us wealth in thousands, heroic strength, keep secure all renown of us!

Soma grants a new life to the old through rejuvenation. Soma, the self-effulgent like the Sun, is prepared by the people. O Divine, so bright flow forth with a roar into the wooden vessels! O Soma, Thou virtuous giveth strength, happiness and infusest excellent deeds. Thou effulgent showerer of rains ordainest laws. O Soma, sought after and made pure by Adhvaryus and priests, Thou flow forth in streams for food, grains and joy of contemplation. Come Thou with gleam and lustre to those who call upon Thee. O mighty Soma, favouring Gods and the sacrifices, flow on in streams to protect us. The great Soma, increases in strength through Yajna and showers bliss like rains. He is effulgent, benevolent, purifier, developer of intellect and approaches us for lifty friendship. O Soma, Thou art realized by the learned men. Thou manifests Thyself and flow on in streams for our wealth, grains and knowledge. Soma streaming on drives away our foes and sinners and marches on to Indra.

III

Soma, flowing in streams, purifying, resplendent, deep like a well, watery in form, residing the place of sacrifice approachest us. The best sacred gifts, Soma the benefactor of mankind, pressed out with stone should be sprinkled all around. Just as the people live in a city, so do Soma pervade all, eclipsing the ever bright rays of the Sun. Thou as expressed in lonely place through contemplation. Just as the Ocean is full of water, so art Soma with the juice of the stalk. O sweet One, giver of joy, remover of inactivity, flow into the wooden vessel for the enjoyment of Gods. Pressed out by Adhvaryus, the swift flowing Soma, goes in greenish yellow streams like an excellent steed in a joyous course.

O Soma, every day Thy friendship hath been my delight. Many pains of birth follow me, please help me overcome these, and grant me salvation. O Pure, Refulgent, when sought for, Thou approachest in rich flow, yellow like gold, much invoked and abundant into the ocean-like vessel with a voice raised loud. The rapturous Soma, the gladdening drink, flow into the vessel from above and spreads ecstasy around. O most wise, pure, watchful, conscious, knowing all, please protect us from all sides with Thy excellent virtues, and fill our sacrifices with sweetness. The expressed, rapturous Soma flows in numerous streams for God. Men prepare it in abundance, pure and bright. Manifest and flow on in streams, O Soma, Thou giver of corns, and joys. Thou art a mighty ocean full of happiness, come to Thy worshippers! The purified souls, immersed in bliss, attain salvation through control of mind, and horse-like restless sense organs. They abandon desires and overcome their sense of egoism.

IV

Expressed and purified by the priests, Soma fills the vessel with swift flowing streams. Just as a powerful courser led by reins is taken to the battlefield, so art Thou taken by the sages to the sacred place of sacrifice, where Thou growest stronger. God, the Creator of speech, the Friend of the holy, ever Pure and purifying. God of the Gods, wishing the world ever well, the Preacher of the Vedas, declares the generations and geneology of the Gods in the beginning of creation. The sages preach the three Vedas in the world, the revealed truth and wisdom of God. Just as the cows go to the cowherd, so the hymns of praise come to Soma, ever longing. Just as a peasant goes to a cattle shed and milks the cows, so goes Soma roaring to the Gods in the sky, expressed, and made pure in a sacrifice by the priests. God Soma, the Father of hymns, the Father of Earth and Heaven, of Agni, the Generator of the Sun, the Father, who begot Indra and Vishnu, is realized by the sacrifices.

Lauded in Vedic hymns, the Dweller in the triple world, Fulfiller of desires. Adorable, the Cause of rains, Giver of life and longevity. All-pervading Lord of treasures, the God showers his blessings. Guardian of all beings, Creator of creatures. Mighty, Roaring like an ocean, expressed by the stones, Soma, Waxeth strong in the proximity of sacrifice. Aloud flows the greenish yellow Soma juice from the wooden vessel, into the sacrificial fire accompanied by Vedic hymns. Ye learned men, meditate on the Soma sacrifice and Vedic speech, O Soma, the embodiment of sweetness, flow forth into the wooden vessels. Thou most gladdening, enrobed in waters, strength giving and excellent drink for Indra!

V

The hero served with Soma goes forth in front of the cars seeking spoils, and thereby mightily pleases his army. He declares his benevolent behests for his friends and takes on himself the formidable onslaughts of the foes. O Soma, Thy streams flow forth, when being pressed and purified. O Pure, Thou refulgent, fillest thy devotees with bliss as does the Sun with his rays the heaven. O men, sing laud to the Gods for obtaining wealth, sing loudly and offer the Soma libation. Let Soma flow forth through the sieve into vessel! O men, Soma the progenitor of heaven and earth, offered in oblation and urged on, goes forth like a chariot to Indra, sharpening his weapons and holding treasures in his hands. Pressed by the ten fingers of a contemplative priest, Soma the gold-hued, resplendent like the Sun, pours forth quickly into the vessel like a fleet mighty courser.

When the sparkling waters strive to cleanse Soma as through he were a courser, and the voices of the singing devotees emulate one another to laud it, Soma flows forth in his wisdom into a vessel as a cowherd goes to stable of cows in order to increase and multiply them. The mighty Soma, enrobed in water, giving happiness, flows forth, infusing strength and joys to Indra. He quells the wicked and slays the enemy, Lord of all, who fulfils desires. O Soma, pure and purifying, pour forth, flow onward into the ocean-like vessel. Soma, the mighty, born of waters, performed a great deed when he gave strength to Indra and generated light in the Sun. Hastening like flood of waters our lauds go forth to Soma. To him they reach with humble adoration, and longing, enter him who longs to meet him.

Chapter Two

I

O friends, for protection of Soma juice, the rapturous drink, drive away the long tongued dog! This Soma, the Lord of wealth, of strength, and purifying, the sustainer of all beings, illumines both the Heaven and earth. Soma, the excellently sweet juice, spreading joy, flows on to Indra. May our libations of Soma reach the Gods! For us flow the Soma streams, pure, benevolent, friends, knowers of the path and the best knowers of our weal. O Indu, shower on us the riches, carved by hundreds, most splendid, thousandfold surpassing light.

The pure souls sing lauds to Indra's dear friend, as in the morning of its life, the mothers lick the new born calf. Soma protects the bold and heroic as a soldier draws his mighty bow for his beloved king. The drops of flowing Soma weave a bright and colourful raiment, amidst songs, for the God. The sages through the sieve purify, the golden hued Soma, beloved of all, who with delightful juices courses to the Gods. O learned men, give dakshina to the Adhvaryus, and other priests who press Soma juices out, without being asked, let not Yajna suffer, but drive away the dog!

II

Benevolent and great Soma manifests himself through life-giving rains. He, the mighty and far seeing hath now mounted the mighty Sun's car, moving in every direction. Let our streams of Soma juice, pressed out flow forth to the Gods! May our enemies, the atheist be ever wanting, and our holy prayers succeed. This exceedingly sweet, most beauteous of the beauteous, mighty as Indra's thunderbolt, the Soma reveals himself in the vessel by its clamour. Just as the milch cow shed milk in streams, so do the juices of Soma flow forth in abundance. Soma, the refined reaches Indra. Soma gains the vessel through hundred paths like a youth who moves with youthful maids. Soma, the joy of Gods, pressed by men, sustainer of heavens, the green hued, the mighty, flows forth in streams like a courser.

The giver of intelligence, the Lord of days, dawns and heavens, life of the rivers, being offered in libation, effulgent having entered the vessel with roar, goes skyward. Having waxed strong in Yajna, He purifies the four, i.e. earth, heaven, space and cardinal points. The seven celestial milch kine pour the milk for Soma from high heaven. Flow forth to Indra, O Soma, well pressed. Let sickness stay afar from us along with wickedness. Let not the double tongued men delight Thy juice, let thy devotees prosper here in the world! The golden hued, wondrous, majestic like a king, roaring Soma delights the sense organs. Being filtered and purified, Thou overflowing the vessel, ascends high in the heaven like a mighty hawk. Just as the milch kine yield milk to their calf, so does sweet Soma flow forth unto Gods. The priests cleanse Soma with waters, blend it with honey and relish its pressing. They revel, hold and taste the gladdening juice.

III

Let these gladdening gold-hued Soma juices, go to Indra and attain light of heaven. O tranquil one, ever vigilant, flow on for Indra, and shower strength that attains light of the heaven! O friends, come, sit down, sing lauds to Him who purifies, adorn Him for Yajna as a child is decked with gifts. O friends, sing hymns to Soma, the purifier, for your joy sweeten him with honey, like a child who is pleased with offering of gifts, etc. Soma, shedding lustre in the sacrifice, dear to men like a child, is far more excellent than any other object, however, dear. O Soma, flow forth in streams for Gods. Thou, sweet and mighty one, come and reside in our vessel!

Soma the pure and purifier, in waves flows on through the sieve of wool, and roars to the accompaniment of Vedic songs. O mighty Soma, flow onto us and grant wealth of milch kine steeds and oxen! The Vedic hymns sing Thy praise for our weal. We know Thee through these Vedic verses. Gold-hued Soma, overcoming all obstacles, flows rapidly through the wool. O Lord shower heroic renown on Thy worshippers! Purifying, the sweet Soma flows, the Vedic verses in seven metres praise Thee aloud!

IV

Flow for Indra, O Soma, Thou so excellent, work-inspiring, blissful, adorable, sweet, mighty and effulgent! Lord of the corns, friend of the learned, God, grant us spendid wealth and glory, remove the cask of clouds! O sacrificing priests! express and pour Him again and again, who is adorable, fast as steed, cause of rains, swims in water and urges light to spread! He is the showerer of bliss, comes in thousand streams, milks the heaven, the Lord of all kinds of riches. He, who is Lord of food and wealth, friend of Gods, giver of handsome bodies and glories, should be invoked.

O beloved, most holy and effulgent God, Thou alone leads the learned to salvation. He floweth forth through the wool, in streams, the gladdening juice, sporting like the waves on water. He, who throws open the strong prison of clouds in the heaven for the beams of light to shine forth, multiplies the kine and horses through copious rains, the conqueror of all. May He remove all our obstacles like a hero in armour.

Aranya Kanda
Chapter Three

I

O Indra, the most Mighty, thunderer, equipped with weapons, handsome, sustainer of earth and heaven, grant us desire-fulfilling food and wealth. He is the Lord of men, all that is animate and inanimate, and all sorts of wealth. He giveth the charitably disposed souls the comfortable means of life. May He grant us desired wealth! He, Self-effulgent, Handsome and Wondrous, provides the charitably disposed with happiness and bliss. O mighty, Refulgent Lord, cut asunder all our three kinds of bondage, so that being free from sin, we may acquire bliss in obedience to Thy Law! O Lord of Tranquillity, Sustainer, Purifier, may be with Thy help, attain desired fruits through our worthy actions!

O God, may all my desires be fulfilled by Thy grace! May He, the most holy, giver of wealth, worthy to be invoked in Yajna, appear unto us. O God, grant us all the wealth and food of the people. We want to divide all these among ourselves equitably. O men, I existed prior to Gods, I am the showerer of true elixir. He, who teaches My divine knowledge, is the benefactor of mankind. He, who does not impart my divine knowledge to other, is destroyed by Me, the Sustainer of all.

II

O Lord, Thou preservest this sparkling milk in white, black and red kine. He illuminates the Sun with light. Finally all things dissove into the womb of Him. He sustains all the worlds, is the Centre of all might; the wicked are killed by His might and He is the source of all. God alone, with His Law, keeps the Sun and Moon interconnected. The same God is Chastiser and Self-effulgent. O

Almighty God, Invincible, defend us with Thy unconquerable safeguards in battles great and small. O Almighty God, this sparking Soma is for Thee. Thou reside in the heart of Thy devotees! O God of opulent wealth. Eternal, when Thou comest in the heart of a devotee to remove the darkness of ignorance, then Thou increasest the bliss of the Earth and sustainest the, heaven!

III

O All-pervading, Lord of all that exist, increase in me spiritual glory, fame and bliss, just as Thou establishes the Sun in space. O tranquil Lord, Chastiser of the proud, may we attain powers and knowledge of all kinds, which shower happiness. Thou art Perfect, grant the eternal soul beatitude in the light and delight of spiritual knowledge. O God, Thou hast created all these herbs, the water and kine like cattle. Thou hast expanded the heavens with its worlds, and hast removed darkness with light. Obeisance to Thee, O Lord, Refulgent, Omnipresent, Illuminator of the Yajna, Adorable in all seasons, Giver to all, Possessor of all beautiful and wondrous objects! O God, Thy subjects on this Earth regard Thy name Om as best of the Vedic speech expressed in twenty-one kinds of metres. These subjects knowing this laud Thee, and the Vedic verses appear glorious with Thy praise.

Just as some waters reach and mingle in the ocean, the others simply manage to reach near; and still some others merge into the ocean, in the form of a river, so do, O God, most Effulgent, Preserver of actions, these Vedic words reach unto Thee. Night, the giver of rest and sleep to the entire world, is here around us. Now Dawn hath come, scattering away darkness with her light. May our speech nobly utter the adorable glory of the Showerer of all joys, Effulgent, All-pervading Lord! May our pure intellect laud Thee, the All-controlling, Omniscient God, just as the newly created sacrificial fire obtains gladdening Soma.

O all learned men, the God, the Earth and Heaven, listen to my prayer! May I never speak unpleasant words for Him, and being in His closest proximity enjoy happiness! May the Earth and Heaven grant me fame! May I attain splendour! May these never abandon me! May I be the proud speaker in the learned assembly! I relate the heroic deeds of Indra, by which He the Thunderer, destroys the castles of clouds and makes waters flow. He scatters the clouds asunder and causes streams to flow forth. I am Agni, by birth I emit light of knowledge, ghee delights me, elixir is in my mouth. I sustain all that exists, in three ways. I am the basis of space, ever effulgent and all best objects am I. The all-pervading Agni guards the orbits of both the moving Earth and the Sun. He guards the gladdening Yajna of the Gods.

IV

O God, Effulgent, Foremost, with Thy grace the tongue in the mouth eats and moves. Thou alone grantest us food, wealth, milk and light to see. O God, it is with Thy grace that spring is pleasant, the summer is pleasant, the rainy season is pleasant, the autumn is pleasant, the winter is pleasant, and the cool season is pleasant. The Omnipotent God hath a thousand heads, a thousand eyes, a thousand feet. He, all-pervading, transgresses the whole Universe. The three-fourths of the God, remains above and aloof from the world. while with the one-fourth He creates and dissolves the world again and again. Pervading the all animate and inanimate objects, He sustains everything.

God is the source of the past, present and future universe, nay He is greater than this universe. God is the Lord of all that grows and the final salvation. God is the Creator and Lord of the universe. He, remaining aloof, creates the Earth, creatures, villages and cities. O all-pervading, Creator of the Earth and Heaven, and all that exists in them, I know Thee as excellent Guardian. Thou overextendest this Earth and limitless Space. May Thee liberate us from sins and sufferings, and giant happiness. O creator of the wonderful Sun, the learned sing Thy laud in Vedic hymns. Let Our souls be in touch with the light of gold, the light of the Sun and the light of Brahman. O God, the Lord of this universe, grant us that might wherewith we may overcome our foes. Grant us abiding wealth and food according to our actions. Make us lethal to our enemies and sins! O kine, in various beauteous forms, may ye ever remain with calves and bulls, yielding milk morning and evening! May this Earth be your extended pasturage, waters fit for your drinking, and thus you be always happy!

V

O God, the Giver of longevity and Purifier of our lives, give us energy and food. Drive away from us the dog like wicked persons. God, the most Effulgent, lords over all the shining heavenly bodies. He creates and inspires fire, water and wind, and is the soul of all animate and inanimate things. He sustains and pervades the Earth, Heaven and Space. The mother Earth moves round her father, the Sun. The lustre of the Sun moves up and between the Earth and the Heaven along with the wind. The Sun, far greater than the Earth, illuminates the Heaven.

Stars and nights disappear at the appearance of the Sun, so the thieves of mind take to flight in the presence of the light of knowledge. The light-emitting and colour-producing rays of the Sun enable all men to behold, like blazing fires. O Sun, Thou relieves us from darkness, maketh all beings see with Thy light. Thou illuminest all shining objects! O Sun, Thou shinest before the Gods, the Earth and the whole world in order to make all see everything. O Pure and the Remover of all calamities! Thou lookest upon all worlds with compassion, as we look upon Thee as our Guardian and Nourisher! O God, the Universal Spirit pervading all, Thou illuminest all the regions and creates days and nights. Thou seest the actions of all creatures as Thou art Omniscient! O Illuminator, Omniscient God, as seven kinds of rays cause to see the resplendent Sun in this beautiful world, so it is the Mantras composed in seven kinds of Vedic metres that make us to attain Thee.

Mahananmyarchika

O all-knowing Indra, direct us on the right path, O Pervading all subjects, reach us how to attain our goal! O Lord of opulent wealth and wisdom, most Conscious, grant us learning, etc. with these lauds! O all-pervading like the rays of the Sun, equip us with learning and wisdom. Thou art Lord of food and fame, the most Mighty, Adorable. Be pleased. Thou Lord, Destroyer of the wicked, the Wielder of the thunderbolt. Grant us spiritual might and opulence, O most Adorable! May Thou ever be blissful! O most Heroic amongst the heroes, the most Adorable, equipped with weapons, most Charitable amongst the rich, urge us to laudable actions for wealth. O Lord of learning. Effulgent like the Sun, Omniscient God, lead us on righteous path. We praise Him alone.

The Almighty God lords over all. We call upon Him, the Unconquerable Hero for our protection. May He take us safe beyond the enemy, so that the truth, the Yajna and the Vedas prevail. We devotees invoke the Unconquerable Conqueror, the Lord of opulence for our protection. May He sweep away our foes. May He completely annihilate our enemy. O Eternal thunderer, grant us bliss, establish us in Thy felicity. O Mighty, Thy nourishment is alone praise-worthy, because Thou alone controllest all. O God, Slayer of the wicked, laudable, we praise Thee. He, the Mightiest, Learned, Friend to all, Blissful and without a second, pervades the Earth and all other worlds.

O Refulgent and Illuminating, Thou art the same as related earlier! O God, Thou art the same as mentioned before! Verily O God, Thou art the same as described earlier! O Nourisher, Thou art the same as described before! O Gods, Ye art all as described before!

Uttararchika/Part Second

Book One
Chapter One

O men, sing forth to God, the Purifier! The learned and sedate men, God loving, blend milk and Soma together for attainment of God. O God, Thou shower happiness on our cattle, happiness on our progeny, happiness on our steeds, people, herbs and plants! The Soma juice, blended with milk sparkles with light. Like a strong courser, roused and sent forth to battle, like the warrior raised to action, the Soma flows forth with speed. Soma, the awakener of intellect, waxing strong in sacrifice, illumines the objects, like the Sun! The streams of Soma, mighty and wise are poured forth, like the steeds issuing from the stable. The fingers of the Ritvij men purify the sweet Soma in the Vat. The streams of poured Soma reach the vessel like the milch kine reaching their shed. They reach the place of sacrifice. O mighty Agni, we kindle and blaze Thee with fuel and ghee. Thou abide in my heart to remove the darkness of ignorance! O Agni, Thou winnest for us great heroic strength and high glory. O Gods Varuna and Mitra, pour nourishment on our pasturage, pour forth sweetness in our atmosphere! Varuna and Mitra gladdened by lauds, growing mighty through Yajna, masters of all, activate noble deeds. O Gods, lauded by Vedic songs, sit in the sacred seats of sacrifice, and enjoy the Soma drink.

O Indra come and drink of this Soma juice expressed for Thee. Come, occupy this sacred seat! Let Thy long maned bay steeds carry Thee here. Pray, come and listen to our prayers. We the priests, engaged in sacrifice, invoke Thee with Thy friend, O Soma drinkers, with our Soma offerings. May both Indra and Agni, pervading the Space, urged by our Vedic hymns, come to our sacrifice to enjoy the Soma juice! Come ye Gods, friends of the soul, and drink this streaming juice! I invoke Indra and Agni, who favour the wise, may They come and sate themselves with the drink! O Soma of heavenly birth, the people here on earth enjoy thy raptures and glory by drinking thee. May the Holy one, giver of wealth and foods unto us, flow to Indra, Varuna and Marut, adorable and worthy of our Yajna. We adore Thee O God, desiring to obtain all the wealth and foods and their equitable distribution amongst us! O Soma, enrobed in waters, purifying all, thou manifests thyself. Thou art lustrous and giver of wealth and happiness. The learned and holy man milks the sweet, excellent, divine, and pure Soma. Thereby he obtains the heavenly Soma juice. O Soma, flow forth and seat thee on the sacred grass! Cleansed and purified by the priests, speed forward. Just as a spirited steed is led by reins, so thou art taken to the sacred seat by the priests, being made sparkling and pure! Thou, well equipped with arms, guardian of the homes, averter of the evils, father and begetter of Gods, mighty, the sustainer of heaven and earth, flows forth in streams!

Just as the unmilked kine low to their calves, so do we invoke Thee aloud, O Lord of animate and inanimate objects and all-knowing! None other like Thee has ever been, nor ever will be. We, men of learning, desiring to obtain kine and horses, praise and invoke Thee! In what manner will He become our friend? With what might, action and conduct? Through wisdom wilt Thou be won over, the ever waxing strong! What excellent and gladdening thing will cause thee burst open the fortresses of the foe? Verily, it is the juice! Do thou, O God, be guardian to thy friends who laud thee for a hundred year! Just as kine low to their calves, so we call aloud upon God, with praises, who is handsome, subdues foes and takes delight in Soma juice. O God, grant us soon, one, who is bounteous giver, handsome, lord of the armies, nourisher like the clouds, rich in corn, kine, other cattle, might and foods! O priests, I tell ye, recite aloud the Brihat Sama for the Yajna, praise God, the Giver of riches, like Children praising their forefather! He, who is adorable, untouched by passions, firm, unconquerable by the foes, grants him wealth and food honourably, who sings His praise and presses Soma for the Yajna. Flow forth thou sweet Soma in streams, expressed for Indra to drink! Subduer of the wicked, pervading the world, reaching the place of sacrifice, Soma hath poured into the golden vat. The best amongst the drinks, adorable, slayer of the foes, the Soma giveth wealth even to the princes.

Flow forth, thou Soma most sweet, inspiring, gladdening juice, for Indra! Having drunk deep of the divine Soma, Indra waxeth strong, wise and spirited, as a strong and speedy steed runs to the battle! May these golden hued, well pressed Soma juices reach the mighty Indra in heaven! This Soma, so well pressed, arouses Indra for conquering the battle. Gladdened by this Soma, Indra, equipped with mighty weapons, wins the foes in war. For protection of the juice, the inspiring drink, drive away, ye friends, the long tongued dog! Like a speedy horse, the Soma, well pressed and purified, flows forth on all sides. The Priests attend Soma, the unassailable, with prayer and devotion. They prepare it for the sacrifice, bounteous, mighty, far-sighted, ever youthful and lustrous Soma, soaring high, hath now reached the mighty chariot of the Sun, which moves in every direction.

We sing to Agni, in every Yajna for acquiring strength. Let us laud the Almighty, Omniscient God, a well beloved friend unto us. He the Almighty, the Protector of our lives, the Guardian, is our Lord! May He defend us in battles and grant us strength! O Agni, come and grow strong with this Soma drink! I sing forth many songs of praise to Thee! Wherever Thou applies Thy mind, there is created a dwelling place. O Agni, let not thy splendour ever harm our eyes and other sense organs! O Lord of us all, accept our devotion! O Peerless one, we call on Thee seeking protection and help. O Indra, we seek thy refuge in all our actions. Thou art suduer of four foes, heroic, effulgent and splendid. We thy friends, have therefore chosen Thee as our succourer. As waters follow waters, we come unto Thee, O Indra, with desires. Just as the ocean swells with rivers, so we increase Thy might every day with our hymns, O thunderer!

Chapter Two

O men, invite Indra, the conqueror, the most bounteous, the giver of wealth, to a drink of Soma with a hymn. He is Indra, praised by many, much invoked, leader of song and renowned of old. Indra, the most active, the giver of wealth and might, and fruits of our actions, binds all with the law. Sing ye friends to Indra, the Lord of bay steeds, the enjoyer of Soma juice. Let us glorify the Lord for acquiring wealth, as men eulogise a noble man, charitably disposed to gain gilts. O good God Indra, Thou grantest us wealth and kine, wisdom and gold, the Lord of boundless power. Indra, we, thy devoted friends, sing thy lauds. The wise also praise Thee with their songs of Chastiser of the wicked, none else have I praised in my Yajna of actions, for I gain light of knowledge through Thy lauds. The ever active wise men, never desiring passivity, merge into Thy bliss. Let our hymns be loud to Indra, the enjoyer of Soma. Let poets sing his praise. We call upon Indra to drink of Soma, in whom all glories rest, in whom the seven officiating priests rejoice. The learned men expand the Yajna during the three days of Triktuka ceremony. Let our hymns aid to prosper it. Hie Thee hither, O Indra, and drink of this Soma, pressed and made pure for Thee! O mighty rayed, scatterer of the mass of clouds, adorable with hymns, for Thy enjoyment hath this juice been prepared. Thou art invoked, O Sun!

O mighty armed Indra, gather for us with Thy right hand, manifold nutritious food and wealth! We know thee, Thou art mighty in deeds, mighty in granting favours! Hero, when thou wouldest give the gifts, neither the sages nor mortal men can restrain Thee like a fearful bull. The Soma being prepared for Thee, I pour it in oblation. Sate Thee by drinking deep of it. Let not the fools and those who mock at Thee, beguile Thee. Leave not the enemy of the Vedic hymns! Here in the Yajna, the learned cheer Thee with Soma juices for food and wealth. Drink to thy fill like a white deer drinking from a lake! Drink of it to thy heart's content, we offer it, O fearless God! Pressed out with stones, cleansed by men and purified through the sieve of wool, Soma juice is like a courser bathed in rivers. Just as cooked barley is sweetened by mixing it with milk for the kine, so we have prepared this excellent Soma for Thy joy. O Lord of opulence, this juice hath been pressed out with much exertion for Thee. Drink of it, O lover of hymns! O Indra, enjoy this juice which gladdens thee so much. Let it cheer Thee up! Let the juice enter both thy flanks, enter Thy head with songs, let it enter with thy arms, with bounty. O Hero! Hie hither. O priests, sit ye down and sing hymns in praise of Indra. Laud him, richest of the rich, who lords over the noblest wealth. May He stand by us in our needs for our wealth. May He come nigh to us with might!

We call on Indra, the mightiest, as friends, in every need, in every fray to succour us. I call Him, the eternal, the giver of salvation, whom my sire invoked of old. If He hears our call, He would come with succour of a thousand kinds of riches! Thou purifiest the Yajna where Soma is pressed for acquiring great strength. In the heaven's first region is His seat, who is most mighty, giver of the fruits of actions and prompt to protect. I invoke Him, most mighty, a friend to aid in war and prosperity! With this hymn, I invoke Agni, the son of strength, dear, wisest envoy, skilled in sacrifice, eternal, messenger of all. See, the brilliant Daughter of Heaven is approaching dispelling darkness of night that we may see. The friendly Lady ushers in the light. The sun, the refulgent star of heaven, ascending pours down his beams together with the Dawn. O Dawn, at thine and the Sun's rising, may we attain our share in your light. O Sun, and Moon, the settlers of all, these subjects desiring light call on you. I invoke you for help, o giver of wealth and wisdom to the subjects. One minded, both of Ye, driven down your car to us, and enjoy this gladdening Soma juice!

Knowing the ancient splendour, the learned men draw the sparkling milk from the Soma plant, giver of wisdom and joy. This Soma is like the Sun, flows forth in seven streams to the vats and to the heavens! He, purifying all, stands above all else as does the God Sun over all. The gold-hued, dazzling God manifests himself for the Gods and flow through the straining cloth to the vat. Soma, well pressed, purified and strengthened by the wise priests flows forth, a God for Gods. O learned men, let this God, opulent and purifying, flow on for other Gods! Like the waves of water. Soma, the excellently sweet, flows forth with intensity to the Gods. The bright and joyous Soma, decked like a beloved son, is pressed and flowed forth by skilled men like a car driven to a battlefield. The rapturous Soma, well expressed, hath flowed forth to our Yajna, to glorify us. Just as the Sun lords over all the world, so does this Soma controls the minds of all. Just as a steed is led by the reins, so is Soma cleansed with fingers. The fingers of the learned priests make Soma flow forth with the stones for Indra to drink. Roaring flows Soma, the friend of Gods, to all sides in streams. Glorious gold-hued, on he flows, for him who expresses it.

Book Two
Chapter One

O Lord of tranquillity, flow forth with thy wondrous aids, Thou foremost of all, purify our hymns and prayers of every sort! O witness to all, flow onward. Thou inspires clouds to rain and our speech to recite hymns, O Sage, O Soma, the Vedic verses rush to sing thy glory! Soma, flow forth, make us glorious and drive away our foes! In thy friendship, O Soma, most mighty, most glorious, may we overthrow all those who war against us! Guard us with those lethal weapons, which Thou hast for the destruction of the wicked! O Soma, potent, bright and mighty, Thou lords over all! O God, throw open for us the gates of riches! O Thou, effulgent and strong, we invoke Thee for thy friendship. Being sprinkled with waters and purified by men, Thou readiest the wooden vessel! O well armed, hie The hither, and shower on us heroic strength! O God, Purifier of the soul, we seek to acquire thy friendly love. O God, be gracious unto us, with thy mighty waves which overflow the filtering sieve. O all purifying Lord, grant us wealth, food and heroic sons!

We choose Agni, the envoy, the skilled performer of the holy rite and instrumental in producing various things. We invoke Agni, the Lord of subjects, the Giver of all objects and much beloved. O Adorable God, bring the Gods hither, Thou art revealed to those who perform Yajna. Thou giveth all desirable things and happiness. We call upon Varuna nad Mitra of pure strength, to drink of Soma juice. I invoke Mitra and Varuna, who by Law sustain the world, and art lords of the shining light. Let Varuna be our special protector, let Mitra guard us with all his protective forces. They both make us rich in wisdom and wealth! The learned singers of Samaveda glorify the god only. The chanters of Rigveda also praise the same God. Let all the Vedas, and speeches of the wise, glorify the Lord of the Universe! O Lord protect us ever in all battles where abundant wealth is gained. O Omnipresent protect us with Thy peerless protective powers. God the Creator hath placed the Sun high in the heaven, so that men may see afar. The Sun draws the water of the ocean up, takes it high in sky and then rains it down. To Sun and Agni we offer our reverent oblations with holy hymns for our protection. The learned priests implore and sing to both these Gods to gain wealth and food and strength. We also invoke them with Vedic verses and oblations for the same reason. O Purifier, Sustainer of the Heaven and Earth, helping us like the Sun to see. Thou strength giving Soma, we call on Thee for winning riches. O Pavaman Soma, gold-hued, offered to Gods in oblation by the priests, Thou flow forth and incite Indra to battle, thine ally!

Just as the bull bellows on seeing the kine, so does Thou ascend to the heaven resounding the Earth and Space with Thy roar. This shout is heard like that of Indra's in the battle. Being cleansed and waxing strong, Thou excellently sweet Soma. flowest forth and soarest high, singing to the Sun. O Lord of the herbs sweet, effulgent, colourful, effused, flow Thou forth for our happiness, urging the clouds to rain! We, thy devotees call on Thee to win wealth and power. The hero in war calls on Thee for aid, men call on Thee on all sides for protection. O wondrous, thunderer, lord of the clouds, chastiser of the foes, mighty and adored, give us ever kine, oxen and horses as a Victorious hero is given far his enjoyment. I sing to Indra, who giveth many gifts, as we all know. I sing his praise, who rich in wealth, bestows upon his eluogisers gifts of wealth thousandfold! Just as a hero destroys the enemy hosts in the battle, just as the streams flow forth from a mountain, so do his gifts flow, who feedeth many a one. O Indra, the thunderer, thy devotees offered thee oblations before. Now Indra listen to him who praises thee, and be master of our house! O All-pervading, adorabie, prayed through hymns, be gracious unto thy devotees, and grant them help and protection! O Soma, flow onward with thy juice, gladdening all. Thou protects the noble and destroys the wicked. Being united with kine like beautiful Vedic verses, fast like a hawk, the Soma rests in his home.

This pure, strength and wealth-giving Soma, loved by all, is obtained in the wooden vessel. He nourishes all the beings and fills the Earth and Heaven with light. Beautiful verses sing the praise of the gladdening drink in joyous mood. When purified, the sparkling Soma flows on in many streams. O Pavaman, grant us thy gladdening, mighty juice which may pervade our five sense organs and whereby we may win riches. Soma, the enhancer of intellect, specially bright, creator of days, dawns and heaven, the filler of rivers, offered in oblation by the learned priests, roaring in the vat, goes high up in the sky. Purified by the sages, flows on the Soma, roaring into vats. From the vats He issues forth shedding nectar through the three worlds, enhances Vayu's strength to make him friend of Indra. This Soma, purifying, makes the mornings shine and makes the rivers flow. Soma, the cheerer and giver of heart's delight, fills the three times seven streams withjoy. Thou art verily the friend of the brave; steadfast and strong art Thou! Thou art praiseworthy indeed! Be Thou our supporter, O Lord of wealth, praised by all the worshippers. O protector of might and armies, taking delight in well pressed Soma blended with milk, remain ever alert like the Veda knowing priests. All holy hymns have magnified Indra, vast as the sea, the best of warriors borne on cars, the lord of strength and horses. May we never, strong in thy friendship, be afraid, O Indra, lord of might! We laud Thee with songs, the never conquered conqueror! The eternal gifts and saving saccour of old never fail him, who gives kine, wealth and food to Thy worshippers.

Chapter Two

These rapid flowing streams of Soma are offered in libation to bring us all felicities. Soma, the remover of afflictions, giver of strength, brings to our progeny easy success. The purifying Soma is eulogised with holy hymns to travel through the space. Pressed for the feast of Gods, Soma giveth us brilliance, beauty and foe subduing strength. O Soma, grant us manifold increase of kine, horses and wealth for our protection. O tranquil Soma, pervading many worlds, the Lord of limitless might and wealth, prayed through Vedic hymns, we seek Thee with sacrifice. We attain Thee, O slayer of the enemies, adorable, door of innumerable mighty deeds! O Lord of the noblest deeds, and the Universe, Thou nourishes the three worlds. The man who desires opulence, therefore, seeks Thy refuge. He, the seer of all, the giver of desired fruit, Lord of the subjects, pervading the whole universe, possess great renown. The revolver of the sun etc. protector of sacrifice, the lord should be contemplated upon by the soul, ever migrating like a bird, O Soma, cleansed by the sages, manifest thyself in flowing streams, and approach us with thy splendour! O Lord, praised through speech, creating life, Thou gold-hued, give wealth, might and happiness to the folk! O Soma, effulgent and purifying, revered by the priests, go Thou to God's resting place! Agni, the lord of the home, ever youthful, bearer of oblations, whose mouth is ladle, He worthy of invocation, is kindled by rubbing together the sticks. O God, Agni, be the sure protector of him, who worships Thee, the giver of manifold gifts! Be gracious unto him, O God, who, rich in sacrifice, would fain call on Thee!

I call on Mitra of holy strength and foe-destroying Varuna, who both give us happiness in our daily activities. Mitra and Varuna, created by God, the absolute Truth, augment the truth and are causes of establishment of contact with God. They pervade all in the form of the universe. Mitra and Varuna are givers of happiness. They of vast dominion, maintain strength and are refuge of multitude. I invoke both Indra and Agni, praised by all since times immemorial. May they never harm us! The mighty Indra and Agni we invoke, may they be kind to us engaged in sacrifice! They both destroy our foes, they both subdue the evil tendencies and drive away everything that may cause us harm. The learned men, who have obtained elixir of knowledge, immersed in joy, preaching it everywhere, realize the bliss in the ocean of their heart. A holy and learned man, practising yoga, attains God, the Embodiment of Truth. Such a man realizes the God through self-control and true wisdom. A Yogi, far-seeing, self-disciplined, guided by wisdom attains God, vast like an ocean.

A wise man preaches all around him the wisdom of God in the form of the three Vedic speeches of Rig, Yajur and Sama. Just as the kine come to their master, so do the hymns reach the Gods. The gladdening Vedic verses long to reach the God. The learned enquire into God with their intellect. Contemplated upon and purifying, the God is eulogised through Vedic hymns, but He cannot be described in words or hymns. O God, showerer of beatitude all around. Purifier, Pervading our souls, come unto us with bliss, wisdom, and let our knowledge grow. O God, not even hundred heavens, hundred earths can match Thee. Not even a hundred Suns, together with the Earth and Heaven can compass Thee, O Chastiser of the wicked! O God, the Fulfiller of desires. Almighty, all-pervading, protect us with all Thy protecting wondrous aids! O God, Destroyer of vice, we of purified heart and engaged in Thy worship, meditate on Thee with a steadfast mind like waters in an ocean. O God, the wealth of the poor, many invoke Thee ever for bliss, just as a thirsty man goes to the place of water. O all-seeing, Foremost, completely Fearless, Thou grantest the learned, the wealth, cattle and food. Therefore, we call on Thee. The Sun enjoys the Soma oblations with a great skill. I, the priest make ye all bow to much worshipped God with my Yedic speech, just as a wright bends his wheel for easy motion. They who give great gifts, love not petty praise; riches come not to a niggard and violent churl. Whatever worthgiving exists in this world, O Lord of wealth, indicates Thy excellence. The priests recite the three Vedas, kine low for milking and the tawny-hued Soma bellows while being offered in oblation. The divine Vedic speech, which is purifying, praises Soma, the Child of Heaven, as does the mother a worthy son, O Soma, make the four, seas full of manifold riches pour from every side for our profit! The excellently sweet Soma juices, pressed for joy, flow in all directions. May these sweet juices reach the Gods! The sages have declared that Soma flows for Indra. Soma, the lord of speech, the mighty, desiring, Yajna, deserves our praise. Of thousand streams, full of juices, lord of speech, nourisher of the sacrificers, manifests himself day by day.

O Soma, the guardian of the knower of the Vedas, thy purity is vast, almighty thou pervades all the organs of the body, but a non-yogi, being raw cannot enjoy this purity. Those who are mature only enjoy this. Soma the brilliant and pure has his seat high in heaven. His threads in the atmosphere glitter with light. The swift flowing juices of Soma protect the sacrifice and then being offered in oblation soar up high in the sky. Inspired by Soma's wisdom, the learned work, the Sun makes the mornings shine and pours rain all around for grains, and the fathers impregnate the womb. O singers, chant verses in praise of the holy, most mighty, munificent, the refulgent Agni! The enkindled in sacrifice, famed and splendid Agni giveth heroic sons and food. May his wisdom come unto us with ample strength! We praise the unconquerable conquering God, the Lord of clouds and mountains who subdues foes, pervades all and creates the worlds. With whatever strength Thou created the Sun and other shining bodies, with the same strength, Thou manifests thyself on the sacred seat of the Yajna. Sages sing Thy praise this day too, as of yore, because Thou releases the waters from bondages of Vritra. O great Indra, listen to my call, the call of him who praises thee. Shower on him wealth of kine and valiant offspring! He praises thee with hymns full of beautiful and deep words. Thou grant him an intellect, full of wisdom, ever-lasting nourisher of Yajna and Veda-loving! Let us praise that God alone, whom Vedic verses have magnified. Him we praise, the Lord of many mighty deeds, to gain his favour.

Book Three
Chapter One

O Purifying God, Thy celestial, all-pervading, gladdening streams flow forth into the vessel. The learned priests express and make Soma bright, who cause the clouds to pour down from the heaven. When golden-hued Soma is cleansed in the Vat, he rests there as one in his house. Then the all-pervading beams of Soma, sent forth from heaven and earth, spread all around. Soma, the all-seeing, mighty, influential, encompasses everything with his rays. O Thou, all-pervading, purifying all, art the Lord of all the worlds! From heaven hath Soma made, as it were, the wondrous thunder and the lofty light of mankind. O Soma, effulgent, thy perfect, gladdening and strengthening juice flows on through the woollen sieve and gets into vat. Thy splendid, mighty and lustrous juice flows all around to spread light and happiness. Thy streams, impetuous, bright and nourishing, flow forth with speed like the beams. We praise the pure Soma, so that we may overthrow the breaker of the law, the uncomfortable anti-social and undutiful foes. The mighty Soma's roar is pleasing like that of the rain. The lightning flashes roam in heaven. O God, Soma, kindly pour forth kine, steeds, gold, heroic sons and food in abundance. O all-seeing, fill the earth and heaven, as does the Sun, the Dawn with his rays. Flow forth around us with Thy gladdening steams like a river flowing to the lower lands. Flow forth, O Thou, beloved flow on every side, all around us, saying, I flow where the Gods abide. Purifier of the unholy, bestower of food, cause Thou the rain to pour down. This Soma, poured down on the straining cloth, reaches heaven in diverse ways through the atmosphere. The sparkling Soma reaches the heaven dazzling the atmosphere, roaring with might. Sweetening the near and distant air, the Soma juices are offered in oblation to Gods. The learned priests press out the golden-hued Soma with stones for Indra to drink.

Just as the beautiful ladies, sisters to one another, resort to their Lord with love, so do the fingers of the priests urge Soma to pour into a vat. Expressed for Gods, O purifying Soma, grant us all kinds of wealth. O Soma, pour down happy rain, regularly and in time for food and the sacrifice. Agni, the guardian of the world, ever watchful, awakener, mighty, handsome, has been born for our fresh happiness and weal. His mouth besmeared with ghee, purifying, he shineth brilliantly for the good of the sacrificers. O Agni, the learned Angiras discover Thee, lying hidden in most woods, going back and forth in search. Thou, called the son of strength, art produced by friction. The sage enkindle Agni, in his threefold seat, the ensign of Yajna and the lord of home. He helps in the performance of the Yajna by manifesting himself on the sacred seat along with other Gods.

Strengthened by sacrifice, this Soma hath been pressed for you. O Mitra and Varuna, listen, ye heroes to this my call! Both the Gods, who never injure anything, have come to their sublime home, the thousand pillared dwelling. They both, lustrous, protector of the sacrificers, shining like the sun, sovereign kings work together in harmony. Indra of great might, armed with Dadhichi's bones, slew ninety nine Vritras! Searching the enemy's head, lying concealed in the mountain-like forts, he found it in the sky. All agree that part of the sun's light is there in the mansion of the Moon. Just as rain comes out of clouds, so this noblest praise is produced from the hearts of learned and meditative men. O Gods, listen to the singer's call, accept his hymns and grant his prayers! O Indra and Agni, urge us not to sin, nor to slander, nor to violence! O Soma, gladdening and mighty, may thou reach Vayu and Marut to drink! Established in heaven, showerer of rains, gladdening, awakener of intellect, Soma looks graceful in the company of Indra, Vayu and other Gods. O Soma, sent by meditation, roaring in thy home, ascend into atmosphere as thy nature dictates.

Soma, thy friendship has been my strength everyday. O nourisher of the world, many afflictions of birth torment me, help me thou overcome these foes! O Peace-giving, sustainer of the world, we ever praise thee, in the morning, during day and in night. Just as birds fly, so may we meditating upon thee, higher than the Sun, attain liberation! Soma, viewed in different forms, overwhelming all the enemies, stimulating the intellect, is cleansed with fingers. The red-hued Soma, hath ascended his seat in the heavens, and

Indra hath approached Soma. O happy Soma, send us now great opulence from every side, and pour riches a thousandfold! O Indra, Lord of the bay steeds, drink of this cheering Soma, pressed out with stones. Just as a well trained steed, driven by the hands of rider, takes us to destination, so is this juice pressed, drink it and be satisfied. Let this drink, thy beloved friend by which Thou overcomes the foes gladden thee, the Lord of manifold riches! O Indra, mark well the praise chanted by me, this laud sung by the learned men. Accept these Vedic verses sung at the sacrifice! All men in one accord should elect their king such a man as is victorious, subduer of the enemies, firm on his seat, mighty, fierce, stalwart and full of vigour. He should be equipped well with weapons for sacrifice and administration. The learned, brilliant, free from all deceit, quick in reciting Vedic verses, bow unto Indra singing hymns. Bards in unison sing to him so that he might enjoy Soma. He, the lord of light, of strong determination, equipped with protective powers, is invoked in Yajna.

I praise him in song, who is the sovereign Lord, moves in chariots unrestrained, slays Vritra, conquers all fighting hosts, and is mighty. O Learned, call upon Indra for his aid, who holds thunderbolt in his hand, is handsome and mighty like the Sun. Soma, the learned Sage of heaven, when pressed, roaring bestows upon us delightful powers. Born pure, great, Soma, the son illumines the Earth and Heaven, his parents! Soma, free from all deceit, loveable, dwelling in high glorious home, flows forth with delight. Soma, the celestial, pure and endowed with splendour, Thou givest immortality to beings. By whom the men spread their Vedic speech, by whom the sages obtain their desires, by whom did they win fame and felicity in the Yajna, may the same God be realized by us! The pure and purifying Soma flows in waves when filtered through the wool, roaring before the chanting of Vedic hymns. The sages cleanse the mighty Soma, sporting above the wool in the wood. The learned praise him of triple height, Mighty like a steed, Soma is released into brakers. He is roaring, while being filtered, glides on.

Soma, the source of intellect, father of the Earth and Heaven; creator of Agni, generator of the Sun, Indra and Vishnu, flows on to sacrificers. Soma, the lord of herbs, the Brahma of learned priests, the leader of poets, the seer of the wise, multiplier of the animals, axe of the forests and hawk among the birds like vultures, etc. goes roaring over the cleansing wool. Just as a river stirs waves, so does

Soma, Pavaman stirs our power of speech, songs and praise. He strengthens sight as does an ox to a cow through insemination. Pavaman, the showerer of rains, dwelling in the sense organs gives them power of cognition. Worship ye well Agni, who helps in your Yajnas, is the lord of the might, brother-like in assistance and refulgent. Just as a carpenter shapes various articles out of wood with his strength, so may the famed Agni stand by us with his might.

This Agni, is the sovereign among all the glorious Gods. May he come near to us with his strength. O Indra, enjoy this excellent, gladdening drink. May Thou enjoy these sparkling streams flowing here at the sacrifice! None can emulate thee Indra in driving a chariot, none can match thee in might, none can overtake thee while you drive a car. O subjects, verily sing songs of praise to Indra, chant his glories, bow to this great and mighty lord, the juices poured forth have gladdened him. O Indra, destroyer of foes, mighty, handsome, manifest thyself, taking delight in juices, drink of this Soma for ecstatic joy. O Indra, fill thy belly with this divine sweet, freshly pressed out juice, which flows singing sweetly. Friend to all like Mitra, impartial like a sage, refulgent like sun, Indra quells the enemy host in Soma's ecstatic joy.

Chapter Two

O tranquil and exultant Lord, Thou art giver of wealth, might, brilliance and glory. Thou pervadest all the worlds. All these men worship Thee with hymns. O omniscient and mighty, purify us. O Soma, seer of men from all sides, purifier, fulfiller of desires, Thou art embodiment of peace. Pour down on thy subjects wealth, food and glory so that we may have strength to live in the world. Just as the beams emanate from the Sun and remove darkness so do the streams of Vedic verses issue forth from Thy purifying self. O omniscient! O Soma, thou art deep like an ocean and purifies space, investing them with strength. O Pure, thou induces the speech, revealing the Vedas in the hearts of the Seers like the Sun in the morning. Purified, sparkling Soma goes skyward roaming amidst the rays of the Sun. Like waters tumbling down a height, the streams of Soma flow forth, being cleansed, all around to Indra. O Pavaman, thou flows to Indra, being purified and offered in oblation by priests. Pressed out with stones and purified, the Soma flows forth swiftly for Indra's delight. Soma. the pure, praiseworthy and nourisher of mankind flows forth, Showerer, of rains, praised by Vedic verses, pure, purifier, wondrous and mighty Soma flows on. Soma, the self pure, purifying others, excellently sweet, expressed, slayer of the foes, is called the gratifier of Gods.

Subduer of all the foes, Soma, the Sage, hath been enrobed in the wool for Gods to drink. He. the Soma, Pavaman giveth to his worshippers manifold riches in the form of kine, etc. Thou purifiest all with thy thoughts and grapest all with thy mind. Grant us grains and purity. Pour on the sacrificers and those who sing thy laud, great fame, abiding wealth and food in abundance! Envoy of the Yajna, wonderful, Soma, thou art the lord of excellent deeds, purifying, praiseworthy like a king and one who enters the hymns. He, the leader of sacrifice, invincible, cleansed by hands, is resting in the vat. Worthy of praise like the Yajna, sportive, giver of heroic strength, to the priests, Soma goest into the vat. Pour on us, O Soma, juices in profusion, all kinds of grains and happy felicities! O Soma, as is thy praise and fame, so do come thou dear nigh unto us and occupy thy seat! Bestow on us kine and steed in great numbers, O Soma, through these days that fly on wings. He who conquering many remains unconquerable, destroys the enemy by laying seize the same Soma come unto us. O Pavaman, settle in the vat with thy excellently sweet streams poured forth for protection. He, the Soma leaving the wooly filter, seats himself on the sacred grass and then flows for Indra to drink. O Agni, thy visible glories are like lightning from the rain cloud and like the light of the coming Dawn. By pervading plants and forest trees, thou crammest by thyself the foodstuff in thy mouth. O Agni, Thou presiding priest in the Yajna, awaker of wisdom, controller of the thought, great or small, we elect Thee Hotar priest of the sacrifice, Thee alone and none else!

O Varuna and Mitra, verily very extensive is your protection. May I attain your kind good counsel! True and guileless Ye Gods, may we gain home, food and remain your friend for ever! O Mitra and Varuna, guard us with your protective forces, defend us with your best defences. May we subdue the wicked with our strong bodies! O Indra, realising thy might Thou arose and shook the jaws, having drunk the fresh Soma, From Indra I receive the knowledge of an eight-footed Vedic verse, with nine parts, which lends strength to the Law. O Indra and Agni, these lauds have been sung for you. You bring beatitude and drink this juice! Come unto us Indra and Agni, leaders of men, with your desired company! Ye both the heroes come to enjoy Soma juice offered in libation. O Soma, come roaming with thy roar, and rest in the wooden vessel, thy dwelling! May water cleansed Soma flow to Indra, Varuna and other Gods! O Soma, bestowing food upon our progeny from all sides, pour on us riches thousandfold! Pressed out with stones by the priests, goes up with speed, the green-hued Soma, in fume from the sacrifice. Just as the cows, which have been milked, go to pasturage, or as rivers flow to the ocean, so do streams of Soma juice flow to the wooden vat for delight. O purifying Soma, bring to us the wondrous, laudable, treasure that exists on earth. O Lord, purifying all men. thou gold-hued, hath manifested unto us. Ye both Indra and Soma, are lords of bliss, kine and speech, as mighty ones, grant our prayers.

We invoke Indra, who like the Sun destroys the wicked, is present with us for our might and happiness. We invoke him in battles great or small. He is our chief commander, may he be our protector, O hero, thou art wellwisher of the army and subduer of all hostile forces. Thou art victor of battles great or small. Thou lord of abundant wealth, givest fearlessness and happiness. O Indra, when battles arise. Thou destroyest the enemy and giveth wealth to thy friends and other noble souls. Yoke thy powerful and delightful steeds, humble the pride of the foes and make us rich! The bright rays of the Sun, enabling creatures to enjoy, drink savoury juices of Soma with delight, diffused all over in space. So do subjects rejoice sovereign. Desirous of his contact, the tawny kine give abundant milk, which is mixed with Soma juice. Thus making Indra strong, they urge him to use his thunderbolt to kill the enemy. The armies of Indra, honour his strength with veneration passing wise and observe his many laws for their own good. Mighty, mountain-born Soma, hath been pressed out in streams for ecstasy. Hawk-like he dwells in his home. Pressed out by priests, cleansed in waters, sweetened and blent with milk. Soma is beloved of Gods. Just as a battle horse is decorated, so do the priests adorn the Soma juice with festivity for eternal life.

O refulgent, Lord of great fame and food, let high and splendid glory shine all around us. Unlock the cask of the middle region! O omniscient, all-pervading, king of all the subjects, pour on us rain, let waters flow from heaven, and develop our strengths of action and knowledge! Soma, the child like grants us lustre in the Yajna, surpassing all things dear, and stands both in the heaven and on the earth. Flow forth in streams through the wool, O Soma for acquisition of wealth. Flow thou, exceedingly rich in sweetness for Gods! Just as the milch kine lick their new born calf, so do our pure hymns caress thee, while thou art being cleansed, O golden hued! O mighty one, thou soars high above the earth and heaven. O Pavaman, thou has enrobed thyself in milk, as it were a coat of mail. Soma, blentded with milk, mighty, infusing vigour, flows for Indra. He slays the wicked, quells malignity, being the lord of home, and giver of bliss. Pressed and blent with milk, flows he in streams, gladdened in the love of Indra, the source of God's joy. Being cleansed, he flows on to perform sacred rites, invested with powers that suit the season, engaging the ten swift fingers of the pressers.

O Agni, refulgent God, we kindle Thee. This fuel which is lighted with thy light, may send forth its flame to thee. Bring food, etc. for thy worshippers! To the Agni, the refulgent Lord, giver of joy, sustainer of the world, wondrous, is offered oblation with the Vedic verse. O bearer of our oblations, grant food to them who sing thy lauds! O glorious god, thou heatest both the ladies in thy mouth. Fulfil our desires O mighty one! Sing ye, a great song to the high Indra, for him who grows food and is worthy of worship. O Indra, thou givest splendour to the Sun, Thou, the creator of all objects, art mighty, the God of Gods! Thou the illuminator of the Heaven, radiant with light, the Gods strive to win thy friendship and love, O Indra! O mightiest Indra, this Soma hath been prepared for you. O potent humbler of our foes, may this juice fill you with vigour as does the Sun, the world with his rays. O hero, destroyer of the foes as the Sun destroys the clouds, mount thy car, in which bay steeds have been yoked. May the pressing stones, with their cloud like voice, well encourage thy heart! Let Indra of indomitable might, admitted by the wise, be brought hither by his strong steeds to our songs of laud and Yajna.

Book Four
Chapter One

The excellently sweet, most rich, the omnipresent, father of Gods, the best of cheerers, most gladdening, the juice loved by Indra, giveth us salvation. The Lord of heaven, green-hued, pleasing to sight, cause of rain, far seeing flows swiftly in thousand streams and singing to the vat. He dwells in the houses where Mitra abides. Soma, thou pressed out by priests, flowing before the rain showers, before the songs and the kine art the Lord of speech. As lord of might thou acquires great spoil in the van of war. The mighty, swift and semen augmenting Soma, is offered in oblation with a desire for steeds, kine and heroic sons. Being cleansed and purified by the fingers of the priests, the Soma, Pavaman flows through the fleecy filter. May these Soma streams pour upon his worshippers manifold treasure from all sides! Flow, thou Soma, beloved of Gods, showerer of rains, fast through the wool and enter into the atmosphere! O sustainer of the world, giver of wealth and food, rest in thy place in heaven as one with power! The excellent and sweet Soma was pressed out to flow in streams while cleansed with waters. The great waters follow in thy wake when thou art enrobed, with milk. Soma, our friend, full of juices, lord of heaven, is cleansed with waters in the wooden vessel. Handsome to look at like Mitra, the green-hued Soma, bellowing like a bull, shines in the company of the Sun. O Soma, the songs of wisdom and action are beautified with thy mighty, wherewith we praise thee for rapturous joy. O Soma, we pray thee for acquiring joy, so that thou mayest have exalted praise. O Primeval Lord, thou art the winner of wealth, heroes and steeds. O Soma, pour on us with thy great strength, the excellently sweet stream of elixir, like a cloud, showerer of rain. O holy and highly famed God, bring us victory and high renown, and make us better than we are! Give us thou all felicities and divine light. Give us skilful strength and mental power, sweep away our foes and make us better! O learned men, cleanse Soma for Indra to drink. Grant us realization through thy help and mental powers, and make us better than we are. O God, may we through thy aids, look upon the Sun. Make us better than we are! O well armed Soma, grant us riches doubly great and make us better than we are! O Conquering but unconquered in battle, give us ample wealth and make us better than we are! The sages magnify thee, O Soma, with their songs. Make us better than we are! O Pavaman, grant us riches and steeds of many kinds and make us better than we are!

Pressed out in streams, sanctified with hymns and praised by speech is Soma, by drinking which one crosses the ocean of life and attains salvation. Swift flows the Soma, giver of riches, effulgent, strengthening and who knows how to protect men. May we obtain the thousands of streams of Soma, the giver of delight! From whom we obtain 3,00,000 delightful streams, the same Soma runs swift giving joy. The strength giving Soma streams are offered in oblation, praised with hymns to obtain greater powers. Soma, the purifier, giver of food and grains beloved like the riches, manifests himself for showering the rains. O God, praised by Jamdagni, pour on us food and nourishment. We, the worshippers, compose songs in praise of Agni, which reach him as if they were a car. O Agni, may we never suffer in thy friendship! O foremost in the Yajna, we the priests serve thee, O Agni, with different kinds of fragrant fuels every day for our fulfilment. Let not suffer in thy friendship! O Agni, may we have ability to kindle thee. Grant thou our daily prayers. O Envoy of the Gods, bring other Gods hither. Through thee the oblations offered reach to other Gods. Let us not, in thy friendship, suffer harm. I sing to Mitra, Varuna and Aryaman, the subduer of the foes, early in the morning as the Sun rises. O learned men, may this prayer bring us gold, and strength. May we be thine O Varuna, O Mitra. May we acquire food and happiness!

Drive the foe away, strike down the enemies that tread the earth, and grant the desired wealth. Give us the wealth we long for, which thou grantest in profusion and which the world craves. O God, grant us the desired wealth found in secret and hidden places. O Indra and Agni, Ye both art priests of sacrifice, well versed in the rites! O Indra and Agni, Ye art subduers of the foe, slayers of Vritra, riders of fast chariots and ever invincible. The learned men press out with stones, the gladdening drink for ye, O Agni and Indra. O rich and excellently sweet Soma, soar high to the lightning girt with air, I sit beside the Yajna altar! The sages, learned in Vedas, laud thee, O Soma, sustainer of the world. Men purify and make thee beautiful. Let Mitra, Aryaman and Varuna drink thy gladdening juice. O Pavaman, giver of yellow, abundant, much desired wealth, thou when purified in the vat, raises thy roar. When pressed out and purified through the wool, thou bellowest in the wooden vessel. Pavaman, blent with milk, reaches the place of Gods. Soma, the son of sea, is cleansed by the ten fingers, before he is seen in the company of the Sun. Pressed out in vat, he effused, flows forth to Indra and Vayu with the rays of the Sun. The sweet and excellent Soma flows on for Mitra, Varuna, Bhaga, Vayu, Pushan and for us.

May our subjects be rich and strong with the favour of Indra. May we wealthy in food, rejoice with them. Just as the axle of a chariot with its wheels carries a car, so do thou, O Indra, grant us our desires, wealth and learning. As a milch cow is to him who milks, we glorify and invoke Indra every day the doer of noble deeds, for our knowledge and protection. Come unto us Indra, and drink of Soma juice offered in libation. Me, being gladdened with juices bestows rich gifts on his devotees. Let us know thee through the learned men, nearest to thee. Come unto us, neglect us not! Like the Dawn, thou hast filled the Earth and Heaven with light. Thou mighty one, the leader of men, thy light, the creator of the world manifests thee; the blessed light reveals thee. As a man controls a mighty elephant who happens in a rut, so do thou possess the power to control the world. As a goat draws down the branch with its foremost foot, so do thou create and sustain this universe with thy powers. O Indra, relax that man's stubborn strength who is bent upon wickedness and trample him down beneath your feet, who desires to harm us. Thy light manifests thy glory. The creator of all objects, thy power manifests thee. Soma, who pleases Gods, bestows riches, land and handsome children, is pressed out by the learned. Soma, the Gods derive pleasure from thee, Thou art our protection and bestower of happiness. O learned men, sing the laud of that Pavaman, who is purifying. Sweeten Soma with mixing milk, honey and other such sacred things, as a child is pleased and decorated with gifts, etc. Just as a calf is nourished by milch kine forward while being pressed and cleansed. He who protects and gladdens the Gods, is adorned by the learned priests. Soma is a great source of strength, and a rich feast for men. He is exceedingly sweet for Gods, effused by the wise. May the Soma juices, that further our weal, friendly, immaculate, benevolent, full of wisdom, flow unto us. The Soma juices, cleansed with purity, blended with curds and milk, of great intellect, flowing forth and set in wooden vat assemble the brilliant sun. Being pressed out with stones, and adorned in many ways, the Soma juices, shower wealth and food on us, the contemplative men, from all sides.

Flow forth thou Soma, swift like wind, the lord of wisdom, purifying, effulgent, to the sparkling lake and bestow wealth, food, etc. on thy worshippers. O Soma, flow on to thy famed ford with pleasant resounding roar and purify us. Just as a man standing under a tree full of ripe fruits shakes many of them down, so do thou shower on us sixty thousand treasures! The two great and mighty tasks perfromed by Soma are: He sends the foe to sleep and slays them, and sweeps away those who are foolish and unfriendly! O Agni, thou omniscient, most praise worthy be our closest friend, protector and our benign deliverer! O Agni, most resplendent, rich and famed, come unto us and give us wealth of knowledge, etc. To thee, O most brilliant, O radiant God, we verily approach thee with prayers for happiness for our friends! May Indra, other Gods and these existing worlds complete our happiness! May Indra along with Aditya, bring fulfilment to our soul, bodies and our offspring. May Indra, Maruts and Adityas send us medicines to heal us! Praise Indra, the mightiest Vritra-slayer, sing to him the song that pleases!

Chapter Two

The God, creator of speech, contributing to the happiness of holy men like a brother, sanctifying, Lord of the Gods, preaching the knowledge of Vedas, reveals the birth of deities. The swan-like discriminating learned men, the friends of God Soma, sing his praise in unison. Like cars thundering on their way, like swift steeds, the pure Soma streams flow for wealth. Flows forth Soma to Yajna from holding hands like chariots urged to speed, like warriors making their progress in the war. Just as kings are graced with lauds and a Yajna with seven priests, so does the Soma adorn himself with milk. Pressed with holy hymns, the Soma streams, the excellently sweet flow in profusion all around! Lustrous like the morning sun, speeding the light of dawn, the Soma juices look somewhat like beautiful canopy. The chanters of old open the doors of hymns, the men who make the Soma come The seven wise priests, sit at a sacrifice and preside at the rites, Soma, the foremost in Yajna, we drink, to see, the sun with our own eyes. We milk the Soma's offspring forth. A lustrous learned man beholds with his eyes all around, the Soma, the source of joy and established in heaven by the sacrificing priests. The learned priests, knowing the right application of Soma. offer it in oblation as the law ordains. The best of all oblations, Soma, the sweet and most excellent, he swims in mighty waters. Soma. the noble, guileless, flows to the place of sacrifice, singing aloud continuously. Purging the hearts around preaching the Vedic wisdom flows forth he. Being purged sits Soma like a king, lording over the warring subjects. Most beloved, gold-hued, through the filtering wool, settles he in the vat, the singer praised with songs. He flows to Indra, Ashvins and Vayu with ecstatic joy. The streams of Soma flow on to other Gods with their prayers. O Ye Heaven and Earth, win us fame, wealth and strength. O God, we choose thee ever, the mighty, giver of peace, wealth and protection, O Soma, thou art excellent, wise and hath an understanding heart, the guardian of us all! Thou art verily our wealth, intelligence, guardian and desire of us all!

Agni created in the beginning, kindled in Yajna is the envoy of Earth, the guest of men, effulgent and the mouth of Gods. O Agni, eternal, God praise and sing for joy at thy coming, as parents do at the birth of a child. O all-pervading, the Gods attain immortality by thy powers following path of righteous actions preached by thee. They all praise Agni, the centre of sacrifice, the abode of riches, conveyor of oblations, embodiment of worship and lord of all. O learned men, sing forth the praise of mighty Mitra and Varuna. Both Varuna and Mitra are God of the Gods, lustrous source of bliss and showerer of rains. So Ye omnipotent Gods, grant us riches both terrestrial and celestial. Great is your command among the Gods. O Indra, wondrous bright, come unto us. These Soma juices, cleansed and purified by active fingers, ever long for thee. Come unto sacrificing, suppliant priests; urged by Yajna, and sped by hymns. Come with speed, O Lord of steeds, to us, the praying men, and enjoy our drink.

O men, glorify that Agni who with his flames encompasses all the forests and leaves them charred and blackened behind. He who gains Indra's favour through oblations in the fire, finds an easy way to riches, across the floods. Both Indra and Agni, bestow on us abundant wealth, fast steeds, and nourishing food. Soma coming like a youth with youthful maids flows on to Indra's appointed place.

The pleasant hymns sung in praise of Soma, the golden-hued echo the sacrificial halls. O Soma, grant us abundant food, which shall yield us ever thrice a day, strength, nourishment and happiness. He who always worships Indra through sacrifice, etc. the lord of devotees, sovereign, subduer of all, remains always untouched by such evils as lust, etc. I laud him, the mighty, unconquerable in war, at whose advent the mighty persons bow in obeisance, the Earth and Heaven bow in praise. Sit down, ye friends and sing forth aloud to him who purifies himself, adorn him for glory, like a child with acts of devotion. O sacrificers blend this Soma, the strength of both the worlds, with milk, as a calf is associated with the kine. O learned sacrificers, cleanse Soma, the source of strength and bliss so that he may gladden Mitra and Varuna. The mighty Soma flows forth in thousand streams through the wool. Cleansed with the waters, blended with milk, the mighty Pavaman flows on in continuous streams. Pressed out with stones by the priests, offered in oblation regularly, drawn up by the clouds, the Soma enters into Indra's stomach.

The Soma juice, which has been pressed out afar or near at hand, or in this land, that expressed in plains, in the midst of householders, or amongst fivefold sacrificers, may shower on us, for our weal, rains and heroic strength. O Agni, I long for thee with speech, because only through thee the speaking fire extends from the heart, the loftiest dwelling place. Thou art alike in all the places, through all the regions. We invoke thee in fights and difficulties. Desiring strength we call thee in battle for aid. O giver of wondrous gifts in strife. O Indra, the most active, grant us strength, valour, and a war conquering hero. O Lord, thou hast ever been to us a mother and a sire. So now, for beatitude, we pray to thee. To thee, much invoked, the master of great might do I beseech. Grant us thou heroic power! O Indra, what wealth thou hast not given me here, that bounty bring to us, filling full both thy hands. Give us that wealth and food, which thou deemest as precious, so that we may know thee as thou art, a boundless giver of gifts! Thy high and famed spirit is spread in all the worlds. With this thou, O thunderer, cleaves even mighty things.

Book Five
Chapter One

The learned in group, cleanse and decorate the Soma, at his advent, the lovely infant. He is a poet by songs, by wisdom a Sage, he flows on singing and accompanied by hymns, to the vat. Beloved of the seers, seer maker, of beautiful gait, inspirer of the poets, praiseworthy, desirous to attain his third form, Soma is most splendid. Established between the earth and heaven, mighty like the hawk, roams in the sky, cleansed with waters, the great Soma, illumines the atmosphere. The Soma juices, satisfying Indra's dear desires, shower satisfaction from all sides. Being pressed and established between heaven and earth, these Soma juices may grant us heroic strength. O Soma, urge Indra's heart to charity. For this purpose I sit in the hall of Yajna. The ten fingers of the priests cleanse thee and then offer to Agni as oblation. The learned rejoice in thee. Being poured, thou art enrobed in milk to be a great banquet to Gods. When cleansed, Soma, green and golden-hued, enrobes himself in milky dress. O Soma, flow forth to thy friend Indra, destroying foes and giving us wealth! May we attain thee, O Soma, the Indra's drink and giver of food, progeny and light to see! O Lord of herbs pour down rain and grains on the eaith from all sides and give us strength to win the war! Poured through the woollen filter. May these pressed out Soma juices grant us great wealth and manly strength! Just as the milch kine run to their callowing, so do Soma juices held in both the hands flow on roaring all around. Beloved of Indra, satisfying and roaring Soma destroys all our enemies. Soma, the destroyer of the godless sits in the place of sacrifice.

Exceedingly sweet Soma juices expressed in sacrifice have been poured for Indra. The learned sacrificers invoke to drink the juices, as kine low to their calf. The rupturous Soma, the wise, dwells in the ocean of heart, on the wave of speech. The beauty of sacrifice, the sage and bard, the Soma is worshipped in the central point of heaven, above the filtering wool. The Indu (Moon) in the sky, holds in close embrace, with his rays, the Soma kept in vats. The Indu, established in an appointed place in heaven, sends forth sweet rays for the speech, urging the speech of men and women, dwells in heaven. O Pavaman, all-pervading, give us riches brilliant with a thousand splendour and ready aid. He, the bard and sage, purified in the place of sacrifice, goes to dear places, far away in the atmosphere. Like the roaring waves of the river, thy juices soar themselves. Urge thou the arrow of thunderbolt in Indra's bow. When pressed out, the verses of three Vedas rise up from sacrificers above the woollen heights. Pressed out with stones, cleansed with wool, the sweet and green-hued, the beloved of Gods, Soma is shed. O most joyous and wise Soma, flow on through the sieve and attain thy highest place. O best giver of joy, anointed well, flow on and enter into Indra's stomach. O Soma, flow forth to him, who enjoying thy wild delights shatters the 810 castles of the clouds. O God, destroy thou the man and his forts, who is the foe of happiness, for the weal of sacrificers! O Soma, finder of steeds, pour on us fast horses, kine and many kinds of foods in abundance!

Sweeping away the foe and godless, Soma manifests himself and flows on to Indra. O Pavaman, grant us great wealth, annihilate our enemies and give fame with brave sons. O Soma, a hundred obstacles have never checked thee when fain to give thy gifts. Thou being pure, give us abundant wealth. Flows forth Soma, the giver of splendour to the Sun and the showerer of rains. Pavaman, high in the sky, goes through the atmosphere, riding the Sun's rays. O learned men, in your sacrifice, make Agni your envoy, who in purifier, firm, best in rites, leader of men, flame crowned and fed with ghee. Just as a horse nighing eagerly for the pasture, Agni comes forth from the sacrificial fuel, then the wind blows with his flames. The path of Agni is black. From the newly born Agni, the kindled flames rise upward, and he as an envoy speedest to heaven to the Gods. Let us make Indra strong to shatter the fort of clouds of demon Vritra. This Indra hath been created for giving wealth, etc. He is of great might, worthy of Soma libation and famed, strong like thunder, ever active, invincible, never failing, showerer of rains, learned in Vedic speech, Indra sustains the world.

O Adharvu, make Soma pure for Indra to drink. The Gods enjoy the excellent and sweet Soma juices. O men, pour out for Indra, the most rich and sweet Soma juice, the milk of heaven!

Flows forth the gladdening juice, sustainer of heavens, the strength of the Gods, hailed by men with joyous shouts. When, he, the gold hued flows like a courser, shows his splendour. Just as a hero takes his weapons in his hands, so does he, desirous of winning happiness, urge Indra, cleansed by learned men, and offered in oblation. O Soma, enter thou Indra's stomach with thy strength, as lightning enters the clouds, and give us strength, wealth and food though our Yajna. O Indra, though thou art invoked by men in the East. West, North and South, thou art everywhere with every man at the same time. O invoked by many, thou resplendent pervadest all men. Though thou art present alike in all the places, be it a beautiful land, or depraved, or dark, or peopled by the rich, yet when the learned men, knowing Vedas call on the thee with Vedic hymns, thou art attained. May Indra listen to our prayer uttered in his praise! May he come unto us with his strength and drink our Soma juice! The denizens of Earth and Heaven seek thee with their spiritual powers, because thy heart longs for heartfelt beautiful feelings and thou all-pervading, most subtle art present everywhere.

God, flow forth to Indra and mount to Vayu as thy nature dictates. O Pavaman, lord of herbs, thou givest fame and wealth. O Soma, go thou unto the lake! Soma, thou flowest forth driving away the foes and chasing the godless afar! Shower on us riches thousandfold, most splendid, that eclipse the light, desired by hundreds. May we live in thy closest proximity. May we be most near to thy bounty full of wealth and food craved by many. This Some, pressed out and urged to flow by Vedic hymns, pours through the wool, spreading joy on all sides. Flow on Soma like a mighty sea, as sire of the Gods! Flow on, and be thou blissful to Heaven and Earth, and all living beings. O lord of tranquillity, mighty, sustainer of the heavens, flow forth and purify us for ever! O men, I laud Agni, your most beloved guest and friend, envoy of Gods like a car. Agni, whom the learned invoke in his two aspects, hath been established among the mortals since times immemorial. O thou most mighty Agni, protect the charitably disposed men, listen their prayers and preserve their children. O Indra dear, ever conquering but unconquered, vast like a mountain spread on all sides, pervading all, come unto us. O truthful Soma drinker Indra, thou verily lords over both the worlds. Thou sustains heaven and gives strength to him who pours libation. O lord of heaven, thou art he, who upholdeth all our cities, slayest Vritra and giveth strength to sacrifice loving men. O Indra, the thunderer, thou art renderer of forts, ever youthful, of unmeasured strength, sustainer of all rites, and much praised. O Indra, upholder of thunderbolt, thou broke open the fortress of Vritra, full of kine. Then, all Gods fearless under thy protection come pressing to thy aid. O men, praise with hymns Indra who reigneth by his might, whose bounteous gifts are thousandfold, ye, even more.

Chapter Two

Guardian of the world, creating beings, pressed with the stones, mighty, the Soma waxes strong. O Soma, for our wealth and sacrifice make Vayu glad, gladden Mitra and Varuna, cheer Heaven and Earth and other Gods. The mighty Soma, cleansed with waters, chooses the Gods, and performs a great deed by granting strength to Indra and light to the Sun. This immortal Soma flows on, like a bird, to settle in the wooden vessels. Lauded by the learned, this effulgent Soma abides in the waters and grants splendid gifts to the devotees. This Pavaman grants all precious gifts to his followers like a hero going forth with his warriors. Pavaman flows on with speed, purifying, like a chariot. He lets his voice be heard by all. Soma, the golden-hued is adorned for gaining wealth by men, devout and efficient in hymns. This God expressed with hymns, flows on fast subduing the foes. This Soma runs in streams to heaven and other worlds, and roars while he flows forth. This Soma, the chief of Yajna, unconquered, goes invisibly to many worlds.

Born for Gods in the beginning, this green-hued Soma, flows through the wool. This same Soma, the doer of many noble deeds from the very birth, flows forth in streams, purifying and giving food. Just as a hero goes in fast chariots, so does Soma go to Indra's settled place. This Soma, performing many noble deeds for the Yajna, in which Gods are fed, flows on. The learned sacrificers adorn Soma, worthy to be adorned, the giver of abundant food. The learned men urge and lead him to the sacred place along the sanctified paths. The lord of liquids and streams, the speedy Soma, is led by priests adorned with gold ornaments, shedding rays like the Sun. Nodding his horns in the heaven like a bull, leading a herd, Soma performs mighty deeds. He, advancing through various rough stages, marches on and drops into the vat. The ten fingers urge him on his course, him who is gold-hued, well-armed and the best source of joy.

This Soma, mighty and pressed out flows to the vat through the long wool of the sheep. The fingers of the learned sacrificers urge the expressed green-hued Soma to Indra for his drink. He, like a hawk settles down amidst the families of men, like a lover speeding to his love. This Soma, the exhilarating juice looks down from heaven, like a child from the lap of his mother. The Soma, the green hued juice, pressed out for joy goes roaring unto the vat, the well beloved place. The gold-adorned ten fingers, cleanse Soma skilfully for acquiring the gladdening drink. This powerful, omniscient, lord of minds, nourisher of all, urged by the learned men, flows fast to the woollen vat. This Soma effused for the Gods, pervading all the places, flows forth to the vat. The immortal, the best drink of the Gods, slayer of the foes, the Soma shines in his place. Urged by the ten fingers, roaring on his way, flows the mighty Soma to the wooden vats. The rapturous, holy Soma lends light to the Sun in the heaven. This invincible lord of speech and might, sheltering all, this Soma soars high with the Sun. Ever praised, intelligent, beautiful, this Soma checking the foes, slays them. The conqueror of strength and winner of happiness, this Soma prepared for Indra, is poured out into the vat. Soma, the head of heaven, is expressed and cleansed in waters by the learned for the weal of the world. Ever conquering, never conquered, desiring kine. longing for gold, this Pavaman hath roared. The mighty, showerer of rains, tawny, purifying, this Soma reaches Indra in the heaven. This Soma powerful, most beloved of the Gods, remover of the sins, invincible, flows forth to the heaven.

The Soma, pressed out for the Gods, slaying the demons, flows on to the holy sieve. Sustainer, far seeing, green-hued, this Soma, flows roaring to the vat, his place of rest. This mighty, fiend slayer, Soma flows forth into the long woollen sieve. This Pavaman, established in the sacrifice of the learned, makes the Sun and the Dawn shine. This Soma, the banisher of diseases, giver of strength, well pressed out, invincible, flows with speed like a courser running to the battle. This splendid, joyful Soma, urged by Adhvaryu, speeds on to the vats. He who reads the essence, the Pavaman hymns, collected by the seers, tastes all the relishing food, purified and sweetened by God Vayu's touch. For him, who reads the Pavaman hymns, the essence of the Vedas, Saraswati pours forth milk, ghee and sweet water. The Soma verses of the Vedas are giver of happiness, bearer of fine fruit and showerer of rains. They form the essence of the Vedas, stored by the Rishis, an eternal elixir for the knower of Vedas.

May the Pavaman hymns bestow on us this world and the next. May they, stored by the sages, gratify our desires! The purifying Pavaman wherewith the Gods ever purify themselves, with that, in thousand streams may the Soma hymns purify us! The eternal Pavaman hymns grant final beatitude, and by their study one attains pure and holy food and immortality. May we approach with great reverence the most youthful Agni, kindled in the place of Yajna, invoked in the homes, vast, shining wondrously between the Earth and Heaven and spreading all around. That Agni, who is lauded in the homes, through his might overcoming all our misfortunes, preserve us and our princes from disgrace and afflictions. O Agni, thou art Varuna and Mitra. Learned men exalt thee with their hymns. Through thee may we gain abundant wealth. Do ye preserve us evermore with blessings. Indra, rich like a cloud in showers, waxeth strong with Vedic lauds. When the learned singers of hymns pronounce Indra, the end of a Yajna, they find all implements of the sacrifice useless. When the learned men magnify Indra with praise, they offer him their gifts.

On flow the splendid streams of Soma, giving joy, the great destroyer, the best rider of the car, gold-hued, in the company of Gods, praised with finest hymns. Pavaman, the giver of might, bestower of wealth and heroic strength, penetrates the whole world with its brilliant rays. The Soma, the best libation, pressed out and cleansed with waters by Adhvarus, is friend of men. Sprinkle forth the same all around. Never conquered, fragrant Soma, being cleansed, flows through the wool. We enjoy thee being effused and mixed with milk. Pressed out, dear to Gods, the performer of sacrifice, pleasing to eyes, far-sighted Soma flows all around. Like a king hath Soma, green and tawny, roared. Being purified, passing through the wool, he speedily flows to his seat, like a hawk flying fast to his nest. Parjanya is the guardian of the mighty Soma plant, who hath made the earth and mountain his home. Just as a groomed steed goes forth to the battle, so do thou flow on all-sides. O Soma, be gracious unto us, drive away all our distresses. Clad in butter, thou goest to thy place. All the wealth that has been and would be, with its full power belongs to Indra. Like a son we enjoy our share of wealth inherited from him, just as the beams of the Sun receive light from the Sun. Praise Indra, who is generous in granting us wealth and gifts. Propitious are the boons he gives. He urges himself to shower gifts and satisfies the desires of his devotees. O Indra. grant us security against that whereof we are afraid. Help us, thou Indra, and drive away our foes! O liberal one, thou art verily the lord of our homes. On thee, of ample bounty, the lover of songs, we call with Soma drink.

Soma, thou art the embodiment of rapture, most strong at sacrifice, and giver of wealth. Flow thou in streams! Thou most delightful, the best gladdener, effulgent, art invincible and ever conquering! O Soma, pressed out with stones, come unto us roaring and bring splendid strength. Flow on, thou Soma in streams for the feast of Gods and reside in our Vats, full of joy. Thy streams delight and exalt Indra. The Gods drink of thee for immortality. O Soma, expressed and cleansed, come unto us showering rains from heaven and with wealth.

O Soma, flow thou in streams to the Gods for their feast. O excellently sweet, come to our vats and take thy seat. Thy swift streams full of joy exalt Indra. The Gods drink thee to gain immortality. Pressed out and cleansed Soma, thou pour on us riches, light of knowledge and rains. The learned cleanse Soma through the fleece, the golden-hued and beloved of the Gods. His exhilarating juices gladden all the Gods. Him, the beloved of Indra, the priests with their ten fingers press out and cleanse with waters, who is full of splendour and a friend of men. O Soma, thou art poured out for Indra, the Vritra-slayer to drink, and for sacrificers give dakshina to the priests. O Soma, thou art pure and mighty like lightning, flow forth and sanctify our deeds so that we may acquire greater wealth and strength. They press them out and cleanse for attaining joy and food. The learned men adorn Soma, the green-hued, new-born infant in the wooden vats. The Gods attain to well expressed and cleansed Soma, the annihilator of the foes. Just as the mothers nourish and strengthen their child, so let our lauds wax him strong, the gladdener of Indra! O adorable, pour blessings on our kine, pour on us many kinds of food and wealth and expand the sea, O Soma! Hie thee hither, O Indra to those who kindle the flame in the Yajna, O thou ever young and friend to us all. Great is their fuel, much their laud, large their supplies, whose friend is Indra ever young. Peerless in fight, the hero leads his warrior chiefs, whose friend is Indra ever young. Indra alone giveth glory to a mortal man, who offers gifts. He is invincible and mighty. Whoever of the many worships thee with Soma, to him Indra giveth tremendous strength. O God, when will you listen to our songs of praise? When will thou trample upon, like a weed, the godless man, who hath no gift to offer? Those skilled in songs, sing thy praise, the expert chanters eulogise thee, Brahmins exalt thee, like a pole, O Indra, doer of countless deeds. When a sacrificer goes from one ridge to another collecting Soma plant and fuel, his toils are taken note of by Indra and he rushes with his attendants to the sacrifice. O Indra, Soma enjoyer, listen to our songs of praise, yoke thy pair of steeds, and hasten to us!

Glorify naught besides Indra, O friends, so shall no sorrow trouble you. Sing only mighty Indra's praise, sing it again and again. O learned ones, sing to him alone, who attracts all the worlds towards himself, is active like a bull, bounteous like a cow, he who is cause both of enmity and peace, munificent, most charitable, and the great protector. As chariots ever conquering, that bring wealth and afford protection, so do our hymns of praise reach Indra. The learned, like the rays of the Sun, the lovers of the sacrifice, attain everything whereupon they set their mind. Thou remover of our debts and subduer of our enemies, pour bliss on us. O Pavaman, sustainer of the Sun, the support of the sky with thy might, thou hastens to pour rain on us. O Soma, the great, we rejoice in thee, effused and realized in a kingdom where all are equal, thou movest about with thy might amidst foes! O Lord of tranquillity, flow thou forth, sweet one to Indra, Mitra, Pushan and Bhaga! Flow forth, thou divine strength giving juice, flow on to thy spacious, finest dwelling place! O Pavaman, let Indra and other Gods drink thy juices for wisdom and gladdening strength! Like the rays of the Sun, the Soma juices, flowing with speed, spread all around. None except Indra purify as does the Soma. Soma, like the child of those who press it out, is first shed and then blent with honey and drunk, which inspires the mind and gives happiness.

Book Six
Chapter One

O well kindled Agni, thou bringest the Gods to him, who offers oblations and gifts to thee. I ever worship thee as thou are giver of beatitude. O sage, the preserver of our body, make the Yajna beneficial to the enlightened persons. I invoke Agni to this our sacrifice, him who is benevolent, sweet tongued and to whom oblations are offered. Agni, come on thy most easy moving chariot, bringing the Gods and accomplish our sacrificial rites. May Mitra, Aryaman, Bhaga and Savitar grant us bliss today with the rising of the Sun. May they guard our home well and bear us safely forward over distress! These self-effulgent Gods and their mother Aditi, whose laws are inviolate, are supreme rulers. May Soma gladden thee Indra, be bounteous, O thunderer, and drive away the enemies of hymns! Crush under thy foot the niggard who offer no gifts. O mighty, there is none to equal thee. Thou art the lord of the expressed and the unexpressed Soma. Thou art the Sovereign of all beings. Vigilant, learned, true, praised with hymns, Soma hath settled in the vats. Him, the Adhvaru couples purify, the skilled leaders of sacrifice. He, purified and decked with the rays of the Sun, pervades both the Earth and Heaven. He whose dear and pleasant streams protect a hero, also grants riches to a sacrificer, as a master to his servant. May he the strengthener of Gods, self-increaser, the settler in the vats, showerer of rains, the handsome Soma, lead us to the place where our sires of old, who knew the path, went and found the light, the bellowing bull, so do the songs of praise reach the reservoir, the God's dwelling place. Flows forth Soma, being expressed and cleansed through the sheep's long wool, and enrobed in a new raiment, as it were. O men, engender Agni, seen from afar, lord of the home effulgent, all-pervading, from two sticks with the strength of your hands! The learned householders set Agni in their homes for all-round protection, him who is eternal, beauteous to behold, mighty and ever revered. O ever youthful, enkindled so well, Agni, shine thou before us at the altar; to thee come continually all oblations and offerings. The Sun hath come revolving and sat in his place— before the mother Earth advancing through the Heaven. The radiance of the Sun, penetrating the body, facilitates the respiration. The mighty Sun illuminates the sky. The Sun shines all the day throughout the month. The Vedic verses are recited in his praise at dawn.

Chapter Two

Let us chant a Vedic verse to Agni, to him who hears from afar! The eternal Agni preserves the life of charitably disposed men. May that most blissful Agni guard our wealth and family, and keep us safe from grief and sin! Ye, let men say, Agni is born, who slayeth enemies and winneth wealth in every battle. O Agni, yoke thy most excellent steeds, swift to bring thee to us. Come to us quickly with other Gods and drink of the Soma at the sacrifice. O Agni, the sustainer immortal, ever bright and effulgent, light others with thy never fading radiance. O learned men, do not expect an Adhvaru to beg, but give him gifts without being asked, let not sacrifice suffer for want of supplies. But drive away the dog and niggard men. Just as a son goes to his mother's lap, or a lover to his bride, so does Soma approach the vat to occupy his seat. The green-hued Soma, sustains both the worlds with his might, and flows forth to the vat to settle in his place. O Indra, since birth art thou foeless and without a rival, seeking friendship in battle. Thou findest not the wealthy to be thy friend, for thy flushed with wine, the godless men, resort to violence, but when thou befriend thy devotees and subjects, the righteous men, they call on thee like a father. May hundreds and thousands of steeds yoked to thy golden car, O Indra, bring thee unto us to drink of the Soma juice! May thy two steeds with peacock tails and white backs, yoked to thy golden chariot bring thee here to quaff the sweet Soma that renders us eloquent. O Indra, lover of the song, drink thou this Soma, full of rapture, expressed with exertion. This savoury juice is excellently sweet and joy giving. O learned men, press ye and pour out him, who is cleansed with water, dwells in wood, is praise worthy and fast like a steed. Of thousand streams, shower of rains, beloved of Gods, divine, rinsed and increased with water, the Soma is great celestial King.

May Agni, bright, kindled, served with oblations and hymns, eager to give wealth, slay our enemies dead. Thou set on the seat of eternal sacrifice, in the lap of mother earth, the father of the heaven, slays Vritra. O Agni, ever active, give progeny with wealth and food that it may shine to heaven. Cleansed and urged, the Pavaman hath pervaded the Gods. This God, expressed, flows forth singing to the vat like a milkman going to an enclosure holding cattle. O Sage, thou robed in fine raiment meet to wear in combat, pronouncing invocations like a seer, watchful, move about the Earth and the Heaven. Beloved Soma, born on earth, more famed than the famous, cleansed on the fleecy height above the vat, roars while purified. Thou art that who ever preserves us with blessings. Come, let us glorify the mighty, pure Indra with pure Soma hymns and pure songs of praise. May he be gladdened with milk—blended Soma juices!

O Indra, come thou pure to us with thy pure powers. Pure. God, send down thou wealth to us. O divine, pure keep us always happy. O Pure, give us pure wealth, pure Indra grant riches to thy worshippers. Pure God, thou dost strike the fiend dead, and giveth thou pure the pure food. We mortals, desirous of wealth, meditate upon Agni's laud today, laud of him who touches heaven in the form of the Sun. He who is lord of the home, abides in the world of men, listens to our songs. That Agni alone giveth happiness. Thou Agni art spread widely forth, worthy to be chosen, Hotar priest, through thee the sacrificers complete their Yajna.

The sacred Vedic verses reveal the secret essence of Soma, who dwells on triple heights and bestows life. Dwelling in the wood, he lavishes all kinds of riches and blessings like an ocean full of treasure. O great hero, the best warrior, equipped with sharpened arms, invincible, the conqueror of the enemy, the fastest in speed, flow thou Soma winning riches. O Lord of vast dominion, spreading fearlessness, grant us heaven and earth with all their fullness. Thou roarest while striving to give us much food, wealth, water, sun and the light. O Indra, thou art far famed, prosperous, and lord of strength, Thou alone, the guardian of men, slayest the resistless foes. O Indra, the most wise, we verily seek thee now, craving thy bounty as our share, like a son to his sire. Thy protection is a great shelter. May thy favour reach us!

O Agni, we worship thee, the best performer of sacrifice, eternal Hotar priest among the Gods, the most skilled in holy rites. I do praise Agni, who lets not the water fall, is beautiful and whose flames are holy. May he win us the favour of Mitra, Varuna and the Waters in the sky! O Agni, the man whom thou protects in the battle and gives strength, becomes the lord of lasting wealth. O Agni, subduer of the foe, no one can vanquish thy devotee, nay very glorious is his strength. May Agni, who pervades the mankind, the winner of fights, grant us riches and fame. The quick moving fingers ten, press out and purify the Soma. He, the gold-hued, son of Surya, flows fast to the vat like a fleet courser. Just as a child is suckled by his mother, or a youth unites with his love, so blended with milk flows Soma speedily to the vat, the settled place. Drink of the sweet Soma juice O Indra and enjoy yourself. Be our friend and sharer of the feast, let thy wisdom protect us well! With thy favours, may we still be strong. Cast us not down before the foe! Guard and succour us with thy protection, establish us in thy favours.

The seven milch kine have shed their pure milk for this Soma. Four other worlds hath he created for his adornment while growing strong through the holy rites. When being offered in oblation with the recitation of vedic hymns, the celestial Soma fills the Earth and Heaven and enrobes himself in the most lucid floods. The learned men know it by grace. May those brilliant rays of Soma, which purifies the food and strength, be inviolate for both the animate and inanimate objects. For this is Soma welcomed as a king by the learned men. Lauded and urged to feast by hymns, the purified Soma flows forth to Mitra, Varuna and Vayu, and to Indra, the thunderer, mighty and car-borne hero. O divine Soma. shower on us the fine milch kine, yielding abundant milk and the raiments that enrobe us meetly. Grant us, O God, gold, silver and chariot horses for our use. Bestow on us divine riches, the wealth contained on earth, and that health and strength wherewith we may enjoy all these possessions. O Indra, the peerless, when thou wast born to remove the darkness, thou did spread the earth and propped the heavens. Then was your Sun created and the sacrifice was produced for thee. Verily, thou art the Lord of all that is there and is yet to be. Thou filled the raw herbs with juices and established the Sun in heaven. Therefore, O learned men, sing ye the Brihad Sama in praise of Indra. O Indra, thou hast drunk the juice which urges you to glorious deeds. Thou the master of bay steeds, art the giver of might, glory and all the pleasures. O God, giver of happiness, gratification, adorable, self-confident, immortal and subduer of the foes, may we obtain thy exhilarating drink. Thou art verily a great hero charitably disposed, and urger of men's desire to good deeds. Turn, thou O slayer of foes, the godless to ashes, like a vessel, sanctified in fire.

Chapter Three

O Soma, pour down on the rain upon us, pour a wave of water from the sky and abundant wholesome food! O Soma, flow forth with thine those purifying streams, whereby the cows and steeds might come to us. O God, most beloved of deities in the sacrifice, pour on us rain in floods from all sides. The learned men listen to thy roar and know it, O Soma. Thou grant us vigour and strength with thy streams flowing through the wool. The Pavaman flows forth, flashing out splendour as of old, and slaying wicked and ignoble beings. O learned men, offer oblations to Indra, who is all-knowing, wanders with speed, never retraces his steps and who fain would drink. O men, come ye nigh, with Soma juices and drinking vessels, to Indra, the great drinker of Soma, the mighty hero and lord of riches. O learned men, if you offer Indra freshly pressed out Soma, he the wise, slayer of the foes, all-knowing, would fulfil all your desires. O Adhvaru, give offering of Soma to Indra alone, for he protects you from all sides, from all violent and presumptuous foes.

O men, sing ye the laud of Soma, the golden-hued, independent of might, the Red, who soars to the heaven with his own might. O Adhvaru, purify through the wool and blend with milk, the Soma, pressed out with stones by the rapid moving hands. Come ye nigh to Soma with humble homage, mix it with the curds and then offer it in libation to Indra. O God, foe-slayer, the seer, mighty and quick, fulfilling the desires of Gods, pour down happiness on kine and other cattle. Thou, the knower of the heart, lord of the heart, art expressed and effused in the vat, so that Indra may drink and be glad. O Pavaman, grant us riches and manly strength, with Indra, our ally. O Sun, thou alone exaltest Indra, the hero renowned for his riches, showerer of rains and who works for men by hurling his thunderbolt. He, with thunderbolt, his weapon, shattered the ninety-nine cloud castles of the fiends and slew Vritra. He, our benefactor and friend showers riches in horses, kine and corn like a full steaming cow. May the effulgent Sun drink the sweet Soma juices, he who grants longevity to sacrificers, urges the wind to blow, nourishes the subjects well, protects them from all sides and pour forth light. The lustrous, mighty, well nourished, sustainer of heavens, showerer of rain and corn, steadfast, subduer of the wicked, killer of the demons, dispeller of the darkness, the mighty aid in overcoming the foe, is the radiance of the Sun. This radiance, the best of radiances, the winner of the world, conquering wealth, all-illuminating, the scorcher, the eternal, subduer of all, mighty as the Sun to see, spreads wide.

O Indra, give us wisdom as a sire gives riches to his son. O much invoked, guide us in this our path, may we ever receive thy light! May we not be overpowered by unknown, malevolent, unhallowed and mighty enemies. May we, with thy help, O hero, in thy obeisance, cross over all the pains and sufferings of the world. Protect us, O Indra, each today, each tomorrow and each following day. Thou preserves thy singers, O lord, through all the days, both by day and night! O lord, doer of many actions, both thy arms are the fulfiller of desires. They wield the thunderbolt to quell the wicked. Thou art dissolver of the universe, exceedingly mighty, passing rich, charitable, all-pervading and lord of the subjects! We, the charitable unmarried men, engaged in devotion and sacrifice, longing for wives and yearning for sons, call upon the omniscient God. Ye, the most dear amid dear speeches, seven-sistered, loved by the sages of old, the Vedic speech, hath earned our praise. May we attain the excellent glory of Savitar, the divine God. May he inspire our intellects. O Lord, make me the son of a sage, skilled in making all kinds of medicines, like an expert craftsman. O Agni, thou purifies our life, pour upon us food and strength and drive away from us the wicked men who are like dogs. May they both Varuna and Mitra grant us heavenly and earthly riches. They are of great might. Desired strength and guileless divine Prana and Apana are obtained and increased through Yajna. Prana and Apana, which make the heavens rain and nourish the corn, pervade the universe. O Agni, the Hotar priest of our rites, ordained by Gods, bring thou the Gods here and complete our Yajna. O Agni, thou most wise in rites, thou knowest all the paths, thou God showest the path with thy might urging thy followers on. O Sage, the mighty lord of sacrifice, thou completest our Yajna. Thou art verily the source of every being and the Sire of power in action.

Pour forth the juices blended with milk, which go quickly to heaven and earth, offer libation to Agni. The priests know well their abiding place of Yajna and come there like the kine with their calves. In all the worlds He was the best and highest whence sprang the mighty one of splendour. No sooner did he bore than he smote the foe, he in whom all who aid him are joyful. Mighty of strength, he strikes terror in the hearts of his foes. Longing to win the animate and inanimate, he is praised at feast and sacrifices. All men meditate on thee with their mental vigour, when they are doubled and tripled with the birth of sons and grandsons. Blend the sweeter with the sweetest. Gain quickly with our sweet that sweet which Indra bestows. He who enjoys Soma juices and barley is verily mighty, great and capable of facing three types of challenges. Let him urge us for performing great deeds. He, with his wisdom, vigour and chivalry scores victoiy by his heroic deeds, subduing the wicked. He granteth splendid wealth to his devotees. He resplendent and mighty overcame the foe in the battle and filled the heaven and eatth with his majesty while waxing strong. One libation he has enjoyed, the other he has left for Gods. O Indra, enlighten us! May true Soma attend upon true Indra!

Book Seven
Chapter One

Laud Indra, O man, with thy speech, as he is known the guardian of the kine, the son of truth and lord of the virtuous. In the sacrifice where the sacred grass is spread, the green-hued Soma is offered in oblation, wherein we sing our songs of praise to Indra. For him the thunderer, the kine have yielded sweet milk to be mingled with juices, which he cherishes exceedingly. O men, draw nigh to Indra, worthy to be involved in every strife. Come, thou most mighty foe-slayer, worthy of our laud, come unto us and our rites. O Indra, thou art the primordial giver of bounteous gifts, thou art true lord of thy devotees. Let us claim alliance with thee, the mighty son of strength and the lord of riches. The learned have realized from the great depth of the heaven the old celestial Soma, the praiseworthy, the joy of Indra. They praise him with their songs, at his birth. Certain learned men, seeing the radiant celestial, water-born Soma from afar, sing his praise. Savitar, open up the heavens to spread it on all sides. Just as a bull is supreme among the herd of kine, so dost thou, O Pavaman, shine with thy might over this earth, heaven and all that exists. O Agni, graciously convey our latest song of praise of our oblation to the Gods. O resplendent God thou givest gifts to thy devotees like an ocean just as canals issue forth from a big river Give us a share of wealth that is found in all the three worlds. I have obtained from my Father the deep Vedic knowledge, and have become effulgent like the Sun. After the ancient tradition, I like the sage beautify the hymns of Veda, whereby I gain strength. Whether praised by seers or not praised by the godless, wax thou strong. O Indra. when praised by me.

O Agni, kindled by friction of the sticks by strength, accept our prayers with all thy fires, with those that are with Gods, with those that are with men, and exalt our hymns! May that Agni come unto us with all his fires, with all his riches for us, for our sons and grandsons. O Agni, thou with thy fires, increases our sacrifice and food. Thou urges other Gods for our sacrifices and wealth. O Soma, the men who trim the sacred grass for a sacrifice, pray thee for fame and strength. So, O hero grant us renown and heroic power. Just as a digs a well with his hands, so thou, O Soma, hast dug for us as it were a well with thy force, a perennial source of water to drink. O Soma, thou hast created the deathless Sun for mortal men, to maintain the Law and loveliness. Thou evermore hast made wealth flow to us. O men, pour out Soma, the sweet juices for Indra to drink, for him who sends forth his bounteous gifts through his majesty. I seeking thy refuge pray unto thee O Indra, O giver of wealth and guardian of life, listen to him who sings thy praise. Never was any hero before thee mightier than thou, none certainly is like thee in riches and praise. The God Agni desires full libation poured to him. So pour ye out, and then fill the vessel again full. The Agni will immediately convey your oblations. The Gods made Agni the watchful Hotar priest of the sacrifice most wise and conveyor of oblations. He grants heroic strength and riches to his devotee, a charitable man.

The most learned dedicate their acts to Agni, the enkindled God, the best prosperer of the sacrificers. May our songs oi praise reach this well kindled Agni. O sacrificers, praise him with songs, who wins thousands at sacrifice and before whoir men shrink when he performs his deeds. Agni, with his splendour, dwelling high in heaven, comes with his might like the Sun, spreading all around the mother Earth. O Agni. thou pourest life, send down upon us food and manly strength, drive thou misfortunes far away! Established before the five classes of priests, the purifier Pavaman, is he to whom we pray and whose wealth is great. O Agni, skilled in thy work, pour down on us manly strength and wealth that nourishes. O purifying divine Pavaman, call the Gods, with thy pleasant and flaming tongue and worship them! O full of radiance, bringer of oblations to the Gods, thou urgest all the luminous bodies. Bring here the Gods to the banquet. O luminous Agni, mighty, feasting on oblations, we kindle thee in our sacrifices. O adorable, effulgent God, favour us with all thy aids in our sacrifices resounding with Vedic hymns. Give us desired wealth, wealth which is ever victorious and invincible. Grant us, O God, pleasant wealth that supports and nourishes life of all for ever, thy favour that we may have longevity!

May our prayers urge Agni forth as a steed is urged in the battle, whereby we may win great wealth. O Agni send us forth thy protection and help whereby we may gain kine and wealth for ourselves. Give us, O Agni, secure and vast riches in steeds and kine, cleanse and purify the sky and moisten the air. Thou hast created, O God, the Sun, the eternal source of light, and other stars and constellations, a great boon to men. O Agni, thou art the most beloved of the subjects, the best, seated in thy place, giver of knowledge. Thou givest longevity to thy worshipper! Agni, the head and height of heaven, is the nourisher of the Earth. He knows the seeds of our actions. Yea, Agni, thou art lord of bliss and the choicest gifts. I, thy devotee, seek refuge in thee. O Agni, thy pure, brilliant, effulgent, blazing high, upward going flames magnify thy glory.

Chapter Two

O Agni, who is thy kin amongst men? Who honours thee with sacrifice? Who art thou? On whom dependent? Thou art verily the kinsman of mankind, their well beloved friend, a friend whom friends may supplicate. Bring Mitra, Varuna and other Gods here to our great Yajna, bring them, O Agni, to thine place. Worthy to be sung and worshipped, dispeller of darkness, finder of the path, showerer of the desires, the cause of rain, Agni is kindled well in sacrifice. Agni, the fulfiller of all desires, is kindled well, like a courser of a hero desiring victory in war. The devotees pray to unto him with oblations. O giver of joys, soft-hearted through prayers, we the sacrificers kindle thee, the effulgent and great. O effulgent Agni, thy blazing flames rise high when thou art kindled! O Pavaman, may my ladles full of clarified butter reach thee. May you accept our prayers and offerings! I pray to Agni, the giver of joy and fruits of our actions, worthy to be invoked in every season, wonderfully lustrous, rich in many ways, may he hear my prayer. Agni protect us with one, protect us with the second, protect us with the third, protect us with the three Vedas. O lord of might, effulgent, guard us by all the four Vedas! We seek thy help, O God, the nearest friend and brother for our weal and that of Gods. Preserve us, thou from each fiend, who offers no gift, save and succour us in every strife!

O effulgent, revolving, radiant Agni, thou art mighty and terrific, pervading all, giver of wisdom. Thou transforms dark Night into shining Dawn with thy radiance. Having swept away the gloom with thy radiance and bringing forth the Dawn, the great Sire's daughter, thou holds the Sun aloft in the sky. Rising with the coining of Dawn, he like a lover follows the blessed Dame. He, of vast radiance, spreading far and wide, enrobes the night with white radiant robes.

With what words should we laud thee, O Agni, omniscient, praiseworthy son of strength! O son of Might, with what may we see serve thee? What reverent word shall we speak? So then, dost thou prepare for us all the happy dwellings and reward our hymns with wealth and corn. O Agni, come here with other Gods, we choose thee as our presiding priest. Thou, best of the priests to occupy the sacred seat, may the preferred ladle full of oblation please thee. O Son of Strength, ladles of oblations are poured forth for thy realization. We pray unto him who is foremost in the Yajna, the guardian of might and food, and whose flames blaze with ghee. May our hymns of laud reach him, who is handsome and effulgent with snake like piercing and shining flames. May our oblations full of devotion, attain him, much lauded, for our help. May our speech attain the son of strength, praiseworthy and giver of knowledge for gaining precious gifts, him, who is immortal, and known among men with his two aspects; as the bringer of Gods from all sides and the giver of sweet foods. Agni, the invincible, moves ahead of his mortal subjects. He is ever new and fast, like a chariot in conveying oblations. A charitable man gains a dwelling from him whose flames are pure, through his oblations to him. Agni, the subduer of enemy forces, the priest of Gods, invincible, is the embodiment of all kinds of foods. May Agni worshipped and satiated, grant us bliss. Let our sacrifices and lauds to him, bring us bliss! O Agni, grant us the determined mind, wherewith success is achieved in strifes. Bring down the manly strength of the foe; we worship thee for the attainment of desired victory.

Give us, O Agni, thou son of strength and lord kine and riches, great wealth and abundant food, O enlarger of our intellect! He, the effulgent, one of the eight Vasus, the most wise Agni, must be prayed with Vedic hymns. O multi-flamed, grant us wealth of many kinds. O Agni, thou of sharp flamed teeth, burn the wicked to ashes by night and when the Dawn appears, O men, longing for food, for ye I glorify Agni with songs, the dear friend, the beloved guest of every home. The sacrificers adore Agni with libations of ghee, praise of songs and gifts. They serve him like Mitra. Much lauded Agni, who conveys oblations to heaven, is over in the service of Gods. I praise Agni, the pure, effulgent, steadfast, wise, bringer of the Gods, kindled with fuel. We implore him with devotion for favour, the sage, guileless, charitable and protecting Lord. O Agni, men have made thee their envoy, offering-bearer to Gods in every age, O immortal and blissful God. They worship thee, who pervades all the fuel, is ever watchful, awakening, mighty and lord of the home. O Agni, thou adorning both Gods and men, moves about Earth and Heaven as envoy of Gods. We lay him to thy regard and gracious care. May thou be kind to us as thrice protecting friendly guard. O Agni, our sacred hymns, like the wives of sacrificers, reach thee in the atmosphere. That Agni is indeed laudable whose three-fold grass is spread unbound and in whom even the waters find rest. His aspect is beauteous like that of the Sun. He showers bliss with his unconquerable aids.

Chapter Three

O Indra, the learned singers praise thee for their satisfaction. The sages sing thy glory in Vedic hymns, thou eternal! Indra increases the manly strength of Soma juices for full enjoyment, and so living men today, even as of old, sing forth their laud to his majesty. O Indra and Agni, the skilled singers, with songs laud you. I too choose you both to bring me food. O Gods, ye both shook down together, with one mighty deed the ninety forts held by the foe. O Indra and Agni, to ye both reach the learned man in the wake of the sacred Law, through their righteous acts. O Indra and Agni, your powers work in harmony, ye both urge the rain to pour down. O hero, the giver of fruits of actions, we pray unto thee to grant us glorious fame with thy all protecting aids. May we follow thee, O giver of wealth, etc. Indra, thou art increaser of our horses and multiplier of our kine, like a deep well full of effulgence. None can impair the gift laid up in thee. Thou grant me whatever I seek. Come to thy devotee, O Indra, and grant him knowledge, wealth, etc. Grant, thou kine and steeds to make us rich! O Maghvan thou bestowest many hundred, ye, many thousand gifts on thy devotee who with Vedic verses, seek thy favour and protection, O shatterer of forts. We send forth our hymns of praise, like first vessels filled with Soma juice, to Agni, who is Hotar priest of men, who grants wealth and bliss. O God, thy devotees and votaries, the charitable men, adore thee with their songs of laud, like a horse drawing a chariot.

Thou, mighty lord of men, bestows wealth both on sons and grandsons!

O Varuna, listen and accept this call of mine. Grant me happiness today, desiring help I pray to thee! O fulfiller of desires, with what aid dost thou delight us? With what help dost thou bring riches to thy worshippers? We call on thee, Indra alone, in sacrifice, in battle we seek thy aid that we may win spoil. With his glorious might hath Indra spread out the Heaven and Earth, with his might hath he lighted up the Sun. In him all creatures abide, in him abide the expressed Soma. O creator of all, bring thyself here, strengthened by oblations, it is thine own sacrifice! Let others in ignorance live in folly, but let us perform the Yajna to completion here! Just as the Sun with his flood of light pouring forth on the earth, engulfs and makes things shine with his seven coloured rays, so does Soma shine forth cleansed with waters. Soma, thou discovered the treasure of Panis. Thou deckest thyself in thy home with the mother-like nourishing sunrays. As the Vedic hymns recited in a sacrifice are heard, as it were from afar, so does thy splendour purify even from distance. Thou nourishes corn with thy rays that sustain the three worlds. Grant us, O Pushan, cattle, horses, abundant wealth and wisdom for our protection O Maruts, the real heroes, mark ye well the sweat of him who toils, and him who worships thee with hymns! May these Sons of immortality listen to our hymns of praise, and be extremely gracious to us. O pure Heaven and Earth, we glorify ye both with our lofty song of praise. Ye both sanctify each other by your own strength and remain in your respective places. Ye both ever further the Yajna. Ye both great ones, promote sacrifice, sit ye around our Yajna! Just as a pigeon turns to his mate, so do we approach Indra, who listens to the prayer of his subjects. O hero, guardian of wealth that gives happiness, praised in hymns, may wealth and fame be ours, who sing thy laud. O lord of several powers, for our protection in this conflict, be over us. We shall talk together for other fights.

O speech, recite Vedic verses at the place of sacrifice, that the cars of the listeners be purified. The sweet Soma is pressed out with stones and poured into the vat. The sages drain the fount with reverence. Let us have no fear, nor be tired in the friendship of mighty Indra. Thy actions are grand and praiseworthy. May we glorify them. O men, on his left side reclines Indra favourably. The Soma juice, blent with the honey of the bee is ready. Quickly come hither, haste and drink. The charity of this Indra does never harm but always does good. O lord of wealth, may these songs of laud exalt thee. The sages, pure and lustrous like sacred fire, have sung these in thy praise. This Indra spreads himself like an ocean, when resorted to by thousands of seers for strength. Real is his majesty, and it is admired at solemn rites and in sacrifices where singers rule.

The Lord of Vedas is he to whom all Aryas are devoted and the world belong. This Vedic knowledge hidden in him, the lord of speech, and leader of men, is revealed to thee. The learned and active sacrificers have sung a song of praise to Indra, expressing sweet juices, that he may shower on them riches, manly strength and filtered Soma. Flow forth to us, O Pavaman, expressed, with wealth in kine and horses and grant our cattle beautiful visage. O Lord of green juice, Soma celestial, lend us splendour as does a friend to friend! Be thou gracious to men! Let us have thy friendship of old. Sweep far away from us the godless fiends, and drive away the false afar! The learned find Soma in streams and balm it with honey. They press it out, cleanse with their fingers and enjoy the juice as it flows like a courser. O learned, skilled in songs, sing to Soma, which flows on like a mighty stream. He glides like a serpent from his slough and runs like a playful flying horse. Foremost, King, watery, set among the worlds, a measure of dates, he, beautiful, mighty effulgent, riding a car of light, showers wealth.

Book Eight
Chapter One

O Agni, the Son of strength, accept this prayer of ours and this our recitation, with all thy fires! Though we worship every God through our sacrifice, but every oblation is offered only to thee. May he, the nourisher of his subjects, promoter of the Yajna, effulgent, adorable, be our beloved. And, may we, the sacrificers, love mutually one another! For you and for us, we call upon Indra, the most high, through Agni. May he be ours and none others. O Indra, showerer of all gifts simultaneously, unclose the door of emancipation to us, obedient to thee. Thou art indeed irresistible, O lord! As the strong bull leads on the herd so he the showerer of happiness, stirs the men with his might. He is irresistible ruler who fulfils all noble desires. O Agni! send us thy bounteous gifts, with thy wondrous protecting aids. Thou art hero and lord of wealth, give safety to our progeny! Thou prosper our sons and grandsons with thy guarding powers, inviolate, never negligent! Keep far away from us all celestial wrath, O Agni, and wickedness of godless men! O all-pervading, with what name shall I describe thou? Thou, defies description! But hide not from us thy Vishnu from, nor keep it secret, since thou did wear another form in battle. O God, pervading all, I, skilled in rules, praise thee, worthy of invocation. Yea, I, poor and weak praise thee, the mighty, who dwells in the realm beyond this region. O all-pervading lord, unto thee I offer my oblation. Let this offering please thee. May these eulogise of mine exalt thee. Do ye preserve us evermore with blessings! O Wind God, I offer thee the main and most sweet oblation in this sacrifice. O mightiy, come thou in haste riding thy steed-drawn chariot to enjoy the Soma drink! O Vayu and Indra, ye both art worthy drinkers of these juices for unto ye both flows the Soma, as do the waters flow to the low plains. Ye mighty twain, lord of strength, come unto us for our protection, and for a drink, riding your fast chariot.

Then Soma pressed out after night, enterest into mighty deeds, when the rays of the Sun impel the golden-hued to flow in streams. We purify this gladdening juice, which Indra in great quantity drinks. The same Soma which kine took in their mouth, and the sages of old and even now drink. The purified Soma they praise with ancient Vedic hymns sitting around. They then supplicate him with hymns bearing the names of the Sun. Pushan, Aryaman and other Gods. With homage, O Agni, I rever thee like a long-tailed steed, thou lord of sacred sacrifice. May the mighty, vast, fast of speed, showerer of rain, our friend, borne of fuel sticks, be ours! Roaming everywhere, thou Agni, protect us from wicked and sinful men from near and far away. O Indra, thou art the subduer of the foes in our battles with the hostile host. Thou art our Sire, all-conquering, the subduer of the curse, the victor of the violent. O Indra, the Earth and Heaven cling close to thy victorious might, as do father and mother to their child. When thou attackest Vritra, all the hostile forces shrink and waxes Indra strong, the showerer of rain, nourishes the Earth. Indra expanded the sky and realms of light in rapturous joy of Soma, when he cleft the demon. Revealing the hidden kine, he drove them forth and flung the fiend headlong down. Call Indra for succour, the ever-conquering God of yours, him who is sung in our praises. He is the hero, whom none can conquer, the Soma enjoyer, ever invincible, the commander of resistless armies. O Indra, bring wealth for us, omniscient, raised in our psalms; project our riches, got in spoil!

That lofty strength and might of thine, the intelligence and matchless thunderbolt of thine, are sharpened by our prayers. The Heaven and Earth augment thy force and fame, the mountains and rivers sing thy laud. O thou, great abode of beings, Vishnu, Mitra and Varuna praise thee, the Maruts get strength in thy company. O Agni, God, thy devotees sing thy praise for strength. Strike thou the foe with terror and disease! O Agni, grant us wealth and kine. O multiplier, multiply us! In the great battle desert us not, Agni, like one bearing a load who castes it aside before the destination is reached. Win the foe and thereby win us wealth! All men and subjects make obeisance to Indra, as rivers bow themselves to the sea. Indra severed the head of demon Vritra with his mighty thunderbolt. That might of Indra was displayed when he brought the Heaven and Earth together, like a skin. O beauteous Indra, come unto us, this happy pair of steeds that draws thy car, are approaching us. O men, bend ye down your heads, for Indra stands amidst water-bearing clouds, pointing the path with his ten fingers.

Chapter Two

The priests prepare excellent Soma juice for Indra, for the mighty hero's joy! A team of two steeds, urged by our hymns, will bring Indra, our friend, here in our Yajna. May he who slays Vritra, drink Soma, and helping us in hundred ways, come to us and stay not afar! May our heart flow unto thee as the river flows into the sea! O Indra, nought emulates thee! Thou watchful Indra, by thy might has obtained Soma offering, which is now inside thee. O Vritra-slayer, let this Soma be enough for you, may it be enough for the three worlds! O Agni, knowable through hymns, help him who knows thee. We sing thy praise for the completion of the sacrifice. May this our God, great, limitless, smoke-bannered, bliss-giving, urge us to holy thought and wisdom! May Agni, like some rich lord of men, the banner of the Gods, refulgent, listen to our songs of praise! O men, sing in unison, the praise of him, the hero, much invoked, the slayer of foes, Indra, the giver like the Earth! He withholdeth not his generous gifts in kine and strength, when he hath heard our songs. May Indra go to godless man's stall of cows and unclose it with his might for us. He created the earth, mid-region and heaven and pervaded all. He thus sustains the whole universe. He, the guardian of the three worlds, the immortal, all-pervading, sustains the creation with his threefold power. Look ye on his wonderful creation, whereby the man performs all his rites. He, the God is the worthy friend of mankind. The learned evermore see God, the all-pervading, within themselves, as men can see the great Sun in the sky. Only the sages, devoted to God, ever active, attain Him, the all-pervading to be attained by all. May the sages help and favour us by making us know the God, the Creator of the worlds, who sustains all.

O God, let none, not even thy devotees, delay thee far away from us. Come to our sacrifice, if already here, listen to our prayer! Just as the flies collect on honey, so do priests collect around the sacrifice and offer oblations to thee. Just as a hero desirous of riches set his foot upon a car, so do the learned men, craving wealth, rest their hope on thee. O men, sing ye the praise of Indra. Recite the eternal Brihat-sama Verses, that he may enlarge your intellects.

Indra hath given a great store of kine, land, wealth, pure and strength giving foods, yea and the Sun. May the Soma drink, blended with milk, pure and sparkling, gladden Indra. The Soma juice hath been shed forth for Indra, the demon-slayer, and for the hero, the giver of guerdon, who sit at the altar. O friends, may ye and we attain this resplendent God, who is so fragrant and whose proximity is a great strength. They filter Soma through the long fleece, the tawny, golden-hued, dear to all, him who flows on to the Gods with his exhilarating juices! O all-pervading, what mortal will attack thee? None! But a devotee of thine longs to offer reverently Soma oblation to thee on the day of Yajna. Urge thou, the mighty ones in battle, who give treasures in charity dear to thee. May we, with thy aid, O lord, pass through all troubles and afflictions! O Adhvaru pour forth the nourishing and gladdening juice, so that the hero who ever prospers us is praised and gratified. O horse-borne lord, none can attain the praise due to you either by might or goodness. We, longing for fame, invoke this God of yours, the lord of wealth, whoever promotes our weal through constantly made sacrifices.

Laud him, the lord of bliss, the envoy of Gods, who bears oblations to the deities. Laud thou O singer, Agni, the great giver, effulgent with flames, eternal, him who is offered Soma in oblation and who bears offerings. O Soma, expressed with stones, urged to flow through the woollen filters, thou enters the vat to settle, as a hero who enters a fort having conquered it. He is filtered through fine long wool on the vat by the learned priests. He is of manly strength like a bull and a courser and one who gladdens. We, the learned men have in the past been making Indra to drink to his fill, he the bearer of thunderbolt. Today as well, bring him the juice expressed in the Yajna, and let him be adorned. Even a thief or a dacoit who waylays, becomes subservient to his dictates. May he graciously accept this our praise and come to us with his wondrous wisdom! O Indra and Agni, in your deeds of might ye adorn heaven's lucid realms. Renowned is this strength of yours. To ye both Indra and Agni go forth our hymns along the path of sacred law. O Gods, your powers work in harmony to lead us forth. Ye both urge us to righteous acts. Who knows what strength Indra wins by drinking Soma juices with other Gods? He, then being satiated with Soma, breaks down the forts in its ecstasy. As a wild elephant in rut, rushes on, this way and that way, and none can check him, so do thou O Indra roam about unrestrained. May he come unto us when

Soma is ready. He, who is of great might, invincible, ever ready to win the battle, steadfast. Indra Maghvan, when he listens to his devotees call, he will tarry not, but come soon!

The strengthening, pure, sparkling Soma is poured forth in libation with the recitation of Vedic hymns. Bright Soma is effused upon the mountains and the earth from the heaven. The swift, sparkling and beauteous Soma flows on driving all the wicked afar! Foe-subduers, sin-removers, equally victorious, invincible, giver of strength. Indra and Agni, I invoke here. O Indra and Agni, skilled singers in Vedic hymns, bring ye lauds! I choose ye both for strength. Together ye both, with one mighty action shook the ninety forts which the demons held. O Agni, kindled by strength, beauteous in visage, we recite Vedic hymns at the place of sacrifice, while offering oblation. To thee we have come seeking refuge, as to the shed from scorching heat, Agni, who shines like gold. Mighty as a hero who slays with shafts, or like a bull with sharpened horns, Agni, thou shatters down the enemy forts! We worship Agni, the lord of ail, truthful, effulgent, eternal and master of Yajna. He, who spreads all around, lends the light to heaven, lord of strength, reveals the seasons. Agni, the primeval cause of what has been and shall be, shines forth as sovereign lord in his various manifestations.

Chapter Three

The wise Agni in the way of old, beautifying his body, is exalted by the learned priests. Here, in this happy sacrifice, I invoke Agni, the Son of strength, whose flames are pure and blazing. O Agni, worthy of reverence from friends, pure and bright, seat thyself with other Gods in this our sacrifice. O Soma, thy streams flow slaying the wicked. Sweep away, thou, the enemy forces that entertain rivalry with us! I conquering the battle with thy aid, where wealth is at stake, and car meets car, with fearless heart I sing thy laud. No evil-minded dare assail this Pavaman's holy Law. Thou crush him who fain would disobey thy law. They send him to Indra to drink, him who is rapturous, tawny hued and giver of felicity. Come, O fndra here, riding thy bay steeds who possess tails like peacock's plumes. None can check thy course. Thou overcomest the opposing forces, as a fowler captures the bird, or as an archer subdues the foe! Indra, the fort renderer, cloud dispeller, the foe-slayer, the rider of the chariot drawn by a team of bay steeds, he shatters even things that stand most firm. As the pools, deep and full, feed the ocean, as a cowherd feeds his cows well, so dost thou nourish the earth. As the milch kine turn to the fodder, and streams flow to the sea, so dost thou reach the sacrifice. Just as a thirsty deer resorts to the pool of water, so should thou come to us quickly to drink thy fill. May the Soma juice gladden thee. O Indra, and gain thy favour for him who pours it. Thou enjoyest the juices shed in the sacrifice and thereby waxeth exceedingly strong. O mighty God, thou blessest the mortal man. O Indra, there is no comforter except thee. Indra I speak to thee. O God. let never thy bounteous gifts and protecting aids fail us! Thou lover of man, pour out to us all the riches.

This Dame, beautiful and bright, the daughter of Heaven, hath appeared after her sister, the Night. The Dawn, red in colour, beautiful, holy and mother of the rays of light, became the Ashvin's friend. O Dawn, thou art verily the friend of Ashvins, the mother of beams art thou, and the ruler over wealth. The beautiful lady, the wonderful dear Dawn, the daughter of Heaven, shines forth scattering darkness. I praise ye high Ashvins. O ye both sons of Ocean, virtuous, mighty and wise ones, give us much wealth through our prayers! Your team of steeds course through the limitless sky like the birds. O Dawn, possessor of good foodstuffs, bestow upon us that wondrous good fortune wherewith we may support our sons and grandsons. O luminous noble lady, possessor of cows and steeds, uttering words true and sweet and doing noble deeds, bestow upon us good wealth. O Lady, enrich with wealth, yoke thy purple steeds to thy car now and cause us to enjoy felicities and delights! O Ashvins, destroyer of sufferings, do ye direct your car unto us, rich in cattle, splendour and gold. May the twins, who are divine and wonder workers, bring us the rays of the Sun, at rosy dawn for obtaining nourishment and peace. Ye both, who brought down the hymn from heaven, a light for men, do ye, Ashvins bring to us strength and food. Agni is the king, whom the milch kine seek as their shed, whom the fleet-footed coursers resort as their stable. O Agni, pour forth food on those who sing thy laud. Agni, God of all, granteth steeds and wealth to men. He giveth readily and the best when pleased. Agni, give food to those who sing thy laud! He is Agni, the praised, to whom the kine go in herds, to whom the racers, swift of foot resort, and to whom our princes go, O lord give food to those who sing thy laud!

O lustrous Dawn, awaken us today to ample wealth, as thou did awake us in the past. O beautiful, enchanting high-born, thou daughter of Heaven, dawn on us today dispelling darkness as thou didest in the past. O sweet Ashvins, listen to my call, the laudatory Vedic praise your desire fulfilling, wealth-giving and beautiful course of conduct. Ashvins, lord of sweetness listen to my call. May I attain you and subdue all my foes, O twain of the golden path, giver of happiness and bringers of rain! Come ye twain to us wearing precious ornaments. Ye Rudras. on your way of gold, promoting the Yajna, mighty and handsome, lord of sweetness listen and accept my invocation!

People kindle Agni with fuel to meet the Dawn, who cometh like a milch cow. The flames of Agni rising from the altar soar high in atmosphere like branches of young trees shooting up. Agni, the Hotar priest has been kindled in the morning for God's worship. He, the pleasing God, rises erect in flames, his radiances frees the worlds from the gloom of night. Having kindled, he destroys the darkness with his pure flames, and then he is offered oblation with the right hand by the priests, which he drinks with his tongues erect. Dawn hath appeared, so wonderful and exceedingly bright, the fairest of the lights. Night has gone away, giving place to Dawn. The bright Dawn, the mother of the Sun hath come, and the dark Night hath sought her own abode. Both akin and allied to the Sun, eternal succeeding each other and mutually effacing each other's complexion, traverse the heaven. They are sisters whose path is unending, they tread it alternately guided by the Gods, combined in purpose though of different visages. They obstruct not each other, nor do they tarry or stand still. The Sun, the bright face of the Dawn, is shining, the recitation of the Vedic hymns has begun. O Ashvins, borne on your car, come you here to our brimming fresh libations. The twain, the frequent guests, scorn not the proffered thing, they are already beside us. They come with speed with their aids, the best guardian of their devotees. Come ye both at early morning, at noon of day, and when the Sun is setting, by day, a night, with most auspicious favour. Not only now.

The Dawns have spread their banner of light over the world in the eastern portion of the firmament brightening all things, like heroes brandishing their weapons in the fight. They, the radiant and progessive mothers of the earth, travel daily on their course. The purple beams of the Dawns have already shot up, they have yoked the red kine. They have made their pathways, as of yore; red-rayed, they have attended upon the glorious Sun. The dawns sing like women engaged in their daily tasks, along their common path bringing, every kind of wholesome food, doing acts of service, and destroying all the sufferings of their charitable devotees. As the Agni is kindled, the radiant Sun rises, and the magnificent joyous Dawn encompasses the world with her radiance. The Sun hath roused the world in sundry ways. The twin Ashvins have harnessed their team for the course. O Ashvins, may your car be swift and smooth. Come unto us with your chariot laden with food and wealth. May your presence be auspicious to us and to all bipeds and quardrupeds. O Pavaman, thy never failing streams flow forth like showers of rain on earth from heaven, which bring abundant wealth. Thou flowest on thy way observing all beloved sacred lore, shattering all obstacles. He, cleansed and adorned sits like a sovereign or a hawk in the wood. So bring tliou hitherward to us, O Soma Pavaman, while being cleansed, all heavenly and terrestrial treasures.

Book Nine
Chapter One

Flow forth the streams of power of this Soma, the mighty one shed, who waits upon the Gods. The learned Adhvarus, the doer of noble deeds, praise with their songs the effulgent, adorable Soma while being cleansed. O opulent, adorable, Soma, thy halos, while they purify thee, are pleasant. Thou, praiseworthy, fill full the sea of bliss! This Brahman, the bringer of different seasons, famed as Indra, him I praise. O lord of strength, to thee alone go forth all praise sung by skilled singers. Like streams on their path, so let bounties flow to thy devotees from thee. We approach thee for help as to a car. O Indra, subduer of the foe, mighty, doer of many deeds, lord of the brave. Great in power and wisdom, in intelligence comprehending all, thou Indra, pervades all with thy majesty. Thou art a mighty God, whose both hands wield the thunderbolt and other weapons that stretch wide on the earth. May that Agni, swift like the steed, effulgent, of many forms, brilliant like the Sun, promote our Yajnas. The twice-born, envoy of the Gods, spread with his radiance in all the three realms, the foremost priest, he is Agni in whom waters abide. The twice-born priest, Agni pervades all the best things for the sake of glory. He who offers oblation to this Agni, hath fine sons. O Agni, we awaken thee with hymns of praise, thou offering-bearer to the Gods like a courser, auspicious and serviceable. Thou art verily the lord and promoter of a real and big sacrifice of a noble, learned and charitable person. Radiant like the Sun, Agni, come to us with all thy manifestations, through these hymns of praise!

O Agni, eternal, radiant, gift of Dawn, give thou this day ample wealth to him who rises early in the morning to pay oblations to the Gods. Thou art indeed the envoy of Gods their beloved offering-bearer and carrier of holy rites. Thou grant us manly strength and high fame in harmony with Ashvins and Dawn! The old Sun hath awakened the new Moon, as it were from the slumber, who revolves among the stars with speed. Behold the high wisdom of God by which greatness, he who died yesterday is living today. Of great strength is the red bird (Sun) with his own might, effulgent hero, who hath no nest to dwell. Whatever, he, the ever active knows, is nothing but truth. He, the conquerer, gives wealth, desired by many. This is the expressed Soma, of which the Maruts, Mitra, Varuna, Aryaman and the twain Ashvins drink. They drink the purified and fresh juice placed in the three places. Indra drinks of the purified strengthening juice in the morning, like a Hotar priest. Truly thou art great, O Sun, verily Surya thou art great. O mighty thou art admired for thy majesty, O God, thou art great by thy greatness! Ye, thou art great, O Sun in fame and wisdom, verily thou art great. By thy greatness, thou art the Hotar priest of all the worlds, foe-slayer, of ever spreading light, never conquerable. Come Lord Indra, with ecstatic joys, come to our sacrifice riding thy bay steeds to our flowing Soma! Come, thou sin slayer, doer of many noble deeds, come to our flowing juice! O Indra, Vritra-slayer, thou drinker of pressed out Soma juice, come, riding thy steeds to our effused juice! Come ye men, with your offerings to the wise and great to obtain his favours. He is the nourisher of his subjects and grants them his grave. The sages ever sing the laud of Indra, far spreading, great and sublime. They never transgress his laws. Indra, whose wrath is irresistible, hath been established king by the singers for victory. Glorify him for he strengthens those whom he loveth.

If I, O Indra, were the lord of riches as ample as thine, I would give them to the singer. O God who scattered wealth, and never desert him in woe. Each day I would enrich him who sang my praise, in whatsoever position he were. No kinsman is better than thou art, Indra, even father is no better guardian. Accept the prayer of one who expresses Soma. mark thou well the hymns of him who sings thy praise, O Maghvan, take to thy innermost heart these lauds! I know and never forget thy lauds and hymns, O Indra, the conqueror, of immense strength. Thy name I ever repeat, O self-effulgent! Many are the ways of thy worship among men and many a tune the pious sage invoke thee. O God, tarry not away from us. Praise the might of Indra, who sets his chariot in the foremost place. He slays the foes, urges us on, protects in the thick of war. The frail bow strings of our weak enemies break at the sight of him. Thou, foeless Indra, made the rivers flow to earth, and killed Vritra. Thou nourishes the subjects, O born foeless, to thee we draw nigh. Let the weak bow strings break upon the bows of our foes. Let our malicious foes be destroyed. Thou castest thy thunderbolt at the hostile forces who wish to strike us dead. Thy generous bounty makes us rich. Let the weak bow strings of our weak enemies break upon their bows. One who praises thee, is bound to be rich, O rich and liberal lord, pervading all. High he would rank certainly who lauds Indra. Does not a wise king understand the lauds of an uneducated man, and the song of praise recited? He does understand and appreciate them. Give us not, O Indra, as a victim to the scornful and the violent, but succour us, mighty one, with thy powers!

Come here with thy steeds, O Indra, and listen to the eulogies of the wise. O lord, giver of comforts of life, grant us pleasures through thy officials who carry out thy behests! The stones press the Soma here like a wolf shaking a sheep. O dweller in paradise, grant us happiness. The stones pressing the Soma juice out, call thee here with their ringing noice. O joyful juices, most sweet, flow for Indra's delight. The Soma, expressed, wise, of manly strength waxeth Indra strong. The Soma juice, speedily as a chariot, is offered in oblation for the enjoyment of Gods. Agni I regard as our Hotar priest, of lofty knowledge, skilled in performing Yajna, radiant, munificent, acceptor of whatever is given with reverence, son of strength, the sage endowed with wisdom, celebrate and virtuous. We, O exceedingly wise Agni, praise thee, as thou art the best, and the most adorable. O Pure God, giver of wisdom, Bull with hair of flames, roaming about in all directions, mighty. Come thou for our protection. He the hero, far shining with brilliant vigour, is the slayer of the foes, like a hatchet he cuts down tress in the forest. Unsparing he sports amidst the foe, at whose contact, whatever is solid and firm dissolves like water, nor does he ever desist from their destruction like an archer who retreats not from battle.

Chapter Two

Great fame and strength are thine, O Agni, thy flames blaze on high. O refulgent one, grant us strength and wealth, thy devotees, thou sage, passing bright with purifying, brilliant sheen thou reveals thyself. Thou guards Heaven and Earth and joins them together as their son. O son of strength, omniscient, be glad with our songs of praise. In thee they have heaped many kinds of foods, the priests from various lands, and of wondrous forms. O immortal, increase our wealth with thy victorious radiance. Thou, handsome to look upon, leadest us to happy Yajna. I laud the sage, who orders sacrifice, and who hath great wealth under his control. Thou bestowest wholesome, plenteous food, and wealth that brings success. They have set Agni before them as a guide, mighty, witness to all, the divine. O celestial one, most famous, with ears to hear, the people in pairs magnify thee with Vedic hymns of praise. He, whom thou makest thy friend, he overcomes all obstacles with thy help, performs great deeds and hath heroic sons, O Agni, fed with Soma, thy blue smoke being kindled is taken up. Thou art the dear friend of the vast Dawns, thou shinest in glimmerings of the night! Him, duly coming, as their germ have herbs received. This Agni hath brought waters to life. So, in the similar way, the forest trees, plants and herbs bear him within them and produce him evermore. Foremost in the Yajna, he grows brighter with oblations for Indra. He shines in the sky far resplendent, and sends forth offspring like a queen.

The sacred psalms love him who wakes and watches, to him come the holy verses of the Vedas, to him who keeps vigil and watches this Soma says, "I rest and have my abode in thy friendship". Praise unto the friends sitting in front, and unto those seated together. I use the many-footed speech of the Vedas. I use the thousand footed speech. I sing in Gayatri, Trishtup and Jagati metres, the Sama Veda that hath a thousand ways. Gayatri, Trishtup, Jagati hymns, the metres united and complete have the Gods created and made familiar friends. Agni is light, light is Agni, Indra is light, light is Surya. O Agni, come unto us gain with riches, pour thou on us from all sides, thy universal stream! If I, were like thee, O Indra, the sovereign over the earth, my devotee would be rich in kine. I would be fain, O lord of strength, to strengthen and enrich the learned, were I the lord of kine and lauds. Thy bounty, God, is a cow yielding wealth, kine and cattle to thy devotees. Ye, streams of water, bring peace and happiness, help ye us to energy and make us look on great delight! Ye waters, grant us potion of the dew, the most auspicious joy that ye possess, like mothers who fondly nurse. O waters, for the removal of impurity you urge us on, and we with speed go unto ye; grant us children who make the proper use of water. May Air breathe his wholesome, delightful and medicinal balm on us to prolong our days of life. Thou art, O God, our father, our brother yea, our friend, so give us strength that we may live! O

Wind God, that store of elixir laid away within thee, give us thereof that we may live! The mighty, of diverse forms, of wings, of beauteous flames, enrobed in seasons and rays of the Sun, refulgent, nourishing the altar, his place of birth, Agni promotes the sacrifice. He, of many forms, lays his seeds in waters and appears on the earth, then establishing his greatness in mid air, roars, the seed of the water-bearing lightning. This Agni, giver of gifts in hundreds, thousands, nourisher of the subjects of the world, assuming thousand robes that suit him, upholds the light of the Sun, and the heaven. People gaze on thee with a longing in their heart, on the strong winged Sun, fast moving, scattering radiance in heaven, gold-flanked, Varuna's envoy, the bird that hasteneth to the west. Established in the sky, the Sun, wearing his multi-coloured weapons, handsome to look on, clad in far spreading form, produces happy rain-bearing clouds. Revolving with great speed in his orbit, and looking on with a vulture's eye, shining with brilliance, the Sun ever lustrous, performs deeds of world weal, in the third region.

Chapter Three

Swift, like a bull with sharpened horns, terrific in attack, awe inspirer among the people, vigilant, matchless hero, Indra defeats at once a hundred armies. Ye warriors, win the war, overthrow the foe with the aids of Indra, the skilled hero, ever vigilant, subduer of the foe, victorious, irresistible, who bears arrows in his hands. He rules with warriors carrying arrows in their hands, and armed with weapons, winner of the battles, drinker of the Soma, mighty, Indra who subdues the enemy hosts, whose bow is ever erect to shoot. He shoots the enemy with his well aimed arrows. O great Indra, attack the enemy at once riding thy war chariot. Thou art slayer of the demons, remover of the enemy, break up of the armies. Winning the battle and driving off the enemy, thou protect the chariots of we warriors! O foremost warrior, mighty, conscious of thine strength, victorious, commander of fine warriors, firm and fierce, Indra, thou mount thy conquering car! O coeval warriors, display your zeal and courage, quiet yourselves as heroes, following Indra, who is cleaver of the mountains, strong limbed, wielder of thunderbolt, who subdues and destroys the enemy forces! May Indra, who with winning strength pierces the cow stall, is pitiless hero, full of righteous wrath, irresistible, subduer of the foe, invincible commander protects our armies in the battles! Marshall thou Indra these forces. The commander should lead the divine army, the conqueror and demolisher of the foe. The hero at the head of the big bands should march on the right. The encouragers should march on the left, and soldiers under Maruts should move on the forefront. Ours is a mighty army of powerful heroes, of Indra, Varuna, Maruts and Adityas. Let the winning shout of these Gods, high minded, skilled warriors, rend the worlds. O Maghavan, let the weapons of our warriors flourish, arouse their warring spirits, urge the speech of the steeds, O Vritra-slayer, and let the din of conquering cars rend the sky. May Maghavan help us when our flags are collected. May our arrows be victorious. May our warriors prevail on the enemy. May Gods protect us at the time of war! Ye Maruts, envelope the enemy army approaching with mighty strength, into thick gloom that not a man of them recognises the other.

O slayer of foes, bewilder the senses of the enemy forces, seize them bodily and depart. Attacking set their hearts on fire with woes that they may abide in utter darkness. Fare forward, O heroes and carry the day. May Indra protect you. May aweful be your mighty arms that none may wound or injure you! O arrow, thou shot from the bow, fly fast to the enemy, strike them, sharpened with our prayers, let none of the foe men be left alive! Let ravens and strong feathered pursue them. Ye, let the vultures feed on them. O Indra, let no sinner escape, let carrion and carnivorous birds devour them. O Vritra-slayer Maghavan, thou and Agni, ye twain, burn down the host of foemen with your flames, the army which comes marching in a war-like show! There where the arrow fall everywhere, may the commanders Brahmanaspati and Aditi protect us well through all our days. O Vritra-slayer, Indra drive away the foe, sweep away the demons, tear thou in pieces the cheeks of the enemy, quell their wrath who threaten us. O Indra, destroy the enemy, humble the foe men, down him who challenges us, rend him down to darkness who wants to injure us! Strong, youthful, unassailable, pleasing, invincible are both the arms of hero Indra. Let these arms be first employed, wherewith Indra won the demons, overthrowing them in the battle!

O King, thy vital parts I cover with armour. May Soma, the lord of herbs, clothe thee in immortality. May Varuna give thee what is more than ample, and may Gods rejoice in thy victory! Blind, O my foemen, shall ye be, even as headless serpents are.

May Indra slay each best of you when Agni's flame hath struck you down. Whosoever of our relations, a godless man wants to kill us secretly, may all the Gods torment him. God is my true armour, my internal armour and protection! Thou, like a fierce wild tiger, roaming in the mountain, hast come to us from farthest place. Indra, now thou crush the foe, whetting thy thunderbolt shaip. Scatter them away who are at war with us! O Gods, may our ears with your grave, hear that which is auspicious. May we attain the ripe age, appointed by Gods, extolling you with our strong limbs and bodies! May Indra, the most illustrious prosper us. May Pushan, the nourisher of all, bless us! May Takshya, the giver of comforts bless us! May Brihaspati grant us his favour. May He bestow on us his blessings!

Atharva Veda

Book One

For Sacred Learning

May the all-pervading Lord of Speech and thrice seven that bear all forms, bestow upon me today their powers. O Lord of Speech and of good come again, with divine mind and let it abide in me, in myself be what is heard. Like a hero who bends the two tips of the bow with its string, so do thou protect us with both thy hands, O Lord of Speech, and let me in, in myself, be what is heard, i.e. the knowledge of the Vedas. Invoked is the Lord of Speech, on us may the Lord call. May we be ever united with the Vedas which are heard, let us never be parted from them.

Charm Against Injury

We know the father of the arrow-bearing hero, Parjanya, the bountiful nourisher, and well do we know his mother, Earth of multiforms.

O bowstring, bend about us, make myself strong as a stone. Do thou hold very far away from us the enemy and the haters.

When the bowstring, embracing the bow, greets with a whiz the hero, do thou, O Indra, keep away from us the shaft and piercing missile.

As between the heaven and earth stands the reed-stalk, so may the Lord stand unfailingly between us and sickness, and discharge of blood.

Charm Against Obstruction of Urine

We know the father of arrow-bearing hero, Parjanya, of hundredfold power; with this charm may I make thy body diseaseless and healthy. May the outpouring on the earth be yours, may it come out of you with a splash. What is accumulated in thine entrails, in thy canals and bladder, may it be released out of you completely with a splash.

May it spilt open like the dike of a canal, that the water be released out completely, with a splash. Unfastened be the opening of your bladder like an ocean, the reservoir of water, and may your urine be released out completely.

As a shaft flies forth, discharged from the bow, so be your urine be discharged out completely, with a splash!

For Blessings from Waters

The mothers go along their paths, sisters of them that make sacrifice, mingling honey with milk.

Ay they who are yonder at the sun, and those with whom is the sun, speed forth this our sacrifice.

I call on the heavenly Waters, wherein our kine drink to quench their thirst; oblations is to be made to the rivers.

Within the waters is *amrit*, in the waters is remedy, by the praises of the waters the horses become vigorous, the kine become vigorous.

To the Waters for Blessings

O Waters, since you are beneficent, so help you us to strength that we may look on to great joy. What is your most auspicious sap, that give us a share, like mothers in their everlasting love. O Waters, you generate us, to you we gladly come for him to possess whom you quicken us on. I beg the Waters to give us remedy, of these streams having mastery of desirable things, ruling over human beings.

To the Waters Seeking Blessings

May the divine Waters be weal for us, for our aid and bliss. May they stream unto us health and strength. Within Waters lie all healing balms. Soma has told me, and Agni, good for all.

O Waters, teeming with medicine, keep my body safe from harm that long I may see the Sun. O Waters of the plains, those of the marshes, and those got by digging, bestow weal on us and also that brought in a vessel and those of the rain be propitious to us all.

Against Sorcerers

O Agni, bring hither the sorcerer that Vaunts himself and the Kimdin, for thou O God, being revered, becomest the slayer of the demon. O most exalted Jatavedas, self-controller, partake of this sacrificial ghee and seasame oil, make the sorcerers howl!

May this oblation bring the sorcerers hither as a stream carries the feam. Let that person, man or woman, who has done this sorcery, speak out. Wherever, O Agni, thou perceivest the brood of these sorcerers, the hidden devourers, do thou, mightily strengthened by our oblations, slay them, piercing them a hundredfold.

To Agni and Other Gods

May the Vasus, Indra, Pushan, Varuna, Mitra and Agni bestow good things on him. May the Adityas and all the other Gods hold him in superior light!

At his bidding, O Gods! let there be light, Sun, Agni and even gold. Inferior to him be his rivals; make him ascend the highest heaven!

With what highest worship, O Jatavedas, thou didest bring to Indra the Soma-draughts, therewith, O Agni! do thou strengthen this man here; give him supremacy over his fellowmen!

Release from Untruth

Homage, to thy wrath, O King Varuna, for all malice do thou know, O mighty one. A thousand others I make over to thee. A hundred autumns shall live this man!

I release thee from the untruth thou hast uttered, and the much wrong done with thy tongue; from king Varuna whose laws are inviolate.

For Easy Childbirth

O Pushan! Let Aryaman as efficient hotar-priest utter vashat for thee. May this woman, herself rightly begotten, be delivered, may her joints relax that she shall give birth.

Four are the directions of the sky, four also of the earth, the Gods together created the foetus. May they open her that she brings forth.

As flies the wind, as flies the mind, and as flies the bird, so do thou, O ten months old embryo, fly along with placenta, may it fall down.

Against Ailments

Release him from (lightning-gendered) headache and from cough, that has entered his every joint. May the cloud-born lightning and born of the wind, strike the forest trees and mountains.

Comfort be to my upper limb, comfort be to my lower limb, comfort be to my four limbs, comfort be to my whole body.

Homage to Lightning

Homage to thy lightning, to thy thunder and to thy bolt wherewith thou strikest the malicious one. Homage to thee, O child of heights, whence thou gatherest energy, be gracious to our progeny. Thou whom all the Gods generate, the mighty one, the Gods created the bolt for thy hurling, do thou, praised in the assembly, be kind to us, to thee as such we pay homage, O Goddess!

A Woman's Incantation Against Her Rival

Her fortune and splendour I have taken unto myself as a wreath from off a tree. Like a mountain with a broad base may she sit long with her parents.

Let this woman be subjected to thee as thy wife, O king Yama, be she fixed to the house of her mother or her brother, or her father!

Oblation for Wealth

May all the streams together flow as weal, together the birds and also the winds. May they all enjoy this my sacrifice as of old, I offer this oblation most humbly.

Come hither straight to my invocation, ye all confluents, increase this man, let every beast come hither, let wealth ever stay in him.

The streams of the rivers which flow together, ever unexhausted, with all these confluences, may the riches flow unto us together.

The streams of ghee and of water and milk which flow together, with all these confluence may the riches flow unto us together.

Against Demons

May mighty Agni, the demon-slayer give us courage against the devourers, who on the night of the new moon have arisen in throngs.

If our kine thou slayest, if our horses or our men, we pierce thee with this lead, that thou may not slay our heroes.

To Stop the Flow of Blood

The women that go yonder, veins in red garments, like brothless sisters, bereft of strength, may stand still.

Stand still lower one, stand still higher one, do thou in the middle stand still. May the tiniest vein stand still, and may the great artery stand still.

Of the hundred arteries, and the thousand veins, and those in the middle, have all really stood still, and then their end have ceased together to flow.

Charm to Remove Unlucky Marks

May Savitar drive out the trouble from her feet. May Varuna, Mitra, Aryaman drive it out from her hands; may Anumati kindly drive it out of us. The Gods have generated this woman for good fortune.

Whatever fierceness is in thyself, in thy body or hair, or in thy look, all that do we smite away with our words of charm. May God Savitar prosper thee.

Against the Foes

Let not the piercing arrows strike us, nor let them hit us. Far away from us, make the volley of arrows fall, O Indra, dispersing on either side.

Dispersing on either side the arrows shall fall, those that are hurled and those that shall be hurled. Ye divine arrows and ye of men, pierce my enemies.

Who so would assail us, whether he be a stranger, or one of our own, the kinsman or the outsider, those my enemies, may Rudra pierce with a volley of arrows.

Him who rivals us, or does not rival, him who curses us in hate, him let all the Gods injure. May my incantation protect me from within.

Against Enemies and Their Weapons

Be kind to us, O God Soma! Be gracious to us, O Maruts, in this sacrifice. May not portent find us, nor an imprecation nor the hateful wrong.

Whatever missiles or weapons are hurled by the malignant today, do ye Gods, Mitra and Varuna, keep them off from us.

Verily a great Governor art thou, wondrous Destroyer of the foes, whose friend is never slain, and is never overcome.

Against Enemies

Thou, Vritra-slayer, lord of the men, giver of blessings, remover of haters, go before us Indra, the Bull, Soma-drinker, bestowing fearlessness.

Smite far away our foes, O Indra, humble him who challenges us. Send him down to nether darkness who would injure us.

Drive away demons and foes, break into pieces the Vritra's jaws. O Indra, thou Vritra-slaying, quell the fury who threatens us.

Baffle the foeman's mind, ward off his deadly weapon who would wound us. Give us protection, keep his murdering weapon afar.

Charm Against Jaundice

Let both the heart-ache and jaundice go up to the sun. In the colour of the red bull we enwrap thee.

With red colours we enwrap thee unto longevity. May this man be free from yellow colour and complaints.

To parrots and to startlings do we give away thy jaundice, and furthermore let it be transferred to Haritala trees.

Against Leprosy

Night-born art thou, O herb, dark, black, sable one. Do thou, rich in colour, stain this leprosy and spot.

The leprous and grey spots, make thou disappear from here. let thine own colour settle, drive away the white spots hence.

Sable is thy secret place, sable thy home, sable art thou. O herb, drive away from here the speckled spots.

The suparna (eagle) was born first and thou wast its gall; then the Asuri woman having conquered gave it to the forest trees for their colour.

She was the first to make this remedy for the leprous spot, this remover of leprosy. She has made the leprous spot disappear and made the skin of even colour.

Even Colour is the name of thy mother. Even Colour is the name of thy father, thou producing even colour, make this spot of even colour!

Against Fever

When Agni entered the waters, the Gods who maintain the law, paid homage, there, they declare, is thy place of birth on high, O fever (Takman), do fuel for us and avoid us.

Whether thou art a flame, or heat, or whether from licking chips of wood thou art born, by name Hrudu art thou, O God of the yellow one, then do feel for us and avoid us, O Takman!

I pay homage to cold fever and to the deliriously hot, to the one that returns every other day, on two successive days, to the fever that returns every third day, be my homage.

For Gods' Protection

Far off be from us your missiles, O Gods, far be the bolt that you hurl!

May a generous king be our friend, may a companion be to us Indra, Bhaga and Savitar of wonderful favours!

O ye brave and high-born ones, like sun in splendour and overthrower of foes, grant us large protection and happiness.

Be thou gracious to ourselves, show kindness to our offspring and advance our joys and happiness.

Against Evils

Thrice-seven, stand the enemy forces yonder on the further spot, like a she-snake, out of their sloughs. We wrap up the eyes of them, the malignant foes, with these sloughs.

Neither have they been ever together, nor could they venture anything being weak. May the enemies, the malignant ones, be unsuccessful like bamboo-sprouts!

Move forward ye two feet, be quick to take us to the houses of our bestowers; let Indrani, the Indra's might, go first, unscathed, unrobbed in front.

Against Sorcerers

God Agni, the demon-slayer, remover of misery, ever victorious, hath come hither onto us, having burnt away the deceivers, sorcerers and double-tongued kimidins.

May the sorcerers eat up her own son, sister and daughter. May the horned-haired sorcerers mutually destroy one another. May these hags be shattered asunder!

An Amulet for Success

With an over-rolling amulet, wherewith Indra increased, with this, O Brahmanaspati, let us increase in royalty.

Subduing our rivals, subduing all niggards, trample thou upon him who fights and abuses us.

Soma and Savitar have made thee increase, and thou hast increased all existence, so that thou mayest be lord of all.

You Sun hath gone up, and this spell of mine that I may be slayer of foes, without any rivals, rival-slayer.

Slayer of rivals, the bull conquering royalty, with royal sway, may I rule over these heroes and the folk.

For Protection of Gods

O all ye Gods, ye Vasus, guard this man, likewise ye Adityas watch ye over him, let none, whether one related or not, nor any deadly weapon reach him.

O all ye Gods, who so of ye art fathers and sons, listen this my prayer; to ye I commit this man. Happy unto ripe age shall ye carry him!

To the Guardians of Quarters

O ye Gods, guardians of the four quarters, do ye liberate us from all fetters, of perdition and distress.

Unmanned I offer sacrifice to thee and make oblation with ghee. May he, the guardian of all directions and hopes, the effulgent, grant us here the best riches.

Blessings be to our mother and father, joy be to our cattle, to beasts and to men! May all well-being and beneficence be ours! Long may we see the Sun.

Cosmogonic

Know ye folk, a great mystery, about to be made known, that which is not found either on earth or in heaven, whereby the plants breathe.

In the atmosphere is their stay, like a station for the wearied the place of support. This the wise know, or perhaps they know not?

What is trembling firmaments and the earth together fashioned, is now in perpetual motion, like the streams of the mighty ocean.

The one Earth has encompassed all; this rests upon the other. Both the Heaven and Earth, the all-possessing I have paid my homage.

To Waters

May these gleaming Waters, all-purifying, who assumed Agni as their embryo, be blessing and pleasant for us!

Amidst whom the king Varuna goes, watching over the truth and falsehood of men, who is of gleaming colours, be blessing and joy for us!

O Waters, behold us with propitious eye, bathe my skin with propitious body, they that are ghee dripping, clean and purifying, let these Waters be blessing and joy for us!

Book Two

The Mysterious

Vena the wise, has seen the Supreme, hidden in the secret cave, wherein all things assume one single form. This, the cause of all spendour, has been milked through things created and the homage paid by heaven knowing men.

May the immortal knowing Gandharvas, reveal that highest hidden, three-quarters of which lie in secret. He who knoweth them shall be the sire's sire.

He, the generator and father of us all, is also our brother. He the knower of all the abodes, all the beings, who is the sole nomenclator of the Gods, of him all beings enquire and desire to attain.

To earth and heaven I have been, I approached the first-born of righteousness, abiding in all beings as speech in the speaker, all-pervading, nourisher is he, is he not Agni?

I went around all the abodes and found there the web of righteousness stretched out, where the Gods having attained immortality enjoyed themselves in the same place of union.

To Gandharvas

The divine Gandharva, the lord of all beings and Universe, the only one worthy to receive homage, to be praised among the subjects, thee being such I meet you through the incantation. O divine God, obeisance to thee, thou abides in all.

Sky-touching, worship-worthy, sun-skinned, remover of the seizure of Gods, the Gandharva is gracious to all. He who is of lord beings, the only one worthy to receive homage, is very propitious.

The Gandharva united himself with the irreproachable ones. He was among the Apsaras. In the ocean is, I am told, their abode, whence they come and go away.

O ye divine Apsaras who dwell in the sky, lightning and in stars, and accompany the Gandharva Vishwavasu, to you I do pay my homage.

They who invoke, fulfil the desires, baffle the mind and arouse interest in the best activities, the divine Apsaras, who have Gandharvas as their consorts, I do pay homage.

For Relief from Excessive Discharges

The yonder spring-water that runs down the mountain, that do I make for thee a remedy, that thou mayest contain a good remedy.

The Asuras have buried deep down this great healer of wounds, that is the remedy of discharges, that has removed the disease.

The ants bring out the remedy from the sea, that is the remedy of discharges, that has removed the disease.

Weal be to us the Waters, propitious be herbs to us. May Indra's bolt smite the Rakshasas, far away from us shall the arrows shot by demons fall!

Charm with an Amulet

For longevity and great joy, we doing no harm, ever vigorous bear this amulet, the remover of obstacles, praiseworthy and destroyer of ailments.

Let this amulet of a thousand virtues, protect us on all sides from convulsions, from acute pain, from violence, from obstacles and from bereavement.

Witchcraft destroyerer is this amulet, similarly it destroys the hostile powers. May this powerful fangidam amulet prolong our life span.

Prayer to Indra

O Indra, be pleased, fare forward and come to us, O hero, on thy two bay steeds. Come fair cne, drink of the pressed out Soma draught, the sweet intoxicant.

Indra, thou aswiftly overcoming friend slew Vritra, spilt Vala, defeated the violent foes like Bhrigu, the wise, in the intoxication of Soma juice.

Now will I proclaim the heroic exploits of Indra, the thunder-armed, who slew the Demon Ahi, disclosed the waters and rent the channels of the mountains.

He slew the Demon lying on the mountain, his divine thunderbolt was fashioned by Tvastar, like lowing kine in speedy flow the descending waters rushed to the ocean.

Impetuous like a bull, he chose Soma, and in three sacred beakers he drank of it, then Maghavan grasping his missile thunderbolt, slew the first born of the Demons.

In Praise of Agni

O Agni, may the favourable seasons, summers, the years, the seers and the things that are true, increase thee. Shine thou with thy bright, beautiful flames and illumine well the four quarters.

Be well kindled, O Agni, and do thou prosper this man, and arise to a great good fortune. O Agni, let not thy devotees suffer, let thy worshippers be famed, and not others.

O Agni, these Brahmins learned in the Vedas, choose thee, be gracious to us in our sacrifice. Be thou, O Agni, the slayer of the foes, conqueror of the hostile people, and keep a watch unremittingly over thine own household.

Charm Against Curses

This God born herb, hated by the wicked, this curse–removing herb has washed away all curses from me, as waters do a foul spot.

The curse of the rival and that from kinswoman, the curse that a Brahmin in fury shall utter, all that be under our feet.

From the sky its root is suspended. From the earth it rises up, with it that has a thousand shoots do thou protect us on all sides.

Protect me, protect my progeny, protect our wealth, let not malice overcome us, let not hostile plots overcome us!

Let the curse go to the curser, our dealings are with him who is friendly. Of the enemy who bewitches with his eye we crush the ribs.

Against Disease

Arisen are the two blessed stars, may they loosen the lowest and the highest fetters of the inherited disease!

May this night fade away, may the bewitchers fade away, may the disease destroying plant fade the inherited disease away.

An Amulet Against Possession by Demons

O thou amulet of ten kinds of wood, release this man from the demon, from the fit that has seized him in the joints. And then, O plant, do thou lead him to the world of living.

This man has come, has gone forth and joined the community of the living. He has become the father of the sons, and of the most fortunate men.

He has now come to his senses, he has come to the cities of the living, for now he has hundred physicians and also a thousand herbs.

For Release from Disease

O man, I do release thee from inherited disease, from the Goddess of destruction, from the curse of kinswomen, from hatred, and from Varuna's fetters. I render thee free from guilt with my incantation, may both heaven and earth be propitious to thee!

May Agni be propitious to thee, together with the Waters, may Soma, together with the herbs be propitious to thee. Likewise I release thee from hatred and the fetters of Varuna. I render the guilters with my charm, may both heaven and earth be propitious to thee!

May the wind in the atmosphere bestow upon thee vigour, may the four quarters be auspicious to thee. Thus I render thee guiltless with my charm, may both heaven and earth be propitious to thee.

An Amulet Against Witchcraft

Thou art spoiler's spoiler, bolt's bolt, and weapon's weapon. Attain thou the better one, fare forward and emulate the equal one.

Dynamic art thou, ever moving art thou, and art destroyer of the charm. Attain thou the better one, fare forward and emulate the equal one.

Attack thou the sorcerer and him who hates us and whom we hate. Patron art thou, splendour-giving art thou, body-guarding art thou. Attain thou the better one etc. etc.

Against Him Who Thwarts Holy Work

Heaven and earth and the vast atmosphere, the Goddess of the field, and the wondrous wide-striding Vishnu, and moreover, the wind-guarded vast atmosphere, let these here be inflamed when I am inflamed!

Hear this, O ye revered Gods! Let Bhardwaja recite praise for me; let him who would injure us, be bound in the fetters and be plunged in misfortune.

Hear this, O Soma-enjoying Indra, with what burning heart I shout to thee. I rend him, as one rends a tree with an axe, him who injures us.

With thrice-eighty Sama singers, with the help of the Adityas, the Vasus and the Angiras—let our father's sacrifices and offerings aid us here—I do seize this wicked with fateful fervour.

O heaven and earth, look after me, may all the Gods protect me. O ye Angiras, O ye Soma-enjoying fathers, let him who does us evil meet with evil.

He who holds us in contempt, O Maruts, he who seeks to abuse our holy practices, may agonies of burning be his portion, may the heavens surround the man with scorching fires the man who hates holy devotion.

The seven breaths and eight marrows, these do I rend for thee with my incantation; thou shalt go to the seat of Yama, escorted by Agni, fitly made.

For an Infant's Long Life

O Agni, thou art giver of life, ghee smeared and ghee backed art thou. O Agni, having enjoyed the sweet pleasant ghee of the cow, do thou protect this boy, as a father does his son.

Put ye, him in splendid garments, nourish him to die in old age, make his life long. Brihaspati, the guardian of the learned, has furnished this garment to Soma for wearing.

Thou has put on this garment for thy joy and has become protector of the people against violence. Many thou live a hundred autumns, and do thou gather about thee the abundant wealth.

Come, step upon the stone, may thy body become strong like this stone, may all the Gods lengthen thy life span to a hundred autumns.

Against Female Demons

There, in the yon house below, let the hags dwell, in the house infernal. There let every debility and every witch find an abode.

Let Rudra, the lord of beings, and also Indra drive out from here the female demons, those sitting on the foundation of the house, let Indra subdue them with his thunderbolt.

A Prayer to Agni

O Agni, thou foe-destroyer, with thy heat be hot against him who hates us and whom we hate! O Agni, use thy rage against him who hates us and whom we hate! O God Agni, with thine gleam, gleam against him who hates us and whom we hate; burn against him who hates us and whom we hate!

Against Demons with a Plant

The Prishniparni, the divine has created prosperity for us and woe for the Goddess of destruction. Since she is fierce and remover of sins, her, the mighty one, have I used.

This Prishniparni was first begotten overpowering, with it I do chop off the heads of the evil broods, as that of a bird.

O Prishniparni, do thou overpower and destroy the blood-sucking demon, and him that would rob us of our health and devourer of progeny.

For the Prosperity of Cattle

Hither let the cattle come that strayed away, whose companionship Vayu enjoyed and whose structure of form Tavastar knows, in this stall let Savitar hold them in place.

Let to this stable cattle flow together, let Brihaspati skilfully lead them hither. Sinivate shall lead hither their Van. Do thou, O Anumati hold them in the stall when they have arrived.

May together the cattle flow, together flow the horses, together men. May the increase in grain flow together. I offer an oblation that causes to flow together!

I pour together the milk of kine, I pour together strength and sap with clarified butter. Poured together are our heroes, constant shall be the kine with me, their owner!

Against Opponents in Disputation

May my rival not win the debate. Mighty and overpowering art thou, O plant. Overcome the debate of those who debate against us, render them sapless, O plant!

An eagle found these out, the boar dug thee out with his snout. Overcome the debate of those who debate against us, render them sapless, O plant!

Indra wore thee upon his arm that he might overthrow the demons. Overcome the debate of those who debate against us, render them sapless, O plant!

For Long Life of a Child

For thee alone, O old age, let this child grow, let not the other hundred deaths harm him. May Mitra, like a provident mother in her lap a son protect him from misfortunes.

May Mitra or helping Varuna in harmony make him one that dies in old age, so may Agni, the hotar-priest, who knows the ways, bespeaks all the births of the Gods.

Agni, thou art lord of all the animals of the earth, those that are born, and also that are to be born. Let not in and out breathings leave this one, let not either friends or enemies slay him!

Let father Heaven and mother Earth, in harmony, make thee one that dies in old age, that thou mayest live in the lap of Aditi, a hundred winters guarded by breath and expiration.

This dear child, lead thou Agni to life and vigour, O Varuna, and king Mitra. As a mother grant him refuge, all ye Gods that he may attain old age.

For Long Life and Prosperity

In the essence of what is earthly bliss, O Gods in strength of body, may Agni, Surya and Brihaspati grant him long life and vigour.

Grant him long life, O ye Jatavedas; progeny, bestow upon him O Tvashtar, impart O Savitar, increase of wealth to him; may he, who belongs to thee, live for hundred autumns!

May our devotion bring us vigour and excellent progeny; do ye both Heaven and Earth grant us ability and prosperity. May, this man, conquering lands with his might, O Indra, subduing his foes, live long!

Given by Indra, instructed by Varuna, sent by Maruts, the mighty, he has come to us. May he be in your lap, O Heaven and Earth, never suffer from hunger or from thirst.

Indra in the beginning having been wounded, made this refreshment, and this divine food, which is yours here. By means of it do thou live a hundred autumns, full of vigour; may it not flow out of thee, the physicians have made it for thee!

For Securing a Woman's Love

As the wind here tears the grass from the earth, so do I tear thy mind, that thou woman mayest love me and not be averse to me.

May ye, O twin Ashvins, unite and bring together the lovers. The fortunes of both of you are united, united are the thoughts and united are the courses.

What is within shall be without, what is without shall be within. Take captive, O herb, the mind of the maidens of many charms.

Hither hath this maiden come, longing for a husband, longing for a wife I have come. Like a loud-neighing horse, I have come together with my good fortune.

Against Worms

With Indra's great millstone that crushes all vermins, I do grind these worms like grains on a grinder.

Both visible and invisible worms have I crushed, not sparing any. We destroy all these worms with our spells.

The Algandus I destroy with a mighty weapon, those burned, and those unburned, they all have been drained of life sap. Present or absent I destroy them all with my spell so that no single worm is left alive!

The worm in the entrails, the worm in the head, the one in the ribs, we crush all with this spell!

The worms that are on the hills, or in the woods, whether in plants or the waters, whether they live within men or cattle, all the breed of them I exterminate!

For Good Health

From both thy nostrils, thy eyes, ears and from thy chin, forth from thy head, brain and tongue I drive the disease away.

From the neck and its nape, ribs and from the spine, from shoulders, upper and lower arms, I drive the disease away.

From Viscara and all within, forth from the rectum, abdomen, from thy stomach, guts and navel I do drive the disease away.

The disease that is in thy every limb, in every hair, in every joint, from all thyself, from top to toe, I do drive the disease away.

For Obtaining a Husband

Unto us, after our liking, O Agni, may wooer come, may he come to this maiden with our fortune. May she, agreeable to wooers, charming at festivals, quickly attain happiness through a husband!

Agreeable to Soma, agreeable to Brahma, brought together by Aryaman, with the unfailing surity of divine Dhatar, do I bestow upon thee a husband and good fortune.

May this woman, O Agni, obtain a husband, for king Soma has made her lovely. May she begetting sons, become the chief queen. May she going to her husband and having good fortune bear rule.

As this pleasant cave, O Indra, giving a safe abode, is to wild animals, so let this woman, O Indra, be favourite of fortune and mutually beloved, and not at odds with her husband.

Ascend thou the full, inexhaustible boat of good fortune and upon this bring here the wooer who shall be of your liking.

Shout to the suitor, O lord of wealth, make his mind bent towards her, turn thou the right side of every suitor towards her according to her desire.

Here is gold and bedellium, and also balsam and good fortune. These have prepared thee for husbands, in order to obtain one who is agreeable to thee.

Hither may Savitar lead the husband who is according to thy desire, do thou assign him to her, O herb!

Book Three

Against the Foe Men

May Agni, the all-knowing, go against our enemies, burning against their hostile schemes. Let the Jatvedas confound the army of our opponents, and deprive them of their hands.

O, ye Maruts, art mighty in such matters, fare forward, conquer and kill them. The Vasus will crush them when implored. Agni, in their vanguard shall skilfully assail them.

Do ye twain, O Indra, Vritra-slayer and Agni, burn against the hostile army who fight against us.

Carried forward, O Indra, by thy two bay steeds, crush the enemies with thy thunderbolt. Slay them, smite that resist, pursue or flee, deprive their schemes of fulfilment!

O Indra, confound the enemy forces. With the blast of fire and of wind, scatter and make them disappear.

Against Enemies

Confounding the mind of our enemies, seize thou their bodies and depart. O Goddess Apava, attack them, bum their hearts with fire, strike them with fits and let them abide in darkness!

Yonder army of our enemies, O Maruts, that comes to fight against us, strike ye it with confounding darkness, that one may not know the other.

For Establishing a King

Rise thou with splendour and go forward as the lord of the people for thy kingdom has come to thee, thou a sovereign ruler. Let all the regions of the compass call thee, O king, attended and revered be thou!

These people, these five heavenly directions shall choose thee king. Rest on the summit of kingship, and then do thou mighty one, give good things to us!

May thy kinsmen come unto thee calling, Agni shall go along with them as swift messenger. May thy queens, thy sons be ever devoted to thee. May thou as mighty one receive rich tribute.

May the twain Ashvins first, then both Mitra and Varuna, all the deities, and the Maruts, call thee. Then put thy mind to the distribution of good things among us.

Hasten forth hither from the furthest distance, both Heaven and Earth shall be propitious to thee. King Varuna himself called thee; do thou come hither!

The wealthy divinities of the road, of different forms, and assembling together have given thee wide domain. They all in accord shall call thee; to the tenth decade of thy life rule here as a mighty king!

An Amulet for Prosperity

Hither has arrived the prana-amulet, with its strength, mighty in slaying our rivals. It is the might of the Gods, the sap of the herbs, may it unremittingly enliven me with energy.

O amulet of prana wood, maintain in me the power of rule, in me maintain wealth. May I be established in the sphere of royalty be the sovereign.

This very dear and my own amulet, that the Gods deposited hidden in the forest tree, the same the Gods shall grant us to wear, together with long life.

This prana amulet, the strength of Soma, has come here, given by Indra, instructed by Varuna. May I shining in splendour, wear it during the long life of hundred autumns!

This prana amulet has ascended upon me in order to give complete unharmedness that I may be superior both to friends and allies.

The skilled chariot builders, the skilful metalsmiths, do them all, O prana amulet, make my aids!

The kings and the king makers, the charioteers, the commanders, and the people around me, do thou prana, make all my aids.

Body protecting art thou, O prana, a hero, brother of me. With the year's brilliancy do I fasten thee, O amulet!

The Asvattha Tree

A male is born from a male, the Asvattha from the Khadira. May it smite my foes, whom I hate and who hate me.

Wipe them out, O Asvattha, my foes as they come forward, thou expeller, allied with Vritra-slaying Indra, with Mitra and with Varuna.

O Asvattha, as thou didst break forth into the great sea of atmosphere, so do thou break out all those whom 1 hate and who hate me.

Let my foes float down like a boat severed from its moorings. Let there be no returning again for those divine away by the expelling one.

I drive them away with my mind, drive them out with my intent and also with my incantation. We thrust them out with a branch of Asvattha tree.

Against Inherited Disease

On the head of the swift-footed stag is a remedy. It has driven the inherited disease away scattering in all directions by means of its horn.

The stag has gone after thee with his four feet. O horn, do thou unfasten the inherited disease (kshetriya) that clings to his heart.

The horn that shines down yonder like a roof with four sides, therewith we drive out every kshetriya disease from thy limbs.

Verily, the Waters are remedial, they are disease expeller, the Waters heal all ailments. Let them relieve thee from kshetriya.

With the fading out of the constellations, and the fading out of dawns, fade out from us every evil, fade out every kshetriya.

Prayer for Authority

May Mitra, the friend like come arranging the seasons and uniting the earth with the ruddy ones. May Varuna, Vayu, Agni grant us great royalty.

devour her own offspring!

What magic spell they have prepared for you and put in a raw dish, or into blue-red thread, or into uncooked flesh, with that same spell slay thou those sorcerers!

Evil dreams, evil living, demons, monsters, hags and witches, all the evil-named, evil-speaking, these we here destroy.

Death from hunger, death from thirst, want of cattle, want of children, all that we drive away, O herb, with thy aid.

Death from thirst, death from hunger, defeat at dice and games of chance, with thy aid, O thou expeller, we here expel all these from us.

This herb, the sole ruler over the plants, with its aid do we drive away all misfortune that has befallen you, do thou then live free from disease!

Prayer to Agni

First of all I worship Agni, the forethoughtful, him of the five peoples, kindled at various places. We pray Agni, who has entered into clans after clans. May he set us free from distress!

O Jatavedas, as envoy of the Gods, carrying oblations, and adapting thyself to the sacrifice, bring to us the favour of Gods. May we be free from distress!

O Agni, the best conveyor, present at every rite, put to service at every course, I praise thee, thou demon-slayer, sacrifice-increaser, offered to the oblation of ghee. May we be free from distress!

We invoke the well-born Jatavedas, the mighty Agni, conveyor of our oblations, belonging to all people. May be free from distress!

With whom as ally the sages did shine in strength, with whom they subdued the demons, with whom did Agni and Indra defeat the Panis, may be free us from distress!

By whom the Gods became immortal, by whom the herbs were made rich in sap, by whom the Gods brought the heaven; may he free us from distress!

He, who is the lord of all that shines, and of that which is born and is to be born, all of it; I rever Agni as suppliant and invoke him. May he free us from distress!

Prayer to Heaven and Earth

My obeisance, to ye, O Heaven and Earth, ye well nourishing, who in accord did spread out in space. Ye being the foundations of all good things, liberate us from distress!

O ye divine Heaven and Earth, much spread, divine, fortunate ones, foundations of all good things, be gracious to me. Liberate us from distress!

I invoke ye, O Heaven and Earth, well spread out, profound, revered by poets of highest penance. Be gracious to me and liberate us from distress!

O ye Heaven and Earth, who bear the *amrita,* the oblations, who bear the rivers, human beings, be gracious to me. Liberate us from distress!

O ye Heaven and Earth, who bear red kine, the forest trees, ye within whom are all creatures, be gracious to me. Liberate us from distress!

O ye Heaven and Earth, who yield sweet drink and ghee, without whom man can do nothing whatsoever, be gracious to me. Liberate us from distress!

As suppliant, I call on ye and praise O Heaven and Earth, that I may be saved from that scorches me, or by whomsoever done, from what is human or divine. Do ye liberate us from distress!

A Prayer to Bhava and Sarva

O Bhava, O Sarva, I adore you, take note of that, ye under whose control is all that shines. Ye who lord over all these bipeds and quadrupeds, liberate us from distress!

Ye to whom belongs all that is nearby and all that is afar, ye who are famed as best shooters among bowmen, ye who lord over all these bipeds and quadrupeds, liberate us from distress!

I invoke the twain thousand-eyed Vritra-slayers. I praise the two formidable ones whose pastures spread out afar, ye who lord over all these bipeds and quadrupeds, liberate us from distress!

Ye two who did much great work together in the beginning and let loose the portent among the people, ye who lord over all these bipeds and quadrupeds, liberate us from distress!

From whose fatal weapons no one either of Gods or men escapes, who lord over all these bipeds and quadrupeds, liberate us from distress!

The sorcerer who makes a charm, or manipulates roots against us, against him, ye formidable ones, send down your thunderbolt, ye who lord over all these bipeds and quadrupeds, liberate us from distress!

O formidable Gods, bless us in battles, !et your thunderbolt visit the Kimidin. I praise Bhava and Sarva, call upon them as suppliant, do ye liberate us from distress!

In Praise of Rice Offerings

The Soma is its head, the Brihat-sama its back, the Vamdeva the stomach of this rice offering; the metres are its two wings, truth is its mouth. This extensive sacrifice born out of tapas is the highest.

Without bones, purified, cleansed by the purifier, effulgent, they go to the shining world. Agni does not burn away their virile element. There in the heavenly abode much pleasure is theirs.

Those who cook such a food offering, poverty comes not to them. Such a man stays with Yama, goes to the Gods, and enjoys Soma drink with Gandharvas.

By means of this rice offering, this extensive oblation, the best sacrifice, he enters heaven, where every kind of lotus grows. May all these streams reach you, in that honeyed and heavenly world. May ponds teeming with lotus await you!

May pools of ghee abound, slopes of honey, streams of milk, water and curds, draughts of wine, flowing in abundance. May all these streams reach you, in that honeyed and heavenly world. May ponds teeming with lotus await you!

Book Five

To Kustha Plant Against Fever

The Asvattha tree, the seat of Gods, is in the third heaven from here. There the Gods procured the Kustha plant, the visible manifestation of immortality.

A golden ship with golden tackle moved about in the heavens. There the Gods procured the Kustha, the flower of immortality.

The roads were golden, and golden were the oars, golden were the ships, on which they brought out the Kustha.

The man here, O Kustha, restore and relieve him; also render him free from disease for me!

From the Gods art thou born, thou art Soma's good companion. Be thou gracious to my in-breathing and my out-breathing, and to this my sight!

Born in the north on the Himavant mountain, thou art brought to the people in the east. There they shared the highest variety of Kustha.

Thou art superior by name, superior by name is thy father. Both of ye drive out all disease and do thou make the fever powerless!

Headache, affliction in the eye, and bodily ailments, all that may Kustha relieve, verily, a powerful divine remedy!

The Healing Plant Laksha

The Night is thy mother, the Cloud thy father, Aryaman thy grandfather. Laksha verily is thy name, thou art sister of the Gods!

He who drinks thee lives, thou preserves, a man, for thou art a sustainer, of all men, and refuge of people.

Tree after tree dost thou climb up like a wench lusting after a man. Conquering, steadfast, saving, verily is thy name.

If a wound is made with a staff, with an arrow or by a flame, of that thou art the remedy, do thou cure this man here!

Thou grows on excellent Plaksha tree, on Asvattha, the Khadira and the Dhava, upon the noble Banyan (nygarodha), and the Prana. Come thou to us, O Arundhati!

Thou gold-coloured, lovely, fiery, of wonderful form, mayest thou go to the hurt, O cure, "Cure" verily is thy name.

Thou gold coloured, lovely, fiery plant, with hairy stem, sister of the waters, O Laksha, the wind is thy breath!

Silaki, by name, thy father, thou goat-brown one, is a maid's son, with the blood of dark brown horse thou hast been sprinkled.

Fallen from the horse's mouth, she ran up the trees, and turned into a winged brook. Do thou come to us, O Arundhati!

Against Demon of Avarice to Arati

Bring riches to us, stand not in our way, O Arati, do not prevent our sacrificial gift as born away. Homage be to the power of confounding, the power of failure, homage to Arati!

To thy minister, who thou put forward as thy agent, O Arati, to him we pay our homage. Do thou not impede my winning!

May our desire, inspired by gods, be fulfilled by day and by night. We follow Arati, homage be to Arati!

We go to invoke Sarasvati, Anumati and Bhaga. Pleasant, honeyed words have I used while invoking the Gods.

Him whom 1 call upon with speech (vak) Sarasvati, the yoke-fellow of mind, shall find faith today, given by the brown Soma.

Do not thou frustrate our desire or speech. Let both Indra and Agni bring us good things. Do ye all, desirous to give us gifts today, be in grace of Arati!

Go thou far off, O failure, we avert thy missile, I know thee, O Arati, to be oppressive and piercing!

Thou can even make thyself naked and cling thyself to people in their sleep, frustrating their plans and intentions.

Thou being great, and of great height, pervaded all the realms, to this golden-haired Nirriti (Death), to thee I had made homage.

To the gold complexioned, fortunate one, reclining on golden cushions, to her, the great, golden-dressed, Arati, have I paid homage.

An Antidote Against Snake Poison

As Varuna, the sage of heaven has given me power, dissolve thy poison with these powerful spells. The poison that is dug, undug and that is inherent, have I seized. Like a stream in a desert thy poison has dried up.

What poison is thine that dries up blood, that I have seized in these. Have I seized thy midmost, thy uppermost sap and also thy lowest, then be gone hence of fright.

My mighty cry is like thunder among the clouds, with my powerful charms do I remove thy sap. I have seized thy poison with men, like light out of darkness, let now the sun rise!

With my sight I smite thy eye, with poison do I smite thy poison, die, O snake, do not live, black upon thee shall thy poison turn!

O Karait, O spotted one, thou grass dweller, brown one, listen me, black ones, repulsive ones, stand ye not on the ground near my friend's house. Listening me well, rest quiet in this poison.

O release thee from the fury of the black snake, the taimataya, the brown one, that which live out of water and from those that live together, like the bowstring is loosened from the bow and the chariots from horses.

Both Aligi and Viligi, both father and mother, we know your relations well. Rendered without your sap what would ye do?

Charm Against Witchcraft

The eagle, discovered thee, with its snout the boar dug thee out, seek thou to harm him, O herb, who seeks to injure us, destroy the sorcerer!

Smite down the evil–doers, smite down the black magicians. then smite down him also who wants to harm us, O herb!

Having cut out a strip from the skin of the sorcerer as if from the body of a stag, do ye, O Gods, fasten upon the sorcerer the spell, like an ornament!

Lead the violence back to the violence maker wizard, grasping it by hand, set it straight before him, that it may slay him, the spell maker!

Let the witchcraft be for the witchcraft maker, the curse be upon him who pronounces the curse. May the witchcraft roll back, like a chariot of smooth wheels, to him that makes the spell.

Whether a woman or a man has made the magic for evil, we conduct the magic back to him, like a horse led by a horse halter.

Whether thou hast been made by Gods or by men, we take back with the aid of Indra as our ally.

O Agni, winner of battles, do thou subdue the foemen. With a counterspell do we hurl back the spell upon him who made the spell.

O skilled piercer, pierce him, do thou slay him who has made the hell. We do not sharpen thee for him who has not prepared the spell.

Go like a son to a father, like a snake walked upon, and bite. Return thou, O spell, to the spell maker, as one released from fetters.

Like a she-deer, like a she-elephant, like a hind in heat go leaping, O spell, to its maker!

Straighter than an arrow may the spell fly upon him, O Heaven and Earth, let the spell seize him again, its maker, like a hunter of a deer!

Against the Enemies of Brahmins

This cow the Gods did not give thee to eat, O king. Do not desire, O prince to devour the cow of the Brahmin, that is not fit to be eaten.

A prince, cheated by dice, the wretched, self-ruined, may by chance devour the cow of a Brahmin, thinking, "let me live today, if not tomorrow".

Enveloped in its skin, the cow of the Brahmin, like a poisonous snake, O prince, is sapless, not to be consumed!

Verily does it take away a prince's regal powers, destroys this splendour, like all-consuming fire. He who thinks Brahmin to be food, he swallows the poison of the taimata snake.

He who slays a Brahmin, thinking him gentle, he who insults the Gods, lusts after riches, in his heart Indra kindles a fire, he is hated both by heaven and earth while he lives.

The Brahmin is not to be harmed like fire, by any one who regards his own body dear. For Soma is his heir and Indra protects him against hostility.

He who swallows down a Brahmin's cow, he does with a hundred barbs, he cannot digest it, he is a fool who devouring a Brahmin's food thinks, "I am eating what is luscious".

Then the Brahmin's tongue becomes a bow-string, his voice a neck of an arrow, his teeth shafts tipped with fire. With these he would pierce those who insult Gods, with bows powered to reach the heart, sped by the Gods.

The Brahmins have sharp arrows and missiles, the weapons they hurl are never in vain. Pursuing him with fervour and fury, even from distance, they pierce him down.

They who were lords of a thousand and were themselves ten hundreds, the Vailahavya, having eaten the cow of the Brahmin, perished.

Verily Agni is our guide. Soma our heir, Indra the slayer of those who curse us. The sages know it.

Like an arrow dipped in poison, O king of men, like an adder, O lord of cattle, is the terrible arrow of the Brahmin. With it he pierces those who insult Gods.

To the Battle Drum

The loud-sounding battle drum, enthusing the warriors, made of the wood, covered with the skin of the cow, whetting the voice, subduing the foemen, thunder thou loudly against them like a lion, sure of triumph.

The wooden drum has thundered like a lion, has roared like a bull at a cow longing to mate. Thou art the bull and eunuches art the enemies, endowed with Indra's overpowering fire!

Like a bull found in a herd, seeking cows, bellow at the enemy, O winner of booty, pierce thou their heart with fire. Let our foes, with their ranks broken, run and scatter.

Conquering the enemy, raise thy roar. Do thou seize that is to be seized, roar in many places. Favour us, O drum, with thy heavenly sound. Bring to us the possession of our enemy!

Hearing thy roar, O drum, that reaches to a far distance, let the enemy's wife aroused by the sound, run in distress to her son, and seizing him by the hand flee, frightened at the clash of deadly weapons.

Mayst thou, O drum, sound the first sound, speak brilliantly over the back of the earth. Open thy wide maw at the enemy host, resounding joyously, O drum!

May thy sound spread out quickly to every side between this heaven and earth. Sound thou, roar swiftly, thunder with resounding noise at thy friend's victory, having chosen the right side!

Made with care may thy sound swell forth, inspire the weapons of the warriors. Allied with Indra, call hither the warriors, and with thy friends smite down the enemy!

Thou art a resounding herald, followed by a bold army, proclaiming news in many places, sounding through the hamlets, winning battles, knowing the way, do thou distribute fame among many in the battlefield!

Aiming at the advantage, conquering booty, O very mighty, subduing the enemy host, thou art made sharp by my song. Do thou, O drum, dance on the booty like a pressing stone on the stoma-stalks!

Subduer of foe men, conquering, overpowering the enemy, eager for fight, overwhelming in victory, spread forth thy sound like a speaker's speech. Speak forth here with force for victory in the fray!

Shaking the unshaken, hastening to the fray, conqueror of the foe, an unconquerable commander in the front, protected by Indra, attending the army, go thou quickly, crushing the hearts of foemen!

Against Fever (Takman)

May Agni drive away the Takman from here; may Soma, the press stone, Varuna of proved skill, the sacrificial altar, the sacred straw, the brightly flaming fuel drive him away and the hateful things.

Thou that makest all men pale, heating them up like a fire, even now, O Takman, mayest thou become powerless. Do thou now go away down or into the depths!

The Takman that is here, spotted, speckled, reddish, him thou O plant, of great power, drive away down the depths!

Prayer to Various Gods

O Savitar, the lord of all men's best designs, protect me in this my prayer, in this my worship, in this my ritual, in this my performance, in this my thought, in this my intention and desire, in this my invocation of the Gods; all hail!

May Agni the overlord of forest trees, protect me in this my prayer, in this my worship, in this my ritual, in this my performance, in this my thought, in this my intention and desire, in this my invocation of the Gods, all hail!

May Heaven and Earth, overlords of bounty, protect me!

May Varuna, the overlord of waters, save me in this my prayer!

May the Maruts, overlords of the mountains, preserve me in this my prayer!

May Soma, the overlord of plants and herbs save me!

May Vayu, the overlord of atmosphere, may the Sun, the overlord of every eye, may the Moon, the overlord of constellations, may Indra, the overlord of Gods protect me in this my prayer!

I send the Takman down below the depths, having rendered it homage. May he, the slayer of the mighty, return again to the Mahavrishavans!

His abode is the grassy Mujavant mountains, and his home is in the Mahavrisha provinces. O Takman, as long as born, so long art thou at home among the Balhikas!

O Takman, ticklish snake like, O limbless one, speak out, go far away. Seek thou the shameless slave girl, strike her with thy missile!

O Takman, go to the Mugavants, to the Bahlikas far away, seek the wanton Shudra woman, give her, O fever, a good shaking!

O Takman, together with thy brother Balsa and sister Cough, together with thy cousin Paman (scab) go away to yon foreign folk!

May the Takman that returns every third day, that comes two days out of three, the constant without a break, and the autumnal one, the cold, the hot, that of the summer, that of the rainy season, be all destroyed!

We send the takman away to the Gandharis, the Majavants, the Angas and Magadhas, like a servant, like a treasure!

May the father of the Maruts, the overlords of the cattle, may Death, the overlord of living beings, may Yama, the overlord of the Fathers, may the fore Fathers, of ancient days, may the Fathers of the succeeding days, and may the Fathers of our fathers protect me in this my prayer, in this my worship, in this my ritual, in this my performance, in this my thought, in this my intention and desire, in this my invocation of the Gods; all hail!

Prayer to Prolong Life

May near things stay near and also far ones. Remain here, go not now, follow not the former fathers, I firmly bind your breath of life.

If any sorcerer has bewitched thee, be he one of thine own men or a stranger, do I proclaim for thee here with my voice both deliverance and freedom.

In case you have deceived or cursed a man or woman in folly, do I proclaim for thee here with my voice, both deliverance and freedom.

If you lie there prostrate as a result of a sin either committed by your father or mother, do I proclaim for thee here with my voice, both deliverance and freedom.

Accept the healing balm your mother and father bring together along with your sister and brother. I make you one who attains ripe old age!

Be thou here, O man, with your soul unimpaired, follow not Yama's two messengers! Come to the cities where the living people dwell!

Return here to our calls, you know the road that lies ahead, the ascent, the climb, the course of every living man!

Do not be afraid, thou shall not die. I shall make thee one who reaches the ripe old age. I have exercised the consumption, that wastes from your limbs.

The limb rending fever, the limb wasting pain, the heart pain and the consumption, all have fled far away, like a falcon, by the power of my voice.

May the two seers, the watchful and the vigilant, the sleepless and that is watchful, guardians of your breath, be alert for your protection by day and night!

We approach here Agni with reverence, may the sun continue to arise here for thee. Arise from the deep pit of death, yea from the darkness, however, profound it may be.

Reverence be to Yama, homage to death, homage to the Fathers, and to them who conduct you. This Agni, who knows how to save do I set forth for this man, that he be free from harm.

His breath may come, his mind may come, his sight and strength may come! May his body resume its strength, let it stand firm and erect on its feet!

Unite him, O Agni, with his breath, with his sight, set his body and its power in motion. Thou knowest the secret of deathlessness. May he now not depart to a house of clay, may he live!

May thy out-breath not srap, may thy in-breath not vanish; let the Sun, the overlord, hold thee up the death with his rays!

His halting and quivering tongue, utters words within. From it have I exercised the consumption, and the hundred torments of the fever.

This world of ours is the most loved of the Gods, unconquered. For whatever, be the death assigned to you when you were born, O men, we call you here, did not before old age!

Book Six

Prayer to Indra Against Demons

O priests, press the Soma and cleanse it for Indra, who shall listen to the praise of devotees and to my call.

Do thou, O exuberant Indra, into whom enter the drops of Soma as birds a tree, drive away the evil brood of the demons.

Press ye the Soma for the Soma enjoyer, the thunder-armed Indra, a youthful conqueror, ruler is he, praised greatly by people. .

For Securing a Woman's Love

Like the creeper embracing the tree on all sides, do thou embrace me, that thou mayest be one loving me and not be averse to me.

As the eagle, flying forth, beats down his wings upon the earth, so do I hold thy mind that thou mayest be one loving me and not be averse to me.

As the sun goes about heaven and earth, thus do I go about thy mind so that thou mayest be one loving me and not be averse to me.

For Securing a Woman's Love

Long thou for my body, for my feet, for my eyes and for my thighs! May the eyes and the hair of thee, lusting after me be parched with love.

I make thee cling to my arm, cling to my heart, that thou mayest be under my control, mayest come to my desire!

May the kine, mothers of ghee, who lick their calves, in whose heart love is planted, make the yonder woman bestow love on me!

For Gaining a Son

The Asvattha has mounted the Shamim, then a male child was born. That verily is the way to obtain a male child, that do we bring to our women.

In the male indeed doth grow the seed, that is poured forth into the women. That indeed is the way to obtain a son. It has been proclaimed by Prajapati.

Prajapati, Anumati, and Sinivali have fashioned him. May Prajapati put elsewhere a female birth, but here may he cause to bear a male.

Against Miscarriage

Just as this great earth bore the seed of all existence, so she may conceive a child and bear a son!

Just as this great earth bears these trees of the forest, so shall thou hold fast thy embryo, to bear a child after pregnancy.

Just as this great earth holds the mountains and the peaks, so shalt thou hold fast thy embryo, to bear a child after pregnancy.

Just as this great earth holds the various living creatures, so shalt thou hold fast thy embryo to bear a child after pregnancy!

Against Jealousy

The first current of jealousy, and the second after the first, the fire, the heart burning, these do we drive away from thee!

As the earth is dead in spirit, more dead than the dead man, and as the spirit of him that has died, so shall the spirit of the jealous person be dead!

The fluttering spirit that abides in your heart, from it do I wipe away jealousy, as the hot air from a skin bag.

Against Fever (Takman)

The fever (Takman) who comes as if from this fire burning and flashing here, may he go away like a babbling drunkard from me. May he, the evil one, seek some other man and not ourselves. Homage be to fever, possessing a burning weapon!

Homage be to Rudra, homage to the Takman fever, homage to king Varuna, the effulgent, homage to heaven, homage to Earth and to the planets!

To thee here, who burns greatly and makes all bodies pale, to thee here, to the red, to the brown, to the Takman, do I reverence.

To the Waters for Cure

The waters flow forth from the snowy heights, and gather somewhere in the Sindhu. May they, the divine ones grant me the healing balm for my heart pain!

The burning sensation that harm my eyes, and that which pains my heels, my fore-feet, may the Waters cure that, they the most skilled physicians!

Ye streams all, whose mistress is Sindhu, whose queen is Sindhu, grant us the cure for that, through this cure may we enjoy you.

Against Sores and Pain

The sores, the five and fifty that have collected on the neck, may they all go away from here like the noise of the disease apakit.

The sores, the seven and seventy that have collected on the neck, may they all pass away from here!

The sores, the nine and ninety that have collected on the shoulders, may they all go away hence!

For Averting Evil

Let me go, O evil, being thou mighty, be kind to us! Set me free and unharmed, O evil, into the world of joy!

If, O evil, you do not leave us, here do we leave you at this parting of the roads. May evil follow another man!

Far off from us may the thousand-eyed immortal evil dwell. Let him strike one whom we hate, and him whom we hate, may he surely strike!

Against Ominous Birds

O Gods, if the dove sent as the messenger of Death, come seeking us, we shall sing praises and worship him. May our bipeds prosper, may our quandrupeds prosper!

May the dove thus sent be propitious to us; may harmless be the bird to us, O Gods. Let the seer Agni enjoy our oblation, let the winged missile avoid us!

May the winged missile not injure us; it makes its track on our hearth, our fireplace. May be it be auspicious to our kine and men, let it not harm us, O Gods.

Against Ominous Owls

May the winged missile fall upon those yonder men. What the owl shrieks, be that futile, or in case the dove makes its track upon the fire place.

To both thy messengers, O Goddess of Death, that come hither, sent or not sent to her house, to the dove and to the owl. This shall be no place to make a track.

It shall not fly hither to destroy our heroes, may it settle here to keep our heroes sound and fit. Send him off to a distant place so that in Yama's abode people may behold you deprived of strength and devoid of power.

To the Rising Sun

This spotted steer has come hither, and has sat on the mother Earth in the east. And now he is marching forward to his sire the Heaven.

He, the Sun moves about the brilliant spaces, from his out-breath pervades the whole Universe. He the bull has looked forth into the heavens.

He is the overlord of thirty domains. The voice, the triple knowledge of the Vedas also abides in its refuge.

Against Hostile Spells

Here has come forth the thousand-eyed curse having harnessed his chariot, seeking out my curser, as does a wolf the house of a sheep owner.

O curse, avoid us as does a burning fire a lake. Strike thou our curser here, as a lightning from the sky strikes the tree.

Whoever shall curse us when we do not curse, and whoever shall curse us when we do curse, him I throw to death as a bone to a dog.

For Splendour

What splendour is in a lion, in a tiger, and what is in and adder, in fire, in Brahmin, the sun, may that blessed Goddess that gave birth to Indra now come to us along with splendour!

What splendour is in an elephant, in a leopard, in gold, in the waters, in kine, and in man, may that blessed Goddess that gave birth to Indra now come to us along with splendour!

What splendour is there in a chariot, in dice, in a bull's strength, in wind, in rain and in thunder, may that blessed Goddess that gave birth to Indra now come to us along with splendour!

What splendour resides in a noble, in a drum, in an arrow's flight, in a man's shout, in a horse's strength, may that blessed Goddess that gave birth to Indra now come to us along with splendour.

A Prayer for Glory

My oblation that increases glory, inspired by Indra, of thousandfold strength, well offered, prepared with strength will prosper.

May it cause me, who offers this oblation to behold the sunlight for long and a rise to royal power.

We honour glorious Indra, rich in glory with glory giving oblations. Do thou O oblations, inspired by Indra bestow upon us royalty. May we be glorious with this thy favour. Glorious was Indra bom, glorious was Agni, glorious was Soma, glorious of all beings am I most glorious.

For Fearlessness

O ye Heaven and Earth, breathe on us fearlessness. May Soma, Savitar render us fearless. May the limitless atmosphere set us in fearlessness. May the oblation of the seven seers set us in fearlessness!

From the four directions, the North and the South, the East and the West let Savitar direct on this village sustenance, welfare, and comfort. May Indra grant us freedom from foes, fearlessness, deflecting the fury of kings.

O Indra, grant us freedom from our foes, freedom below and above, freedom behind and before,

For Atonement of the Sin

Go far away, O sin of the mind, why do you utter things improper? Go from here, I do not desire you. Go and live in the trees and forests. My mind shall be with our kine and homes.

If any wrong has been done by us, O Agni, waking or sleeping, by cursing or illwill, put it far away from us, all that is evil and disagreeable deeds!

If we have done any thing wrong, O Indra and Brahmanaspati, let Angiras, the wise, protect us from distress and difficulty!

Exorcism of Evil Dreams

You, who are neither alive nor dead, the immortal child of the Gods are you.

O sleep, Varunani is your mother, Yama your sire, Araru are you by name!

O sleep, we know thy birth, you are the child of the divine sisters, the instrument of Yama. You are termination, you are death. Do we know you, O sleep. Do you preserve us against evil dreams!

As men pay off a sixteenth, an eighth, or the entire debt, so do we send forth every evil dream from us upon him who hates us.

For Winning a Husband

Here comes Aryaman, with his locks dishevelled in front, seeking a husband for this spinster, and a wife for him without one.

This spinster, O Aryaman, has grown weary of going to the weddings of other maids. May now, O Aryaman, the other women come to her wedding without fail!

Dhatar, the creator sustains this earth, he sustains the heavens and the sun. Let Dhatar provide this spinster with a husband after her own desire!

Against Discord

May you agree, be united, may your minds be in harmony, just as the Gods of yore sat in harmony to their position of oblation.

May their counsel be same, same their gathering, their aim the same, same their thoughts. The same oblation do I offer for you, may you both enter together into the same thought!

What varied food I consume often times, and my gold, my horse, and also mine kine, goats and sheep, whatever I receive as a gift, may Agni, the hotar priest, render that into propitious gift!

Whatever gift do I receive in sacrifice, out of sacrifice, granted by the Fathers, granted by men, which excites my mind with joy, may Agni, the Hoter priest, render that into a propitious gift!

The food that, O Gods, I improperly eat, and promise intending to give it, or not to give it to the Brahmins, may that by the greatness of great Agni (Vaishwanara) be propitious and honeyed for me!

Let your bodies be united together, may your minds and your aims be united together. Brahmanaspati has brought you together, Bhaga has brought you together.

Harmony of the mind for you, also harmony of the heart, besides with the aid of Bhaga's exertion, do I render you in harmony.

As the Adityas are united with the Vasus, as the severe Rudras are united with the Maruts, without any grudge, so, O three named one (Agni), without any grudge, do thou render these people of one mind!

For Matrimonial Bliss

Through this auspicious oblation, let this man be flourished again, may he grow superior to his wife that they have brought for him with his sap.

May he grow superior to her in strength, superior in royalty. May these two grow rich in thousandfold wealth, that is inexhaustible and full of splendour.

Tvashtar generated a wife for thee, and for her a husband in thee. May Tvashtar grant both of you a thousand lives, may he give you a long life!

For Happy Conception

Thou art a holder, thou boldest both hands and drives away the demons! This amulet, hath become the obtainer of progeny and wealth!

O amulet, hold wide the womb, so that the embryo be placed into it, do thou bestow a son, do thou make him come here, thou comer!

The amulet that Aditi wore, when she wanted a son, may Tvashtar fasten upon this woman that saying, "she shall beget a son"!

For Procuring a Wife

I take a name of him who comes here, who has come, and is coming, I call the name of Indra, the Vritra-slayer, the Vasus of the hundredfold strength.

By which path the Ashvins carried away Surya, as a bride, Savitar's daughter, by that, Bhaga has told me, thou shalt bring a wife!

With thy wealth-giving, great, golden hook, O Indra, O overlord of strength, grant thou a wife to me who seeks one.

For Imparting Swiftness to a Horse

Be thou, O steed, as swift as the wind, being yoked to the chariot, urged by Indra go fast as the mind. May the all-possessing Maruts yoke thee, may Tvashtar put swiftness into your feet!

With the swiftness, O courser, that has been put into you in secret, also that which has been given away to the eagle, to the wind, with that speed, O steed, do you, being strong, win the race, reaching the goal in the contest.

Let thy body, O steed, leading a body, run, a pleasure for us and a delight for you. A God, not stumbling, great, he shall find his own light in the heaven, as it were!

For Relief from Distress

The many plants whose sovereign is Soma, of hundredfold aspect, begotten by Brihaspati, may free us from distress!

May they free me from the distress arising out of a curse, and also from that which is of Varuna, besides, from Yama's fetters, from each and every sin against the Gods!

If we have transgressed any law waking or sleeping, if with sight, with mind or if with speech, may Soma purify these for us!

For Victory in Battle

Victorious is the sacrifice, Victorious is Agni, Victorious is Soma, Victorious is Indra. We devotees of Agni, reverently offer this oblation so that we may subdue all the hostile armies!

Hail be ye, O wise Mitra, O Varuna, increase ye here our kingdom with honey so that it be rich in offspring, drive away afar the misfortune, remove from us far away any committed sin!

May ye be inspired to follow this hero, be close, to Indra, O friends who subdues armies, conquers cattle, is thunder-armed, overthrows the enemy host arrayed, slaughtering the foe with his might!

For Securing a Woman's Love

As this draught horse, O Ashvins, comes on, so may thy spirit come on and move together with me!

I draw your mind to me, as does a chief stallion the female side horse. Like a stalk of the grass torn by the wind, so may thy mind twine itself to me!

For a Child Born at Unauspicious Time

Since yore, O Agni, thou hast been praised at sacrifices as hotar priest and even now a new thou shalt be our priest, O Agni, gratify thine own self and grant us good fortune.

Born under Jyesthaghni constellation, or under the Vikritan, do thou protect him from being uprooted by mulabarhana. May Agni conduct him across all misfortunes unto long life of a hundred autumns!

On the tiger day was the hero born, born under an auspicious constellation, he became rich and brave. May he not slay his father, may he not harm his mother that gave him birth, when he grows up!

Against Insanity

O Agni, free this man for me, who here bound and well secured cries so loudly. Thenceforth he shall make a due share for thee, when he is released from insanity!

May Agni calm down thy mind if thy mind is disturbed. Skilfully do I make a remedy so that thou mayest be freed from madness!

Made insane by the sin against the Gods, or by the demons, for you skilfully, do I make a remedy so that thou mayest be freed from madness!

May the Apsaras restore thee, may Indra, may Bhaga restore thee, may all the Gods restore thee so that thou mayest be freed from madness!

For Expiation of Sins

From sin we have committed knowingly or unknowingly, deliver us from that, O Gods one and all!

From the sin, I committed awake or asleep sin-inclined, may both past and future set me free, as if from a wooden post to which I was bound!

May I be released from sin as if from a pillar, or from dirt and filth after a bath. May all the Gods clear me from sin as ghee is pure after passing through a sieve!

Asking Forgiveness for Debts

The food that I eat, the debt that I owe and not returned, and my offerings to Yama which ever sustains me, O Agni, may I be freed from all these debts, you who know how to unfasten all the fetters.

Being just here before you, we give this gift back, we restore it, O Agni, the grain that I have eaten having borrowed it, so that I may be released from guilt of that.

Free from guilt of debt in this world, free from guilt of debt in the higher world, free from guilt in the third world may we be, and also in the world of Gods, and in those of the fathers, on all our paths may we remain free from the guilt of debt!

A Prayer for Attaining Heaven

If we have harmed space, earth and sky, or if we have ever offended the father or mother, may this Agni of the house, absolve us from that and conduct us safely to the world of well-doing.

May the Earth our mother, Aditi the boundless, our kin, and space our brother, preserve us from damnation. May our father

Heaven grant us prosperity from the world of the Fathers. May I attain the world of my kindered ones, and having reached here, may never lose the heaven!

In that divine world where men of good deeds and pious acts revel, their bodies made free from disease, free from lameness, or any other defect, their limbs made whole, there in the heaven may we behold our parents and our children!

A Prayer for Auspicious Day

When the stars appointed Shakadhuma their king, they bestowed upon him auspicious day saying, "This shall be his dominion".

May we have auspicious day at noon, auspicious day at eve, auspicious day in the early morning, and also auspicious day in the night!

For day and night, from the stars, from the sun and moon, do thou, O king Shakadhuma, make auspicious day for us!

To thee, O Shakadhuma, sovereign of the stars, who made auspicious day for us at eve, in the night and by day, let there be ever homage!

For Gaining a Man's Love

Down from the head unto thy feet I implant passionate longing. Ye Gods send forth the passionate love, may you man burn for me!

O Anumati, give assent to this plan, fit it well, O Akuti! Ye Gods send forth the passionate love, may you man bum for me!

Even if thou hast run away three leagues, five leagues, the distance covered by a horse in a day, from there thou shall come back, thou shalt be the father of our sons!

A Prayer of Power Through a Girdle

The God who has bound this girdle round us, who fastened us together and joined into me, the God at whose divine direction we move, may he head us to the other shore and may he liberate us!

O thou daughter of Faith, born out of fervour, sister of the seers who fashion the world, grant us, O Girdle, powers of thought and wisdom, also grant us fervour and Indra's manly vigour!

For Luxuriant Hair

O herb, thou art born divine, on the divine mother Earth, We dig thee up here, O mitani, so that thou mayest quicken the growth of the hair!

Strengthen thou, the old ones, generate the new and render them luxuriant that has come forth!

The hair of thine which falls down, and that which is broken root and all, upon it do I sprinkle here the all-healing balm of the herb!

For Promotion of the Growth of Hair

This herb which seer Jamdagni dug up to promote the increase of his daughter's hair, that one Vitahavya has brought from Asita's house.

They (hair) had to be measured with a rein, and were measured out after with stretched arms, May the black hair grow as do the reeds, on thy head!

Make thou the roots firm, draw out the ends, stretch out the middle, O plant. May the black hair grow as do the reeds, on thy head!

For Rendering a Man Impotent

O herb, thou art reputed as one of the best plants; change this man for me impotent who wears his hair dressed!

Do thou turn him impotent, him who wears his hair dressed, likewise change him into one that wears a hood! Then may Indra crush both his testicles with the two press stones.

Impotent one, I have made thee impotent. O eunuch I have made thee eunuch, O weakling, into a weakling I have made thee. A hood we set down upon his head!

The two tubes, created by the Gods, in which reside man's virility, them I break with a club.

As women split reeds with a stone for a mattress, so do I split thy member.

For Bountiful Barley Harvest

Spring up, become abundant, grow thick with thy own strength! Burst all vessels fashioned to contain you! May lightning from the heavens not smite you!

O divine barley, spring up tall as the sky in response to our call and be inexhaustible like the ocean!

May those who attend you be inexhaustible, inexhaustible their barns who offer you in sacrifice, also those who consume you shall be inexhaustible!

Book Seven

The Gods Sacrificed to the Gods

Through the sacrifice the Gods sacrificed to the sacrifice. Those were the first established rites. Their greatness increased and they ascended to heaven where dwell the ancient Gods, who had attained perfection.

Thus sacrifice came to be and it manifested itself. It was practised and then it increased. It became overlord of the Gods. May it bestow wealth upon us!

The Gods offered sacrifice to the Gods through oblation. The immortals worshipped the immortal with immortal mind. May we also enjoy ourselves in the highest heaven. May we see with wonder the rising of the sun!

When using the man for their oblation the Gods made the sacrifice, but still more powerful was the sacrifice they offered with invocation.

In Praise of Pushan

On the forward pathway has Pushan been born, on the distant path of heaven, on the distant path of the earth. He comes to both the dearest abodes, hither and yonder, knowing each path.

He knows and traverses all these heavenly realms. May he guide us by that path which is most secure and free from fear, granting us our wellbeing protecting our heroes. May he lead the way who foreknows.

O Pushan, we worship you that we may never be harmed. We take up stance, O Lord, in thy domain.

May Pushan put his right hand to protect us, may he restore us what we have lost, may recover that which we have lost!

Protection Against Lightning

With thy broad thundering, which elevated by the Gods, pervades all this, with that lightning do thou not ruin our grain, nor do thou destroy it with the rays of the sun.

For Success in the Gathering

May both the assembly and meeting, the two daughters of Prajapati, favour me! May he, with whom I shall meet, aid me, may I, O Fathers, speak what is pleasant among those who have assembled here!

We know thy name, O assembly; verily, 'sport' is thy name. May all those who sit there in assembly speak in harmony with me!

Of these who have assembled together I take to myself the splendour and discernment. Of all the assembled, O Indra, make me successful!

If your mind has gone away, or has been chained either here or there, that we cause to return here. Let your mind rest in me!

Against Enemies

As the rising sun takes to himself the glory of the stars, thus do I take away the strength of both the men and women who hate me.

As many of enemies as look upon me. as I come along, of those who hate me do I take to myself the strength, of them who sleep while the sun rises!

I offer my song of praise to Savitar, of true impulse, wealth-giving, exceedingly wise, most dear and possessed of real strength.

His lofty splendour stretches far and wide, his light shines brightly in his creation, golden-handed, measuring the heaven by his appearance, he traverses the sky.

It were you, O God, who inspired our first father of old, granting him height and breadth in space. May we also enjoy, O Savitar, desirable things in abundance day by day!

The adorable Savitar bestowed upon our Fathers wealth, skill and life. May he drink Soma at the sacrifice and take delight in our offerings. In his ordinance walks the pilgrim!

Prayer to Sun

Come ye together with prayer to the lord of heaven, He is the one, the all-pervading, mighty guest of people May the ancient one, abide in the present. Him, the one, the many follow on the track.

This one is a thousand for our sight, inspiration to the poets, light far extending.

The effulgent one sends together the Dawns, blameless, like–minded, most splendid, for the benefit of the entire Earth.

Prayer to Vishnu

Of Vishnu, now I would declare the mighty deeds, of one who measured out the earthly realms, who established the highest region, striding out thrice, he, the wide-striding one.

For this his heroic deed is Vishnu praised, like some fearful wild beast, prowling the mountains and saying, "From far off place may he come hither".

He, upon whose three wide extended paces all living beings dwell. Widely, O Vishnu, stride out, widely make us to live, enjoy the oblation. O ghee-wombed one, make us drink the ghee-like life-giving sap and prolong the master of sacrifice on and on!

Through all this world strode Vishnu, thrice he planted his foot, and it collected in his footstep's dust.

He strode three steps, he whom none can harm, the guardian of all, ordaining his high decrees!

Look ye here the deeds of Vishnu, whereby he, the friend of Indra, close allied, has allowed his holy works to be seen.

The princes ever behold that loftiest step of Vishnu, laid as it were, an eye stretched in heaven.

Between Wife and Husband

The eyes of both of us be of honey aspect, our foreheads be gleaming like an ointment. Put me thou within thy heart, may we two of us be together in mind.

I wrap thee in my garment produced by Manu, so that thou mayest be wholly mine also, mayest not speak of another woman!

For Securing Love of a Man

I dig out this remedy (herb), drawing towards me the eye and causing lover's tears. It returns one that has gone away, and gladdens him that comes to me.

By this herb did Indra allure away Asuni from the other Gods, therewith do I subject thee, so that I may be very dear to thee!

Thou art like Soma (the moon), thy face is turned towards the Sun. It is also turned towards all the Gods, as such we invoke thee here!

In this matter my speech carries weight, not yours. In the assembly, verily, do thou speak! May you be mine alone and not even mention another woman.

Whether you are beyond the haunts of men, or whether beyond the stream, may this herb, as if a captive bound, shall bring you back to me!

To the Divine Falcon

Across the waters, across the waters, the solar Falcon, the men beholder, has penetrated the unerring path to his desired resting place. Through all the lower realms may he wing his way here, the auspicious one, accompanied by Indra!

May this divine Falcon, observing men, the thousand-footed one, having a progeny a hundred-fold, vigour-giving, grant us an abundant source for oblation, as he did to our Father in days of yore!

To Soma and Rudra

O Soma, O Rudra, chase asunder the disease that has entered our dwelling. Drive Nirrti away, and set aside from us any committed sin.

O Soma, O Rudra, give us for our bodies all needed remedies to heal and cure. Loosen from us any committed sin that is still inherent in our bodies.

Charm Against Jealousy

From folk belonging to all peoples, away from the Sindhu river thou hast been brought here. From a distance, I think, has been brought the remedy of jealousy.

As if a fire is burning him, as if a conflagration burning forest in all directions, this jealousy of this man do thou quench, as fire is appeased with water.

For Success at Dice

As the lightning strike the forest trees irresistibly, so would I today irresistibly beat the gamesters with my dice.

Whether they be quick or slow, the fortune of these people irresistibly shall come together from all sides in my winning hands.

I invoke with reverence Agni, who is lord of riches, here attached he shall heap up again for us. I win wealth for myself as if with booty-winning chariots. May I sing skilfully the song of praise to the Maruts.

May we, with thee as ally, conquer the enemy troops; do thou help us to gain our portion in every conquest. Make for us, O Indra, wide space and easy going path, O Maghavan, do thou crush the manly power of our foes!

I have won thee out, I have also won the reverse, as a wolf shakes a sheep, so do I pluck thy winnings!

For Concord

May we be in harmony with our own men, in harmony with strangers. Do ye O Ashvins, establish harmony among us!

May we be harmonious in our own mind thought, may we not fight with one another, which is displeasing to the Gods. May not there arise the din of frequent battle destruction; may the arrow of Indra not fall, when the day has come!

For Health and Long Life

When thou, O Brihaspati, did liberate us from Yama's yonder world existence, and from hostile scheme, then did the Ashvins, the physicians of the Gods sweep away death from us, O Agni.

O in and out-breathings, go together with the body, do not desert it, may these by thy allies here. Live and prosper a hundred autumns. May Agni be the best shepherd and overseer!

The vital breath that has been dissipated afar, thy in and out-breathings, may they come once again. Agni has taken them up from the lap of Nirriti, and them I again implant into thyself!

Let this breath leave not this man, let not out–breath desert him and depart. I consign him to the Seven Seers, may they lead him into happy old age!

Enter ye in-breathing and out-breathing, like two oxen into a stall. Let this man here prosper in the treasure of old age unharmed!

We do drive into thee thy life breath. I do drive not consumption from thee. May this divine Agni give us life from every side!

Ascending to the highest firmament, out of darkness to the Sun, the God of Gods, we have attained the highest light.

To Indra and Varuna

O Indra and Varuna, true to law, Soma drinkers, drink this pressed Soma, the giver of rapturous joy. Let your chariot come to the feast of the Gods, to sacrifice, as it were home, so that you may drink.

O Indra and Varuna, drink to your fill, ye bulls, of this most sweet and rich Soma. This juice is poured out that ye may quaff. Be seated here on this sacred grass and revel.

Against Ominous Black Bird

What this black bird flying out towards me has dropped here, let the waters protect me from all that misfortune, from all that distress!

What this black bird has brushed here with thy mouth, O Nirriti, may Agni, the lord of the house, release me from this sin!

A Prayer for Joy

May the wind blow us joy, may the sun shine down joy upon us, may the days pass with joy, may the night be full of joy, may the dawn shine forth joy for us!

For Curing Apakit Sores

Ye Apakits shed easily from that which sheds easily, more non-existing than that which do not exist at all. Ye are more sapless than the sehu, more dissolving than the salt.

The Apakits that are on the neck, likewise those which are upon the shoulders, the ones which are upon the perineum, may they fall off themselves!

To the Maruts

O Maruts, ye consuming Gods, here is offering, enjoy this ye Maruts, to aid us, O foe-slayers!

Maruts, the man who would slay us before we can think, the very inimical, let that man be tangled in the fetters of hate, smite him down with your most flaming weapon!

May the Maruts of the year, well singing, wide dwelling, gracious and well attended, release us from the bonds of sin, they the much heating, jovial and revealing ones!

To Varuna

O king Varuna, thy golden dwelling is built in the waters! May the king that maintains the laws release us from all the bonds!

Loosen us from the uppermost fetters, O Varuna, loosen down the lowest ones, loosen the middlemost ones, so, that, O Aditya, we may live in freedom, freed from guilt in thy realm!

Release us, O Varuna, from all fetters, that are the uppermost, the lowest, and those that are imposed by Varuna. Drive away from us evil-dreaming and distress, then we may go to the world of the pious ones!

Against Bad Luck

Fly forth from here, O evil sign, be gone from here, fly forth to yonder places. With a metal hook we fasten thee to him who hates us!

This unauspicious flying sign which has alighted upon me as a creeper upon a tree, that mayest thou put away elsewhere from here, O golden-handed Savitar, granting wealth to us!

A hundred and one are the signs that are born with the body of the mortal man, the worst of these we send forth away from here, the auspicious ones do thou Jatavedas, hold fast on us!

These signs here I have separated, like cows scatted on a barren. Let the auspicious signs stay, the foul ones I have made to vanish.

Book Eight

For Long Life and Health

O man, take thou hold on your share of immortality, so that you may attain old age without mishap. I bring back thy life and spirit, do not vanish into shadow and darkness, do not perish!

Go forth thou unto us the light of the living. I take you forth to a life of hundred autumns. Releasing you from the fetters of death and malediction, I extend further your thread of life to a longer time.

From the wind have I fetched thy breath, from the sun thy sight, I strengthen your mind in thee, let your limbs in harmony, speak with thy tongue without stammering.

I blow upon thee the breath of bipeds and quadrupeds as one blows a fire just kindled. O Death, to thy sight, and to thy breath, homage I have paid.

Let this man live, let him not die, this man we now revive, here, I prepare a cure for him. Death do not smite this man!

The lively, life-possessing herb, the powerful, potent here do I call, to bring freedom from harm to this man once more.

Bless thou this man, do not seize him, release him, though he be yours. Let him remain here, O Bhava and Sarva, be ye gracious, protect him and grant him full old age, drive away distress!

May the missile of Gods avoid thee, I make you emerge from darkness, I have made thee safe from death. I have removed thee far from the flesh-eating funeral pyre (fire). I set a protective enclosure for thee for your preservation.

We preserve him from death's gloomy path, which is thine, O Death, and allows no return. Protecting him from the descent to darkness, we make a covering for him, with this our prayer.

To thee now we give the in-breath and out-breath and a ripe old age, death at its end, and wellbeing. All the messengers of Yama who move about, I drive them far away.

I sweep away to a distant place distress, destruction, the flesh-consuming demons, every rakshas of evil power, them I slay, as it were, into darkness.

I snatch away thy life breath from immortal Agni, the ever living, all-knowing Jatavedas, so that you may remain unharmed and mayest be immortal in alliance with him. I perform this rite for thee, let it help thee to achieve perfection.

May Heaven and Earth be propitious to thee, never distressing, ever giving fortune. May the Sun shine weal upon thee. May the wind blow auspiciousness to thy heart! May the divine streams, rich in sap, flow propitiously in thee!

May the herbs be propitious to thee. I have uplifted thee from the lower to the higher realm. There may both the Sun and Moon, the boundless ones preserve you!

The garment that envelops thee, that which wraps at the waist, that we make auspicious to thy body, a soft caress to your body!

When thou shavest us as a barber with a very sharp razor, our beard and hair, may our faces shine bright, but the length of our life may remain uncurtailed!

May barley and rice be propitious to thee, never may they cause balsa or any other disease. Let them free thee from consumption, and free thee from distress!

Whatever thou eatest or drinkest, of grain, of field, or of milk, edible or non-edible, all these do I render free from poison!

Now we commit you to both the day and night, to them both we give you. Preserve ye this man from the clutches of the demons who seek to devour him.

A hundred, a thousand years, two, three or four generations we grant thee. May Indra and Agni, may all the Gods grant thee this boon without enmity!

We commit thee now to winter, spring and summer. Let the rainy season, in which the herbs grow, be pleasant to thee!

Death is overlord of bipeds. Death is the lord of quadrupeds but thee I rescue from his clutches, so do thou not be afraid!

Do not be afraid, thou shalt not die, unharmed one, thou shalt not die. Men die not at that or go to the lowest darkness.

At that place where this holy word is uttered, a defence unto living, every being, verily lives the ox, the horse, the man and the kine.

May it protect thee from thy peers, from evil spells, from thy kinsmen and their wiles. May ye be deathless, immortal, surviving, may thy life breath never leave thy body!

The deaths that are a hundred and one, and the powers of doom that are to be combated, may the Gods free thee from that, by the power of Agni, Vaishvanara, the universal lord!

Thou art Agni's body, ready to protect, foe and demon-slayer art thou, rival-slayer, likewise the expeller of disease, the healing herb, putudry by name!

An Amulet Against Witchcraft

This attacking amulet, a hero, bound on a hero, is full of might, foe-slaying, a true hero, a very effective protection.

This amulet slays enemies, makes mighty heroes, is powerful, vigorous, fomidable, as a hero advances to meet the sorceries and annihilates them.

With this amulet Indra slew Vritra, with its aid he, filled with wisdom, destroyed the Asuras, with it he conquered both the heaven and earth, with it he conquered the four quarters.

This amulet of sraktya wood assails and attacks, forcibly removes and controls the enemies. May it protect us on all sides!

Agni hath said this, and also Soma hath said this; Brihaspati, Savitar, Indra, may these Gods, the divine priests, drive the sorceries back with this amulet upon the sorcerer!

I interpose heaven and earth, also the day and also the sun. May these Gods, the divine priests, turn the sorceries back with this amulet upon the sorcerer!

The folk who make amulet of sraktya wood their armour, like the sun ascending the sky, it subdues and drives away the sorceries.

With this amulet of sraktya wood, as if with a seer full of wisdom, I have won all battles, I smite down the enemies and the demons.

The sorceries that arise from Angiras, that arising from Asuras, the sorceries that are self-made, and those brought by others, may these, of both types, go away to the distances across ninety navigable streams!

Upon this man shall the Gods tie this amulet as an armour, Indra, Vishnu, Savitar, Rudra, Agni, Prajapati, Paramesthin, Viraj, Vaishvanara, and all the sages!

Thou art the prince of the plants, as if an ox among the moving creatures, as if a tiger among beasts of pray. This amulet that we did seek, that have we found, a protector on our side.

He who wears this talisman, verily becomes a tiger, likewise a lion, a bull, likewise a curtailer of the foes.

Apsaras slay him not, nor Gandharvas, nor mortal men, he rules over all the quarters who wears this amulet.

Kashyapa did create thee, Kashyapa did produce thee, Indra bore thee in human battle, and wearing thee he conquered in the strife. The Gods made this amulet of thousandfold strength their armour.

Whoever wants to harm thee with magic, with consecrations, whoever desires to harm thee with sacrifices, him strike thou back, O Indra, with thy thunderbolt that hath a hundred.

May this attacking amulet, vigorous, all-conquering, verily defend our progeny and wealth, a very auspicious defence!

Eliminate our foes in the south, eliminate them in the north, eliminate O India, our foes in the west. Place light, O hero, in front of us, in the east.

A protection for me be the heaven and earth, a protection the day, a protection the sun, a protection for me be both Indra and Agni. May Dhatar assign an armour to me!

The formidable defence of Indra and Agni, which not all the Gods together can pierce through, may that great armour protect my body on all sides, so that I may attain ripe old age and long life.

This divine amulet has ascended upon me unto great unharmedness. Assemble ye together around this post that protects body, provides threefold armour in order to grant vigour.

In this may Indra implant manliness, do ye, O Gods, assemble around it in order to gain long life of a hundred autumns, that he may reach ripe old age.

May Indra, the bestower of welfare, the lord of the people, Vritra-slayer, subduer of the foes, he who conquers and is unconquered, the soma-drinking bull, that makes one fearless, bind this amulet on thee. May it defend thee on all sides, by day and by night!

To Medicinal Plants for Restoration of Health

The herbs that are brown, and that are white, the red ones, the spotted ones, the sable and black herbs, all of them do we call.

Ay they save this man from the disease of consumption sent by Gods, the herbs of which heaven has been the sire, earth the mother, ocean the root.

The waters were in the beginning, and the heavenly herbs, they have driven out from every limb the sinful consumption of this man.

The herbs that spread forth, the bushy ones, single-seathed ones, those that creep along, do I invoke. I call on thy behalf the herbs and plants that have shoots, that contain stalks, that spread out their branches, and those derived from all the Gods, the strong ones, which provide life to men.

With that power which is yours, ye mighty ones, with the power and strength which is yours, with that do ye, O herbs, release this man from this disease. Now do I make a cure.

These various plants, lively, by no means harmful living herbs, disease removing, flourishing, rich and sweet, do I invoke to free this man from harm.

May all the forethoughtful, intelligent plants come hither, aid to my spell so that we may bring out this man out of distress.

They are the food of Agni, embryo of the waters, they that grow up renewing themselves, the fixed, that bear a thousand names, the healing ones, may they all come hither!

The plants whose womb is Avaka, whose sap are the waters, the sharp thorned, shall thrust away distress!

The herbs that release from Varuna (dropsy), are formidable and remove poison, also those which remove balsa and those which ward off witchcraft, shall come hither!

The plants which have been bought, the very potent ones, that which are praised shall protect in this village the kine, the horses, the men and the cattle!

Honeyed are the very roots of these herbs, honeyed the tips, honeyed their middles, honeyed their leaves, honeyed their blossoms. Partaking of honey, they are a food immortality. May they yield ghee and food and above all the cattle!

However many may be these plants in number and kind here on the earth, may these, the thousand-leafed, release me from death and distress!

Tiger-like is the amulet of these herbs, a saviour, guardian against evil. May it sweep away afar from us the disease and the demons!

As if at the roar of a lion do they tremble, as if at the roar of the fire, they quake before the plants that have been brought hither. May the disease of kine, and of men be driven away by these herbs across the navigable streams!

These herbs released from Agni, the Vaishvanara, may spread over the earth, go ye, whose king is the forest tree!

The herbs, coming from Angiras, and those which grow on mountains and plains, rich in sap, shall be propitious to us, and soothing to the heart!

These herbs which I know, and those which I behold with my eyes, the known ones, and those we know not, and those invested with power, may all these herbs note my words, that we may bring this man into safety out of distress!

A Charm Against the Foe

May Indra, shake the enemy, Sakra, the mighty hero, who splits the forts, so that we may slay by thousands the armies of our enemies!

May the rotten rope, breathing on it, turn into a stench against the yon enemy army. When shall they see from afar our smoke and fire, fear shall set into their hearts.

The atmosphere was the net, the great quarters of the space the stakes of the net. Therewith the mighty Indra encircled the enemy and scattered away the army of the Dasyus.

Verily great is the net of mighty great Indra, wealthy in steeds, therewith do thou, enfold all the foes, so that no one of them may be released!

Great is the net, O mighty Indra, a hero, equal to a thousand warriors, and who hast hundredfold strength. With that net Indra slew a hundred, a thousand, ten thousand and a hundred million foes.

This great world was the net of this great mighty Indra. With this net of Indra I enfold all you enemies in darkness!

With debility, great dejection, failure and misfortune, with fatigue, weariness and confusion do I enfold all you enemies!

To death do I assign them yonder, with fetters of death in which they have been bound. Them I conduct as captive to the messengers of death!

Lead ye them, O messengers of Death, ye messengers of Yama, enfold them. Let them in thousands be slain, may the Bhava's club smash them!

The Sadhyas go holding up with might one stake of the net, the Rudras another, the Vasus one, still another is upheld by the Adityas.

Let all the Gods go pressing from above with force, let the Angiras go on slaying the great army in the middle!

The forest trees and growths that are like trees together with the plants and herbs, bipeds and the quadrupeds, all do I impel to slay the yonder army!.

The Gandharvas and Apsaras, Serpents, the Gods and the pious men, the Fathers, the Visible and invisible beings, do I impel to slay the yonder army.

Scattered here are the fetters of death, when stepped upon thou shalt not escape. May this hammer slay yonder army by thousands!

The sacrificial hot drink that has been heated on fire, this oblation shall slay in thousands. Do ye Bhava and Sarva slay yonder army!

May they fall into death's snare, into hunger, exhaustion, into deadly weapons and fear. O Indra, O Sarva, do ye slay yonder army with trap and snare.

Do ye flee away, O foes, being conquered repelled by or incantation, do ye run away. None of the yonder army shall escape when repulsed by Brihaspati.

Let their weapons fall down from their hands, let them not be able to fix the arrow on the bow. And then our arrows shall strike them, fearing much, in their vital parts.

May heaven and earth together yell at them, and the atmosphere, along with the Gods. May they not find a helper nor a supporter, mutually smiting one another may they go unto death!

The four quarters are the she-mules of the chariot of Gods, the sacrificial cakes are their hoofs, the atmosphere the seat, heaven and earth the two sides, the seasons the reins, the intermediate realms the attendants, speech the road.

The year is the chariot, the full year the body of the chariot, Viraj the pole, Agni the front part, Indra the left stander, the moon the charioteer.

Do thou conquer on this side, on this side do thou conquer away, conquer fully, hail! Let these here be conquered, let those yonder be conquered, hail to these here, wail to those yonder! Those yonder do I wrap in blue and red!

Book Nine

A Prayer to Kama

The foe-slaying bull Kama, adored with ghee, oblation sacrificial butter, worshipped from all sides, do I desire to aid. Do thou, O praised for thy great heroism, make my enemies fall down.

That which is not pleasing either to my mind or my sight, and that which does not give me pleasure or gnaws me, that evil dreaming do I fasten on my foe. Lauding Kama, may I go up!

O Kama, do thou fasten on him the evil-dreaming, lack of progeny, distress, homelessness, who desires to harm us, O formidable one!

Thrust forward, O Kama, let them, my foemen, go to ruin, thrust them to the nether most darkness, do thou, O Agni, burn to ashes their dwellings!

O Kama, that which fulfils our desires, is called thy daughter, the speech, and the sages call that speech as Viraj. Therewith do thou avoid my enemies, let all, the life and cattle avoid them.

With the might of Kama, of Indra, of Varuna, of Vishnu, with the strength of Savitar, with the force of Agni, the hotar-priest, do I thrust forth my foemen, as a skilled poleman thrusts forth a boat on the waters.

May Kama, my mighty and formidable master, make me without enemies. May all the Gods be my refuge, may all the Gods come in response to this invocation of mine!

O sages, enjoying this sacrificial ghee, with Kama as your leader, revel here to render me without foes!

O Kama, allied with Indra and Agni, do ye make my foes fall down. O Agni, do thou burn to ashes the homes of them fallen to the nethermost darkness!

Smite thou and make them fall down to utter darkness, O Kama, them, my enemies. Let them be all senseless, strengthless, let them not live another day.

Kama hath slain my enemies, he has rendered for me wide space to dwell and prosperity. May the four quarters do me obeisance, may the six wide ones bring ghee for me!

May they drift away downward, like a boat detached from its moorings, thrust them away from the shore with the missiles, of them let there be no return again!

Agni is repeller, Indra is repeller, Soma is repeller, may all these repelling Gods repel my foes!

May my enemy, being hated by friends, deserted by heroes, being avoided by his own kinsmen, wander forth. Do thou, O formidable Gods, massacre my foes like the lightning striking the earth!

The great earth bears the lightning, those that are fallen and weak and those strong and not fallen. May the Aditya, arising with might, thrust down my foes with force, the great one!

O Kama, what pleasant, triple guarding, unpierceable armour thou hast, therewith thou thrust away my foes, let life, creatures and breath avoid them.

Wherewith the Gods thrust away the demons, wherewith Indra hurled down the Rakshasas to the darkness, therewith do thou, O Kama, thrust forth far from my enemies!

Kama is the first born, not the gods, nor the Fathers, nor mortal men, attained him. Thou art superior to them all, always great, so to thee as such, O Kama, do I render my obeisance!

O Kama, thou art the eldest of all, greater than the expanse of earth and heaven, altogether mighty. To you we render obeisance!

O Kama, thou art the eldest of all, greater than the quarters and directions, the expanses and vistas of the space, altogether mighty. To you we render obeisance.

O Kama, thou art eldest of all, greater than all things moving and inanimate, than the ocean, O passion, altogether mighty. To you we render obeisance!

Verily thou art beyond the reach of wind and fire, the sun and moon thou, O Kama, art superior to them, altogether mighty. To you we render homage!

In many a beautiful form, O Kama, you manifest yourself. May all these forms be implanted in our hearts. Send forth evil things elsewhere.

Incantations Concerning a House

We hereby unfasten the bonds of the pillars of this house, of numerous treasures, of the supporters and also of the cross beams!

What of you is bound, O you, who contain all treasures what fetters and knots are there. I unloose with a powerful spell, like Brihaspati breaking open the cavern.

The sorcerer stretched out the rope, he tied and made the firm knots. We loosen them with Indra's aid like a skilled slaughter cleaving the joints.

We unfasten the bonds of your beams and clasps, of your thatch and of your sides, O thou house, that holds all riches.

We unfasten the bonds of clamps and clasps, of all that binds now the lady of the building.

What hanging loops are there bound within you for enjoyment, we do unfasten them. May the mistress of the house, when established within be propitious to us!

Vessel of oblation, hall of Agni, abode and domain of the wives are you. O divine dwelling, you are the seat of the Gods.

The thousand-eyed net, stretched out, propped on the central beam, well tied and fastened, do we unfasten with holy word.

May he, who receives you as a gift, and by whom you are build, O queen of the houses, may both these enjoy long life and attain ripe old age!

Do thou, firmly fastened, tied and well adorned, come here to your master. Your limbs and joints we now unfasten.

He who collected the timber, O house, and constructed your walls, he the most exalted Prajapati created you for the increase of progeny!

Homage to him, homage to the giver, homage to the lord of the house, homage to Agni and homage to him who performs the rites, we pay.

Homage to kine, homage to horse, to all that is born in the house, O house, rich in progeny, we unloosen your bonds!

Within your innermost being, you cherish Agni with men and cattle. O house, rich in progeny, we unloosen your bonds!

Between heaven and earth what expanse there is, I accept that together with this house. The space that it encloses I make a container for treasures. I accept this house for the owner.

Rich in food, rich in milk, with firm foundation built upon the earth, treasure of all nourishing, O house, harm not those who receive you.

Wrapped in grass, clothed in straw, the house, like night provides rest to its dwellers. Built firm on the earth, she stands like a she-elephant on her feet.

I loosen and remove the covering of your reed. What Varuna has tightly bound, let Mitra unfasten again in the morning.

This dwelling built with worship, designed by the wise, may Indra and Agni, the Gods immortal, preserve the house, the seat of Soma.

A nest is placed upon a second, a vessel laid upor another, thereby a mortal is born, from whom all things originate!

This house is built with two sides, with four sides, with six sides, with eight or ten. In this mistress building Agni lies like an unborn babe in the womb.

For Removing Sickness

Headache, earache, anaemia, and all that afflicts your head, do we expel out of you by our incantation.

From your two ears, from each part of them, the earache, and the pain, all that afflicts your head, do we expel out of you by our incantation.

That consumption may be removed from your ears and from your mouth, all that afflicts your head, do we expel out of you by our incantation.

Whatever makes a man dumb or blind, all that afflicts your head, do we expel out of you by our incantation.

Limb-splitting, limb-wasting pain, the ache that ails all the limbs, all that afflicts your head, do we expel out of you by our incantation.

The fever that attacks man each autumn, whose fearful aspect makes one tremble, the Takman we do expel by our incantation.

The deadly Yakshma that creeps along the thighs, and also goes to the groins, the disease within your limbs do we expel by our incantation.

If the disease be born out of love or hatred, by heart's affliction, the balsa from your heart, from your limbs do we expel by our incantation.

The yellow jaundice from your limbs, the colic from your belly within, the Yakshma that plagues you from within, do we expel by our incantation.

May this disease turn into ashes, may it become sickening urine. The poison of all Yakshma I have exorcised from you.

Forth from office let it run out, the rumbling from your belly, the poison of all Yakshma I have exorcised from you.

Out of your stomach, out of your lungs, out of the navel and the heart, the poison of all Yakshma I have exorcised from you.

Those gnawing pains that cleave asunder the crown and rush against the head, let them go forth out at the orifice, without harm, free from disease!

The piercing pains that rush into the heart and travel along the spine from head to foot, let them go forth out at the orifice, without harm, free from disease!

The stabbing pains that rush into the sides, and pass along the ribs, let them go forth out at the orifice, without harm, free from disease!

The piercing pains that rush into the sides, and pass along the ribs, let them go forth out at the orifice, without harm, free from disease!

The piercing pains that rush on crosswise and penetrate into the stomach, let them go forth out at the orifice, without harm, free from disease!

The piercing pains that creep along the intestines, and confound the entrails within, let them go forth out at the orifice, without harm, free from disease!

The pains that suck out the marrow, and split apart the joints, let them go forth out at orifice without harm, free from disease!

The pains that intoxicate the limbs, the wasting Yakshma, the colic pains, the poison of every wasting disease I have exorcised from thee.

Spots that erupt out and abscesses, rheumatic pains, and disease of the eye, the poison of every wasting disease I have exorcised from you.

Forth from your feet, your knees, your hips, from your buttocks, your spine, from your neck and from your head, I have made all sickness vanish.

Book Ten

The Amulet of Varana Tree

This is my Varana amulet, a lusty amulet that destroys my rivals, with it do thou seize your foes and shatter those who would harm you!

Shatter them, crush them, take hold of them, this amulet shall be thy vanguard in front, with the Varana amulet the Gods did ward off the attack of hostile demons day after day.

This Varana amulet, thousand-eyed, all-healing, yellow and golden, it shall subdue the foes, do you in front lay low them who hate you!

The Varana will ward off the sorcery that has been practised against you, this will preserve you against danger from men, this will protect you from all evil!

This divine tree of Varana shall ward off the disease that has entered this man, the disease that the Gods, too, have warded off.

If in sleep you behold an evil dream, if a wild beast run a violent course, from excess sneezing, from the evil call of a bird this amulet, the Varana shall protect you.

From Arati, from Nirriti, from sorcery, from distress, from death and deadly weapons, the Varana shall protect you.

The sin that my mother, that my father, that my brothers or that we ourselves have committed, from that this divine tree will protect us.

Confounded and thrust forth by Varana my enemies and my rival kinsman have gone to the gloomy world, let them go to the nethermost world of darkness.

May I remain unharmed, with unharmed kine, long lived, with all my men. May this Varana, this amulet protect me on all sides of space!

This Varana on my breast, the royal, divine tree, shall drive away my foemen, as Indra the Asuras, the demons!

Long lived, a hundred autumns old, do I bear this Varana. May it grant me both royalty and authority, cattle and might.

As the wind breaks the trees with force, the giant trees of the forest, so do you break my enemies, those born before and after. The Varana shall protect you!

As both the wind and the fire consume the trees, the forest trees, so do you consume my enemies, those born before and after. The Varana shall protect you!

Do you cut off, O Varana, them before their appointed time, before their mature age, them who strive to harm him in cattle, and threaten his royal authority!

As the sun shines resplendently, as in him effulgence has been implanted, so shall the Varana amulet implant in me fame and prosperity, shall sprinkle me with brilliance. May it cover me with glory!

As effulgence is in the moon, and in the sun, that beholds men, so shall the Varana amulet implant in me fame and prosperity, shall sprinkle me with brilliance. May it cover me with glory!

As effulgence is in the earth, as in the Jatavedas, so shall the Varana amulet implant in me fame, etc. etc.

As glory is in a maiden, as in a given chariot, so shall Varana amulet implant in me fame, etc. etc.

As glory is in the soma-juice, brilliance is in honey mixture, so shall Varana amulet implant in me fame, etc. etc.

About Skambha or Cosmic Creation

In which of his limbs does penance dwell? In which of his limbs is right deposited? In what part of him abides the vow? In which of his limbs is truth established?

From which of his limbs does fire come forth? From which of his limbs issues and blows the wind? From which limb does the moon take the measuring rod when he measures the form of great Skambha?

In which of his limbs does the earth reside? In what limb is the atmosphere situated? In which of his limbs is the space set? In which of his limbs is set what is beyond the space?

Desiring what does Agni flame up high? Desiring whom the wind so eagerly blow? On whom do the compass points converge? Tell me of that Skambha, who may he be?

Where do the half months go, where the months together with

the year in harmony go? Where do the seasons go, together or alone? Tell me of that Skambha, who may he be?

Desiring whom to attain the two sisters run, day and night? Desiring whom to attain, the waters flow? Tell me of that Skambha, who may he be?

The One on whom Prajapati leant for support when he established the world? Tell me of that Skambha, who may he be?

What was that highest, the lowest, and what was that midmost Prajapati created of all fonns and by how much did he enter the support himself? What did not enter, how much was that portion?

By how much did Skambha enter the creation? How much of him lies along that will enter in the future? In that one limb that he fashioned thousand fold, by how much did Skambha himself enter?

By whom man knows the worlds and that which envelopes them, the waters and Brahman, in which are found both the existent and the non-existent? Tell me of that Skambha, who may he be?

By whom the highest penance, waxing forth maintains the greatest vow, in whom unite the cosmic Law and Faith, the Waters and Brahman. Tell me ofthat Skambha, who may he be?

In whose one limb all the Gods, thirty and three in number are set together? Tell me ofthat Skambha, who may he be?

In whom both death and immortality are set together, as man? To whom belong the swelling ocean and the veins that runs within man? Tell me of that Skambha, who may he be?

Of whom are the four cardinal directions and the swelling veins? In whom has the sacrifice strode forth? Tell me of that Skambha, who may he be?

Whoever knows the Brahman in man, they know the highest One. Those who know the most high One, or Prajapati, the lord of creation, know the supreme Brahman. They therefore know the Skambha also.

Whose head is Vaishvanara, the universal fire, whose eyes the Angirases are, and whose limbs are the demons. Tell me of that Skambha, who may he be?

Of whom they say Brahman is the mouth, the honey whip the tongue, of whom they say Viraj is the udder, tell me of that Skambha, who may he be?

From out of his body they carved the verses, the sacrificial formulas were fashioned from his shavings. His hairs became the hymns, Atharvans and Angiras the mouth, tell me of that Skambha, who may he be?

The branch of non-existence, that extends forth, men regard to be the highest thing, the other, the lower one, the branch of existence, they regard as inferior, and them who adore it.

In whom do the Adityas, Rudras and Vasus abide together, in whom are the worlds set together, that in which what is and what is to be, are established together? Tell me of that Skambha, who may he be?

In whom the Gods, knowing Brahman, worship the supreme Brahman, he who knows the Gods eye to eye is verily a seer, a knower.

Great are the Gods who were born out of non-being, that one limb of Skambha men call non-being beyond.

When the Skambha, generating forth, evolved the Ancient One, he who knows this limb also knows by that knowledge the Ancient one.

It was he in whose limbs the thirty-three Gods shared severally the portions among themselves. So verily the knowers of Brahman also know the thirty-three Gods.

People know the goldenembryo as the supreme, inexpressible. Yet it was the Skambha in the beginning who poured forth that gold on the world.

In the Skambha are contained the worlds, in him penance and law are established. You I know. O Skambha, eye to eye, as wholly set in Indra.

In Indra the worlds are, in Indra is penance, in Indra is law, you O Indra, I know eye to eye as wholly established in the Skambha.

Before the sunrise, before the dawn, man calls name after names. This unborn came to being with full sovereignty beyond which there is nothing else existent.

Homage to him of whom the earth is model and the atmosphere his belly, who made the sky his head. Homage to this supreme Brahman!

Homage to him of whom the sun is eye, and the moon that grows anew, whose mouth is Agni. Homage to this supreme Brahman!

Homage to him whose in-breath and out-breath is the wind, of whom the Angirases are the eye, who made the four cardinal points foreknown. Homage to this supreme Brahman!

The Skambha upholds both heaven and earth, the Skambha supports the wide space, the Skambha sustains the vast six directions, by the Skambha is the whole world pervaded!

Homage to him who is born of toil and penance, has pervaded all the worlds, who has made Soma all his own. Homage to this supreme Brahman!

How does the wind cease not to blow? How does the mind take no rest? Why do the waters, seeking to attain the truth, at no time cease flowing?

A great wonder in the midst of creation strode, in penance on the water's surface. In him are established whatever gods there be, like the branches of tree round about the trunk.

Unto whom do the Gods always with two hands and feet, with speech, with ears and with sight bring tribute unmeasured in a well measured sacrifice. Tell of that Skambha, who may he be?

In him there is no darkness, no evil exists in him. In him are all the three lights that are in Prajapati, the Lord of creation.

He who knows the golden reed standing in the waters, he truly knows the mysterious Prajapati.

It is by the Skambha that these two, heaven and earth remain established in space. In Skambha abides all things that have a soul, and all that which winks and closes the eye.

Three generations have already gone, the others settled down about him, the great measurer of space stood on high. The golden one entered into green gold plants.

One is the wheel, twelve are the bands, three are the hubs — who understands it? Therein are fixed three-hundred and sixty pins, and pegs that are firmly fixed.

This, O Savitar, do thou know, six are twins, one is born alone and the twins desire to unite with him who of them is born alone.

Though manifest, yet it is hidden, mysterious, by name the ancient, the great mode of being. There in the Skambha are set this all, therein are established all that stirs and breathes.

One-wheeled, one-rimmed, it rolls forth, thousand-named, forth in front, down behind. Withahalf of itself it created all existence, what has become of the other half that remained?

The one carries the five onward, with five side horses, yoked, also drawing. One beholds of it the not yet gone and not what is gone. The distant is the nearer, the nearer the more distant.

A bowl is there with aperture sideways and the bottom upturned. In it is deposited glory of all forms, thereon sit together the seven sages, the keepers of it, the great sphere.

The verse which is applied in front, and that which behind, and that which is applied in all cases, and the verse by which the sacrifice proceeds forward, that I ask of you, which one it is of all the verses?

What moves, what flies, what stands, and what breathes, what does not breathe, winks the eye, that abides into only one, though varied in form, sustains the earth.

Bearing water in a pitcher on high like a water bearer, all see him with their eyes, but all know not him with the mid.

Whence does the sun rise, and where does he go to rest, that same I think to be the Supreme. There is nothing whatever that goes beyond.

The Sun, the yellow swan, flying to heaven on a thousand days flight gathers all the Gods in his bosom, viewing all the worlds together.

By truth he blazes on high, by Brahman he beholds below, by breath he breathes across the realms, he on whom rests the Supreme.

A beautiful maiden, never aging, an immortal, dwells in a mortal house. He for whom she was created, lies prone, and he who made her has grown old.

You are woman, you are man, you are boy and a maiden too. You are the aged man tottering with a staff. When born, you manifest your face everywhere.

He is both their father and also their son, at once the eldest and the youngest. The one God penetrates the each mind, the first born and yet even now within the womb.

From fullness he pours forth the full, the full spreads out merging with the full. May we know from whence is he thus poured out?

The lotus bloom of nine doors, covered with the three strands is a great marvel within. This is it that the Brahman knower knows.

He who knows the self, desireless, wise, immortal, self-existent, full of fresh sap, wanting nothing, unaging, ever youthful, will never be afraid of death.

Book Eleven

O Agni, come thou into being, Aditi here, in her travail desiring sons, she is cooking the rice dish for Brahmans. The Seven Seers, who created the beings, may thy churn thee, along with progeny.

Make the smoke, O ye lusty friends, unharmed go ye to the contest. This Agni here wins battles, commands warriors, with his aid Gods conquered the demons.

O Agni, thou has been kindled to a great heroism, to cook the Brahman's ricedish, O Jatavedas. The Seven Seers who created the beings, have generated thee, do thou grant this woman wealth along with heroes!

Burn, O Agni, be thou kindled with the fire-wood. Mayest thou bring hither skilfully the worshipful gods making the oblation, cook for these Brahmans, do thou make this man rise to the highest heaven!

The threefold share that is yours of old is set apart, of Gods, of Fathers, of mortals. Know ye the shares. I divide them for you. The share that is of the Gods shall protect this woman.

O Agni, mighty, conquering, thou subduest without fail, bow down our hateful foes. May this measure, that is being measured, and has been measured, make the fellows bring tributes to thee!

Mayest thou in the company of thy fellows be endowed with milk, urge this woman to grant heroism. Ascend thou aloft to the summit of the heaven, which they call the heavenly world.

May this great Earth, graciously accept this sacrificial hide. Then may we proceed to the world of heaven!

Join thou these two press stones on the hide, crush well the Soma shoots for the sacrificer. O Earth, crush and smite down those who are hostile to this woman, bear her progeny aloft, elevate!

Seize into thy hands, O hero, these two press stones that grind together. The reversed Gods have come to the sacrifice, whatever three boons thou choosest, I shall here procure for thee unto fulfilment.

This is thy purpose, and this thy place of birth. May Aditi, mother of heroic sons, take hold of thee. Thrash them out who are hostile to this woman; bestow wealth alongwith heroes upon this woman!

These maidens (waters) have come hither, adorning themselves. Arise, thou woman and gather strength. To thee, who is well spoused by thy husband and by thy progeny made rich in progeny, the sacrifice has come, receive thou this water vessel!

A Prayer to Bhava and Sarva

Bhava, O Sarva, be auspicious, do not be against us, ye lords of beings, lords of cattle, homage be to ye twain! Let not your arrow fly even after it has been fitted on the bow and drawn. Do not harm our bipeds and quadrupeds!

Make not our bodies for the dog, or the jackal for the buzzards, the vultures, and the black birds, that are greedy. O lord of cattle, let thy flies and birds not get us to devour!

Homage do we pay. O Bhava, to thy roar, to thy breath, and to thy harming qualities. Homage do we pay, O Rudra, to thee, thou thousand-eyed God!

We pay homage to thee in front, above, below and from every side and from heaven. Homage be to thine atmosphere!

To thy face, O lord of cattle, to thy eyes, O Bhava, to thy skin, to thy form, to thy appearance and to thy aspect from behind homage be!

May we never be in conflict with Rudra, the blue crested archer, the thousand-eyed, mighty one, the half slayer!

May Bhava steer clear on all sides from us, as fire the waters, may he steer clear from us. May he never scheme against us homage be to him!

Four times, eight times, be homage to Bhava, ten times be homage to thee, O lord of cattle. Thou art the master of these five kine, horses, men, sheep and goats!

Thine are the four quarters, thine the heaven, thine the earth, thine, O mighty one, this wide space, thine is all that has a soul and breath upon the earth.

Thine is this vast vessel, holder of riches, within which are contained all beings. Be auspicious to us, O lord of cattle, homage be to thee! Let the jackals, the evil portents, the dogs go away from us, away the mourners who bewail with disheveled hair!

O crested God, thou who bears a golden bow which smites thousands, that slays husbands, Rudra's arrow, a missile of Gods, flies far, homage be to that, in whatever direction it flies from here!

He who lurks in order to attack thee, O Rudra, him thou pursuest from behind like a hunter chasing a wounded animal.

Bhava and Rudra, allied in harmony, both mighty unto heroism, homage be to them, in whatever direction they may be.

Homage be to thee coming, O Rudra, homage to thee going, homage be to thee standing, and also homage be to thee while sitting.

Homage in the evening, homage in the morning, homage by night, homage by day, both to Bhava and Sarva I have paid homage!

May we never cause offence to Rudra with our speech, him who hurls, his shafts, sees all, is thousand-eyed and manifoldly wise.

We go forward to greet him that has dark horses, is black, sable, destructive, terrible, who made Kesin fall down from his car, homage be to him!

Do not let fly at us thy club, thy missile, be not angry with us, O lord of cattle. Shake over the heavenly branch some other than us, homage be to thee!

Harm us not, bless us, be not incensed, let us not be in conflict with thee!

Be not greedy for our kine, our men, and goats and sheep. Speed forth thy missile, O mighty one, elsewhere to strike the progeny of the blasphemers!

Homage be to thy shouting hosts, O God, homage be to thy long haired ones, homage be to them who are revered, homage be to thy devouring hosts!

In Praise of Prana or Life Breath

Reverence to Prana, who is the lord of all this world, who has been the master of all, on whom all things are based.

Homage, O Prana, to thy roaring, homage to thy thunder, homage, O Prana, to thy lightning, homage to thy rain!

When Prana with thunder roars over the herbs, they are impregnated and burst forth in abundant blossoms full of pollen.

When Prana thunders over the herbs in due season, then all things rejoice greatly on the earth.

When Prana has watered the wide earth with rain, then the cattle rejoice thinking, "verily, we shall have in plenty".

Then plants converse with Prana, drenched with its moisture and say, "verily, thou hast prolonged our life, thou hast made us all fragrant".

Homage be to thee, O Prana, when thou arrive, and homage when thou go. Homage be to thee standing and homage be to thee when you sit quiet!

Homage be to thee, O Prana, when breathing both in and out, to thy turning, too, this side or that, to the whole of thee homage be!

Grant us, O Prana, thy dear form, and that, one still dearer, and likewise thine healing power, that we all may live!

Prana clothes all the beings, as a father a dear son Prana, verily, is the lord of all, whether they breathe or they breathe not.

Prana is death, Prana is fever, worshipped by the Gods. Prana establishes in the highest world him who speaks the truth.

Prana is Viraj, Prana is guide, adored by all things, Prana is sun, he is moon, he is also the lord creator of all things, the Prajapati.

The eight-wheeled mover having one rim, thousand syllabled, forth in front, down behind. With one half it has generated all existence, of its other half what sign?

He is the lord of all that moves and of all that is born, to thee being such, O Prana, possessing a swift bow like the rest, be homage!

He is the lord of all that moves and all that is born, untiring, wise by Brahman, let my prayer bring Prana to my aid!

Upright among the sleeping he keeps vigil. By no means does he fall prostrate. No one so ever has heard of his slumbering among the sleeping.

O Prana, do not desert me, thou art indeed, I, like the embryo of the waters, I hold ye fast to me that I may live!

Rice and barley are his in-breathings and out-breathings, Prana in the ox that draws. Prana is set in barley as in-breathing and out-breathing in rice.

A man breathes in, he breathes out in the womb, quickened by Prana, he is born once more.

They call Prana Matarishvan, the mighty wind or the breeze. The past and future, forsooth, exist in him, all things are supported on Prana.

When quickened by thee, O Prana, the divine plants, those grown by men, of the Atharvans, and those of Angirases spring forth to birth.

When Prana has poured down upon the earth as rain, then herbs spring forth and plants of every kind.

He who knows thee thus, O Prana, and that on which thou art supported, to him all will offer tribute in yonder highest heaven.

All these beings, O Prana, owe tribute to thee, so shall they offer it to him who hears you, O famed one!

He moves among the Gods as an embryo, then having arrived, and being in existence, is reborn. He has entered the son, he, the father, who was, has been and shall be!

When he rises as the sun bird from the waters, he does not withdraw his foot, forsooth if he did, there would be neither today nor tomorrow, there would be neither night nor day, nor would dawn appear.

In Praise of Brahmachari

The Brahmachari sets in motion both the heaven and earth. In him the Gods are in harmony. He sustains heaven and earth, he fills the teacher with creative fervour.

The fathers, the folk and all the Gods severally follow the Brahmachari. The Gandharvas follow him, six thousand three hundred and thirty three. He fills all the Gods with tapas.

When the teacher takes the Brahmachari under him as a disciple, he makes him an embryo within him. He bears him for three nights in his belly, and when he is born the Gods assemble to see him.

This piece of fuel is earth, the sky the second, and the atmosphere also he fills with the piece of firewood. The Brahmachari fills the worlds with fuel, girdle, austerity and creative fervour.

Born prior to Brahma, the Brahmachari, clothed in heat, by creative fervour did he rise. From him was born the Brahman, the highest Brahman, and all the Gods together with *amrita.*

The Brahmachari advances kindled with fuel, clothed in black antelope skin, consecrated and bearded. He moves from eastern to the western ocean, grasping the worlds he shapes again and again!

The Brahmachari, generating the Brahma, the waters, the

world, Prajapati, Parmesthin and Viraj, having become an embryo in the womb of immortality, became verily Indra, and pierced the demons.

The teacher fashioned out both these hemispheres, the wide and the deep, earth and heaven. The Brahmachari preserves them by his creative fervour, in him the Gods are harmonized.

This wide earth and the heaven the Brahmachari brought hither as alms. Having turned them into two fuel sticks, he worships them, upon them all beings rest.

Prayer to Gods for Deliverance

We address Agni, the trees, the plants and the herbs, Indra, Brihaspati and Surya. May they all deliver us from distress!

We call on God Savitar, Dhatar and Pushan. We call on Tvashtar, the first born. May they deliver us from distress!

We address the Gandharvas and Apsaras, the two Ashvins and Brahmanaspati, the God called Aryaman. May they deliver us from distress.

Now do we call Day and Night, Surya and Chandrama, all the Adityas we call. May they deliver us from distress!

Vata we address, Parjanya, the atmosphere, and the quarters of the space, and all the regions we address. May they deliver us from distress!

May Day and Night, and also the Dawn, free thee from curses! May God Soma, whom they call Moon, deliver me from distress!

The earthly, the divine cattle, also the beasts of wild we address. Likewise we address the hawks and the birds. May they deliver us from distress!

Now we address Bhava and Sarva, and Rudra, the lord of cattle, their shafts do we all know well. May these be ever auspicious to us!

We address the heavens and the stars, the earth, the yakshas, the mountains, the seas, the rivers and the ponds. May they deliver us from distress!

We address now the Seven Sages, the divine waters, Prajapati.

We address Fathers with Yama as their chief. May they free us from distress!

The Gods dwelling in heaven, and those who dwell in the atmosphere and the mighty ones who are set on earth, may they deliver us from distress!

The Adityas, the Rudras, the Vasus, the Atharvans, the Angiras, the wise, the gods in heaven, may they deliver us from distress!

We now address the sacrifice, the sacrificers, the verses, the chants, the remedies, the ritual formulas and the invocations. May they deliver us from distress!

The five kingdoms of herbs with Soma (Moon) as their chief, we address and also the sacred grass, hemp and barley. May they deliver us from distress!

We address the niggard and demons, the serpents, the pious folk and fathers, the hundred and one deaths. May they deliver us from distress!

The seasons we address, the lords of the seasons, the sections of the year and the winters, the summers, the years and the months. May they deliver us from distress!

Come ye Gods from the south, from the west, come ye along from the east. From the east, from the north, all the Gods, mighty shall assemble here. May they deliver us from distress!

We speak now to all the gods, of true agreements, promoters of righteousness, together with all their consorts. May they deliver us from distress!

We speak to the lord of existence, and him who controls all the existence, all the existence assembled. May they free us from distress!

The five divine regions, the twelve divine seasons, the fangs of the year, may they all be propitious to us.

The *amrita* bought for a chariot, which Matali knows, that Indra deposited in the waters; that *amrita,* O waters ye give us!

Book Twelve

A Hymn to the Earth

The great truth, inviolable law, consecration, austerity, prayer and sacrificial ritual, sustain the Earth. May she, the mistress of what is and is to be, spread wide to provide us ample space.

Untrammled in the midst of men, the Earth, possessed of the ascents, slopes and plains, bears various healing herbs. May she spread wide to provide us joy!

On whom are the oceans, the rivers, the waters, on whom have come forth food and ploughman's crops, on whom moves all that breathes, and that stirs. May she give us the first draught!

The four quarters belong to Earth, on her grows food, on her grow the ploughman's crops. She bears all that breathes and that stirs. May that Earth grant us kine and food in abundance!

On whom the people in yore spread themselves far and wide, on whom the Gods defeated the demons, the abode of kine, of horses and of birds. May this Earth grant us good fortune and splendour!

Bearing all, holding treasure, firmly established, golden bosomed, sustainer of life, bearing the Vaishvanara, the universal fire, whose hero is Indra, may she prosper us!

Boundless Earth, whom the Gods, sleepless defend all the time with great care, may she yield us honey so desired, and pour on us splendour!

Earth who in the beginning was water upon the ocean, whom the seers discerned with their spiritual powers, whose eternal heart covered in truth abides in the highest heaven. May she bestow upon us strength, splendour and highest royalty!

On whom the waters flow, always the same, night and day, ceaselessly, may this Earth, of many rivers, yield us milk and pour on us her splendour in plenty!

May this Earth, whom the Ashvins measured, on whose vastness Vishnu strode, whom Indra, the mighty lord, freed from enemies, release milk for us like a mother to her son!

May thy hills, O Earth, thy snow-clad mountains, thy forests, be pleasant to us. Brown, black, red, of varied forms, firmly established is this Earth, protected by Indra. I, unharmed, unconquered, unharassed have my abode on this Earth. Grant us, O Earth, those vital refreshments, which are confined in thy middle, in thy navel and those within thy body, purify us fully. She is mother, I am Earth's son, Parjanya is my father, may she ever preserve us!

The Earth on which they enclose the sacred altar, on which a group of men make the sacrificial offering, on which are fixed the sacrificial posts, tall, bright prior the sacrifice, may this Earth grant us increase.

Those who would hate us, fight us, O Earth, who would oppose us mentally or with deadly weapons, do thou deliver them to us, before they act.

All beings born of thee, go about on thee, thou bearest all the bipeds, quadrupeds. To thee belong these five races of men, those mortals on whom the rising sun pours forth his immortal rays.

May all the creatures, without exception, yield to me the honey of speech, O Earth, grant me this boon!

The mother of all plants and begetter of herbs, firmly established Earth, sustained by law, is auspicious and pleasant, may we ever dwell on her moving about here and there.

O Earth, thou has become great, as a great station, great is thy motion, great thy stirring and thy quaking. The great Indra ever protects thee. O Earth, make us shine like burnished gold, may nonesoever hate us!

Agni abides in Earth, in the plants, the waters contain Agni. Agni is in stones, Agni is in the heart of men, within cattle, in horses there are Agnis.

Agni hashes heat from the heavens, the vast atmosphere here belongs to Agni, Agni, it is that is kindled by the mortal men, as conveyor of oblation, the ghee bearer.

May the Earth, clad in fire, black kneed, grant me sharpness of intelligence and splendour.

On the Earth the mortal men offer sacrifice to the Gods and well prepared oblations. There they live on food and nourishment, may that grant us life and breath, allowing us to attain ripe old age.

O mother Earth, fill me with that fragrance in plenty, which is there in the herbs, in the waters and in thee, and which is shared by the Gandharvas and Apsaras, let no one ever wish us ill!

What fragrance of thine has entered into the lotus bloom, wherewith the Gods were filled at the wedding of Surya's daughter, O Earth, in the beginning, instil in me that fragrance, may no one ever wish us ill!

The sweet smell which is there in men, in women, in pleasure, what is in heroes, in horses, what is in wild animals and in elephants, in a maiden, instil in me that fragrance in abundance, let no one ever wish us ill!

Earth is made up of rocks, stone, and dust. Earth is held together, consolidated, to this golden visaged Earth I have paid homage!

Upon her stand the forest and other trees firm, unshakable, this Earth sustaining all we now address, that is held together, consolidated.

Whether we stand erect or sit, whether we walk forth or remain still, whether we walk with right or left foot, never may we stagger!

The purifying Earth, I call, the patient one, increased by worship, that bears nourishment, prosperity, food, ghee and strength, O Earth, may we sit down upon thee!

May purifying water flow over our bodies, that which defile, we deposit on him who hates us. I do purify myself as with a purifier.

May all thy directions, to eastward, to southward, northward, and westward, receive me graciously whenever I go about them. May I never fall down when standing on thee!

Do not push us aside from front or behind, from above or below. Be kind to us, O Earth. Let not robbers waylay us on our travel, keep away from us the deadly weapon!

A great much of thee as my sight may reach, O Earth with the Sun as my ally, so far may my sight never fail from one year to another.

Whether I remain lying, turn upon my right side or my left side, or lie stretched upon my back, I feel your pressure all over my body, be soft and gentle, O Earth, thou bed of all!

Whatever of thee, O Earth, I dig up, let that quickly grow, let me never hit thy vitals, nor thy heart, O purifying Earth!

Let thy cycling seasons, thy hot season, thy rainy season, thy autumn, winter, cool one and spring, let thy arranged seasons, thy nights and succeeding days, O Earth, yield us their milk!

This cleansing Earth, one trembling on the Serpent, who protected the fires that were within waters, who chastized the God insulting demons, has chosen Indra as her mate and not Vritra, surrendering herself to the mighty one, the lusty bull.

On the Earth are made the altars to hold oblations, and the sacrificial posts are erected, on her the Brahmins, the knower of sacrificial formulas, chant their Verses, on her the hotar priests set before sacrifice, may that Indra enjoy Soma!

On her the sages in yore, the Seven Seers, the maker of beings, sang holy hymns while performing sacrifice and doing penance and thereby caused the kine to generate!

May the Earth grant us abundant wealth that we desire. May Indra lead us followed by Bhaga!

May the Earth, where mortal men sing and dance in gay abandon, where they fight resounding it with cries of battle and beating of the drums, push far away our rivals, and free us from our enemies!

The Earth where food grows, rice and barley are produced, whose are these five races of men, the sap-enriched Earth, the spouse of Parjanya be homage!

On the Earth the Gods made castles, in the vast plains men waged the war, the Earth, the mother and womb of everything, may Prajapati make all her regions pleasant for us!

May the treasure bearing Earth and also the secret wealth in many places, the generous giver of good things, grant us besides gold and gems, her special favour!

May the Earth, bearing diverse people of diverse speech and customs in several places, yield me a thousand streams of wealth, like a steady milch cow that never resists the milking hand!

The hard stinging serpents and scorpions, that lie lazily hidden chilled with winter, and the worms, all that move about in the early rain, may all that creeping ones, not creep on us. May thou be gracious to grant us all that is auspicious!

The many roads thou hast for people to go upon, the track for the chariot, and for the cart, by which the mankind travel, used by both good people and evil, may we choose one free from foes, free from robbers. May thou be gracious to grant us all that is auspicious!

The mother Earth bears on her bosom both the fool and the wise, she bears the death of good as well as of evil one. She in accord with the boar, opened herself to the wild hog.

O Earth, thine wild beasts, dwelling in woods, lions, tigers, man-eaters that misfortune stalking about, and the demons, do thou chase away from us afar!

The Earth, on whom the bright and the dark, the day and the night in association, though separate, are disposed, the vast Earth, often drenched and made fertile with rains, may settle us graciously in each well loved abode!

Both Heaven and Earth and the atmosphere in between have given me this vast expanse. Agni, the Sun, the Waters, the Gods have jointly given me this wisdom.

In villages, in forests, in places where men gather, in market places, in assemblies may we ever speak that which is pleasant about thee.

O mother Earth, do thou graciously settle me down that I may be at my ease, in harmony with the heaven, do thou set me, O poet, in prosperity!

Book Thirteen

A Prayer to Rohita (The Ruddy Sun)

Rise up, O steed, that art within the waters, enter into this kingdom, full of pleasantness. Rohita, the red Sun, who has generated all this, shall bear thee well to sovereignty!

Up hath risen the steed from within the waters; ascend thou upon the clans that are sprung from thee. Providing Soma, the waters, the herbs, the kine, make thou the bipeds and the quadrupeds to enter here!

Do ye, O mighty Maruts, sons of the spotted mother, allied with Indra, slaughter our foes, Rohita, the red Sun will listen you, he who gives liberally ye thrice seven Maruts who take delight in sweets together!

The Red One has ascended the heights, he has mounted them, he, the seed of women, has mounted the womb of births. He taking hold of these women has discovered the six wide directions, and seeing in advance the road, he has brought here the kingdom.

Here, for thee Rohita has brought thy kingdom having dispersed thy enemies. He has rendered thee fearless. To thee, as such, the heaven and earth together with Revati and Sakvari will yield gifts at thy desire.

Rohita generated heaven and earth, there the most high one stretched the thread, there the one-footed Aja (Sun) did establish himself. He fixed the heaven and earth with his might.

He made heaven and earth firm, he established the sky, by him the firmaments were measured out, by him the gods obtained immortality.

Rohita scanned all the forms, while ascending his climbs and then having ascended the sky with his great might, be shall annoit thy kingdom with milk and ghee!

Thine clans, who came into being out of creative fervour, have come hither in the wake of the young one and its mother Gayatri. May they enter into thee with propitious mind, preceded by the ruddy Calf and his mother!

High on the firmament Rohita has stood, the young poet, generating all forms. As Agni he shines with brilliant light, in the third space he did assume beautiful forms.

Rohita is the father and mother of sacrifice, to him I offer oblation with speech, hearing and mind. To him go the Gods with favouring spirit. May he cause me to ascend with ascensions of the assembly.

This clothes himself in the womb of the earth, this one clothes himself in heaven, and in the atmosphere. This one on the summit of the ruddy sun has entered into the heavenly worlds.

O lord of speech, bring into being good cheer and spirit, cattle in our stall, children in our wombs, Right here be our life-breath in our friendship, O highest one, I clothe thee in life and honour.

May God Savitar and Agni enwrap thee in honour, may Varuna and Mitra deck thee in splendour. Striding upon all powers of grudge come thou here to make this kingdom rich in nice things!

Thou, O Rohita whom the spotted cow, yoked at the side, draws, goest with brightness, causing the water to flow.

She that is ruddy and devoted to Rohita, as Rohini his mistress of beautiful complexion, generous, great, very majestic, may through her we win booty of all forms, may we overcome all the battles through her!

The Sun's tawny bright steeds, the immortal ones, always draw the easy moving chariot. Rohita the ghee-drinking, the brilliant God has entered the spotted heavens.

Measure thee out this cow, rich in milk, dripping with ghee. This is the God's milch cow that does not resist. Let Indra enjoy Soma, let there be wealth, let Agni sing hymns of praise, do thou push away the foes!

Do thou, O divine Sun, beat down my rivals, strike them down with stones, with thy rising, let them be hurled to the nethermost darkness!

In splendour thou goest to the cardinal points and quarters, in splendour in the right of cattle and races of men, splendid in the lap of the earth, of Aditi, the boundless. May I be splendid like Savitar!

Below the higher realm, above the lower one, the cow has stood up bearing her calf with her foot. Whither has she gone, to what quarter, verily, has she turned away? She is not in this herd!

One-footed, two-footed, four-footed is she; eight-footed, nine-footed, the thousand-syllabled line became she. Out from her flow forth the oceans on the earth.

Establishing cold and heat, using the mountains as sacrificial posts, using rain as sacrificial ghee, the two fires of Rohita, the ruddy, performed the sacrifice!

The fire of the Ruddy one is kindled by Brahman. From it heat, from it cold, from it sacrifice came into being.

Having fashioned the earth into sacrificial altar, having made the heavens sacrificial gift, then having made heat into sacrificial fire, the Ruddy one created all that has soul, with rain as sacrificial ghee.

He who kicks a cow with his foot, and he who urinates towards the sun, such a man do I tear out the root, thou shalt hereafter not cast a shadow!

He, the impeller Savitar goes across the heaven, looking down upon the back of the sky with pleasure.

He goes through the heavens, covered on all sides by rays, as great Indra.

He is the creator, he is the sustainer, he pervades all as Vayu, the highest.

He is Aryaman, he is Varuna, he is Rudra, he is the great God. He is, forsooth, Agni, he is also the Sun, he is indeed great Yama. On him attend ten young ones, united and possessing one head.

They spread out forward from behind, when he rises and shines forth in many ways.

His is this troop of Maruts, he pervades as if hung in slings.

He goes to the heavens, covered on ail sides by rays, as great Indra.

There are his nine vessels, these are his nine-fold posts.

He looks upon the creatures, both that breathe and that do not, for their weal.

Power entered into him. He is One, the Single, only One. In him all the gods are unified.

Both fame and glory, fruitfulness and fertility, Brahman splendour, food and nourishment, belong to him who knows the God as single One.

Not second, not third, also not fourth is he called, not fifth or sixth, not also seventh is he called.

Not eighth, not ninth, also not tenth is he called.

He watches over all existent beings over both that breathes and that breathes not.

Power entered into him, he is the one, single, only one.

In him all the Gods are unified.

Book Fourteen

Nuptials

By truth is the Earth sustained and by the Sun the Heavens. By law stand the Adityas and Soma maintains his place in the sky.

By Soma are the Adityas strengthened, by Soma mighty is the Earth, likewise Soma in the midst of all these stars hath his seat.

One thinks himself to have drunk Soma when they have crushed the plant. Of Soma the Brahmins truly know as Soma no one ever tastes.

Thought was the pillow of her bed, sight the ointment, earth and heaven were her treasure when Surya went to her husband.

The hymns were the cross bars, Kurisa meter adorned the can, the twain Ashvins were the bridesmen, Agni the leader of the train.

Soma was he who wooed the maid, both the Ashvins the groomsmen when Savitar bestowed his willing Surya upon her husband.

Her mind was the bridal chariot, the heaven the canopy, white were both the steeds that drew it when Surya went to her husband.

Kept steady with verse and chant, the horses went peacefully, the ears were the two wheels, the track was wandering in the sky.

Be ye not parted, be ye two just together, attain the full age of your life sporting with sons and grandsons and rejoicing well in your own house.

May thou bear sway over thy father-in-law, over thy husband's mother, over the sisters of thy husband and also over his brothers.

I hold thy hand unto good fortune, so that with me as husband thou mayest attain ripe old age. Gods Bhaga, Aryaman, Savitar and Purandhi have given thee to as one as a wife.

Thou art my consort and I thy husband by law. Bhaga hath grasped thy hand, Savitar has grasped thy hand.

Be my wife unto prosperity. Do thou abide with me as thy husband for a hundred autumns, rich in progeny. God Brihaspati has given thee to me.

Tvashtar decked thee with this raiment at the direction of Brihaspati and consent of the sages. Therewith may Savitar and Bhaga envelop thee like Surya with children,

May Indra, Agni, Heaven and Earth, Matrisvan, Mitra and Varuna and also twain Ashvins the Maruts, Brihaspati, Soma and the Brahmins enrich this woman in offspring.

First of all Brihaspati did the hair on the head of Surya. Similarly, O Ashvins, do we deck will this woman for her husband.

This is that beautiful form in which this bride has dressed herself. I wish to know mentally the wife moving about. I shall go after her with learned friends, who knowing shall have unloosened the fetters.

Clean were the chariot wheels as thou went, wind was the axle fixed there, a chariot fashioned out of mind did Surya mount when going forth to her lord.

The bridal pomp of Surya, which Savitar sent off, moved long. In Magha days are the oxen slain, in the Phalguns is the wedding.

When, O Ashvins, ye came as wooers on your three wheeled car unto Surya's bridal, where was one wheel of yours? Where stood ye for pointing out?

Ye two lords of splendour, when ye twain the Surya's wooing came, then all the Gods agreed to your proposal. Pushan as a son chose you father.

The two chariot wheels, O Surya, the Brahmins know by seasons, the one kept hidden, that, forsooth, the sages only know.

Let Bhaga lead thee by the hand, and conduct the forth by a chariot. Go to the Ashvin's house to be household's mistress and speak as such to the people assembled.

Happy be thou and prosper with thy progeny, be vigilant to rule over thy household. Unite well thou with thy husband. So shall ye advance in age and speak to the assembled people.

Knowing the form of this woman as the basis of my mind. I loosen her in me. I do not eat stealthily; I have released myself from the fetters of Varuna by my mind.

O woman, I release thee also from Varuna's fetters, with which the auspicious Savitar bound thee, O bride, I make for thee here wide abode and easy path, with thy lord.

For thee, with bridal train, they first carried about Surya in the bridal car to her home. Mayest thou Agni give to us husbands the wife with progeny.

Agni hath given the spouse again together with splendour and long life. May he who is her husband live long, a hundred autumns may he live.

Soma got her first as wife, the Gandharva was her next husband and Agni the third, and Agni has given to me together with riches and sons this my wife.

Your favour hath come, O ye Gods of abundant wealth. Our longings are stored up, O Ashvins, in your hearts. Ye lords of splendour, have become our twin protectors. May we as dear ones, attain Aryaman's abode.

Do thou, rejoicing auspiciously, grant wealth and heroes, to be praised. Make an easy ford, well provided with drinks, O lords of splendour, remove the spiteful stump.

The herbs that are there, the rivers, the fields and the forests, may all these, O bride, protect thee from the demons, having offspring for thy husband.

O bride, be thou pleasant to father-in-law, pleasant to husband, pleasant to home, pleasant to the clan. Be thou pleasant unto their prosperity!

Marked with signs of good fortune is this bride, come ye all and look at her. Wishing her good fortune go asunder and away with ill-fortune.

Ascend here the couch with gracious mind and deliver children for this man, Indrani rising with good awakening. Mayest thou behold the Dawn tipped with light.

The Gods in the beginning lay with their wives in close bodily embrace. O bride, of beautiful form, unite thou with thy husband like Surya to have offspring.

May Prajapati bring forth children for you two. May Aryaman unite you by day and night. Not inauspicious, enter thou this world of thy husband, bring weal to our bipeds and weal to quadrupeds.

To Surya and to the gods, to Mitra and to Varuna, unto them who know the thing, I have paid this homage.

Unite, O Indra, then two spouses like two Chakravakas. May they be surrounded by their progeny, live out their long life happily!

He and I, share you, song am I, earth you are. Let we together dwell here generating children!